The Campaign on the Loire 1870–1871: Orléans and Le Mans

Quintin Barry

Helion & Company

Helion & Company Limited
Unit 8 Amherst Business Centre
Budbrooke Road
Warwick
CV34 5WE
England
Tel. 01926 499619
Email: info@helion.co.uk
Website: www.helion.co.uk
X (formerly Twitter): @Helionbooks
Facebook: @HelionBooks
Blog: https://helionbooks.wordpress.com/

Published by Helion & Company 2025
Designed and typeset by Mach 3 Solutions (www.mach3solutions.co.uk)
Cover designed by Paul Hewitt, Battlefield Design (www.battlefield-design.co.uk)

Cover: The storming of the railway bridge near Orléans by the I Bavarian Corps, 11 October 1870. (Artwork by Christian Speyer)

ISBN 978-1-804517-82-6

British Library Cataloguing-in-Publication Data.
A catalogue record for this book is available from the British Library.

Publisher's Note: A Tribute to Quintin Barry

It is with profound sadness that I write this tribute to my friend and colleague, Quintin, whose passing during the preparation of this book has left an immense void. Over the past two decades, Quintin and I forged a close and rewarding friendship, and I had the honour of publishing 19 of his remarkable works, including this one.

Our relationship began in a modest yet fitting way – through Quintin's regular orders as a Helion customer, driven by his passion for military history, particularly for the German Wars of Unification. This shared enthusiasm quickly blossomed into frequent conversations and meetings, as we explored the joys and challenges of uncovering obscure titles. Our discussions often strayed beyond military history, enriched by Quintin's brilliant mind and insights from a distinguished career in law.

In 2008, Quintin and I embarked on a memorable tour of the 1866 battlefields in Bohemia, where we navigated the terrain – sometimes literally driving over fields – to gain the views and perspectives we sought. This was a truly unforgettable journey, as was a subsequent exploration of the 1870–1871 battlefields on the Somme. These trips exemplified Quintin's deep curiosity and enthusiasm for matters military and historical.

Above all, I will always remember Quintin as a modest, erudite, and warm friend and colleague – qualities that shone through in both his friendships and his writing. It has been a privilege to bring his works to readers around the world, many of whom have shared their admiration for his scholarship, clarity, and engaging style.

Though his voice is now silent, one final work remains to be shared: his study of the Battle of Beachy Head in 1690. While I mourn the end of his work as an author and miss our conversations, it is important to also celebrate the legacy of a truly extraordinary author. Quintin's enthusiasm, professionalism, and depth of knowledge were unparalleled, and it was a joy to collaborate with him.

Quintin's presence will be deeply missed, but his work and memory will act, I believe, as a fitting legacy.

Duncan Rogers,
Helion & Company,
January 2025

Contents

Preface

The campaign on the Loire was in many ways the most dramatic, and most important, of the various campaigns of the German Army during the winter of 1870–1871. It was fought for the most part in dreadful weather conditions which subjected its participants to extremes of physical hardship. The culmination of the campaign was the Battle of Le Mans, and this tested the armies on both sides to an even greater extent than the months which had gone before.

Michael Howard, in his classic account of the Franco-Prussian War, wrote of the period during which the German Second Army advanced on Le Mans: 'There followed six days of campaigning which remained like a nightmare in the memories of all the participants, French and German alike.'[1] Fought in the bitterest winter weather, through a countryside criss-crossed by narrow twisting roads, many of which were frequently almost impassable, the troops on both sides had to cope with conditions even more appalling than those which they had encountered previously. For the French, it represented the last hurrah of the one army that had realistically offered a fleeting prospect of being able to relieve Paris. And for the Germans, it finally disposed of such a possibility once and for all.

The Franco-Prussian War generated an enormous literature during the ensuing four decades, which reflected the huge military interest in all aspects of the German Army which had won such a stunning victory. In November 1870, Helmuth von Moltke, as he presided over the operations of the various German armies in the field, had mused on the question whether a trained army or a militia was preferable, correctly foreseeing that it would be answered by the outcome of the war, when every state would then imitate the example of the victors. During the second phase of the war, the extraordinary success of the Government of National Defence in putting large armies into the field gave France at least the hope that they might overcome the battle-hardened veterans opposed to them. In the end, though, Moltke's question was conclusively answered in favour of a trained army. After the war, Alfred Chanzy, ending his account of the 2nd Army of the Loire, pointed to the fact that all the nations of Europe were reforming their military systems, and called on France to do the same; failure to do so would, he wrote, be fatal.

Thus the development of every army in Europe was profoundly affected by the lessons to be learned by the military profession; this extended not only to the effect of the latest weapons employed, and the performance of an army based on universal service, but also to the organisation and management of the German armies. In particular, the huge logistical demands made upon the German and French armies demonstrated the extent to which modern warfare would in future be very different.

1 Michael Howard, *The Franco-Prussian War* (London: Rupert Hart-Davis, 1961), p.399.

The flow of new works on the Franco-Prussian War naturally declined sharply after the First World War, but it has never dried up altogether, as historians have sought to approach it from different angles. The reviewer of a recently published history of the war suggested that Michael Howard's account was 'perhaps too sanitised, too cerebral, but this one brings the opposite impulse, an unwillingness to spell out broader implications.'[2] Not everyone will agree with the reviewer's opinion of either of the two books; but neither this latest work nor any of those that succeeded Michael Howard's book can match his outstanding account of the war.

The campaign on the Loire confirmed that, in the Chassepot rifle and the mitrailleuse the French possessed infantry weapons which were far superior to those of their opponents. But it also confirmed that the German artillery would almost always be decisive in ensuring German battlefield superiority. Perhaps most strikingly, the war had also shown that the management skills of the Prussian General Staff, so carefully developed by Moltke ever since he succeeded to the post of its chief, represented the way forward for military leadership.

The Loire campaign also illustrated some of the command problems that could arise as a result of the interaction of very differing personalities. On the German side, for instance, it was only after Moltke, extremely dissatisfied with the proceedings of the detachment under the Grand Duke of Mecklenburg-Schwerin, intervened, that the difficulties were resolved. He replaced its chief of staff, Colonel von Krenski, with the temporary appointment of the Prussian intendant general, Albrecht von Stosch. The latter was, indeed, one of the outstanding heroes of the Loire campaign, whose achievements did not go unnoticed by his colleagues and by historians alike, even if the convention that Royal army commanders should have the credit for victories won was what weighed with the press and the general public.

For the French, the indomitable Alfred Chanzy was by some way the ablest of their generals; notwithstanding the series of defeats sustained by his 2nd Army of the Loire, he never gave up. Less fortunate was General Claude d'Aurelle de Paladines, whose tenure in command of the Army of the Loire was marked by the abominable mistreatment which he suffered at the hands of Charles de Freycinet, the 'delegate' appointed by Leon Gambetta to support him in carrying out his duties as Minister of War. Freycinet thereby had the effective conduct of the armies of the Government of National Defence, a position to which he brought vast enthusiasm and determination, but no military experience whatsoever. His efforts to do everything in his power to launch the French armies in an attempt to relieve Paris, and to energise their more cautious commanders, are easily understood. But his insulting treatment of decent and competent military professionals was ultimately counter-productive. D'Aurelle's dignified account of his leadership of his army convincingly recorded his relationship with Freycinet, unlike the latter's memoir, which was at times extremely untruthful.

On both sides there were many other commanders who played important parts in the struggle on the Loire, but in the end its great heroes were the ordinary soldiers whose loyalty, courage and endurance illuminated the campaign. The recollections of some of those in less senior positions, such as the Prussian Hans von Kretschmann, and the French Roger de Mauni, give a real sense of what it was like to be fighting on the Loire in the field during the fearful winter of 1870–1871.[3]

2 Pratinal Anil, review of *Bismarck's War* (London: Allen Lane, 2023) in *The Observer Magazine*, May 28 2023.

3 Hans von Kretschmann, *Lettres* (Paris: Henri Charles-Lavauzelle, 1904); Roger de Mauni (D. Clarke, ed.), *The Franco-Prussian-War* (London: Longman 1970).

The location of the German forces (blue) in the series of maps covering the Le Mans Campaign is taken from Volume IV of the German Official History. The location of the French forces (red) is included by way of a general indication of their whereabouts.

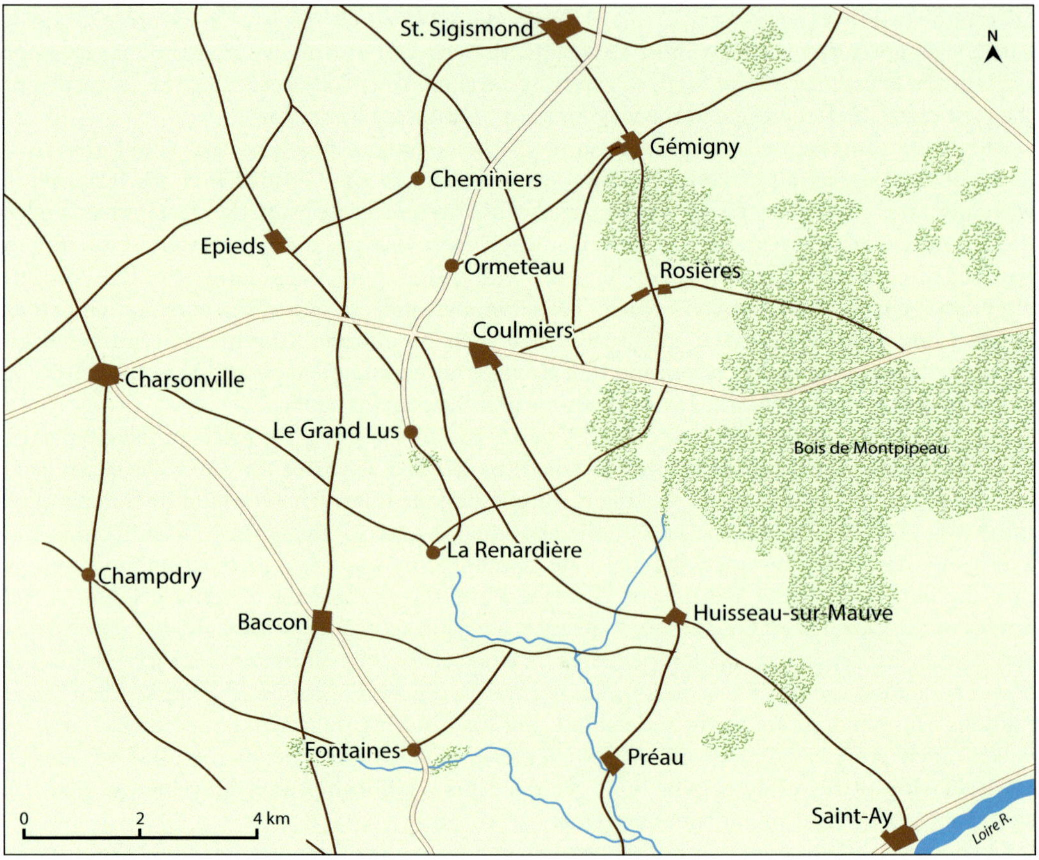

Map 1. Coulmiers, 9 November 1870.

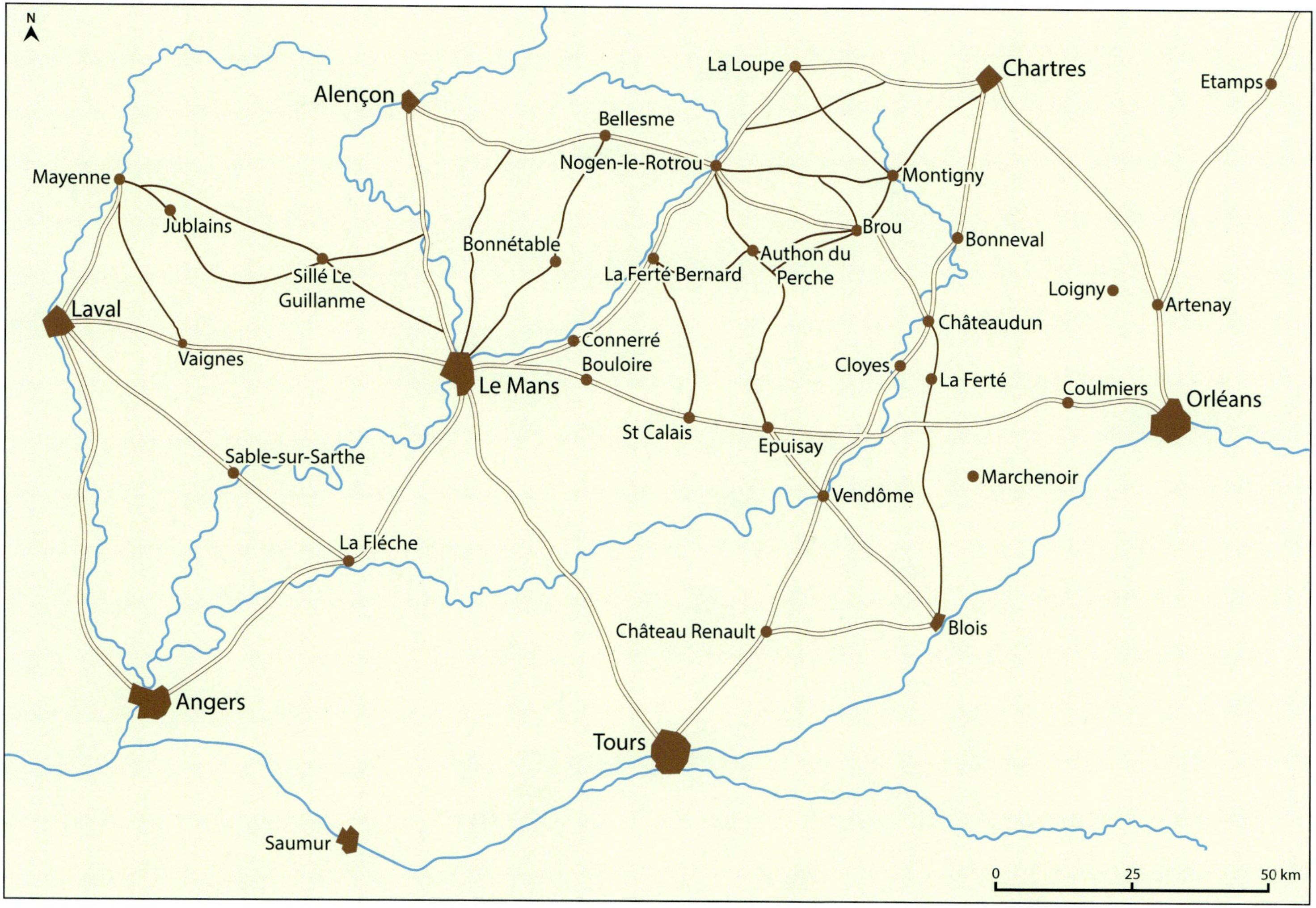

Map 2. Perche, Beauce and the Loire Valley, November 1870.

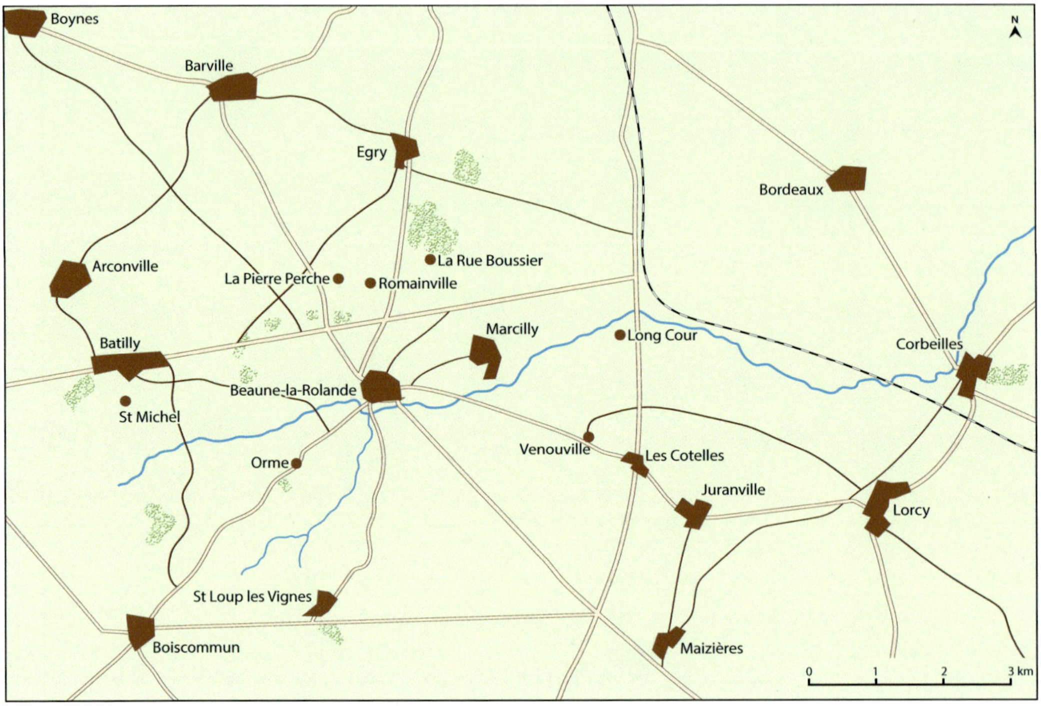

Map 3. Beaune-la-Rolande, 28 November 1870.

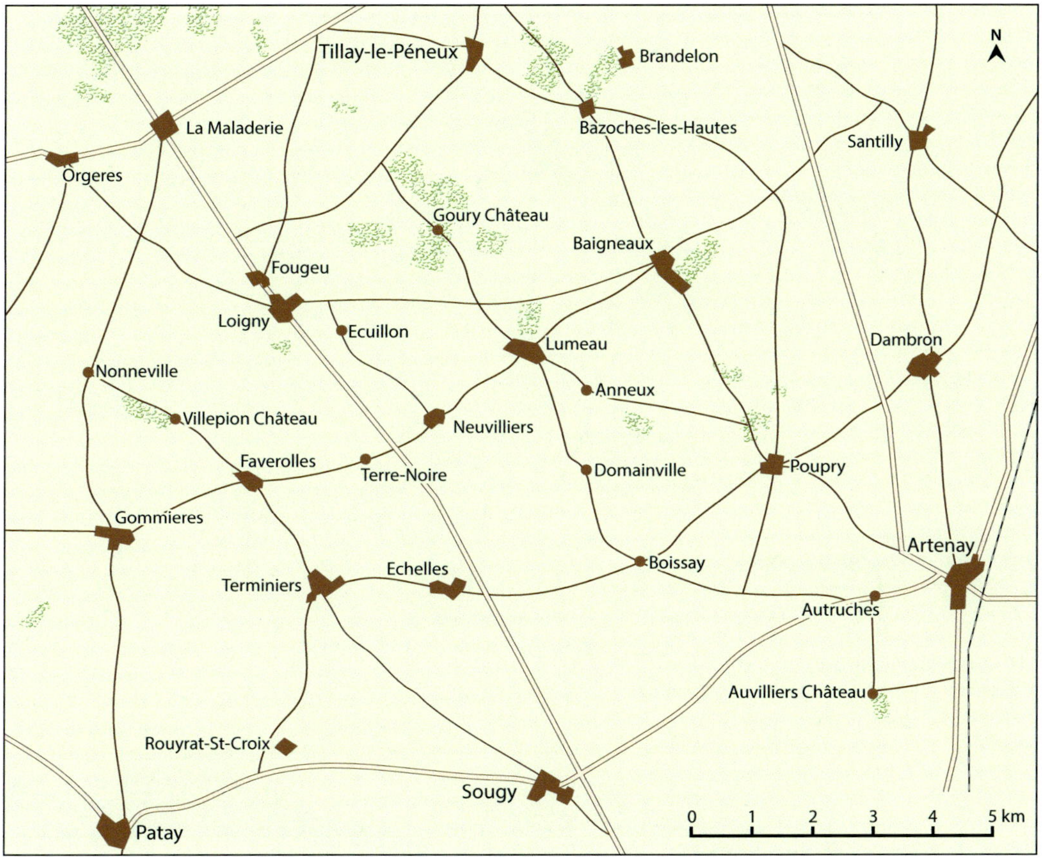

Map 4. Loigny-Poupry, 2 December 1870.

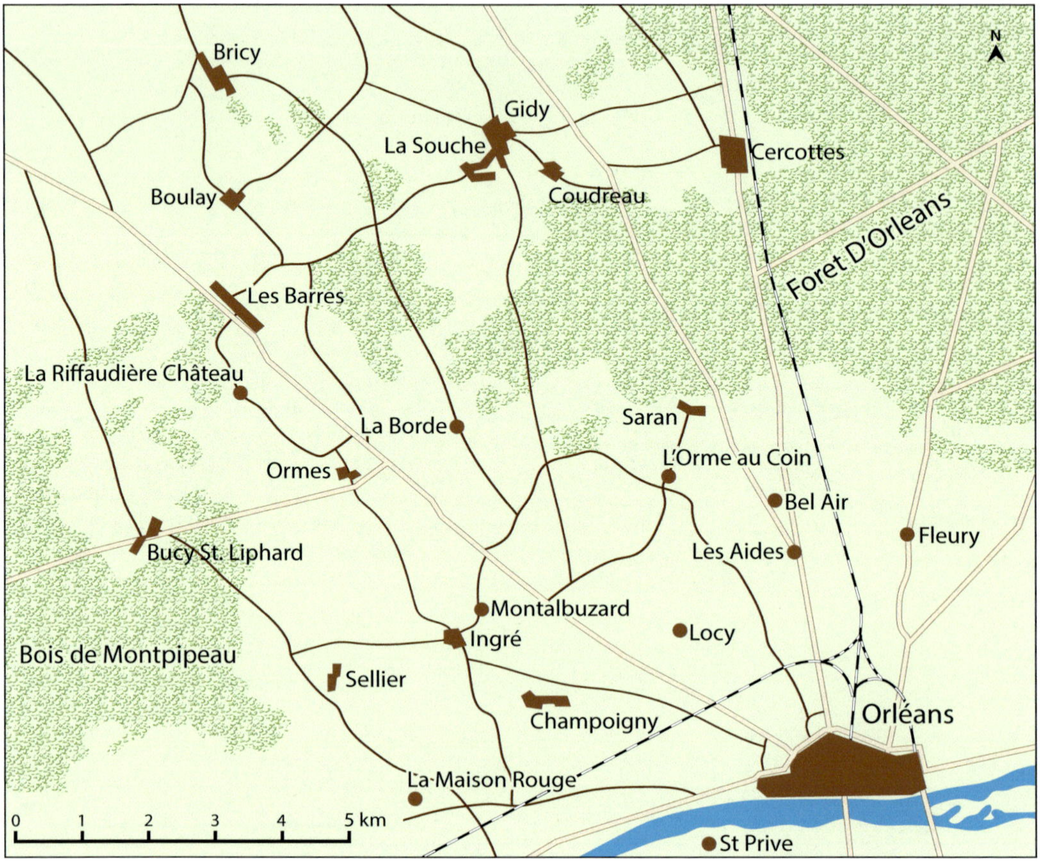

Map 5. Orléans and surroundings, December 1870.

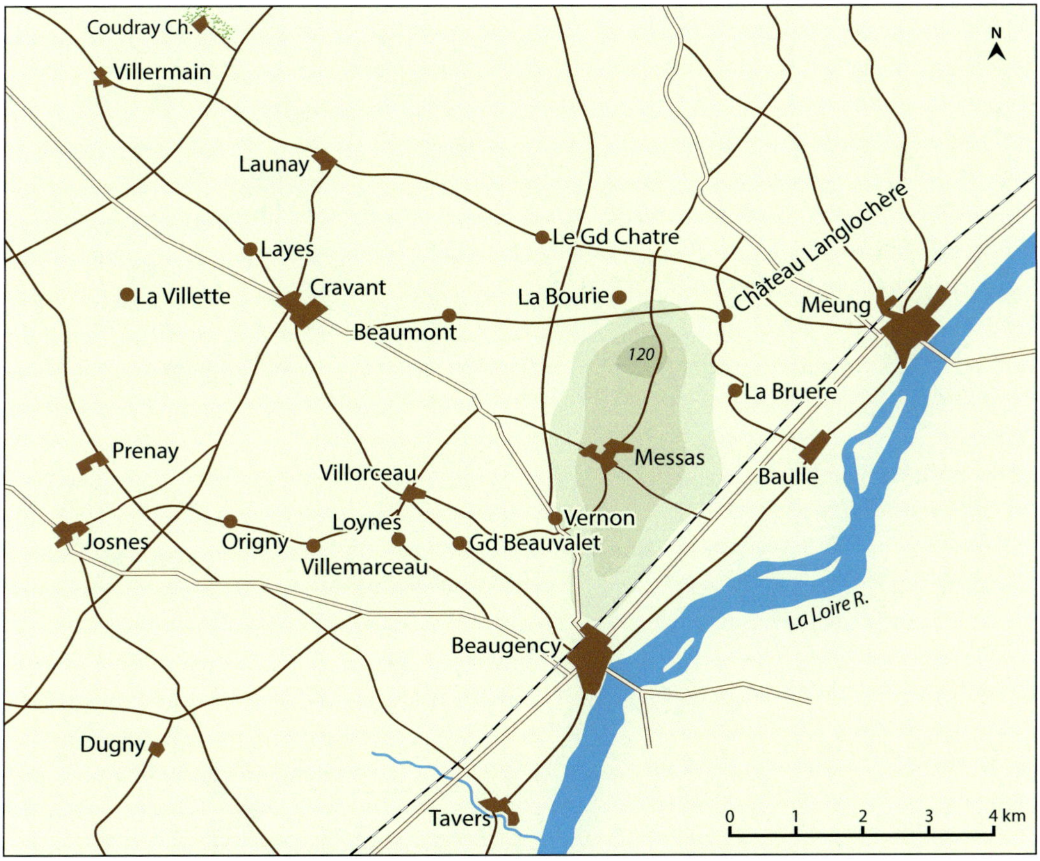

Map 6. Beaugency, 7-11 December 1870.

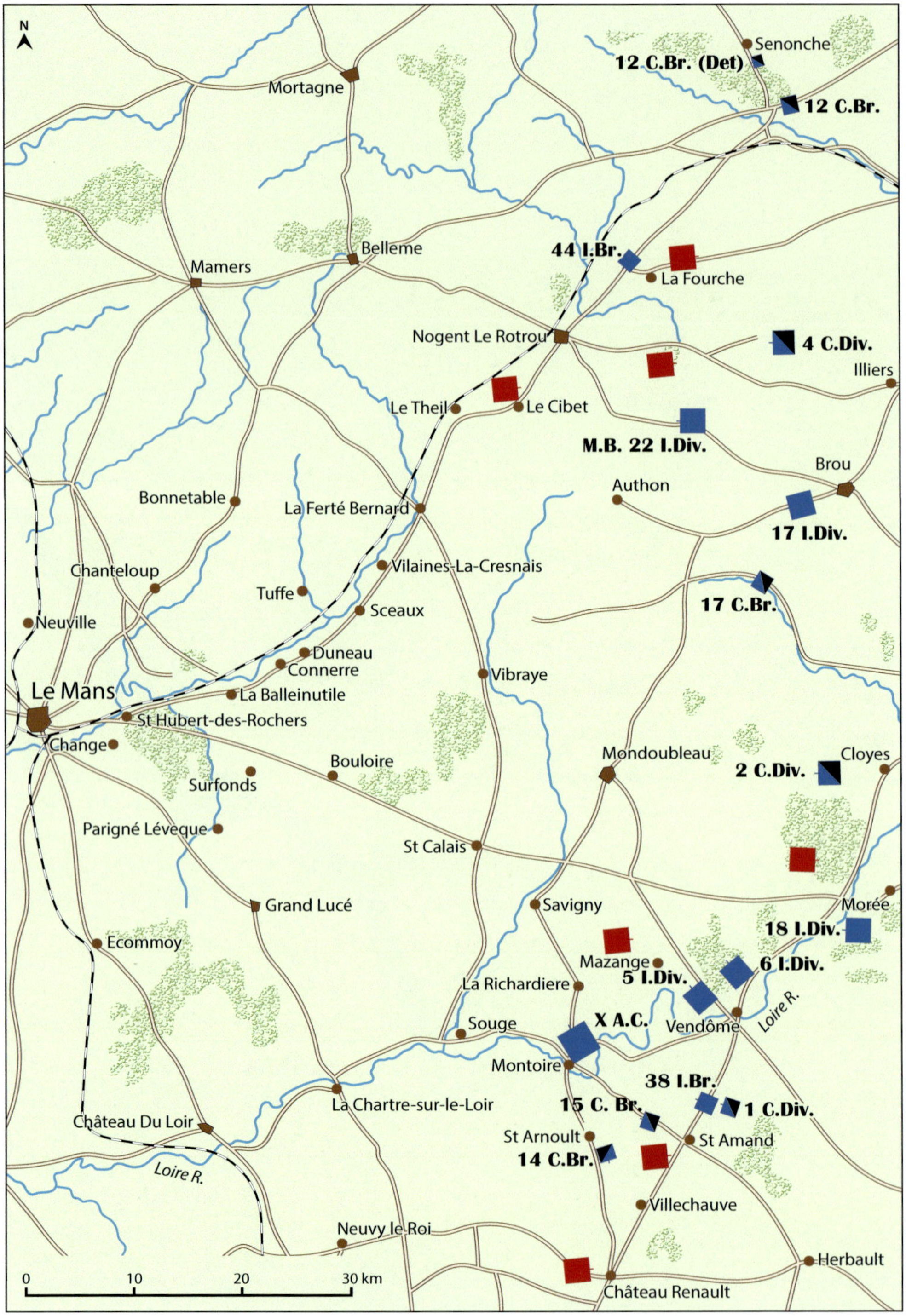

Map 7. The advance to Le Mans, 6 January 1871.

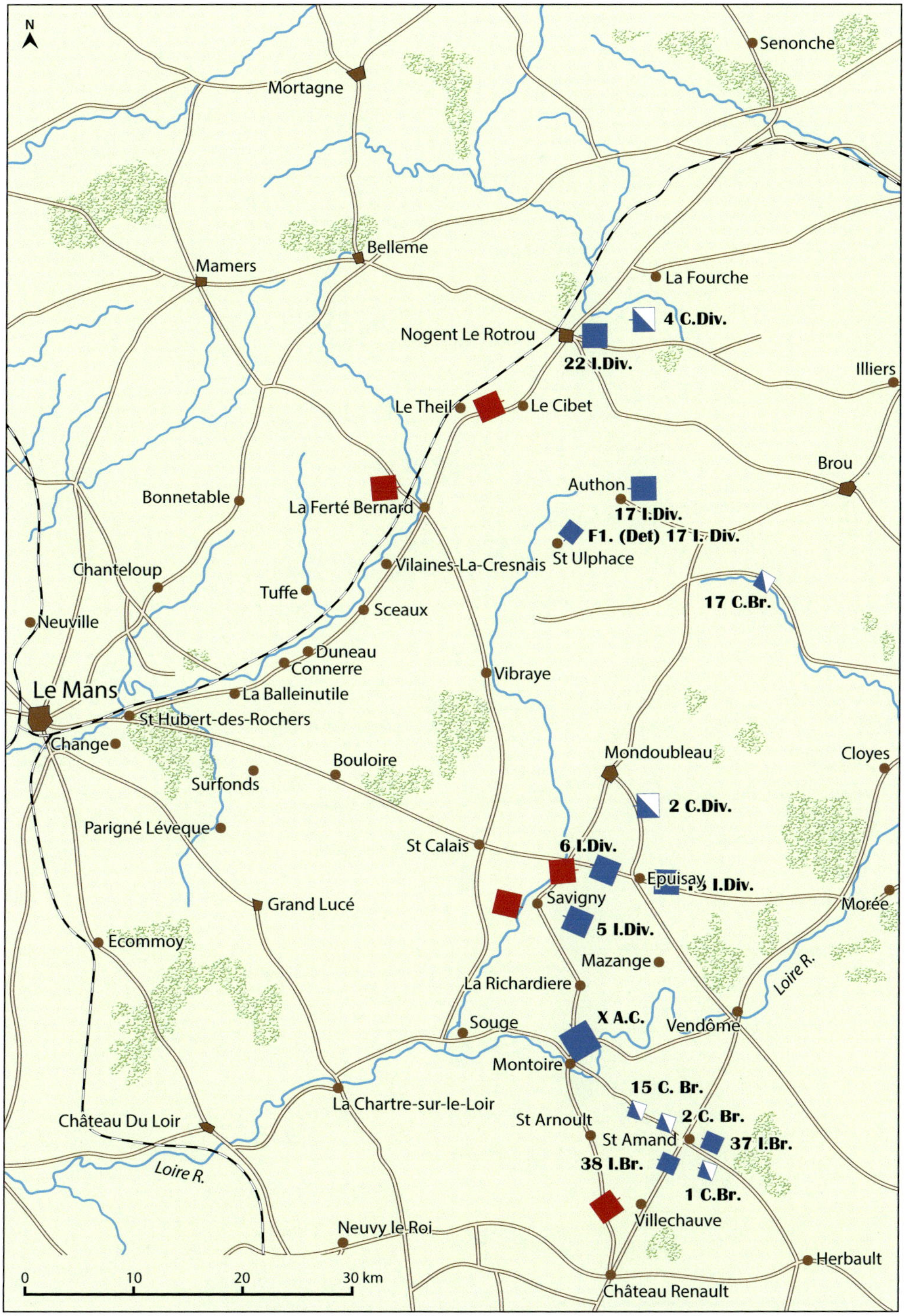

Map 8. The advance to Le Mans, 7 January 1871.

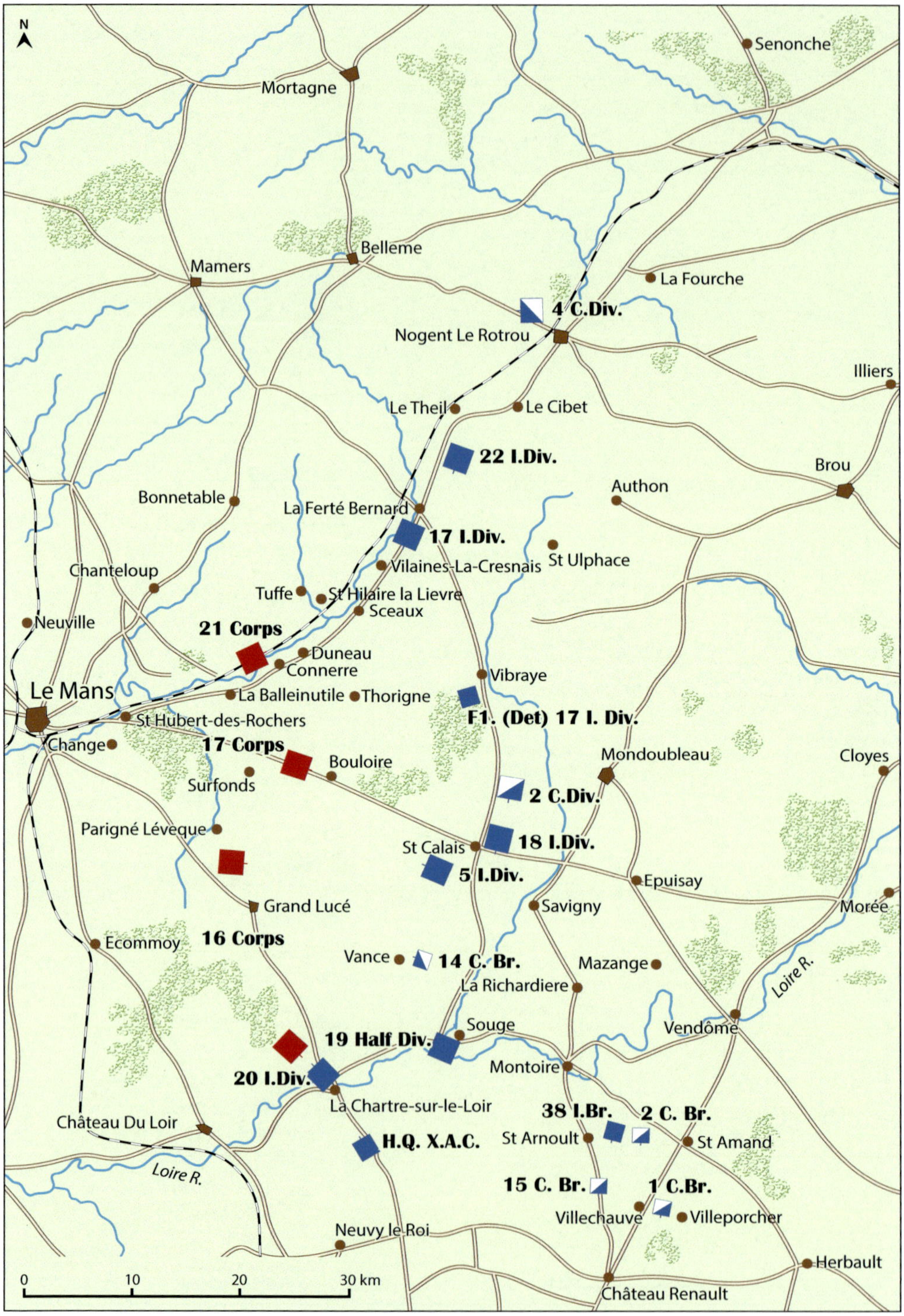

Map 9. The advance to Le Mans, 8 January 1871.

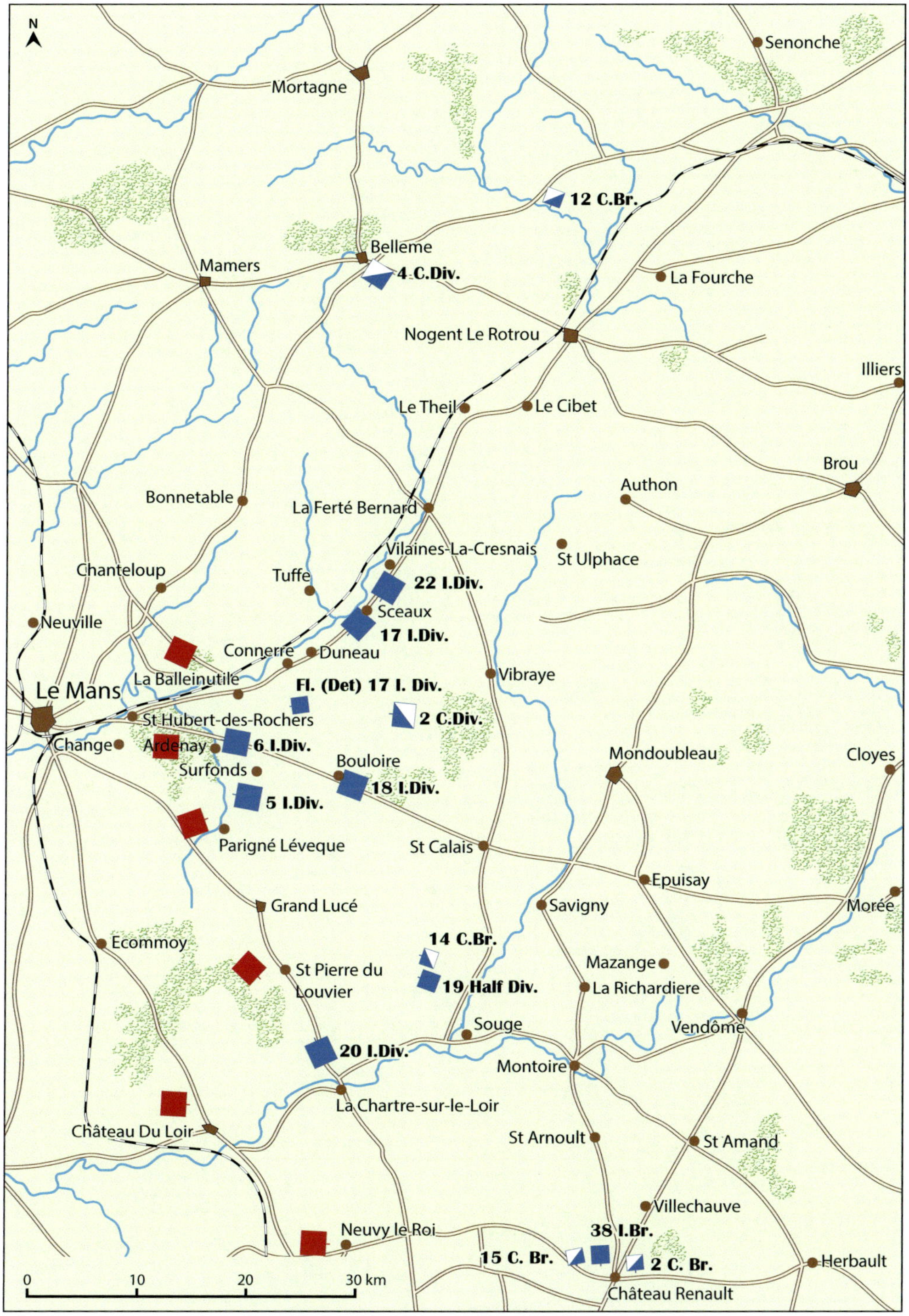

Map 10. The advance to Le Mans, 9 January 1871.

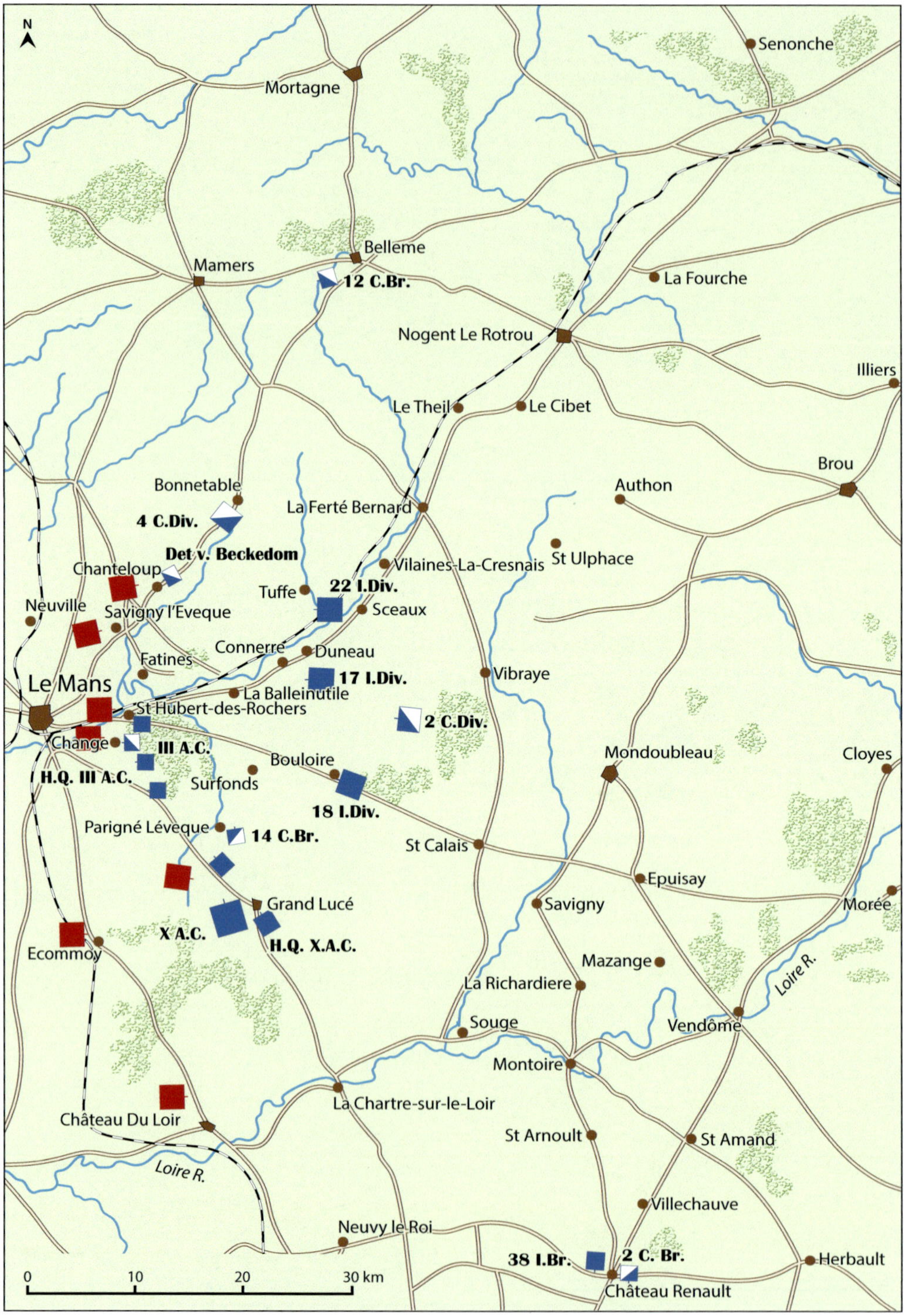

Map 11. The advance to Le Mans, 10 January 1871.

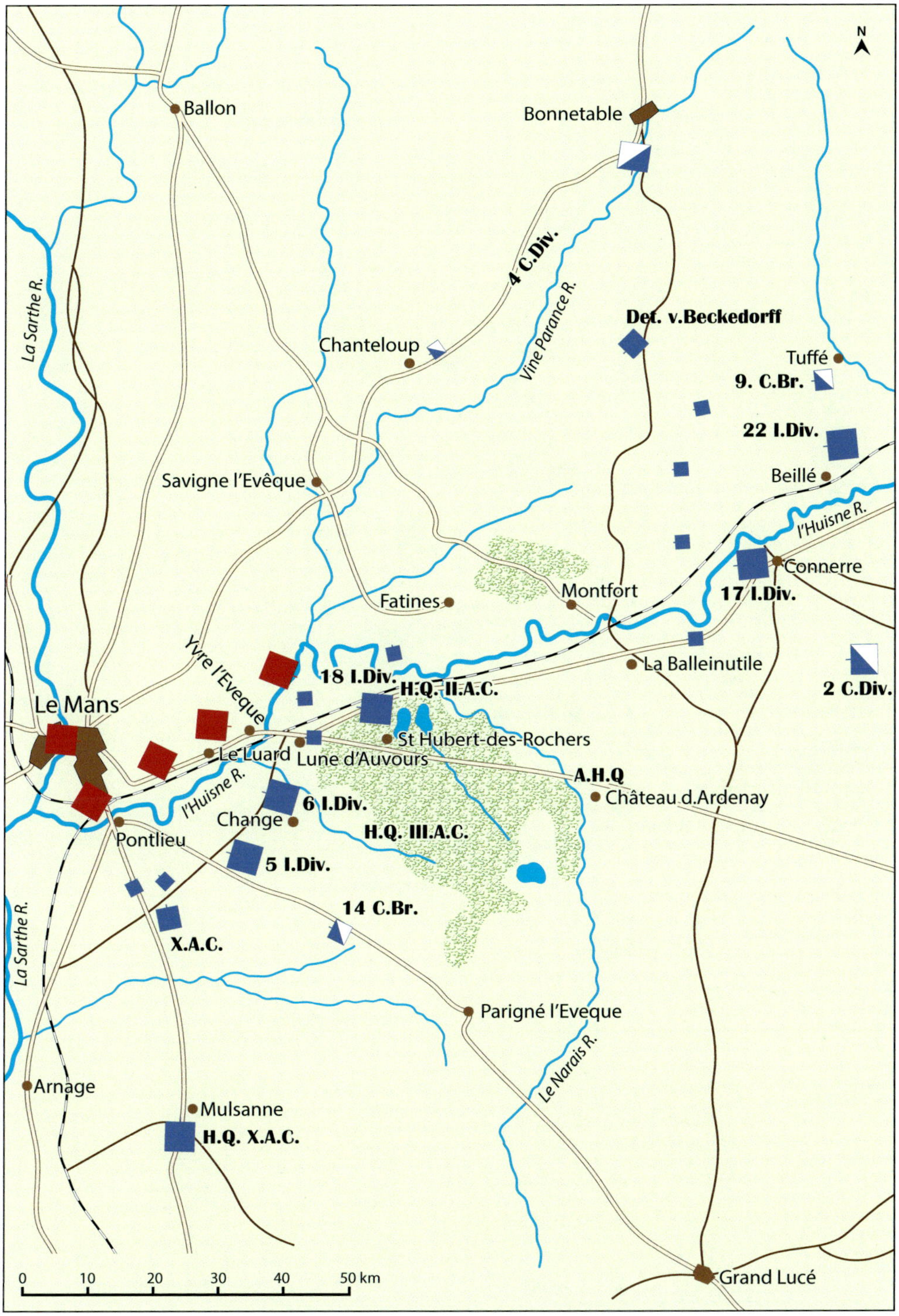

Map 12. The advance to Le Mans, 11 January 1871.

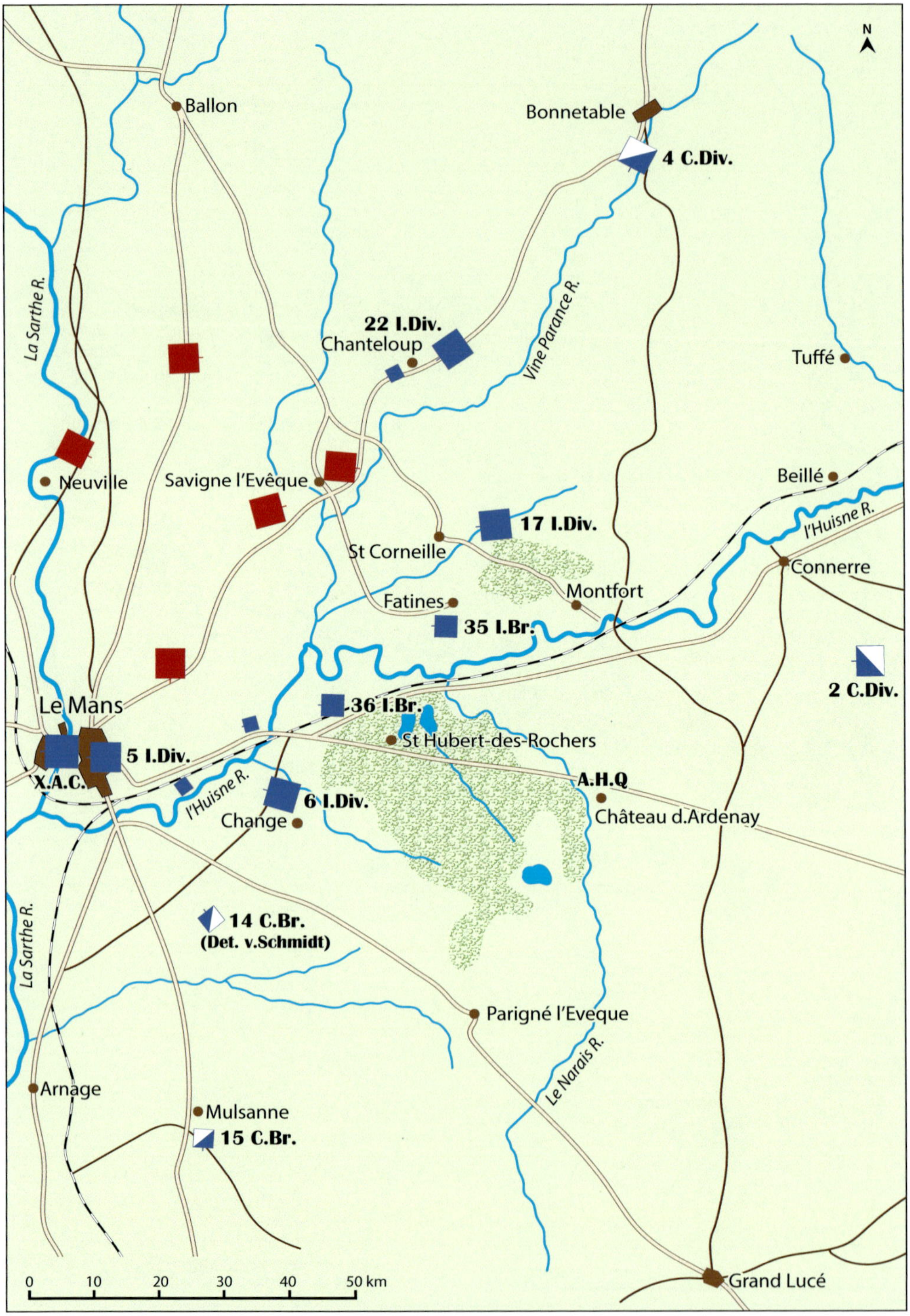

Map 13. The occupation of Le Mans, 12 January 1871.

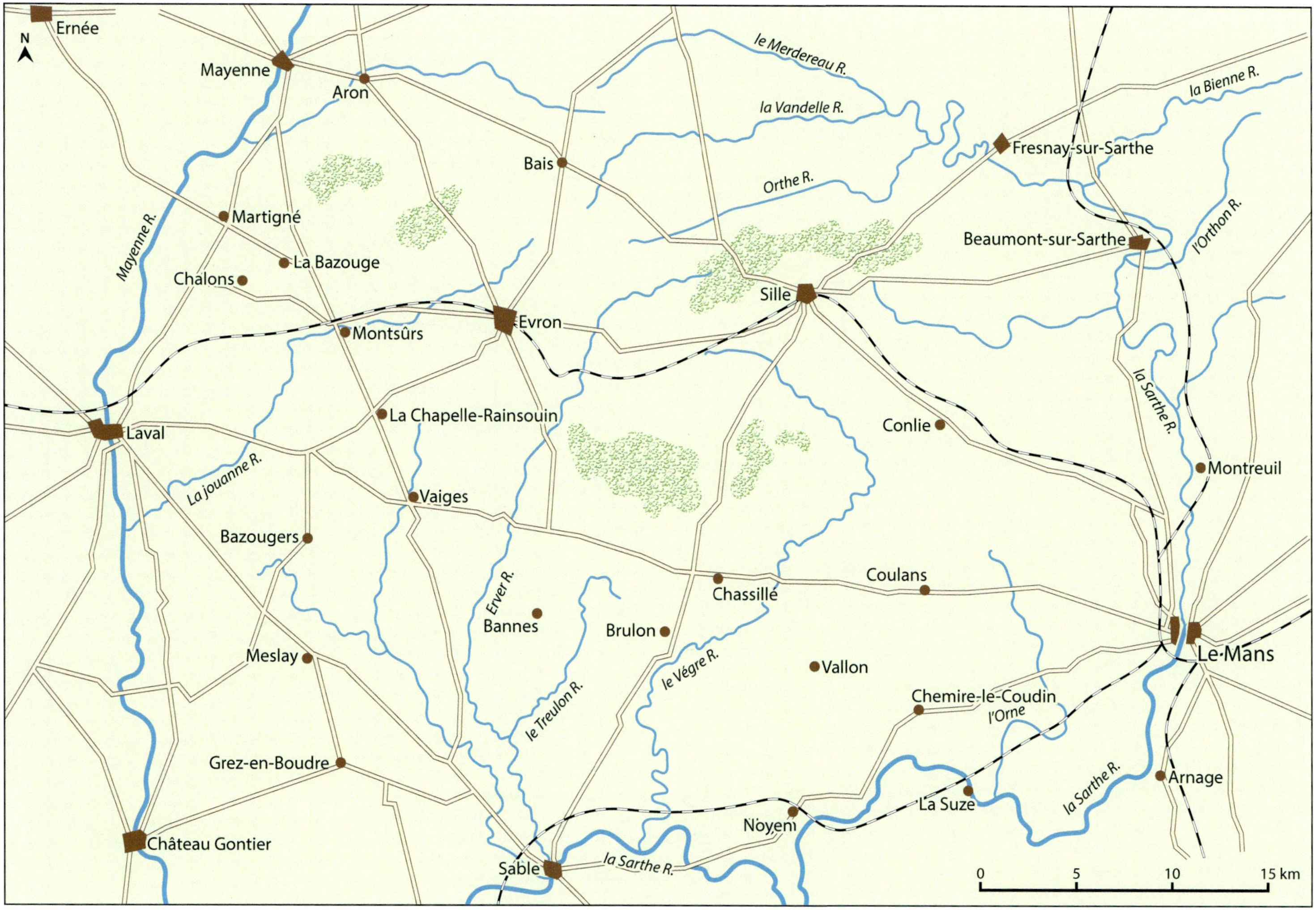

Map 14. The pursuit of the French, 13-18 January 1871.

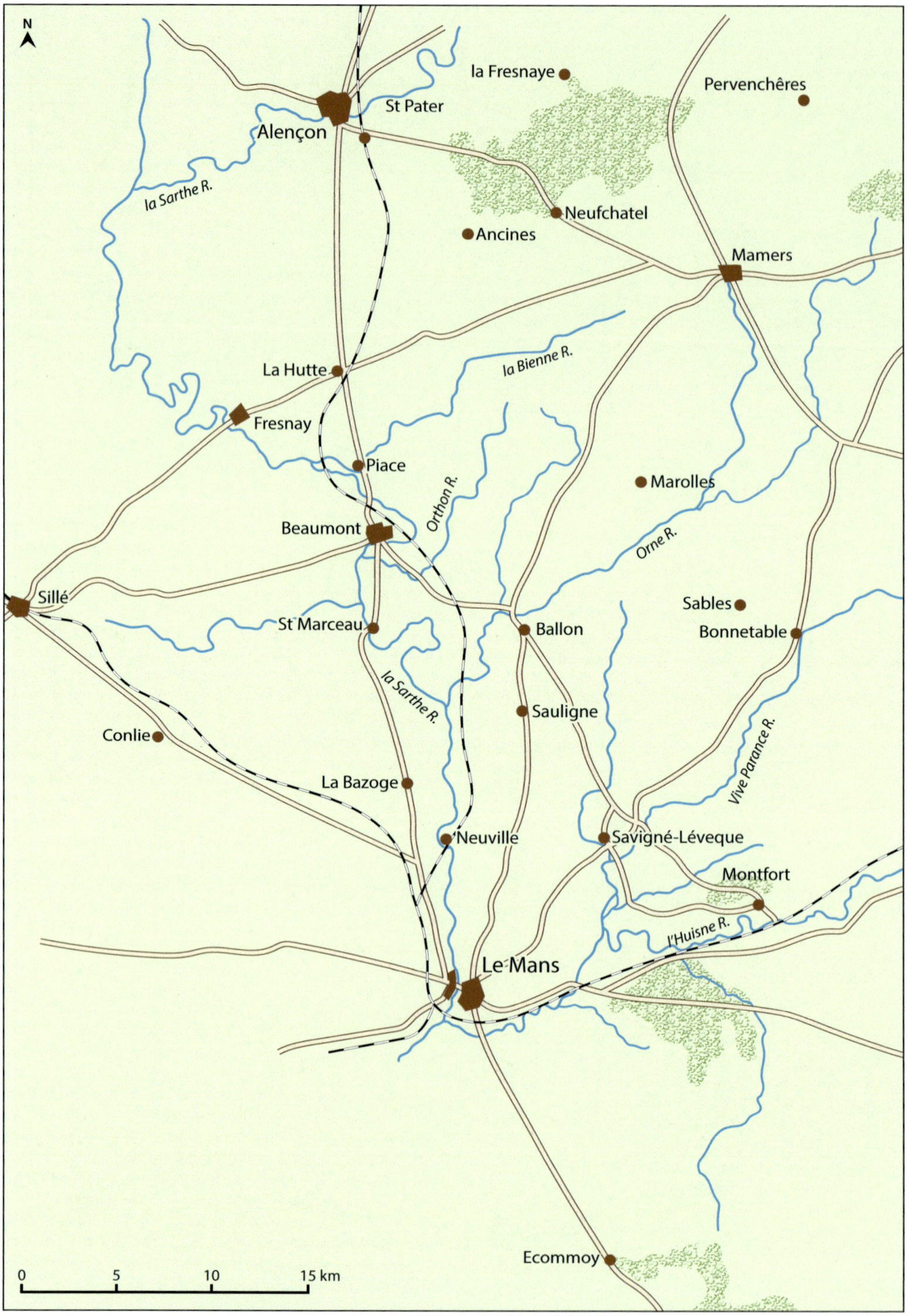

Map 15. The French retreat northwards, 13-15 January 1871.

1

The Capture of Orléans

Following the crushing victory of Sedan and the subsequent advance across France, Helmuth von Moltke completed his scheme for the investment of Paris at his temporary headquarters at Château Thierry on 14 September 1870. Its objective was simply stated: 'The march on Paris has as its end, above all, to cut off communication between the city and the exterior, and to prevent any revictualling and all attempts to lift the blockade.'[1] He went on to identify the positions to be taken up by the various units of Third Army and of the Army of the Meuse; the former would cover the southern sector of the investment, and the latter the northern sector. It would be an immensely complicated military operation, and to France, and the rest of Europe, it seemed scarcely conceivable that it could be undertaken. Moltke, though, calmly went about ensuring that the investment of the city was completed as quickly and thoroughly as possible.

The investment was completed with the defeat, on 19 September, of the offensive launched by General Auguste Ducrot at Châtillon in the direction of the Versailles Road. The attack quickly broke down under the fire of the German artillery, and the French troops streamed back into the city with cries of '*Nous sommes trahi*!' Ducrot attempted to make a stand behind the fortifications of the Châtillon Redoubt, but by mid-afternoon he was forced to abandon the position. Crown Prince Frederick William of Prussia, the commander of Third Army, watched the engagement from just south of the Croix de Bernis. His army included both Prussian and Bavarian units; he wrote in his diary:

> I could not today make out with any clearness who had most to do with it, whether Prussians or Bavarians; but this much was certain, that both sections had afforded one another mutual assistance, and that, while V Army Corps, by my orders was pushing its advance right up to Versailles, the Bavarians in the section allotted them were actually able to occupy an entrenchment with seven abandoned guns in it.[2]

Next day the Crown Prince rode over the battlefield with his chief of staff, Lieutenant General Leonhard von Blumenthal, and was very struck by the view of the city: 'A noble prospect here

1 Helmut von Moltke, *Correspondance Militaire* (Paris: Henri Charles Lavanzelle, n.d.) vol. II, pp.375–376.
2 Crown Prince William (A. R. Alliinson, trans.), *War Diary* (London: Stanley Paul 1927) p.126.

lay before us; Paris lay directly under our very feet, shining clear in the sunshine with its sea of houses, the richly gilded dome of Les Invalides and the numerous forts.' Later, they rode on to Versailles, where their headquarters was to be established. On the terrace of the palace he cast his mind back to the visit he had paid there with his father in 1867 as a guest of Napoleon III and Empress Eugénie, 'who did the honours with an amiable courtesy which charmed us. How swiftly has the star of the Imperial pair faded! Now Prussian uniforms enliven this superb scene of French pomp and pride!'[3]

On 19 September the Royal Headquarters was established at the Baron de Rothschild's château at Ferrières, and it was here that Bismarck engaged in negotiations with Jules Favre, the French Foreign Minister of the Republic, which ultimately proved to be abortive. Moltke, though, was hopeful that the war might end quickly; he wrote to his brother Adolph on 21 September: 'I cherish a private hope that I may be shooting hares at Creisau by the end of October.'[4] In the context of the military situation at that time, with armistice negotiations continuing, Moltke's hopes of an early peace were perhaps not unreasonable.

Meanwhile he had to concentrate on the practical tasks of establishing the investment of Paris. In the letter to his brother quoted above, he reflected on the difficulties faced by his field artillery:

> We are placed at present in the awkward position of having to submit to being fired at without being able to answer in like manner, for our 4-pdrs cannot possibly compete with the 74-pdrs in the forts. The siege train, which is conveying over 100,000 hundredweight of ammunition cannot be brought on very quickly, there being but a single line of rails.

In ordering up the siege train, he did so as a military necessity, but he was not at all enthusiastic about conducting formal siege operations or undertaking a thorough bombardment of the city. He intended to pursue a patient strategy, even though he entirely appreciated that the process of starving out Paris was going to be a very slow one.

Once the investment had been completed, responsibility for ensuring the security of the units besieging the capital fell to the respective headquarters of Third Army and the Army of the Meuse. For the moment, at the end of September, there were no French organised units capable of interfering with the investment, but it was not to be expected that this would continue to be the case. In particular, there was already a threat from the *franc-tireurs*, which necessarily hampered the German lines of communication. It would be for the cavalry divisions operating behind the lines of the investing armies to monitor the French and anticipate any concerted attacks.

On 23 September Moltke drove out from Ferrières to see the lines of investment for himself. He took with him two of his most trusted staff officers, Colonel Paul Bronsart von Schellendorff and Lieutenant Colonel Julius von Verdy du Vernois. The latter described the trip in his diary:

> After having reached the outpost line, we went on foot to a small building on the other side of it, a kind of garden pavilion, standing high on the slope which descends steeply

3 Crown Prince, *War Diary*, p.128.
4 Helmut von Moltke (C. Bell & H. W. Fisher, trans.), *Letters to his Mother and his Brothers*, (New York: Harper Bros, 1893), p.193.

> to the Marne. The little building had been put into a state of defence, and we had a good view of the neighbouring forts through the loopholes. We could see plainly some *gardes mobiles* on the ramparts, and we overlooked that part of the town between the forts and Mont Valerien. The railway bridge across the Marne, at our feet, as well as several other bridges were blown up. As we are not in a position to attack the fortifications on this side, the blowing up of these means of crossing would really have been our business, to protect ourselves against a surprise here, but the French have been so kind as to save us the trouble.[5]

Visits such as this to the front line were not without risk; two days later Verdy recorded that the little house had been demolished by French shells.

It had always been part of French military strategy that Paris should be defended, rather than being declared an open city. The chain of forts which had begun being built during the Thiers administration formed a perimeter of some 40 miles, meaning that the line of works to be erected and defended by a besieging army was itself some 50 miles in length. The total strength of the forces investing the city was around 150,000 men, with 620 guns; with this the Germans had to enclose an enemy force of more than double their numbers. The defence of Paris would give the Government of National Defence the time it required to raise fresh forces in the provinces with which to continue the war. It meant, though, that the principal strategic focus for all the French military operations must be the relief of the capital. It also meant that most of the troops available to Moltke after the Battle of Sedan were themselves pinned down, both at Metz where the Army of the Rhine was invested, and at Paris. As Colonel Lonsdale Hale wrote, the loss of mobility can be extremely dangerous for an invading army:

> Not merely is time afforded to the invaded for fresh preparations for defence, but the prestige inherent in the continued offensive is lost; the invaded have time to recover their self-possession and morale; and they attribute to the invader either exhaustion arising from his previous efforts, or an acknowledgement of inability to pursue owing to the numerical weakness of his forces.[6]

Although the forces available to Moltke to conduct the investment of Paris were considerable, they were barely enough for the task. Inside Paris, there was an enormous pool of men to be drawn on for the defence of the city. General Louis Trochu, who had become President of the Council on the establishment of the Government of National Defence, and commander-in-chief of the army, had available the two new regular corps that had been formed in Paris, the 13th and 14th. The former had been at Mézières when the Army of Châlons had surrendered at Sedan and Vinoy, its commander, had succeeded in extricating it and bringing it back to the capital. Some 10,000 men had also escaped; there were 3,000 marines and 8,000 sailors. These regular troops amounted to 106,000 men. In addition, there were over 100,000 *gardes mobiles*; the *Garde Sedentaire*, which comprised all male citizens between 25 and 35 years of age, amounted to around 200,000 men; and a large number of private volunteer formations added

5 General Julius von Verdy du Vernois, *With the Royal Headquarters in 1870–71* (London: Keegan Paul Trench and Trübner, 1897) pp.166–167.

6 Colonel Lonsdale Hale, *The People's War in France, 1870–1871* (London: Hugh Rees Limited, 1904), p.24.

to the numbers available. On 14 September a huge review took place in the Champs Elysées, which Trochu later described:

> More than a million human creatures, soldiers and sailors in uniform, National Guardsmen and armed civilians, and watching crowds filling with their intermingled and tightly squeezed ranks the great roads which stretched from the Place de la Bastille to the Arc de Triomphe, through the boulevards, the Place de la Concorde and the Champs Elysées! At every window of surrounding buildings, on the balconies and the terraces there were further ranks of moving heads, of flags, of patriotic emblems. Every voice was shouting, all arms were moving, it was a delirium.[7]

Although the Government of National Defence had, anticipating the investment of the capital, sent some of its members as a 'delegation' to Tours to represent it in the provinces, the Government of France itself remained in Paris, as Gambetta's message to the *préfets* of the 89 *départements* made clear: 'Our new Republic is a Government of National Defence, a Republic of battle to the last against the intruders. Gather around you citizens who, like yourselves, are animated by the lasting desire to save the country, and are prepared not to shrink from any sacrifices.'[8] Although there was a considerable body of opinion in favour of committing all available forces to a guerrilla war, Gambetta among others soon grasped that the need to relieve Paris meant that properly organised and equipped troops, given as much training as was possible, must be put in the field without delay. There was a large pool of men available, and those called up were given intensive basic training, but in many of the new units that came into being the equipment was inadequate. Roger de Mauni, enrolled at first with the *gardes mobiles* of the Seine, wrote in his diary:

> We begin our target shooting today, and it is to be continued tomorrow. A great number of our *mobiles* have been sportsmen, and take a much better aim than one would expect. Our muskets are detestable, and it is aggravating to hear them spoken of as being so excellent. As we cannot be convinced on this point, they talk of giving us others. It looks as if they were trying to amuse us; if so, the attempt is not very successful.[9]

Moltke was perfectly aware that sooner rather than later the forces being assembled in the provinces would move forward in an effort to relieve the capital. By the end of September there had been assembled on the Loire the newly constituted 15th Corps, under the command of the experienced 66-year-old Edouard de La Motte-Rouge, about 60,000 strong. It was still however, in a relatively disorganised state. It included three regular line regiments; the remaining units consisted of two-thirds *régiments de marche* and one-third *gardes mobiles*. In the north-west, General Fiereck was attempting to bring together a force based on seven regular battalions and two marine battalions. The rest consisted of various units of *franc-tireurs*, *gardes mobiles*, *gardes nationales* and armed civilians. In the coming months this force, known as the Army of the West, was given credit by the Germans for being a good deal stronger, and much

7 General Louis Trochu, *Oeuvres Posthumes* (Tours: Perrin et Cie, 1896), vol. I, pp.218–221.
8 Hale, *People's War*, p.23.
9 Roger de Mauni, *The Franco-Prussian War* (London: Longman & Co., 1872), p.32.

better organised, than was in fact the case. In the north-east of the country a force of about 14,000 men under General Gudin had been assembled around Rouen and Elboeuf, while a force of 4,000 men at Vernon and Dreux maintained contact with the forces on the Loire and covered the important railway links from Rouen to the west and south. Finally, in the south-east, General Cambriels was assembling a corps at Besançon, intended to cover Lyon.

It was not easy for the Germans to gather firm intelligence about the actual strength of these new French units, but such information as was received did not suggest that at the moment they presented a serious threat. Some of those on Moltke's staff, such as the quartermaster general, Lieutenant General Theophil von Podbielski, were inclined to write them off altogether, describing them as 'ragamuffins'.

Blumenthal had established the headquarters of Third Army on 20 September in the prefecture, where he was very comfortable. He was, therefore, not at all pleased to learn that it was proposed to locate the Royal Headquarters at Versailles as well, writing in his diary:

We shall, I suppose, have to move out of our beautiful palace and seek some humbler abode. I do not mind that so much, but the close propinquity of the King's headquarters has its drawbacks, especially for me, as I have not always sufficient command over myself to return the diplomatic or evasive answers to all the unnecessary questions and unsolicited conundrums set to solve. I am afraid that I shall again become somewhat caustic or brusque without wishing to be so, and shall get myself disliked.[10]

The rear of the Third Army was covered by the 2nd, 5th and 6th Cavalry Divisions, commanded by Lieutenant Generals Count zu Stolberg, von Rheinbaben and von Schmidt respectively, and before the end of September these were each reporting stiffening resistance from *franc-tireurs*. As a result, these units required infantry support which was provided by von der Tann's I Bavarian Corps. This, which formed part of Third Army, had been standing in reserve, in cantonments around Longjumeau, from where it pushed some infantry units forward in the direction of Pithiviers in support of the cavalry scouting towards Orléans. Six infantry battalions in all were assigned to this task. They were not, however, in the best of health; they had previously been involved in dealing with the vast number of prisoners taken at Sedan, as well as clearing the battlefield and collecting and sorting the captured war materiel, before marching to Longjumeau. The official history noted:

> The pernicious consequences of the unhealthy detention before Sedan began to make themselves seriously felt. Typhus and dysentery were the prevailing illnesses; according to the unanimous opinion of the doctors they were chiefly contracted in the trying duties after the Battle of Sedan, when the troops had to pass days and nights in swampy bivouacs, under an incessant downpour of rain, and breathing air tainted by the exhalations of putrefaction.[11]

Although the bulk of the French forces designated as 15th Corps, concentrating to the south of Paris were largely assembling behind the Loire, a force of *gardes mobiles*, covered by a cavalry division under General Reyau, had been posted around Orléans. Patrols from Rheinbaben's 5th

10 Count Albrecht von Blumenthal, ed., *Journals of Field Marshal Count von Blumenthal for 1866 and 1871* (London: Edward Arnold, 1903), pp.141–142.

11 Captain Hugo Helvig (Captain George Schwabe, trans.), *Operations of the I Bavarian Corps* (London: Henry S King and Co, 1874), p.105.

Cavalry Division operating westwards from St Germain de Laye encountered resistance at Les Alluets, but supported by two Bavarian battalions soon cleared the place; the French retired to Vernon. The Bavarian infantry occupied Maule; the 12th Cavalry Brigade, under Major General von Bredow advanced to the line of the Eure, and broke up the railway at Mantes.

The 6th Cavalry Division had marched south westwards, and on 2 October met a body of French troops based on Epernon. Two days later its 15th Cavalry Brigade, supported by Bavarian infantry, drove the French out of Epernon, inflicting some 75 casualties.

Following his appointment to command the 15th Corps, Motte-Rouge had been to Tours to get instructions from the delegation; as he left, one of its members said to him: 'For God's sake do something or other as soon as you possibly can. Public opinion insists on it.'[12] In response to this Motte-Rouge moved his corps up to Orléans and Gien, and on 5 October sent Reyau to advance through Artenay on Toury. There he encountered two brigades of Prince Albrecht's 4th Cavalry Division, which withdrew slowly towards Angerville without being pursued; a detachment of the division which had been at Pithiviers supported by an infantry battalion retired in the evening to Étampes.

News of the French advance was at once reported to von der Tann, and to the headquarters of Third Army, as well as to the Royal Headquarters. There, next day, Moltke sketched out a plan for the I Bavarian Corps to attack the enemy in front, while the 22nd Infantry Division (Major General von Wittich) and Stolberg's 2nd Cavalry Division attacked the flank.[13] Blumenthal, who not infrequently assigned to himself the credit for decisions of this kind, wrote in his diary that he approached Moltke, 'and proposed that a force consisting of the I Bavarian Corps supported by the 22nd Division, together with the three cavalry divisions, the whole under General von der Tann, should move against the Army of the South and give it a sound drubbing.'[14] According to the Bavarian official history, it was at noon on 6 October that orders reached the I Bavarian Corps to concentrate at Arpajon, while the 22nd Division moved to Montlhéry.

The area in which Motte-Rouge was operating was to be the scene of considerable activity in the coming weeks. It was well suited to operations designed to lead to an advance for the relief of Paris, as the German official history recorded:

> The central course of the Loire, a stream of considerable breadth and some six or seven feet in depth, at whose northerly bend the town of Orléans forms a convenient bridgehead for forward movements from the southern provinces in the direction of Paris, separates two districts of very opposite character. The Beauce Plateau rising on the right bank and sloping towards the river district of the Seine is broadly undulating, and gentle, wooded spurs, a result of its natural fertility, cultivated like a garden, studded at intervals with stone farmsteads, intersected by numerous roads and surrounded with extensive woods. Little rills trickle for the most part within narrow folds of the ground and run with a northerly direction towards the Seine; their margins are bordered by narrow tracks of meadow land. South of the Loire spreads the sandy and stony Sologne. There also, is found a sufficient network of roads for the movement of troops; for the deployment of large bodies of cavalry

12 Hale, *People's War*, p.32.
13 Moltke, *Correspondance Militaire,* vol. II, pp.409–410.
14 Blumenthal, *Journals*, p.146.

> and artillery difficulties are interposed by the numerous ponds and marshes bordered with fir-copses, with which this generally inhospitable waste abounds.[15]

The openness of the country enabled the French to make good use of the power of the Chassepot, and it was impossible for cavalry to surprise a body of infantry if the latter displayed ordinary caution. The Bavarian official history explained the problems faced by von der Tann:

> The plains of La Beauce, therefore, had their drawbacks, for cavalry could not, at a distance of more than a thousand yards, hope to make a successful attack even on raw troops if armed, as in this case, with a good and powerful firearm. The enemy's infantry was able to hinder the movements of the cavalry by covering large spaces with a crossfire from the numerous but widely scattered farms. Our infantry had to perform the hardest and most thankless task in the engagements in this district. When on the offensive, it had to advance without cover, and when on the defensive it had to rely on villages and farms as its only *points d'appui*. It was impossible to make a gradual advance and at the same time to keep up a fire on the enemy's position, or to move in small bodies from cover to cover. The skirmishers were forced to extend in long thin lines, while the supports could not be massed.[16]

Von der Tann's Corps was composed of two infantry divisions, each of two brigades, from which several battalions had been detached, a cuirassier brigade of eight squadrons, two regiments of divisional cavalry, and 112 guns. Its numerical strength was about 16,000 infantry and 1,600 cavalry. The 22nd Division comprised some 5,500 infantry, four squadrons of cavalry and 24 guns. Finally, the 4th Cavalry Division was composed of 24 squadrons and 12 guns. At Arpajon, von der Tann resolved to await a French attack in a position stretching from Bruyères to St Germain and then, as the battle developed, to move to the offensive with one or both wings.

However, when no sign of an enemy advance appeared, von der Tann was ordered, on the night of 7/8 October, to take the offensive in a southerly direction. It would be his task to clear the country south to Orléans, and westwards to Chartres; then to occupy Orléans; and, as circumstances permitted, to advance on Tours. He was given in addition Stolberg's 2nd Cavalry Division of 24 squadrons and 12 guns, bringing his total strength to 21,500 infantry, 6,700 cavalry and 160 guns.

Moltke, in one of his regular letters to Major General Gustav von Stiehle, the chief of staff of Second Army at Metz, told him on 9 October of Reyau's advance and the steps that were being taken to deal with the French forces on the Loire: 'If the Army of the Loire does not retreat of its own accord, there will be a decisive battle in the outskirts of Angerville. To tell the truth, in front of Paris, we are for the moment without reserves.'[17]

When von der Tann's movement began, Motte-Rouge pushed forward a small force as far as Artenay, four miles north of the forest and a dozen miles from Orléans. Blumenthal had sent Major von Hahnke to von der Tann's headquarters with orders to push on as quickly as

15 (Captain F. C. H. Clarke, trans.) *German Official Account of the Franco-German War 1870–71*, (London: HMSO, 1877) vol. III, p.147.
16 Helvig, *Operations of the I Bavarian Corps*, p.122.
17 Moltke, *Correspondance Militaire*, vol. II, p.413.

possible, and on 10 October at 6.00 a.m. the advance began. Pushing down the high road, the 1st Bavarian Brigade encountered French forces at Dambron; these soon withdrew towards Artenay. Meanwhile the commander of the 1st Bavarian Division, Major General von Stephan, brought up his 2nd Brigade to drive back the enemy to the east of the road. Von der Tann, accompanying his leading troops, anticipated fighting a major action, and assembled a gun line in an arc around the north of Artenay as far as Poupry, behind which the rest of his force remained in reserve.

Further to the west, Prince Albrecht had heard the sound of gunfire, and swung back towards the Paris high road. At Ouvans, some three miles west of Artenay, his horse artillery opened fire on French troops in Autroches and Château Auvilliers. By 3.00 p.m. this attack on his flank led Motte-Rouge to conclude that his position at Artenay was indefensible, and he ordered an immediate retreat which deteriorated into a rout. To the east, at Arblay Farm, a French battery was caught in the open by three squadrons of hussars from the 10th Cavalry Brigade, and dispersed with the loss of 250 prisoners. On the main road, a body of French infantry, around 600 strong, was surrounded and taken prisoner at La Croix Briquet. The French, in great disorder, fell back into the Forest of Orléans. Von der Tann had sustained some 200 casualties; the total French losses are not recorded but included 1,500 men taken prisoner.[18]

Blumenthal, when the news of the victory was reported to him, was delighted. He had been certain that 'nothing will convince sooner of our power than the knowledge that we can prevent the formation of new armies.' This extremely premature judgement appeared to be confirmed by the news, and he was pleased to hear all about it, 'as I had had so much difficulty in getting this expedition sanctioned.'[19]

On 11 October von der Tann continued his advance in the direction of Orléans. He was optimistic that he could capture the city without undue difficulty. The bulk of his troops marched down the high road, with the 22nd Division on his right, while his cavalry fanned out towards the west. Motte-Rouge, however, had been sufficiently dispirited by the action at Artenay to conclude that he could not successfully hold any position north of the Loire, and his troops had already begun to cross the river. He assigned a force of 15,000 men to cover this movement, and part of this body took up an entrenched position at Ormes, from where a field artillery battery fired vigorously on the advancing 22nd Division. Wittich brought up seven batteries which quickly silenced the French battery. Meanwhile his leading unit, the 44th Brigade, took cover as far as it was able and awaited the advance of the rest of the division. Wittich developed his attack on his right, following which the 83rd Regiment led by Colonel Marschall von Bieberstein, stormed the village, though not without suffering some considerable loss. It was in German hands by 2.00 p.m., and Wittich's two brigades continued their advance, supported by the 1st Bavarian Brigade.

On von der Tann's left, the rest of his corps advanced on Saran, where stiff resistance was encountered before the position was finally cleared and the Bavarians could resume their advance on Orléans. Meanwhile, on the high road, the 3rd Bavarian Brigade had encountered less resistance until it reached the northern part of the built-up area at the suburb of Bel-Air. Here they met very stiff opposition. Although the ground was unfavourable to the deployment of artillery, four guns of a 6-pdr battery were brought into action at the High Road and near a windmill to

18 *Official Account*, vol. III, pp.154–156.
19 Blumenthal, *Journals*, p.153.

the west of it. The infantry forced their way into the nearest farms of Bel-Air, but here the attack bogged down. Schumacher, the brigade commander, committed his two remaining battalions but although first they made some progress, their advance was then stalled.

Meanwhile the 4th Brigade had been in action with its three 6-pdr batteries to the south of Saran, advancing against les Aydes, which was defended by the 5th Battalion of the Foreign Legion. Here, too, extremely stiff resistance was encountered, and it took a long struggle before the village was finally captured. To the west, the brigade reached Grange des Groues and St Jean de la Ruelle, where they began a prolonged exchange of rifle fire with the French skirmishing lines deployed on the railway opposite.[20]

The French had fortified and strongly occupied the railway station at Les Aubrais. This was successfully stormed by a column led by Colonel Narciss, and he pushed on to attack the gasworks to the south; the French, however, launched a series of counter-attacks in an effort to retake the position, inflicting considerable casualties on the Bavarian infantry, which were compelled to fall back to the railway station. The French followed this up with a further series of attacks. These were ultimately beaten off, and the Bavarians in their turn launched a series of counter-attacks of their own, which ultimately succeeded in retaking the gas works and the adjoining vineyards. Von der Tann had been taken by surprise by the fierce resistance offered by Motte-Rouge's rearguard, but he was nevertheless determined to take Orléans by nightfall, and he ordered an advance by his right wing to achieve this. At 5.00 p.m. he directed the 1st Bavarian Brigade to come between the 43rd Brigade and the 4th Bavarian Brigade. Major General Dietl, the commander of the 1st Brigade, then struck off from the high road into the vineyards at Le Grand Orme which he reached just after the 4th Brigade was regrouping there after an unsuccessful assault on the railway embankment. It was only after the 32nd Regiment had crossed the embankment from the west by a route pointed out by Lieutenant Colonel von Heinleth, von der Tann's chief of staff, that the enemy fell back into the suburb of St Jean.

Led by Heinleth, the 1st Bavarian Regiment, which had been in reserve on the High Road, dashed through the suburb as far as a toll gate across the road, where it was brought up short by a hail of rifle fire and grenades. Forcing its way in through a side entrance, the regiment drove the enemy before them by two parallel streets. During the advance into the outskirts of Orléans, none of the attacking columns had much idea of the progress being made by the others, because of the disadvantages of the terrain and the way in which the vegetation impeded movement.[21] Each column directed itself, so far as it could, towards the spire of the cathedral, which could be seen in the distance in the fading light.

By 7.00 p.m. the advance through the city had reached the central Place du Martroi. The 43rd Regiment, pursuing the French as they retreated to the suburb of Bannier, advanced towards the bridges over the Loire. Von der Tann, however, riding into the city with Wittich, feared that in the darkness any close pursuit of the enemy could lead to dangerous confusion, and he contented himself with ordering the occupation of the city, seizing the most important buildings and the bridges over the Loire; the troops bivouacked in the larger open squares. One battalion of the Bavarian *Leib-Infanterie* was ordered to occupy the Mairie, in the city centre:

20 *Official Account*, vol. III, p.161.
21 Helvig, *Operations*, p.136.

> This battalion advanced through the dark and silent streets with band playing and drums beating, and was greeted at La Place Martroi by the ringing cheers of the 1st Regiment. The flames of the bivouac fires, which had been hastily kindled, lit up the martial groups, and the outlines of the gigantic statue of the Maid of Orléans, which towered over the foreign soldiers, as they exulted in their victory.[22]

During the night, the 1st Bavarian Division crossed the river to occupy the suburbs on the left bank, while the 2nd Division occupied the eastern part of the city, and the 22nd Division the western part. The battle for Orléans had turned out to be a much more severe engagement than the Germans had expected. Von der Tann had, though, successfully achieved the first of his objectives. The total German casualties amounted to 59 killed and 873 wounded; French casualties were very much higher, and included some 1,800 prisoners.[23]

Moltke, in his own account of the war, noted that the French rearguard had covered the retreat of the 15th Corps, 'for a whole day against superior forces, with praiseworthy determination.' Reflecting on the difficulties of the terrain, he added:

> In the open field, where skilful handling of masses is possible, it would soon have been defeated; but in street fighting, unflinching personal courage is all that is needed in the defender, and the latest recruits of the newly created French levies did not lack that attribute.[24]

Having taken Orléans and the Loire crossings, it was hoped at Versailles that von der Tann would be able to follow up his success by advancing south to the hugely important arsenal town of Bourges. Blumenthal wrote to von der Tann to this effect, suggesting also the possibility of advancing westwards to Tours, but he left it to him to decide his movements in the light of the circumstances of the moment. Von der Tann, hearing that the French forces immediately opposed to him were being reinforced, and that Bourges had been fortified, concluded that his relative weakness in infantry made an advance deep into the inhospitable region of the Sologne altogether too risky. He limited himself to holding Orléans and the line of the Loire.[25] Since it appeared that comparatively small forces were all that was needed for this purpose, the 22nd Division and 4th Cavalry Division on 16 October were ordered to return to Third Army, after first dealing with the substantial bands of *franc-tireurs* which had appeared at Châteaudun and Chartres. The *franc-tireurs* had now begun to make a considerable nuisance of themselves in the rear areas of Third Army.

The Bavarian official historian was at some pains to refute the suggestion that the period of three weeks during which von der Tann was in occupation of Orléans was a time of rest and recreation. The general situation was 'so doubtful and uncertain' that the demands made on the troops of the I Bavarian Corps were considerable:

22 Helvig, *Operations*, pp.154–155.
23 *Official Account*, vol. III, p.162.
24 Field Marshal Count Helmuth von Moltke, *The Franco-German War of 1870–71* (London: Harper and Brothers, 1907), p.148.
25 *Official Account*, vol. III, p.164.

It was a long time before the effects of this so-called rest in Orléans ceased to be felt by some of the troops, more especially by Major General von Orff's battalions and General Barnekow's hussars, upon whom the severe outpost duty on the left bank of the Loire devolved, and by the cuirassier brigade, which hardly passed a day, from 20 October to 9 November without an alarm.[26]

26 Helvig, *Operations*, p.164.

2

Gambetta and Freycinet

The principal reason which led the Government of National Defence in Paris to send three of its members to Tours to represent it as a delegation was to ensure access to the representatives of the leading European powers, who had left Paris before the completion of the investment. The delegation was also intended to serve as a means of communication with the provinces. However, its members were neither united in their view of the way to proceed nor were they particularly effective; Crémieux and Glais-Bizoin have been described as 'elderly, inexperienced and talkative,' and they were at odds with the third member of the delegation, Admiral Fourichon, the Minister of Marine, who also held the portfolio of War Minister.[1] Their differences arose particularly over the relationship with the provinces, and Fourichon ultimately resigned as War Minister on 3 October.

From Paris, the government had decreed that national and municipal elections should take place on 2 October. It was a decision which caused consternation among the prefects, all of whom had been appointed by Gambetta when he assumed office as Minister of the Interior. Practically all of them saw the likely outcome of such elections as producing a hostile majority in the National Assembly. However, with the breakdown of the armistice negotiations between Bismarck and Jules Favre, the Foreign Minister, at Ferrières, the situation was seen in Paris as having entirely changed; to hold constituent elections taking place without an armistice was seen as offering a serious threat to the conduct of the national defence, and would be practically almost impossible. Accordingly, the government decreed that these should be postponed indefinitely.

At first, this decision was welcomed at Tours, and in instructing the prefects that the elections were to be postponed, the delegation told them to provide for the situation in the meantime by '...the maintenance of the existing municipalities or by the nomination of provisional municipalities.'[2] In the days immediately following, however, a different view began to emerge. In the face of the bad news from all quarters reaching the delegation, its members reversed their previous endorsement of the Paris Government's decision. The independence of the delegation had greatly increased as a result of the Germans locating, and cutting, the cable in the Seine which had been the means by which the Government could communicate with the provinces.

1 Howard, *Franco-Prussian War*, p.238.
2 J. P. T. Bury, *Gambetta and the National Defence* (London: Longman Green and Co, 1936), p.111.

Its members now felt that the burden of responsibility which rested on them was too great, and on 1 October decided that elections should after all be held, citing 'a general demand of the departments' for this, and asserting that it was an 'unavoidable necessity.' Clement Laurier, serving at Tours as Deputy Minister of the Interior, justified the decision in these terms in a letter to Delpech, the prefect at Marseilles:

> Elections are for us the principal element of national defence. Through them we shall acquire the authority we lack and we shall be able to say that we represent something sacred .... Without a constituent we shall never be able to inspire France with the energy she needs. Remember that the greatest national effort in our history was made by the convention.[3]

In Paris, on the evening of 1 October, Gambetta brought the news of the delegation's decision to a meeting of the government ministers. They were indignant at this act of insubordination on the part of the delegation. Gambetta argued that it was essential that a decree should be issued immediately forbidding the proposed elections, and stating that any which might be held were to be regarded as null and void. This was readily agreed. Gambetta also suggested that the only way to sort things out, as well as bringing greater determination to the conduct of affairs by the delegation, was to send 'a man of energy' by balloon to Tours.

Over the next two days the question of who should go was debated at length. Various candidates were put forward and in the end the choice came down to Favre and Gambetta. The former had put forward Gambetta, and he was not himself prepared to undertake the task, although as Foreign Minister he was perhaps the logical choice. Favre argued that whoever went must be able to obtain the agreement of the prefects; all of whom had been appointed by Gambetta, while he personally knew none of them. Gambetta, he contended, 'would have an influence over them which I could not pretend to have. His youth, his zeal, his popularity, seemed valuable qualities for ensuring the success of his mission.'[4] Another valid consideration was the relative age of the two men. Jules Favre was 61 years old; Leon Gambetta only 32. Balloon flights were still in a fairly basic stage; a younger man would be better able to cope with the dangers to which he might be exposed.

Gambetta accordingly accepted that he should be the one to go to Tours. J. P. T. Bury suggests that his initial reluctance was formal rather than profound, and that he grasped the opportunity with both hands: 'A show of reluctance to the entreaties of his colleagues was doubtless all the easier when there was no other candidate eager to accept a journey so hazardous. But once he had accepted, he was full of optimism, and already saw himself triumphant at the head of a nation in arms.'[5] Favre later wrote that Gambetta had not sought the assignment, and that he had not foreseen the development of the authority with which he was about to be invested:

> But he devoted himself to the noble and sacred task of saving his country, and the strength of his desire made him believe that he possessed the power to realise it. 'I shall return with

3 Bury, *Gambetta*, pp.112–113.
4 Jules Favre, *The Government of the National Defence* (London: Henry S King and Co, 1873), p.181.
5 Bury, *Gambetta*, p.115.

> an army,' he said to me, in a private conversation, 'and if I have the glory of delivering Paris, I will ask no more of fortune.' [6]

It was not until 7 October that a favourable wind and the absence of any fog made it possible for Gambetta to depart. He was accompanied only by the pilot and by his faithful secretary, Eugene Spuller, when he boarded the balloon *Armand Barbés*. Wrapped in a fur cloak and wearing a fur cap, he was understandably pale and nervous, but had the presence of mind to wave a tricolour as the yellow balloon ascended. After its launch from the Place St Pierre, the balloon hovered dangerously close to the German siegeworks before drifting north-east at a height of 2,000 feet. Two abortive attempts were made to land, but were thwarted by German patrols which fired on the balloon. Ultimately it came down near Épineuse, west of Compiègne; Gambetta was unscathed apart from a grazed hand, and he made his way to Amiens, from where he left for Tours. En route he paused at Rouen, where he made a passionate speech to the *garde nationale*, calling on every man to do his duty: 'If we cannot make a pact with victory, let us make a pact with death.'[7]

He arrived at Tours soon after midday on 9 October. 'Fatal balloon!' Glais-Bizoin thought, when he learned that Gambetta had brought with him the decree cancelling the elections. The British Ambassador also heard the news of the balloon's arrival with regret, not out of any feelings of antipathy to Gambetta, but because he saw at once that it would mean the prolongation of the war. [8]

Gambetta's first task was to ensure the cancelling of the elections in accordance with the decree, brushing aside the arguments which were put forward in their favour. In the event, the delegation bowed to the inevitable without much protest, and Gambetta turned to the much greater task of inspiring France to resist the enemy. He issued a vivid proclamation calling for victory:

> We must set all our resources to work – and they are immense. We must shake the countryside from its torpor, guard against stupid panic, increase partisan warfare and, against an enemy so skilled in ambush and surprises, ourselves employ ruses, harass his flanks, surprise his rear and finally inaugurate the national war. The Republic appeals to all for help; its government will avail itself of all zeal, of all force of capacity. It is its tradition to call to its aid young leaders. We will do it. Heaven itself will soon cease to be favourable to our adversaries; the autumn rains will set in, and the Prussians, so far from home, disquieted, anxious, worried by our population now awakened, will gradually be decimated by our arms, by hunger, by natural causes. It is impossible that the glory of France shall be quenched forever, that the great nation will allow its place in the world to be determined by an invasion of 500,000 men. Let us rise en masse and die rather than submit to the shame of dismemberment.[9]

6 Favre, *National Defence*, p.182.
7 Douglas Fermer, *France at Bay 1870–1871* (Barnsley: Pen and Sword Military, 2011), p.30.
8 Lord Newton, *Lord Lyons: A Record of British Diplomacy*, 2 vols (London: Thomas Nelson & Sons, 1913) vol. I, p.325.
9 Hale, *People's War*, p.45.

The decision to send Gambetta to Tours completely changed the way in which the war would be conducted thereafter. His effect on the administration there was immediate. Arriving to find that Fourichon had resigned his office as Minister of War, he saw at once that he must succeed him, and that in this way he would be able to impart to the war effort the kind of energy that it required. Gambetta's assumption of the office of Minister of War was opposed by Crémieux and Glais-Bizoin; but he had been given a casting vote, and with support from Fourichon he got his way.

At Versailles Moltke clearly saw the change that had come over the French. In the following month, musing on the new situation in which his armies found themselves, he offered a characteristically detached and intellectual view:

> We are now living through a very interesting time, when the question of which is preferable, a trained army or a militia, will be solved in action. If the French succeed in throwing us out of France, all the powers will introduce a militia system, and if we remain the von der Tanns, then every state will imitate us with universal service in a standing army.[10]

Moltke had perfected the organisation of the Prussian General Staff to produce a system of military management that had proved itself on the battlefields of Bohemia and Alsace-Lorraine. As its leader, his ability at all times to bring a thoughtful and analytical approach to decision making gave him an authority which was largely unchallengeable. Professor Ritter wrote of him:

> Moltke's attitudes were never purely personal, but always governed by objective considerations, and there has scarcely ever been a general less influenced by passion, more given to ice cold reason. It was precisely this unswerving objectivity that gave him such a lead over more wilful and emotional men.[11]

His military leadership was characterised by his use of general directives rather than specific orders. These were defined in the *official history* as 'communications from a higher authority to a lower one, which convey guidelines rather than definite orders for immediate action. These guidelines should serve as a precept for subsequent decisions that must be taken independently.'[12] Moltke was able to depend on the understanding of his intentions on the part of the officers of the General Staff in the field, a body of men whom he had personally selected. An American historian has described the way in which the role of chief of staff of operational units had evolved since Moltke took office:

> During the time he was serving as chief of staff the peculiar status of that official in relation to the commanding general was more firmly established. The General Staff officers serving in armies, corps and divisions tended more and more to represent the General Staff. The

10 Prinz Kraft zu Hohenlohe-Ingelfingen, *Aus Meinem Leben* (Berlin: Mittler & Söhne, 1907), vol. IV, p.421.
11 Gerhard Ritter, *The Sword and the Sceptre* (London: Allen Lane, 1972), vol. I, p.194.
12 *Official Account*, vol. I, p.155.

> relationship of Moltke to the Crown was similar to the relationship of the lower chiefs of staff to their respective commanders.[13]

The dual nature of this command structure generally worked extremely well, but inevitably there were occasional stresses. This was illustrated by one such issue recorded by Blumenthal in his journal for 2 December, when his army commander, the Crown Prince, expressed his dissatisfaction with the chief of staff because the latter had issued orders without reference to him:

> In the morning the Crown Prince was very much put out that I had not had him called, as he said he ought to be informed of all orders as soon as they arrive. I said to him that I could not think of waking him for such details; moreover, that it came into my province, and not into his, to issue the subsequent orders. I told him that I was not in the position of an adjutant who merely had to carry out orders; that I was only too willing to leave him all the honour of the command and do all the work, but that my position could not be reduced to that of an adjutant. He saw my point, but he has not a very clear comprehension of his position in the command. With the greatest possible kindness and geniality, he replied that I could do anything I wished, and that he would in no way hinder me nor raise difficulties; but he must be told of everything, especially when an order has come direct from the King. It is not possible for him to feel offended, as he is always governed by the very best intentions, but he does not grasp the exact relationship in which I stand to him.[14]

At all levels, Moltke's policy ensured a consistent and methodical approach to decision making. Herbert Rosinski, examined the thoroughness with which the German armies became imbued with Moltke's military philosophy:

> His appointment as head of the General Staff, without effecting any fundamental changes in the constitution or methods of that body, marked an epoch in its development owing to the immediate intensification of all its activities. The career of its members was regularised, a more intimate contact with the general life of the army assured by the regular interchange of staff and regimental duty; its theoretical work – particularly the study of military history, the compilation and interpretation of statistical and other information, and the cartographical service – was revived and greatly expanded; the tactical and strategic thinking of the General Staff was much improved by the better adaptation of tactical exercises and 'staff journeys' to wartime conditions and by their extension to cover strategical issues proper.[15]

There could scarcely have been a greater contrast with the armies of the French Republic, where the relationship between civil and military leaders was very different from that enjoyed by Moltke. Bismarck, for all his reservations about the attitude of some members of the Prussian General Staff, accepted that they knew their business. He had an unwavering respect for Moltke's professional ability and, except in the instance of his determination to launch a bombardment

13 Colonel J. D. Hittle, *The Military Staff: Its History and Development* (Harrisburg, Pa: Military Service Publishing Co, 1949), p.66.
14 Blumenthal, *Journals*, pp.211–212.
15 Herbert Rosinski, *The German Army* (London: Hogarth Press, 1939), pp.127–128.

of Paris, did not generally interfere. In that instance, he was motivated by his political aim of bringing the war to an end as soon as possible.

The new French Government approached the conduct of military operations in a very different spirit. Gambetta saw it as essential to revolutionise the way in which the Ministry of War was managed, announcing: 'I have determined to quit the usual paths. I wish to give you young and active chiefs capable by their intelligence and their energy of renewing the prodigies of 1792. Therefore I have no hesitation in breaking with the old administrative conditions.'[16] One casualty of this approach was General Lefort, who had been in charge of the War Ministry since it arrived in Tours. In the face of complaints from Gambetta of delays, he soon resigned, saying: 'I told him that we would go no faster without departing from routine. I added that we might do things faster but that disorder would result.'[17]

The Ministry of War that Gambetta found at Tours was, in his immediate judgement, unable to meet the demands made on it:

> It had only three departments instead of ten, and its personnel was no more than a quarter the War Ministry's normal peacetime strength. The sudden change in routine did not make for increased efficiency, and it was hampered all the more by lack of archives and material which had been left in the capital, and upon which its smooth running depended. Even six weeks after Sedan there were still generals who had no maps by which to conduct their operations.[18]

Although the Ministry had, before Gambetta's arrival, succeeded in raising the 15th Army Corps under Motte-Rouge, as well as the nuclei of several other units, it appears that Lefort and his officers had not expected that the Army of the Loire would undertake any substantial military operations. He later stated that he had worked to create an organised force because he believed that it might strengthen France's bargaining position in any peace negotiations. And many of the officers in key positions lacked confidence that the new levies being raised would be able to stand up to the German invaders after the crushing defeats of the Imperial armies.

From the outset, Gambetta was determined that it should be he who made the key strategic decisions. He took these frequently and with a total disregard for the professional advice which he was offered by the military. One of his first acts on reaching Tours was to publish a decree, on 14 October, that created an auxiliary army which comprised all the forces outside the regular army, placing its men on an equal footing to the regulars in respect of rank and pay. In addition, the ordinary rules as to promotion were suspended in order to encourage talented younger men, and commands were interchangeable between the regular and the new auxiliary armies.

Gambetta, with all the responsibilities which he had assumed since coming to Tours, realised at once that he could not 'enter into the thousand details of the complicated and absorbing administration' such as the War Ministry, and he sought a deputy on whom he could rely to put his policies into effect. Prior to Gambetta's arrival, Crémieux had been about to appoint a deputy who would relieve him of part of the burden of responsibility which he carried – this was Charles de Freycinet, an unknown civil engineer whom Gambetta had previously appointed

16 Bury, *Gambetta*, p.136.
17 Howard, *Franco-Prussian War*, p.241.
18 Bury, *Gambetta*, pp.134–135.

as prefect of the Département de Tarn et Garonne. The appointment had been much resented locally, since Freycinet was perceived as being a reactionary, and he was soon forced from office. Proceeding to Tours he was appointed to the Armaments Commission, where he gave considerable thought to the way in which the nation should best be able to mobilise its industrial resources and manpower. In conjunction with Jules le Cesne, the president of the Armaments Commission, he published a memorandum calling for the root and branch reform of the War Ministry; this appeared a few days before Gambetta's arrival. In this document Freycinet argued that the Minister of War should be a civilian, that a Military Council of War should be established advising him on the conduct of operations, and that a civilian 'delegate' should be appointed to take over all questions of administration and organisation.[19]

Gambetta found that the recommendations in Freycinet's memorandum corresponded so closely to his own ideas that he realised that here was the man to serve as his deputy, and within days Freycinet was appointed to the post of 'Delegate of the Minister of the War Department, and charged with the direction of the services in his stead and within the limits to be traced by the Minister.' Bury speculates that the contrast with the passionate and mercurial Gambetta, 'no less completely in temperament than in appearance,' was a factor in the appointment of the 'frigid, methodical, cautious and calculating' Freycinet as a man in whom he could place complete confidence.[20]

Michael Howard, in assessing the effect of the reforms that Gambetta and Freycinet introduced, points out that they went far beyond the reorganisation of the War Ministry, suggesting that they understood one aspect of modern war better than the professional soldiers on either side. Civilians were not only converted into soldiers; civilians from professions of all walks of life were conscripted to employ their particular skills, 'in a common enterprise in which the movement of armies was only the final result.' This, in Howard's view, gave the organisation of the national defence, 'an amplitude which far surpassed anything on the German side, and which was not to be seen again until the First World War was far advanced on its course.'[21]

Gambetta's confidence in Freycinet meant that the newly appointed Delegate could move fast, which was what the situation demanded:

> Gambetta gave his Delegate entire freedom to proceed with his plans of reorganisation, and bade him spare neither men nor money in the interests of the defence. It was Freycinet who reformed the War Office, enlarging it and creating new departments to correspond with the 'immense extension of the forces of national defence,' which was Gambetta's aim. It was Freycinet who was responsible for the most important measures for the organisation and training of new levies. 'When M. Gambetta was present at either Tours or at Bordeaux, I was accustomed to visit him at the prefecture .... to inform him of the events of the day and to discuss important measures,' he wrote later.[22]

When Gambetta was away, Freycinet was in absolute control of the War Ministry; and it was he who was the effective director of military affairs. Gambetta described himself as a 'will

19 Howard, *Franco-Prussian War*, p.242.
20 Bury, *Gambetta*, p.131.
21 Howard, *Franco-Prussian War*, p.243.
22 Bury, *Gambetta*, pp.131–132.

supplying an impulse' rather than a military specialist, though his remained the ultimate decision in questions of key importance.

Although it is not unreasonable to say that without the impetus provided by Gambetta and Freycinet, the War Ministry could not have raised, in the time available, anything like such considerable forces, they were seriously prejudiced by the lack of really competent senior officers. It was understandable that Gambetta should seek youthful and energetic leaders, but such men needed time to prepare themselves. For the moment Gambetta and Freycinet had to make the best of the senior officers available. Confronted with the news of Motte-Rouge's defeat at Orléans, and his abandonment of the city, which Gambetta received in an extremely critical telegram from Cochery, a former deputy for Orléans, Gambetta did not wait for further news; that evening he replied to Cochery, 'I share your opinion about la Motte-Rouge. He is replaced by General d'Aurelle de Paladines.'[23] This snap decision to sacrifice Motte-Rouge to satisfy public opinion was, however, not encouraging to the professional soldiers in their opinion of the capability of their new civilian masters.

In thus abruptly dismissing Motte-Rouge, Gambetta was glad of the opportunity to demonstrate the new spirit of determination with which he intended to infuse the War Ministry, even if the haste with which he took the decision deprived him of making a more considered assessment of the general. The new commander to whom he turned was an extremely competent, though cautious, soldier who had led a division in the Crimea. D'Aurelle was a firm disciplinarian and capable organiser who quickly gained the confidence of his troops.

In the aftermath of the loss of Orléans, the immediate question was where to make a stand against the Germans if they should push down into the Sologne. Von der Tann, of course, had soon concluded that a bold advance towards Tours was altogether too risky, but Freycinet had in the meantime decided that the battered 15th Corps should take up a position at Salbris, behind the River Sauldre, and on 15 October issued orders to d'Aurelle to this effect. At the same time, with a view to frustrating any sudden thrust from Orléans westward, he ordered the newly formed 16th Corps to assemble at Blois. In the first instance the command of this unit was given to General Pourcet, newly returned from Africa, however it was not very long before his unfitness for the post became apparent.

The decision to stand at Salbris was a sound one. Freycinet wrote later:

> As for the camp at Salbris, it became the veritable cradle and school of the Army of the Loire. It was here that General d'Aurelle, with the firmness and vigilance that did him honour, began to restore to the army the order and discipline which had disappeared. In less than a week, the change brought about in the aspect of these troops was apparent.[24]

Gambetta was later to claim that when he first arrived at Tours, the Army of the Loire, 'counted scarce 18,000 men, disunited and lacking in determination.' His distortion of the facts was characteristic, but a letter which he wrote on 24 October was much nearer the truth, when he reported to Paris: 'I have supplied Thiers with positive information concerning the position and state of our troops.... He has been able to convince himself that an Army of the Loire 110,000

23 Bury, *Gambetta*, p.138.
24 Charles de Freycinet, *La Guerre en Province* (Paris: Michel Levy Frahier, 1872), p.72.

men, well-armed and well equipped really does exist.'[25] Lefort was subsequently to assert that 70,000 men were under training at the end of September, and that 15th Corps was fully organised, while the formation of 16th Corps was well advanced by the time of Gambetta's arrival at Tours. Many years later, Freycinet was similarly disposed to understate the military resources immediately available at that time; he wrote of the total numbers available across France to resist the invaders:

> In all 40,000 regular troops, as many national *gardes mobiles*, five to six thousand cavalry and 100 cannon.... Such was the sum of our resources with which to repulse an invading army which already disposed of from 700,000 to 800,000 soldiers in perfect organisation, 2,000 cannon not including siege batteries and powerful reserves on the Rhine.[26]

Of course, this assessment took no account of the men under arms in the cities under siege, or of those already in the process of organisation or available to be called up. France had huge reserves of manpower upon which its new leaders could draw. Nevertheless, it is still true that with the arrival of Gambetta the process of raising new armies soon greatly accelerated.

Freycinet, whose appointment was on 10 October, waited a week before sending his first letter to d'Aurelle. The letter was written in Freycinet's own hand. D'Aurelle suggested that he deserved a little indulgence, seeing that he was writing for the first time about military operations and strategy. Nevertheless, d'Aurelle was surprised to read what Freycinet had to say, as he sardonically observed in his memoirs:

> Here, certainly, was a lengthy lesson on the art of making war, given by a mining engineer and improvised professor of tactics and strategy; from the first day he took up his duties he believed that he had found the way to defeat the Prussians: 'To take them between two fires and inflict cruel surprises on them.'[27]

It was the start of a relationship that was never one of mutual respect. D'Aurelle was nettled to receive another letter from Freycinet of 17 October, in which the Delegate wrote that he had heard that the camp of the Army of the Loire was not properly guarded at night, and that it was possible to reach the headquarters without encountering a single patrol. D'Aurelle indignantly recorded that there had not been a single instance under his command of any post being surprised or captured.[28]

The troops that comprised 15th Corps at Salbris were reasonably well equipped, but as other units were formed it was found that there were inadequate arms available for them:

> This shortage, and the no less serious shortage of officers and men able to train the new levies, would preoccupy the War Office throughout the national defence, and none of the measures designed to relieve the situation, the acceleration of home ammunition manufacture, the purchase of arms abroad, and the creation of an auxiliary army, proved a complete

25 Bury, *Gambetta*, p.140.
26 Bury, *Gambetta,* pp.141–142.
27 General d'Aurelle de Paladines, *La Première Armée de la Loire* (Paris: Henri Plon, 1872) p.36.
28 d'Aurelle, *Première Armée*, p 3.

> remedy, for the truth was, as George Sand said, the government had 'many too many men to have enough soldiers.'[29]

On 14 September, Gambetta had initially demanded the enrolment of all volunteers, unmarried men or childless widowers between the ages of 21 to 40, in companies of mobilised *gardes nationales*; subsequently this was extended by a new decree calling up all the remaining able-bodied men between 21 and 40. He boasted to Jules Favre that these measures would produce a reserve of nearly 2,000,000 men. The actual numbers recruited did not exceed 250,000 men, and their military value was disappointing. Admiral Jauréguiberry, who would prove to be one of the most capable of the commanders in Chanzy's 2nd Army of the Loire, was to report in due course on their deficiencies:

> Unhappily one is forced to admit that in general they have rendered scarcely any service, and that their ignorance of the business of war, their indiscipline and want of steadiness in presence of the enemy have frequently been the cause of serious repulses[30]

At Salbris, however, d'Aurelle had made immediate and substantial progress in making the 15th Corps into an effective combat formation. This corps, and the 16th Corps, contained the bulk of those remaining of the old Imperial Army outside Paris together with retired service men recalled to the colours. D'Aurelle worked tirelessly to raise their morale, regularly visiting each of his regiments. A devout Catholic, he appointed chaplains to the army whose presence was welcomed by the men they served. Unfortunately, the qualities and attitudes of the commander of the Army of the Loire, which contributed so much to its recovered effectiveness, ensured a pronounced lack of sympathy between d'Aurelle and Freycinet. The general had the military man's distrust of politicians, accentuated by a dislike of republicanism, while his professional caution was a constant source of dismay to Gambetta and Freycinet.

In his memoirs, d'Aurelle offered a decidedly unflattering picture of Freycinet:

> The Delegate of the Minister of War is short, thin and scrawny looking, very inflexible, finding it difficult to assume a pose which reflected the importance which he wished to convey. His face is pale, and he appears exhausted by the work and the long hours. His hair is grey, cut short; he is scarcely 43 years old but nevertheless seems prematurely aged.[31]

The relationship between the two men was never going to be very good; as time passed it steadily deteriorated.

At the War Ministry there was a growing opinion that an effort should be made to recapture Orléans. Any hesitations about such a forward move were dispelled by the receipt, on 21 October, of a message from Jules Favre to the effect that Trochu was contemplating an assault within 20 days on the German lines of investment, 'passing over the bodies of the enemy.' However, this plan was for an advance in the direction of Le Havre along the right bank of the Seine; and even before he heard of this Gambetta foreshadowed the rejection of the scheme, writing to Favre

29 Bury, *Gambetta*, p.144.
30 Bury, *Gambetta*, p.145.
31 d'Aurelle, *Première Armée*, pp.40–41.

on 19 October that the actual position of the troops required to cover Bourges, Dijon and Lyon did not seem to him to allow the realisation of Trochu's plan for some time. Everything in fact favoured the adoption of the direct route to Paris, and the recovery of Orléans as the first step on the way as being likely to inspire French public opinion.

Accordingly, Freycinet convened a meeting at d'Aurelle's headquarters at Salbris to discuss his plan of operations. It was attended by d'Aurelle, Pourcet, Martin des Pallières, the commander of the 1st Division of 15th Corps, and Borel, d'Aurelle's chief of staff, together with a staff captain. Freycinet brought with him two of his own staff, Auguste de Serres and Sourdeaux.

Freycinet later gave an account of the discussion in his war memoir, which he said lasted three hours. He put forward his proposals for the operation to recover Orléans; these provided for the 2nd and 3rd divisions of 15th Corps, together with 16th Corps, to advance along the right bank of the Loire on Orléans, under the personal command of d'Aurelle. Martin de Pallières, with the 1st Division of 15th Corps, which was much the largest, would cross the river above Orléans, at Gien, and fall on the enemy's rear as he was engaged with d'Aurelle.[32]

D'Aurelle later disputed the accuracy of Freycinet's account of the discussion which, he wrote, gave the meeting much more importance than it actually had. In particular, he challenged the suggestion that the possibility had been considered of either launching an offensive to the east to cut German communications, or alternatively a direct march on Paris to raise the siege.[33]

The two accounts do agree that d'Aurelle raised objections to the operation against Orléans, contending that the troops were too young, especially those in 16th Corps, to undertake a campaign in the open field. D'Aurelle, in his account, referred also to the fact that the troops were not used to coping with exhausting marches and were insufficiently equipped. The operation, he said, risked running into the army of Frederick Charles, which was reputedly the best German army, which had for three months held in check 200,000 French troops at Mets. D'Aurelle summed up the end of the discussion: 'The idea of taking Orléans prevailed, advancing on the city from Blois, and for the moment there was no other objective. This was the only scheme considered; there was no discussion of the possibility of marching on Paris.'[34]

D'Aurelle added a further comment on Freycinet's part in the debate, to the effect that his voice had not carried much weight during the discussion, 'And if, as he seeks to insinuate in his book, he had asserted his authority to ensure that his opinion prevailed, none of the generals present had been disposed to submit to his will without protest.'

A further meeting was held on the following day, this time at the War Ministry at Tours. On this occasion Borel, alone among those present at Salbris, had subsequently been giving thought to the implications of what was proposed. In particular, he was concerned about the difficulty of forcing an entry to Orléans if the enemy entrenched themselves there. According to Freycinet his objections were overcome by the production of a plan of Orléans which showed sufficient routes into the city.[35] Returning that evening to Salbris, d'Aurelle and Borel put in hand the necessary orders for the operation. During the discussion at Tours, it had been agreed that the advance would be made solely from Blois, and not by Gien, and d'Aurelle wrote at once to Pallières to inform him of this, and to set out the outlines of what was proposed. The intention

32 Freycinet, *Guerre*, pp.79–80.
33 d'Aurelle, *Première Armée,* p.39.
34 d'Aurelle, *Première Armée*, p.40.
35 Freycinet, *Guerre*, pp.80–81.

was that the movement would be commenced on 27 October, with the object of reaching Orléans on 1 November.

To the dismay of those at Tours, d'Aurelle sent a telegram on the evening of 28 October announcing that he had been obliged, due to bad weather, bad roads and the defective equipment of part of the artillery for the 15th Corps, to postpone the movement. In addition, d'Aurelle later recorded that the cavalry was not in the best condition, while no precautions had been taken to ensure that the railway administration would be able to disembark the horses when they arrived at their destination.

This, however, was only part of the problem. Nothing effective had been done to prepare the railways for the complex task of moving a large body of men in a short time. Civilian traffic continued; troops were left aboard trains for four hours because of miscalculation of the time required to disembark them; the stations were unprepared to receive them; and it was at once clear to d'Aurelle that his troops could not possibly be launched in an attack without a breathing space. In his account, he wrote merely that he had been obliged to postpone for one day the march of the army.[36] Gambetta telegraphed in reply that the movement of the army on Orléans must, for the moment, be suspended. There is some suggestion that the possible start of armistice negotiations – Thiers was in Tours at the time with this in mind – may have contributed to Gambetta's decision.

At all events, Freycinet wrote to d'Aurelle on 29 October confirming that:

> We are obliged, in the face of your telegram of last night at 10.20 p.m., to renounce the magnificent part which we have been preparing to play and in which in my opinion, we must succeed .... You know how to prepare and organise an army; you have proved this at Salbris. Employ your talents to prepare and reorganise in one complete body the five divisions which you actually have around Blois.

Freycinet reluctantly accepted d'Aurelle's decision, but he ended his letter with a firm reiteration of his insistence on an early advance:

> As soon as you feel you are in a state to march towards the Prussians you will tell us. Meanwhile, remain vigilant, fortify your positions and keep an eye on the area between Blois and Salbris, to prevent an advance by the enemy towards Tours and Vierzon.[37]

This letter crossed with a further letter from d'Aurelle setting out in some detail his reasons for postponing the advance:

> The plan which was adopted was premature, by reason of the degree of organisation of the troops which must take part in its execution. However, with an effort, it will be possible to achieve it and obtain good results, above all if it remains a secret. Unfortunately, everything has turned against us; continuous rain for several days has sodden the terrain making it impracticable for artillery and held up supplies and ammunition, imposing great hardship on our troops .... and the secrecy on which we have counted is not secure.[38]

36 d'Aurelle, *Première Armée*, pp.59–60.
37 d'Aurelle, *Première Armée*, pp 60–61.
38 d'Aurelle, *Première Armée*, pp.62–63.

Freycinet's letter of 29 October had brought with it the news of a crucially important command change. Already conscious of Pourcet's deficiencies as a corps commander, he now told d'Aurelle that the latter would be transferred to other duties. Two days later General Alfred Chanzy was appointed to command 16th Corps.

The 47-year-old Chanzy had, on the outbreak of war, been serving in Africa, where he had earned a good reputation. He was, however, apparently regarded with some disfavour at the War Ministry because of what were believed to have been his contributions to the press, and he began the war without an operational command. After the proclamation of the Government of National Defence he arrived at Tours where in due course he was appointed to command the 3rd Division of 16th Corps. The appointment to take command of the corps would prove to be one of the most inspired decisions taken by Freycinet.

As his forces uncomfortably made their way into their assigned positions to commence the attack on von der Tann's force, d'Aurelle and Freycinet continued to exchange correspondence which did little to improve the opinion which they had of each other. A dispatch dated 5 November from Freycinet told the general to prepare as if he intended to advance on the following day, and to do so unless he received an order to the contrary. Later that day, a letter from Freycinet on the subject of the advance warned d'Aurelle: 'it is possible that political circumstances may oblige us this evening or tomorrow to rescind this decision in which case I will telegraph you; but for now, I repeat, you must act as though the movement was irrevocable.' Another letter followed: 'Good luck and the grace of God! You bear at this moment, general, the fortune of France, and never has a man been given a greater opportunity. You can rescue our country from the depths in which it has been plunged for three long months.'

D'Aurelle observed that these letters made it extremely difficult to issue precise orders for a movement which on one hand was to be considered irrevocable and on the other might be postponed.[39]

39 d'Aurelle, *Première Armée*, pp.90–91.

3

Coulmiers

Von der Tann's decision not to advance into the Sologne had released Wittich's 22nd Division and the 4th Cavalry Division for other duties, and it was decided that his task should be to clear the western flank of the German lines of communication before returning to the investment lines around Paris. Blumenthal issued the necessary orders to Wittich on 16 October:

> As the neighbourhood of Châteaudun and especially that of Chartres is in the hands of *gardes mobiles* and *franc-tireurs*, who are continually threatening the rear of the army before Paris, you are given the duty of clearing the enemy out of those districts; for this purpose, you will, as circumstances may require, form from your division flying columns which are to return generally to Paris by Châteaudun, Chartres and Dreux. Your departure is fixed for the 17th, but you have perfect freedom to halt when you please, and complete liberty in your choice of action.[1]

Wittich was a highly regarded divisional commander, to whom Blumenthal could safely give such independence to deal with a tricky assignment.

As Wittich advanced, he found that all the villages between Tournoisis and Châteaudun had been virtually abandoned. When on 18 October his advance patrols approached Châteaudun they found that it was defended by a force of 1,200 *franc-tireurs* and *gardes nationales* under the command of Colonel Lipowski, which had occupied strong entrenched positions around the town, from which cavalry alone was unable to dislodge them. Accordingly, at about 1.00 p.m. Wittich brought up infantry and artillery but soon found that the enemy were putting up a stiff resistance. As night fell the Prussian infantry, led forward by three officers from Wittich's staff, had succeeded in taking several barricades at the entrances to the town, but encountered bitter opposition from its defenders, who fought from house to house. Many of the buildings of the town caught fire as the battle raged with great intensity; it was not until 3.00 a.m. of the next morning that resistance finally ceased and Lipowski withdrew into the suburb of St Jean and further, in the direction of Nogent le Rotrou.[2] Each side had lost about 100 men killed and

1 Hale, *People's War*, pp.38–39.
2 General von Wittich, *Journal de Guerre* (Paris: R Chapelet et Cie, 1902), pp.87–88.

wounded in the fighting; in addition the French left behind 150 prisoners when they retreated. It was estimated that 235 buildings were destroyed by fire during the course of the battle.

Wittich's next objective was the City of Chartres, towards which he advanced on 20 October. His cavalry patrols reported to him that it was held by between 7,000 and 8,000 men together with artillery. No trace of enemy troops was found at Houdouenne and Morancez and the inhabitants there told his patrols that all the bridges over the Eure had been ruined. In order to ensure that he could cross the river at Thivars he occupied it at dawn on 21 October with an infantry battalion; his orders for the rest of his force were to cross the river with the object of attacking Chartres from the south-east. A force of marines and *gardes mobiles* moved out of the city to block his advance but were soon driven back by artillery fire. On Wittich's right, and around to the north-east his cavalry closed on Chartres, while other cavalry units cut the railway line to Le Mans.[3]

When Wittich reached Morancez, Lieutenant Colonel von Heuduck brought the local *curé* to him, together with the mayors of several places on the road to Chartres. They begged him to spare their villages, to which he replied that he would burn to the ground all those which had fired on his troops. The *curé* pleaded for Chartres to be spared; Wittich said that he intended to enter the city that day, either by force of arms or amicably. If it was defended, it must expect to share the fate of Châteaudun.

At about 1.00 p.m. the prefect of the Départment arrived at Wittich's headquarters accompanied by the Mayor of Chartres. After some discussion, in which Wittich made it clear that he would stand no nonsense, it was suggested that the prefect should surrender the city, upon terms that the *gardes nationales* should surrender their arms; that the regular troops should evacuate the city, and that this should then be occupied. Wittich gave him until 3.00 p.m. to think it over, warning him that if these terms were not agreed, he would almost immediately commence a bombardment. He wrote in his journal:

> The appearance of a battery of guns made a considerable impression, and the capitulation was agreed; but I declared that I would consider it null and void if a single shot was fired on my troops inside or outside the town .... After the convention was agreed, the town was able to feed the troops and satisfy the requisitions arising from military needs.[4]

When Blumenthal received the news of the occupation of Chartres, he approved a suggestion from Wittich to send only a flying column to Dreux, while the rest of his force remained at Chartres. He now had in his mind the possibility of launching an offensive against Blois and Tours, reuniting Wittich and von der Tann for the purpose, and he wrote in his diary: 'This nest must be smoked out. The Crown Prince has consented to my plan, and now I have sent Bronsart to Moltke to communicate it to him. I am sure he will have no objection, but it is to me like a millstone round my neck that I am not allowed to do anything independently.'[5]

Blumenthal had, meanwhile, to consider the situation of von der Tann's force in Orléans. On 19 October he received a telegram from him to the effect that he could not remain any longer at Orléans, because of the assembly of strong French forces at Gien. He proposed that he should pull out of the city and take up a position at Pithiviers, 24 miles to the north, where

3 Wittich, *Journal*, p.97.
4 Wittich, *Journal*, pp.98–99.
5 Blumenthal, *Journals*, p.168.

the terrain was better suited to the employment of cavalry and artillery. In reply, Blumenthal told von der Tann to stand fast for the present, since he was as yet in no danger, the French not having concentrated their forces and still being 32 miles away from the city. Orléans was to be evacuated only in the presence of far superior French forces. In response to this, von der Tann deployed his forces to meet an attack from the west, since the French troops at Gien appeared to have retired. His cavalry patrols continued to warn of enemy movements which plainly indicated the likelihood that the French were preparing to take the offensive.

At Versailles, Moltke was becoming increasingly frustrated by the lack of any activity on von der Tann's part. As he made clear in a letter to Stiehle of 1 November, he was optimistic about the overall situation, complacently remarking that, 'the south of France will hardly make great efforts on behalf of Paris.' It was in this frame of mind that he wrote to Blumenthal on the following day:

> His Majesty the King considers it inadmissible that General von der Tann should remain any longer in an entirely passive attitude; His Majesty wishes, on the contrary that this officer and General Wittich use the troops available to take the offensive and seek to prevent the movements which the enemy appeared to be carrying out completely undisturbed.[6]

This suggestion came as an unpleasant surprise to Blumenthal, who commented in his diary:

> I cannot say that I at all approve this idea, for it throws my plan to the winds, which has hitherto been followed, of remaining quiet until all should be ready for a big stroke. It may easily lay us open to defeats in detail. I drove over to Moltke at once, and we came to terms as soon as he had heard what I had to say. He now desires nothing more than that they should make reconnaissances in force, which they are both doing.[7]

Blumenthal had now reached the conclusion that the French advance, when it came, would be from the west rather than the south. He correctly placed 16th Corps at Blois, but had got it into his head that the rest of the Army of the Loire was now concentrated at Le Mans:

> Opposed to them stands Wittich with his single division. I do not actually believe that he is in any great danger, as his division is more effective than a whole French army that has been brought together as this one has; still, it is high time that these impudent folk should have their corns trodden upon.[8]

Since the Crown Prince was going over to see the King, Blumenthal asked him to seek permission to support Wittich with the 4th Division which had just arrived outside Paris, and then allow him, with von der Tann, to take the offensive. He gloomily recorded that it was all in vain, because the King regarded the position in front of Paris to be extremely hazardous, and would not agree any troops being sent away. Blumenthal wrote that he had 'not been so depressed for a long time, or so despondent as I am today.'

6 Moltke, *Correspondance Militaire*, vol. II, pp.439–440.
7 Blumenthal, *Journals*, p.179.
8 Blumenthal, *Journals*, p.181.

Although the visit of the Crown Prince had met with no success, Moltke was himself still turning over in his mind the possibility of launching an offensive against the French forces in the west. Another attempt by the Crown Prince on 5 November failed to change his father's opinion, but Moltke let Blumenthal know that he did intend to make such a move in the future. On 7 November he was able to announce that a detachment (*Armee-Abteilung*) would be formed to undertake the operation, under the command of the Grand Duke of Mecklenburg-Schwerin. It was to consist of von der Tann's I Bavarian Corps, the 17th Division (von Schimmelmann), the 22nd Division and the 4th and 6th Cavalry Divisions. All told it would comprise 36,300 infantry, 9,200 cavalry and 208 guns. Blumenthal was to decide when the operation would start, and the force would remain under the orders of the Third Army.[9]

Blumenthal was 'gratified' to hear the news. He still remained convinced that apart from 16th Corps at Blois, the bulk of the Army of the Loire was at Le Mans. Meanwhile von der Tann reported that he was expecting to be attacked; Blumenthal comfortably observed in his diary that he did not anticipate any such thing as the enemy could not be ready for it yet. This was on 7 November; the next day Blumenthal met with the Grand Duke, who came to receive instructions. He impressed Blumenthal as being 'so quick and smart in apprehending his task that I have the greatest hopes of him.' Later, reading a telegram from von der Tann that strong enemy forces were advancing from Beaugency, he concluded that a battle was nearer than had been supposed, 'by those in the counsels of the King,' evidently having put out of his mind his smug conviction of the previous day that the enemy could not be ready yet. Instead, he wrote: 'All my prayers and entreaties have been in vain, and now people will not be surprised that it should have made me ill. My conscience is, however clear. I did all I could, and never hesitated, and God will show who was right.'[10]

In his diary, the Crown Prince reflected a widely held view about the Bavarians and their dependence on Prussian support, when he wrote loftily and rather unfairly:

> General Von der Tann again reports that an attack is imminent; they seem to be in a state of nervousness there, knowing no Prussian helmets to be any longer in the immediate neighbourhood. It is wonderful how strong is the moral influence our arms exercise over the Bavarians, the very people who once laid such stress on their military independence and distinctive character.[11]

It was becoming clear that before the newly formed detachment could embark on the operations assigned to it, the I Bavarian Corps would have to face an attack from the Army of the Loire. Von der Tann had been feeling distinctly uneasy since the closing days of October. After a sharp engagement with a force of *franc-tireurs* at Binas on 25 October, he had to face a stronger force which emerged on 31 October from the Forest of Marchenoir to drive back a foraging party of Bavarian cuirassiers. The arrival of cavalry reinforcements drove the French back, but reports from patrols confirmed that substantial French forces were moving forward on a wide front. To the north, Châteaudun had been reoccupied, while the French were moving towards Orléans

9 Moltke, *Correspondance Militaire*, vol. II, pp.468–469.
10 Blumenthal, *Journals*, p.184.
11 Crown Prince, *War Diary*, pp.185–186.

along the right bank of the Loire. Patrols also reported increased French activity in the Forest of Orléans.

Matters were clearly coming to a head, and on 7 November von der Tann pushed Stolberg's 2nd Cavalry Division forward to test French strength beyond Baccon and Ouzouer le Marché, supported by one and a half battalions of infantry. The French outposts fell back into the Forest of Marchenoir, and Stolberg pursued them in order to ascertain the strength of the force sheltering there. Concentrating at Marolles, he advanced westwards, meeting strong French forces sent forward by Chanzy from St Laurent and Autainville. Stolberg put his infantry in defensive positions between Marolles and Vallière, where they were attacked by forces which considerably outnumbered them. After an hour Stolberg, learning of further French forces advancing from Vallière which threatened his line of retreat, broke off the action and fell back towards Baccon under cover of a horse artillery battery firing from a position south-east of Chantôme. The Bavarian official history noted:

> The enemy's infantry was far superior in numbers to our own, and in the bearing, as well as the handling, of his troops there was a marked improvement over all the detachments with which we had come into collision at the outposts since the occupation of Orléans.[12]

It was an ominous sign that the efforts of d'Aurelle and his senior commanders were beginning to bear fruit. Stolberg's reconnaissance in force had achieved his object, but not without considerable loss; his casualties amounted to 28 killed, 51 wounded and 64 taken prisoner.

D'Aurelle had begun his forward movement on 7 November, as Stolberg's reconnaissance had discovered. It did not, though, begin well; as his columns moved through the Forest of Marchenoir in pouring rain, there was serious confusion, and he would have liked to pause to sort this out, but Freycinet insisted that the advance must continue. For his part, von der Tann realised during 8 November that he could remain in Orléans no longer; it was evident that the enemy was seeking to cut off his retreat:

> In reflecting on the measures to be taken in the course of the next few hours, one idea was constantly present in General von der Tann's mind, viz. to follow the orders from Versailles and not to give up Orléans without a struggle, or without proving the superiority of the enemy's forces. In upholding this principle, the idea of evacuating Orléans and of falling back upon Chartres or Toury, upon a point between these two places, or upon Orgères, had necessarily to be given up. He at once decided to accept the challenge, and, as the initiative was left to him, he had to decide where the battle was to commence. To remain in the town of Orléans would have been a strategic and tactical absurdity, and this course was not taken into consideration. The army was weak in infantry, but comparatively powerful in cavalry and artillery.[13]

The superiority in numbers which d'Aurelle possessed was overwhelming; Von der Tann had 14,543 infantry, 4,450 cavalry and 110 guns. The French forces closing in on him numbered 72,000 infantry, 7,200 cavalry and 160 guns. Clearly von der Tann must fight a defensive battle,

12 Helvig, *Operations,* p.174.
13 Helvig, *Operations*, p.178.

and he must, as a matter of urgency, select the position in which to receive the enemy. This must be chosen to enable him to fall back towards the road to Paris; he must not let himself be forced back towards Orléans. Two positions were considered; one, to the north, at St Péravy la Colombe, would certainly enable retreat if necessary to the Paris road, but it seemed at least possible that the enemy, instead of launching an attack there, would simply mask the position and proceed to occupy Orléans. This would put von der Tann in the position of having abandoned Orléans without a struggle and he might have been thought to be deliberately offering battle in a position in which the enemy would not accept it. His orders on the point were explicit. The alternative was a position at Coulmiers, where the terrain favoured the use of both cavalry and artillery, and which the French would be more or less obliged to attack; if defeated, Von der Tann could retreat without difficulty towards Artenay and Toury. At Versailles, nothing was done to amend von der Tann's orders that he was not to abandon Orléans without a struggle unless he was faced with overwhelming superiority, no doubt in part because a retreat from the city would afford the enemy the chance to claim it as an important success.

During the night of 8/9 November, the Bavarian troops began to pull out of Orléans. Von der Tann left the Bodyguard Regiment in Orléans temporarily, in order to be able to hold the city and in particular to protect the field hospitals remaining there should there be no battle on 9 November. The temporary bridges over the Loire were broken up. Von der Tann himself left Orléans during the evening for Ormes, and in the early hours of the following morning rode to Huisseau where he learned that strong French forces were now advancing from Cravant and Messas. Shortly after this, skirmishing commenced at the German outposts near Baccon, and it was evident that the attack was imminent. Von der Tann knew that he would have to meet this on his own; although Wittich had begun his march to his support from Chartres, he would not arrive during 9 November.[14]

The Bavarian official history described the position which Von der Tann's corps had taken up:

> Coulmiers, which lies on the road to Ouzouer le Marchè, consists, like all the villages of La Beauce, of stone houses, and has a massive castle with an extensive park. This park, which lies at the south-western extremity of the village and is surrounded by a thick, quick-set hedge and ditch, was the key to the defence of Coulmiers, and its importance was enhanced by the fact that the main attacks of the enemy were made on that side of the village. From Coulmiers the ground falls gently for some distance towards the west, where it again rises, forming a valley, in which lies a group of houses, Carrières les Crottes, close to the road.[15]

Schumacher, the commander of the 2nd Division, was naturally aware that an attack was imminent and he had already ordered the occupation of Coulmiers, thereby anticipating von der Tann's intentions. The Bavarian commander intended to post his left wing on the little River Mauve, facing the French advance from the direction of Randonneau and Baccon, aiming to launch an attack himself from Coulmiers in a south-westerly direction. When firing broke out, von der Tann sent orders to the *Leib-Infanterie* in Orléans to move to join his left wing by way of La Chapelle.

14 *Official Account*, vol. III, p.271.
15 Helvig, *Operations*, p.187.

In taking up this position and thus avoiding being trapped in Orléans, von der Tann had adopted the correct military response to d'Aurelle's advance; by meeting the troops of 15th and 16th Corps advancing from the west, he gave himself the opportunity, if he was successful, of dealing subsequently with Pallières. Freycinet's scheme by which the separate French forces would encircle the Bavarians was thereby disrupted, since Pallières' advance could not yet take effect. However, von der Tann had not anticipated having to face an attack in such strength, nor had he expected that the French would be attacking to the north of Coulmiers. Howard points out that in fact d'Aurelle might still have encircled the Bavarians if he had taken the advice which he received from Chanzy to launch his attack with a stronger left wing in order to drive the Germans back on the Loire. As it was, the two divisions of 15th Corps advanced on Coulmiers itself, while Chanzy's 16th Corps attacked further north towards the Châteaudun Road.[16]

When the battle began, the French advanced to the assault with a confidence and skill which took the Bavarians by surprise. They were supported by their artillery to much greater effect than had been the case during the early stages of the war, since their gunners were now using percussion fuses which exploded on impact. The successful action on 7 November against Stolberg's reconnaissance had lifted the morale of d'Aurelle's troops to an enormous extent. He had left Poisly, where he had been overnight, and arrived before Baccon at 9:30 am, where he watched his troops going into action: 'The French army was deployed for battle in two lines, in admirable order. Everything demonstrated their confidence.' Before firing broke out, d'Aurelle noted: 'A solemn silence reigned over this large plain, where soon would sound the noise of cannon. In the ranks a profound calm; the troops were in perfect order, seeming as if prepared for a review.'[17]

At Coulmiers, Schumacher extended his defensive position north of the village to Carrières les Crottes and Ormetau. Into this triangle he put the 4th Bavarian Brigade. The weather was cold; the early mist was dispersed as the sun came up. At Huisseau, von der Tann reviewed the reports reaching him of the French advance which as far as he could tell seemed to be coming from the direction of Meung. To meet this, he moved the 1st Bavarian Brigade forward to La Renardière, and the 3rd Bavarian Brigade towards Château Prefort. The 2nd Bavarian Brigade was for the moment held in reserve with the corps artillery at Bonneville.[18]

D'Aurelle had ridden forward to reconnoitre as his troops advanced and he now brought up four batteries to an ideal artillery position near Champdry, from where they opened fire on Baccon. Behind this village the leading troops of the 1st Bavarian Brigade moved up to La Rivière, supported by artillery to the north of La Renardière. As the French advanced south of Champdry through Les Barchats, their artillery there soon overwhelmed the Bavarian horse artillery battery at Baccon. To the south, the 3rd Brigade had reached Château Prefort, taking up a position on the banks of the River Mauve. As the morning passed without a French attack developing in this sector von der Tann, who was now himself at Coulmiers, ordered that the brigade move through Huisseau to reinforce La Renardière, where the principal French thrust was developing. This meant that for two critical hours this brigade had no influence on the outcome of the battle. Its presence at Château Prefort had however discouraged the French from attempting to turn von der Tann's left flank.

16 Howard, *Franco-Prussian War*, p.298n.
17 d'Aurelle, *Premiére Armèe*, p.102.
18 *Official Account*, vol. III, p.271.

Meanwhile at the other end of the line Chanzy's advance was led by Barry's 2nd Division. Advancing through Champdry it was held up for a while by a Prussian battery to the north of Baccon. The 1st Division, led by Admiral Jauréguiberry, advanced on Barry's left through Charsonville towards Cheminiers, north of Schumacher's positions around Coulmiers, which they threatened to outflank. To meet this, Schumacher posted a battalion at Vaurichard together with the 5th Cavalry Brigade. Orff's 2nd Brigade was now brought up from the reserve at Bonneville and moved towards Champs, with the support of the 4th Cavalry Brigade from St Sigismund.

The huge French numerical preponderance was now beginning to have its effect, and Chanzy's corps began a general advance, with Barry moving through Saintry towards Coulmiers, and Jauréguiberry on the other side of the main road in the direction of Ormeteau. Behind them, Chanzy concentrated a line of guns on either side of the main road in their support.[19] In response, the Bavarians brought up two batteries from the corps artillery to strengthen their line of fire at Coulmiers, one to the south of the park and the other at Ormeteau.

On the far left of the French advance, Reyau's cavalry had encountered the Bavarian Cuirassier Brigade at Renneville and around La Vallée. By now, all along the northern part of von der Tann's front there were intensive artillery exchanges, but further south things were not going well for the Bavarians. Peytavin's Division of 15th Corps had taken Baccon, and brought up artillery on either side of the village, which poured a heavy fire on the defenders of La Rivière; by now this village was in flames, and they retreated to the castle, and to La Renardière, to await the next assault. Dietl, the commander of the 1st Brigade, held on as long as he could; but his troops were driven out of the farm of La Grande Motte on the left of La Renardière, and he fell back first to the Clos farm north-east of the village, and then into the Bois de Montpipeau, which he held for the rest of the day.[20]

At about 3.00 p.m. the 3rd Brigade arrived after its march from Château Prefort, and took up a position on Dietl's right, while also sending two batteries and an infantry battalion to support Rudolf von der Tann's 4th Brigade.

North of Coulmiers, the Bavarians had been endeavouring to hold the quarries at Carrières les Crottes, but were overwhelmed by the repeated assaults by Barry's Division, and they retreated into the park at Coulmiers. South of the park, the French artillery firing from Le Grand Lus drove back a Bavarian battery which retreated half a mile eastwards. Three batteries between Ormeteau and Coulmiers were however successful in preventing Barry's attempts to outflank the village on its northern side.[21] The two infantry battalions at Ormeteau and between that place and Vaurichard were able to maintain their position.

However, by now von der Tann had committed his last reserves except for two companies of the 12th Regiment and the 1st Rifle Battalion:

> The enemy's artillery and infantry fire increased every moment in intensity, and his troops were turning our left flank more and more, and pressing forward against the park from the south. About 3.00 p.m. two French 6-pdr batteries were brought up to Grand Lus, and with the batteries at Saintry, Epieds and Villevoindreux, opened a crossfire upon our

19 *Official Account*, vol. III, p.273.
20 *Official Account*, vol. III, p.275.
21 Helvig, *Operations*, p.201.

position at Coulmiers, which far surpassed in violence all that had gone before, and showed that the enemy wished to strike a final and decisive blow, and that he was bringing up considerable troops from La Renardière.[22]

Von der Tann's position was becoming critical. Deplanque's brigade, of Jauréguiberry's 1st Division, had occupied Cheminiers and Champs. Orff, though, was able to deploy his brigade on the right of a strong artillery position to the east of Champs, and from there was able to overwhelm the French artillery which had been supporting Deplanque's advance. Now Orff, driving the French out of Champs, pursued his counter-attack by launching an assault on Cheminiers, which was fiercely defended by Jauréguiberry's men, and Orff, aware that the position at Coulmiers was deteriorating, broke off his attack and took up a position to cover any northwards retreat of the corps.

This was something that von der Tann now realised he must consider. He had the alternative option of trying to hold on to his position until nightfall, but this would entail the risk of heavy losses, and he decided that he must break off the action, and retreat towards Artenay. At 4.00 he issued the necessary orders; it was his intention, in order to ensure the safety of the troops investing Paris to the south of the city, to form a junction with Wittich's 22nd Division which was hurrying from Chartres to join him.[23]

For von der Tann, extricating his troops was not easy. In the centre, the struggle for Coulmiers Park had reached a climax. French infantry had broken in again on its north-western side, while four battalions threatened it from the south-west. Colonel von Ysenburg, the commander of the 13th Bavarian Regiment, gave orders for a gradual retreat, the houses in the village being defended to the last minute to cover the withdrawal. Further north the retreat from Ormeteau was covered by sustained artillery fire, and the French made no attempt to pursue. Ysenburg collected up all the men he could find, from whatever unit, and formed a skirmish line behind which the 4th Brigade was able to effect an orderly retreat.[24] Once Coulmiers was evacuated the 1st Brigade was ordered to fall back through Coinces and Sougy towards Artenay, and this too was carried out in good order. As the Bavarians pulled back, the French artillery continued to fire on them until prevented by the increasing distance and the oncoming darkness.

In his memoirs, d'Aurelle recorded his justifiable pride in the victory which his men had won. He reserved special praise for Jauréguiberry who, arriving the day before to take command of a division of infantry, had, 'by his sangfroid and audacity, astounded his young soldiers. Electrified by his example, they had attacked with the bayonet at Champs and Ormeteau.'[25] He went on to deal with the criticism which had after the battle been expressed about his failure to pursue the enemy, giving his reasons for not doing so: 'The battle had not finished until nightfall: the cavalry which, launched on the enemy's line of retreat, would have been able to begin the pursuit and bring good results, had returned to its cantonments at Prenouvellon.' This was a decision taken by Reyau, the cavalry commander, and it appears that he took it on his own initiative. In addition, fearing that his advance might be turned from the north, Chanzy had refused his left flank. It is also true that the French cavalry, had it taken up the pursuit, might not have fared

22 Helvig, *Operations*, p.202.
23 *Official Account*, vol. III, p.278.
24 Helvig, *Operations*, p.208.
25 d'Aurelle, *Première Armée,* p.109.

well against the battle-hardened troopers of von der Tann's cavalry. Perhaps the most compelling reason for not seeking to follow up the retreating enemy was, however, the expectation at French headquarters that a counter-attack would be launched on the following day.

Total losses sustained by the Germans in killed wounded and missing amounted to 1,308. French casualties are rather more uncertain, but were of the order of 1,800. Chanzy reported the total losses of 16th Corps at 1,284.[26]

Freycinet, to whom of course d'Aurelle had reported the success of the day, sent a telegram of congratulation in which he announced the promotions of Borel, Peytavin and Longuerue. He ended this by warning d'Aurelle to redouble his vigilance in case of an enemy counter-attack. D'Aurelle moved his headquarters to St Péravy on 11 November, where he met with his generals, colonels and the heads of the various services. He was entitled to feel the great satisfaction which he expressed to them. He made known his intentions as to the establishment of strong positions in front of Orléans. In covering Orléans in this way, d'Aurelle had considered that it would have been preferable to move further north, as far as Artenay, where the left flank of the army could rest on the River Conie; but although this offered a good position for defence it had in his eyes one serious disadvantage – it would have meant a substantial extension of his front line. To his mind it was essential to keep his army concentrated, to maintain their organisation, their discipline and their readiness to resist a further Prussian advance on Orléans.[27]

The recapture of Orléans was a major symbol of the determination and ability of the Government of National Defence to carry on the war, and its members justifiably felt exultant:

> Unfortunately, however, the military value of the success was negligible in comparison with its moral effect. Gambetta naturally made the most of the first victory of any significance gained by the French during the whole course of the war, but the actual achievement was from a military point of view more a matter for regrets then congratulations, since the opportunity to surround the whole Bavarian force had been lost, and the inexperienced French troops were in no condition to follow up their success to advantage.[28]

Von der Tann had retreated slowly northwards, hampered by roads which were rendered almost impassable by the heavy rain and snow which began to fall in the early evening. His 1st Division and the 4th Cavalry Brigade finally reached Artenay at about midnight. His western flank was covered by the 3rd Cavalry Brigade and the Bavarian Cuirassier Brigade, while the rearguard was composed of the 3rd Brigade and the 5th Cavalry Brigade. The position which he took up between Gemigny and St Sigismund was quite close enough to the battlefield if the French had been disposed to attack it; but the truth was that both sides were exhausted, and there was never any likelihood of this. On the following day von der Tann continued his retreat to Toury, where he took up a defensive position astride the main road. He had a major scare later in the day when reports reached him that the French were advancing on Artenay, and he took the precaution of beginning a further retreat to Angerville, but when this was found to be a false alarm he returned to his position at Toury. It was there that he learned of the incorporation of his corps in the detachment of the Grand Duke of Mecklenburg-Schwerin.

26 General Alfred Chanzy, *Deuxième Armée de le Loire* (Paris: Henri Plon, 1874), pp.30–31.
27 d'Aurelle, *Première Armée*, p.122.
28 Bury, *Gambetta*, p.180.

The mood of the Bavarians was not unduly cast down. They had fought bravely and skilfully at Coulmiers, and their official history recorded their response to the events of the battle:

> Although the general feeling was not cheerful, it could not be described as despondent. The consciousness of having done their duty to the fullest extent, and the conviction, which was forced upon officers and soldiers alike, that they had only given way before overwhelming numbers of the enemy, prevented our troops from suffering the moral effects of a defeat. On the other hand, their state of bodily exhaustion was such as to render it doubtful whether they could resume the fight on the following day.[29]

At Versailles, the news of the battle was received calmly. Verdy wrote in his diary:

> As we had anticipated, General von der Tann was engaged with the Army of the Loire yesterday and has been compelled to retreat before superior numbers and evacuate Orléans. We now hope that he will succeed in forming a junction tomorrow or the day after with the supports which are already on their way, and that the Grand Duke of Mecklenburg, who has taken command of the force, will be strong enough to drive the enemy back again.[30]

Blumenthal reported the news of Coulmiers in his diary without comment, save to remark that the French were in great numerical superiority, and that it meant that no offensive movement could be immediately attempted. In the evening he met with Moltke to discuss the situation and found that they were of the same mind. Moltke had received the news of Coulmiers without dismay; he sent a telegram to Stiehle to speed the progress of the Second Army across France: 'Strong enemy forces advancing from the Loire close to Orléans. It is necessary to hasten the march of the Second Army. IX Corps cannot have a rest day on 11 November and must reach Fontainebleau by 14 November.'[31]

As further information came in with regard to the Battle of Coulmiers, the mood at Versailles was rather more upbeat. The Crown Prince wrote in his diary on 11 November:

> Today it is now plain that General von der Tann has come off quite well. Posted in a position well adapted for defence, he repulsed three well supported French assaults energetically and brilliantly, and only when he realised the superiority of the enemy numbers did he voluntarily evacuate the field as dusk was coming on, without ever being attacked or hard pressed. The enemy appears not to have sent a single man in pursuit; indeed, a French report speaks of a check to their left wing.[32]

Alfred von Waldersee, one of the King's aides-de-camp, was also sympathetic to von der Tann, writing in his diary:

29 Helvig, *Operations*, p.209.
30 Verdy, *Royal Headquarters*, p.210.
31 Moltke, *Correspondance Militaire*, vol. II p.473
32 Crown Prince, *War Diary*, pp.187–188

Yesterday came the unpleasant news that Tann had evacuated Orléans. As always happens with failure, severe judgements were at once passed on Tann, but soon it came to be realised that injustice was being done to the blameless and gallant General. He had frequently reported that a storm might be expected to burst upon him.[33]

33 Field Marshal Alfred von Waldersee, (F. Whyte, trans.) *A Field Marshal's Memoirs* (London: Hutchinson & Co, 1924) p.80

4

The Grand Duke's Detachment

Moltke followed up his telegram to Stiehle urging Second Army to make haste with a letter, dated 10 November, which he had begun a day or two earlier. In this, after confirming the outcome of the Battle of Coulmiers, he went on to consider its immediate consequences:

> A concentration of all the troops under HRH the Grand Duke in the neighbourhood of Angerville-Toury can be effected the day after tomorrow. If, contrary to expectation, the hostile Army of the Loire is able to advance yet further, we shall have to reckon with certainty on sorties in greater strength than hitherto from all sides of Paris, the main attack being against the southern portion of the investment .... In a few days we shall be able to determine whether the left wing of the army will not be more usefully employed on the left bank of the Loire and in the country between the river and Paris.[1]

The suggestion that part of Second Army might operate south of the Loire was interesting; Moltke still had not lost sight of the possibility of acting against Bourges, but for the moment it was with the situation at Artenay that he was immediately concerned.

Once it had been decided to form the detachment, Blumenthal had given to the Grand Duke the objectives at which he was to aim. These were based on Blumenthal's current assessment of the situation, which was entirely inaccurate, based as it was on his conviction that the bulk of the Army of the Loire was to be found at Le Man. The task allotted to the detachment was to:

> ...break up the Army of the Loire now in process of formation, and to compel it to retreat by Le Mans. If 15th and 16th Corps are to be found north at Bourges and Le Mans, they may perhaps be driven apart, and their reunion rendered impossible. A further (subsidiary) object would be the destruction of the hostile communications between Tours and Rouen, as well as the utilisation of the occupied territory for the supply of the army. In order to make the communication with the superior command better and quicker, the capture of one or two locomotives would be beneficial. Reports by telegraph to be made frequently to Versailles.[2]

1 Moltke, *Correspondance Militaire*, pp.476–477.
2 Hale, *People's War*, pp.72–73.

By the time that the Grand Duke and Colonel von Krenski, his chief of staff, had effectively taken up their duties, the situation had been changed by the Battle of Coulmiers. During 12 November, reviewing such information as was available to them, they concluded that the enemy were no longer before Orléans, but were on the move behind the screen of Fiereck's Army of the West to unite with the forces at Le Mans and with them to attack, through Dreux, the western side of the investing lines around Paris. Accordingly, they issued orders that on the following day the whole of the detachment should turn around and on its then left, its present right, should wheel facing north-west towards the line Chartres-Dreux. It would in fact mean turning its back on the enemy.

By nightfall on 12 November, before the orders for this move had been sent, the detachment was in a defensive position facing south astride the high road from Orléans to Paris, 18 miles from the former and 47 miles from the latter. I Bavarian Corps and the 2nd Cavalry Division were at Toury and Outarville, the 17th Division was 8 miles to the rear. Seven miles west of Toury, at Allaines, stood the 22nd Division, and 5 miles to its right rear was the 4th Cavalry Division at Ymonville, on the road to Chartres. The 6th Cavalry Division was at Chartres, which is 27 miles north-west of Toury. The detachment's advance guard was three miles south of the latter place, at Tivernon.

On the following day, after the planned movement had begun, the Grand Duke and Krenski were astounded to receive from the headquarters of the Third Army the following message:

> His Majesty the King has, at an audience today [12 November] given orders to the commander-in-chief of Third Army to inform your Royal Highness that His Majesty does not wish your detachment to take the offensive unless very special reasons not known here should make it necessary. IX Corps, under General von Manstein, has, with special view to this, been so directed that its advance guard arrives at Fontainebleau on the 14th, crosses the Seine on the 15th, and can connect with you on the 16th. Success seems the more certain thereby, as General von Manstein would perhaps be able to act on the flank of the enemy, who does not expect him.[3]

Confronted with these explicit instructions, the Grand Duke halted the march of the detachment with the exception of the 22nd Division, which continued its march alone to Chartres. The Grand Duke, in issuing his previous orders, had taken the precaution of letting Blumenthal know what he was doing. Third Army's chief of staff received the news of the decision that the detachment was to stand fast calmly enough, but on the following day got into trouble when he forgot to send to the King the information that the 22nd Division would continue its march to Chartres. This prompted an irritable entry in his diary that he had become 'a veritable reporting machine.' He disapproved of what he saw as a decided tendency to dictate every move to the Grand Duke: 'If I were in his place, I should report nothing, but just cut the telegraph wires.'[4]

The news that the Grand Duke had continued the march of the 22nd Division came as a surprise to Blumenthal and to the Crown Prince, his royal master. It was also a surprise to Moltke who made it clear that he considered it necessary to send a reminder at 12.55 p.m. on the 14 November of what was required of the detachment:

3 Hale, *People's War*, p.90.
4 Blumenthal, *Journals*, pp.188–189.

> General von Manstein can, on the 16th, arrive with IX Corps at Étampes, to which place he has been directed by the supreme headquarters. It is, therefore, only there that the concentration of a large force can be effected most quickly. The road from Orléans to Paris must not be left open, if the enemy advances by Artenay.[5]

Moltke was annoyed at what he saw as the unnecessary division by the Grand Duke of his forces. Blumenthal grudgingly agreed with him, but noted that they did not know the Grand Duke's reason for so doing.

On 14 November Moltke, after his visit to Blumenthal, took the opportunity to write again to Stiehle at considerable length with an update on what had been happening and a review of how he saw the situation. He was dissatisfied with the failure of the cavalry to keep in touch with the enemy after the Battle of Coulmiers:

> The reconnaissance on the 11th did not obtain sufficient information; on the 12th, Pithiviers was found unoccupied, and beyond Artenay there was no enemy found. According to our estimate, the Orléans Army consists of 15th and 16th Corps, numbering 24 Line (*Marche*) regiments, and, with *gardes mobiles*, may be over 60,000 strong. The artillery has presumably been collected together from the fortresses; the Algerian troops may be the nucleus of the army. The French give their losses on the 9th as 2,000, and the Army of the Loire has, apparently, not considered itself strong enough to advance with more fighting direct on Paris, the only way by which a real success is to be obtained. It appears that it is endeavouring to turn our position to the west, a position it does not consider advisable to attack. On this march it would be able to unite with the new formations for which Nogent le Rotrou is the central point, perhaps even with the 30,000–40,000 *gardes mobiles*, by whom generals Briand and Bourbaki, on the line Pacy-Vernon-Les Andelys, and as far as Gournay have for a long time held our detachments in check in this direction .... Gambetta is well aware that Paris cannot hold out without relief. Should, therefore, the departure of that army to the west be confirmed, the Grand Duke will move parallel to this march until the possibility of a decisive attack is offered to him. Then the important place of Rouen will be his next objective. Subject to the foregoing, the protection of the Paris-Orléans road must be undertaken by Second Army alone. The road cannot be left entirely open for any time, and the Grand Duke cannot be weakened by detachments.[6]

Moltke still wanted an operation south of the Loire, but he accepted that for the moment this was not feasible, and he continued his letter to Stiehle with an outline of what Second Army was to do:

> The only thing to be done is to continue the advance from Fontainebleau and Sens, first in a westerly direction. Whether X Corps will be directed on Gien on the Loire, will be better determined on the 19th instant. The recapture of Orléans, and the crossing of the river by Second Army to the left bank will be much thereby facilitated. For the speedy approach

5 Hale, *People's War*, p.92.
6 Moltke, *Correspondance Militaire*, vol. II, pp.480–482.

> of HRH Prince Frederick Charles, we are very grateful; it has pulled us through a sort of crisis.[7]

At Versailles, the unease felt about the Grand Duke's decision was general. The Crown Prince, having commented on this, added, in an echo of Blumenthal's view: 'Still, he must know what he is about, being there on the spot; so I prefer not to scare him with questions and instructions rather than interfere with his independence.'[8] Those around Moltke were less tolerant; on the same day Verdy wrote in his diary:

> We can make nothing of the operations of the Grand Duke of Mecklenburg, it being not easy at this distance to judge of what is going on on the spot. One of us will probably have to go there. It is Bronsart's turn and, as he has now recovered from a slight indisposition, it is likely to be he.[9]

The Grand Duke had responded during the evening of 14 November to the Crown Prince's reminder earlier in the day, suggesting that, in order that he could carry out the duty of protecting the investment line of Paris against attacks from Orléans, and to enable him to control the forces concerned, Manstein's IX Corps should be placed under his orders. Manstein, although at this time receiving orders direct from Moltke, still formed part of Second Army, and there was no likelihood of the Grand Duke's request being granted.

Fritz Hoenig, in his history of the campaign on the Loire, recorded the doubts held at the Royal Headquarters:

> Anyhow, affairs from the 10th to the 14th were not so managed as to raise high expectations from the detachment, and had there been no special considerations to be taken into account, it would perhaps have been even at that time a question whether it might be advisable on the whole to allow the detachment to continue in existence after the arrival of the Second Army on the scene, or at least to consider whether the staff work was in proper hands. These matters were discussed at the time in Versailles and among the General Staff, but no decision was taken.[10]

During 14 November the detachment was picking up further information which seemed to indicate that the Army of the Loire might indeed be swinging around to the west, when both the 5th and 6th Cavalry Divisions reported enemy activity in their front, which apparently centred on Dreux. At Bu, six miles to the north of Dreux, cavalry patrols encountered unexpectedly strong opposition, and were later driven back from the village by a force of two companies of marines and three battalions of *gardes mobiles*, with artillery support. On the basis of this encounter, and information gathered from local residents, the cavalry sent back reports to headquarters indicating a total of 12,000 French infantry, with eight squadrons and eight batteries as being in the area. This was a substantial force, and on receiving this news Moltke took steps to

7 Moltke, *Correspondance Militaire*, vol. II, pp.482–483.
8 Crown Prince, *War Diary*, p.190.
9 Verdy, *Royal Headquarters*, p.211.
10 Hale, *People's War*, p.93.

support the 11th Cavalry Brigade which had taken up a position at Houdan. On 15 November he ordered the 2nd Guard Landwehr Brigade of five battalions, together with the 2nd Heavy Reserve Battery of the Guard, to move off from the Argenteuil peninsula to Neauphle.[11]

The Grand Duke, meanwhile, deployed his principal forces facing north-west, his intention being to cover the investment lines. The 22nd Division and the 6th Cavalry Division remained at Chartres; I Bavarian Corps was quartered on the Volée Brook, on either side of the road from Chartres to Ablis, and the 17th Division was moved to Rambouillet. The 2nd and 4th Cavalry Divisions continued to scout south and south-west from Toury and Voves.

Moltke's response to the information reaching him indicated how sensitive he was to the possibility of the French threatening the investment lines from the west. Bu is only 26 miles from Versailles, and there had been only cavalry between the French and the siege lines. Blumenthal, although he considered that the movements being reported by the cavalry were merely a blind, was pleased with the return to Third Army of these reinforcements.

The march of the 22nd Division to Chartres had of course been in breach of the instructions issued from Versailles, and the further movements ordered by the Grand Duke compounded his offence. Whatever might be the thinking of the Royal Headquarters, he and Krenski were now perfectly convinced that the French were planning to launch an offensive from the west, and they felt obliged to take steps accordingly.

On 15 November Moltke issued an order to Third Army which seemed to recognise this. The detachment was now released from its duty to cover the Orléans-Paris road, and instead was now given the exclusive task of covering the investment of Paris from the west. It would thereafter be for Second Army to deal with any enemy threat from the south. Moltke, disliking the way in which the detachment had been divided, recommended to Blumenthal that it should, 'concentrate immediately and take the offensive against the enemy forces reported to be marching from the area of Dreux and Chartres. The Royal Headquarters has sent no communication on this subject to HRH the Grand Duke.'[12] At the same time Moltke directly instructed Manstein, who was around 30 miles to the east of the Orléans-Paris road, that he was now responsible for covering this possible line of the French advance. Moltke reminded him that substantial French forces had been identified to the south of Artenay. He sent a copy of these instructions to Second Army, adding that, as soon as circumstances permitted it should itself take the offensive towards Orléans and beyond.

The Grand Duke had told von der Tann that he anticipated that the enemy intended, 'either to make a long turning movement against Versailles, or to advance against Chartres and turn our right flank,' and the orders which he had given to the various units of the detachment for 15 November reflected this. He saw the centre of the threatening French concentration as being at Châteauneuf en Thymerais, about a dozen miles north-west of Chartres. He moved his headquarters to Nogent le Roi, on the right wing of the 17th Division. Schimmelmann, its commander, had gone sick and had been replaced by Lieutenant General von Tresckow, the Chief of the Military Cabinet. Moltke was increasingly dissatisfied with the performance of the detachment, and he told Blumenthal this on 16 November:

11 Official Account, vol. III, p.283.
12 Moltke, *Correspondance Militaire*, vol. II, pp.486–487.

> Moltke came to me today, and complained that the Grand Duke reported so little, and said I ought to write to him to take the offensive. That is not at all necessary. The Duke will do that of his own accord, and up to now it seems to me that he has done perfectly right. He remains concentrated, as it appears, between Chartres and Maintenon.[13]

The task which had been set for the Grand Duke was one of considerable difficulty. It was to seek out, and destroy, an enemy force of unknown strength, the position of which was uncertain. He had a force of 110 squadrons, 52 battalions and 220 guns, supported by lengthy trains, and he was advancing into broken, close and wooded country criss-crossed by narrow roads and lanes, unsuitable for his cavalry and artillery; with the lanes making scouting particularly difficult, he was able to gather little information about the size and movements of the enemy in his front. Hale observed that it was 'dissemination rather than concentration that was the principle guiding the Grand Duke's operations, adding that the staff work appeared to be indifferent.'[14] It was a recipe, if not for disaster, at least for a serious setback.

Moltke had come away from his latest meeting with Blumenthal without feeling any reassurance about the concerns which he expressed to him, and thinking it over he decided to send Krenski a memorandum to guide him in carrying out his difficult mission. He wrote the memorandum on 17 November and in it he restated that the only duty of the detachment was to prevent hostile forces advancing from the west towards the left bank of the Seine. He pointed out that the detachment had numerous cavalry at its disposal which enabled it to discover what the enemy was doing. He went on to emphasise his key point:

> There is no question that you should attempt to defend each of these roads by a separate force; on the contrary, I count on you attacking on the road on which the strongest enemy column advances. Your success on a single road will prevent all movement of the enemy on the others. You will certainly achieve this if you keep your forces closely together. Generally speaking, his Royal Highness's detachment has as its mission not to occupy territory but to carry out a war of movement, which is also the only way in which the troops can be kept supplied .... The delicate point of your mission is to discover exactly the centre of gravity against which you take the offensive with all your forces; this will guarantee your success.[15]

In writing this, Moltke may well have felt it should not have been necessary to point out such basic principles, and his confidence in Krenski was obviously weakening. In fact, by the time this letter reached the detachment on 20 November it had already been operating for several days in a manner directly contrary to its central principle.

Fritz Hoenig was unimpressed by this memorandum, pointing out that the Royal Headquarters did not grasp the great extent to which the population were taking part in the war, nor the topographical conditions of the region in which the detachment was to operate, arguing that the formation of the theatre of war in no way lent itself to the 'Moltke idea'. The enemy could be driven back, separated, destroyed at certain points, but there were always roads open to him

13 Blumenthal, *Journals*, p.192.
14 Hale, *Peoples War*, p.101.
15 Moltke, *Correspondance Militaire*, vol. II, pp.491–492.

into which they could escape, and by use of the telegraph and with the help of the population receive timely warning of the movements of the detachment.

At Versailles, Blumenthal was contemptuous about what he perceived as a jittery attitude at the Royal Headquarters. He noted on 17 November that the detachment would next day attack the enemy in the Châteauneuf-Brezolles-Dreux position: 'God grant that he may defeat him, for that will soon bring the war to an end. If only the King with all the princes and his staff would go away, we could make short work of the business, and soon bring peace within measurable distance.'[16]

It was an entirely characteristic, if completely wrong-headed, comment.

Moltke, meanwhile, had received a response from Stiehle to his letter of 14 November, reporting on the position of the units of Second Army, and telling him of Frederick Charles's view of the situation. The Prince had now set his mind on the recapture of Orléans as his principal objective, rather than the destruction of the Army of the Loire. In his letter of 16 November, Stiehle wrote:

> By the capture of Orléans his Royal Highness believes he can best carry out the duties assigned to him of 'protecting the investing army against Orléans.' Afterwards, according to circumstances, his Royal Highness intends to move down the river by Bourges on Tours with IX Corps on the right bank and III Corps on the left bank of the river. There is no risk in the operation, although *à cheval* the river, because between Orléans and Tours there are, exclusive of both places, five permanent bridges, and also III Corps has with it its pontoon train. If a portion of the II Corps could be employed to occupy Orléans, where all the trains must remain, the operation would be thereby facilitated.[17]

Frederick Charles was setting himself an enormously ambitious programme, and he had insufficient forces to carry it out even if they all arrived promptly. As they marched westwards through population centres which were increasingly hostile it was beginning to be apparent that the inhabitants were no longer as overawed by the marching columns as had previously been the case. Von der Goltz, in his history of the campaign, wrote:

> Already it had become known through the outspoken remarks of the population which eyed, with a certain amount of contempt, the weak marching columns of the advancing Second Army that, on the Loire, was assembling an army numbering hundreds of thousands, well equipped, and animated with the highest spirit. The expression '*La belle Armée de la Loire*' was heard here and there. On the German side this was at first regarded as mere rodomontade, as an exaggeration due to the constitutionally excitable temperament.[18]

X Corps, commanded by General von Voigts-Rhetz, in particular experienced this kind of reaction from the civilian population after the news of Coulmiers had spread. On 13 November, when arriving at Châtillon sur Seine, the hostility was so marked that Voigts-Rhetz sent to the 39th Brigade, following a day's march behind the leading units, a message that the town had

16 Blumenthal, *Journals*, p.193.
17 Hale, *People's War*, p.115.
18 Colmar von der Goltz, *Gambetta et ses Armées* (Paris: Librairie Sandoz, 1877), p.79.

only just been evacuated by French troops, that there were armed parties in the neighbouring woods, and that casualties must not be left behind but must be brought along in waggons. He added that bodies of men coming up to join the army should move in bodies of at least 300 to 400 men.

X Corps was led by the 38th Brigade, which was two days' march ahead of its rearmost unit, the 40th Brigade. On 18 November the 38th Brigade encountered such strong resistance in front of Joigny that all three arms had to be brought into action before the enemy was driven back to Auxerre.

Moltke had by now come to realise that an offensive towards Bourges could not, for the moment, be undertaken. He was also no longer persuaded that the Army of the Loire had marched off to the west. His letter to Frederick Charles of 18 November made this clear; it also emphasised that the question of how Second Army would be deployed once it was concentrated would depend on the developing situation, particularly as to the advance of the detachment:

> It does not yet appear possible to decide on the dispatch of X Corps to Bourges, since one cannot yet judge eventual necessity of employing all the forces of Second Army against Orléans and Châteaudun.... The reconnaissance of the next few days will show whether the principal forces of the Army of the Loire are still near Orléans or perhaps a little to the west towards Châteaudun. Information as to this will be sent as soon as possible.[19]

Frederick Charles and Stiehle shared Moltke's concern to obtain reliable intelligence as to the location and movements of the enemy, and they ordered Manstein, who at this time had the 1st and 2nd Cavalry Divisions under his command, to ensure that he undertook thorough reconnaissances; this, he was told, was of the primary importance, and he was to send an officer every day, by midday, to Second Army headquarters with the information obtained. Manstein, however, was already on the case, and at 6.30 p.m. on 18 November he telegraphed both to the Royal Headquarters and to Second Army information that had been collected:

Enemy outposts on the line St Germain le Grand – Ruan – Dambron; a detachment at Chilleurs aux Bois, bivouac fires on the line Bougy – St Lye and the south of Artenay. According to a consensus of reports, the enemy is preparing a defensive position at St Lye and Chevilly.[20]

While the Germans were endeavouring to build up their knowledge of French movements and intentions, a material difference of opinion had arisen between d'Aurelle and Freycinet as to what the Army of the Loire should be doing. On the morning of 12 November an important conference was held at d'Aurelle's headquarters attended by Gambetta and Freycinet, Borel and Pallières were also present. Gambetta withdrew after a short while to compose a proclamation to the soldiers of the Army of the Loire:

> Your courage and your efforts have at last brought us victory after three months .... Under the leadership of vigilant and faithful chiefs you have found again your discipline and determination. You have recovered Orléans for us, taken from troops for a long time accustomed to victory .... You are today on the road to Paris. Never forget that Paris awaits us

19 Moltke *Correspondance Militaire*, vol. II, pp.493–494.
20 Hale, *People's War*, p.121.

> and honour demands that we should wrest it from the grasp of the barbarians who are threatening it with pillage and fire.[21]

Before the campaign to recover Orléans had begun, on 27 October Freycinet had written to d'Aurelle to tell him that, for the moment, the objective was to occupy the city. In this letter Freycinet told the general what was expected of the army:

> Once your army is at Orléans (if God wills that it should arrive there), and without losing a moment, you will give orders to establish a fortified camp around the city, able to contain 150,000 to 200,000 men. You must immediately fortify and arm the most defensible locations so that your army may there be able to defy all attacks from the Prussian armies, if they attempt to dislodge you. Establish at Orléans a defensive point against an enemy advance.[22]

This was a policy statement with which d'Aurelle was entirely in agreement and when, on 11 November, he had met with his senior leaders and announced to them that this was what would now be done, and gave orders to his artillery and engineers to carry out the necessary work, his decisions were greeted with unanimous approval.

D'Aurelle was soon to learn that this no longer constituted the limit of the government's ambition. When he came to write his memoirs he took particular exception to a passage in Freycinet's own book, in which he had written: 'after the taking of Orléans, if we had marched on Paris, we should have succeeded.' Freycinet went on to blame d'Aurelle for failing to take the offensive at once. This was entirely unjust; the victory at Coulmiers, energising though it was to the army and the government, had not come close to creating the conditions for an immediate march on Paris, which could only have ended in disaster. D'Aurelle set the record straight: 'The commander-in-chief well knew what it was possible to ask of his army; in spite of all the courage of which it had given such proof, to march on Paris after Coulmiers was a senseless and rash advance, which would expose the army to certain destruction, encouraging a general belief in something that could not be achieved.'[23]

But in his memoirs Freycinet went even further in his efforts to destroy d'Aurelle's military reputation, claiming that at this crucially important conference the general, judging that it was dangerous to remain at Orléans, 'had proposed to evacuate Orléans immediately, and to retreat to the former positions at Salbris, behind the Sauldre.' Freycinet explained how he had resisted such a proposal, pointing out its destructive effect on the national morale.[24] So far-fetched a proposal was this that, as d'Aurelle not unreasonably remarked, it was impossible for Freycinet to have misremembered it being put forward, and it perhaps puts into context many of the observations which Freycinet, in his memoirs, was to make about d'Aurelle.

The Army of the Loire now set about establishing the fortified camp around Orléans, identifying a number of key positions at which extensive entrenchments were dug and artillery positions prepared. These would be occupied by 15th and 16th Corps, and in Pallières and Chanzy

21 d'Aurelle, *Première Armée*, p.131.
22 d'Aurelle, *Premiere Armée*, pp.132–133.
23 d'Aurelle, *Premiere Armée*, pp.133–134.
24 Freycinet, *Guerre*, p.102; d'Aurelle, *Premiere Armée*, p.135.

in particular d'Aurelle possessed commanders of marked ability, upon whom he was able to rely. 15th Corps was screened by its cavalry on its right at St Lye; the 1st Division (Pallières) was between there and Chevilly, the 2nd Division (Martineau de Chenez) was in position from Chevilly to Gidy, and the 3rd Division (Peytavin) from Gidy to Boulay. 16th Corps, on the left, was echelon and between Coinces, St Péravy and Champs, with the second division between Germigny and Coulmiers, its 2nd Brigade standing in reserve at St Lyphard; the 3rd Division was also in reserve at Barres. The cavalry of 16th Corps covered the extreme left of the Army of the Loire, at Coulinelle, Tournois and Nids.[25]

The more or less continuous failure of understanding between d'Aurelle and Freycinet was particularly apparent in the different views which they took of the overall strength of the Army of the Loire. In addition to 15th and 16th Corps in their positions around Orléans, it had, in theory, four additional corps. On the immediate left was 17th Corps (de Sonis) at Châteaudun; beyond this, at Le Mans, was the Army of the West, under Fiereck, now designated 21st Corps. On the right of the army, at Gien, was 18th Corps, to which Bourbaki, newly arrived from the north, would be appointed; for the moment it was led by its chief of staff, the youthful Colonel Billot. Finally, in the Saône Valley, there was the body of troops under Crouzat; this force, now designated 20th Corps, was ordered by Freycinet to move by rail to the Loire, taking up a position between 15th and 18th Corps. These last four corps were not yet fully organised; they consisted of troops which had received a minimum of training; and in many instances were still poorly equipped. To Freycinet, the total strength of these forces was so considerable that it justified the extravagant plans which he had for their employment. In his correspondence with d'Aurelle he set out their paper strength and the way in which they should be deployed. D'Aurelle regarded such letters as examples not only of exaggeration, but also duplicity, but he patiently responded to them in an effort to get Freycinet to understand the reality of the situation. It was necessary, he wrote, to reduce the estimate of 250,000 men that Freycinet claimed were available: 'I will make every effort to make the best of the troops entrusted to me, but it would be dangerous to rely on the deceptive mirage of figures on paper and take them for reality.' He added that to put in hand a plan to link hands with Trochu in Paris, it would be necessary to learn what was going on there and what Trochu's intentions were.[26]

Gambetta had been kept informed of the correspondence between Freycinet and d'Aurelle, and was accordingly fully aware of their deepening mutual mistrust, and on 20 November he wrote personally to the general in order to reinforce the burden of Freycinet's correspondence. He set out three principles which d'Aurelle should follow. First, the most reliable and disciplined troops should be posted on the wings of the army. Secondly, Orléans must be the base of operations, as Salbris had been in the past, and it was from there that the great movement on Paris must be launched. Finally, therefore, d'Aurelle must consider the preparation of an operational plan having Paris as its supreme objective.[27] When he read this, d'Aurelle noted that in fact, for all the grandiose indications of Freycinet as to what could be achieved, no specific order had yet been given for a forward movement on Paris; the only instruction he had received had been to fortify himself around Orléans.

25 d'Aurelle, *Premiere Armée*, pp.161–162.
26 d'Aurelle, *Premiere Armee*, pp.187–188.
27 d'Aurelle, *Premiere Armee*, pp.189–190.

While engaging in what was an increasingly unsympathetic correspondence with d'Aurelle, Freycinet was becoming anxious about a possible threat to Tours posed by the movements of the detachment. And, indeed, it seemed to Krenski and the Grand Duke that perhaps they should be making Tours their ultimate objective. It had appeared previously that the enemy was in some force at Dreux, thus on 17 November Tresckow with the 17th Division was ordered to march directly on the town, while to the south Wittich and the 22nd Division advanced towards Châteauneuf. I Bavarian Corps was directed on St Cheron; on the left, the 6th Cavalry Division accompanied the advance which was in effect a wheel to the right. Dreux was taken without difficulty, and it was clear that the French were in fact not in any great strength to the immediate front of the detachment.[28]

It was with the thought that they should be advancing towards Tours that Krenski and the Grand Duke decided on a further change of direction – to move south-west on Nogent le Rotrou and thence towards Le Mans before intending subsequently to turn south on Tours. This meant that the detachment must wheel to its left, pivoting on Châteauneuf. It was now in the much more difficult country of the Perche, and the short foggy November days made considerable demands on the troops and their leaders, and would demand above all highly efficient staff work. 18 November turned out to be a truly dreadful day for all concerned, and Krenski's staff did not distinguish itself. The extent to which the leadership of the detachment had lost the plot is to be seen by the fact that since 12 November the detachment had already made a wheel en masse three times. These manoeuvres had been carried out without undue difficulty, though they had failed to achieve their objective of engaging with the enemy. On 18 November everything went wrong; it was a day for the troops concerned which, in Colonel Hale's words, 'was never to be forgotten.... Moreover, the detachment had now thrust itself into a veritable hornets' nest, and there would necessarily be an accompanying sensation of stings. As a warning and as a really profitable example of thoroughly bad leadership and bad staff work, the movements of the 18th are worthy of consideration in detail.'[29]

Tresckow's Division, marching west from Dreux to Brezolles, got only as far as Laons, about five miles short of its objective, 'as the roar of artillery resounding from the south had caused it to halt for a considerable time and send out reconnoitring detachments.'[30] Wittich, marching from Châteauneuf to La Loupe, also failed to reach his destination, being held up at first by parties of enemy troops which obstructed his departure from the area around Châteauneuf; the 44th Brigade had to move north to deal with them. While this was being done von der Tann's Corps came up to the rear of the 22nd Division. The Grand Duke refused to permit Wittich to halt to allow the Bavarians to pass across the front of his division, with the result that when they arrived they had to make their way through the columns of the 22nd Division. In its turn, this meant that the 42nd Brigade was obliged to halt, and could not get through Châteauneuf. The 43rd Brigade in its turn ran into such fierce resistance at Digny that Wittich was obliged to seek support from the 4th Bavarian Brigade (Rudolf von der Tann) which set off for Digny, without pausing to cook a meal, with three battalions, a 4-pdr battery and a half squadron of light cavalry:

28 *Official Account*, vol. III, p.297.
29 Hale, *People's War*, p.109.
30 *Official Account*, vol. III, p.297.

> During the march, darkness had set in and was rendered more intense by the thick fog, which lay over the country ever since the morning; not a shot could be heard from Digny; all was quiet, and it appeared probable that the Prussians had in the meantime occupied the village, but, as soon as the column had reached the first houses of Digny, it was received with several volleys. The village was still in the hands of the enemy.[31]

In the prevailing conditions, von der Tann forbore to launch a night attack.

Further south, the 4th Cavalry Division, advancing towards Illiers and Bonneval, encountered the enemy but was unable to drive the French out of Illiers, and in the evening fell back to Nogent sur Eure and Dammarie.

The troubles of the detachment were not ended by the fall of night:

> Many detachments had been on the march since the morning, and even during the frequent halts had obtained no real rest, and were now obliged to seek their cantonments amid the darkness, which, owing to the mist, had set in at 4.00, only to find them either occupied by the enemy or in flames, and were obliged to drive the enemy out of their quarters or to bivouac in the cold without fires.[32]

After such a difficult day Krenski and the Grand Duke had no choice but to order that the following day be a rest day. The order announcing this, issued on the evening of 18 November, commenced as follows:

> In today's advance the army encountered opposition at almost all points. This, and more especially the victorious action in which Wittich's Division was engaged, have enabled us to accomplish our object of ascertaining the strength and position of the enemy. It appears that our enemy belongs to the Army of the West (General Fiereck) and is based upon Le Mans.[33]

This extremely disingenuous order may, or may not, have deceived its readers among the troops under the command of the Grand Duke and of Krenski; but the fact was that they were still none the wiser about the enemy force which they thought they were pursuing or the direction which it was taking.

The detachment spent its rest day in sorting itself out and preparing to continue its movement in a south-westerly direction on the following day. The reports received during the day pointed to a general withdrawal in that direction by the French, and suggested that the enemy was strongly occupying Nogent le Rotrou, so it was towards Nogent le Rotrou that the detachment advanced on 20 November. The 17th Division marched to Senonches, on the right of the advance; the 22nd Division moved to take up a position at nightfall on the line La Loupe – Courville. It had been intended that I Bavarian Corps should concentrate at Ardelles and Favière, but at 8.00 a.m. news came from the 4th Cavalry Division that the French were advancing from Bonneval and Illiers towards Chartres. This information arrived while von der Tann was conferring with

31 Helvig, *Operations*, p.224.
32 Helvig, *Operations*, p.224.
33 Helvig, *Operations*, p.225.

the Grand Duke and Krenski, and the decision was at once taken to alter the Bavarians' direction of march. The 1st Division reached Champrond en Gatine, and the 2nd Division reached Courville.

They were seriously handicapped by lack of maps; when the 2nd Brigade of the 1st Division arrived at Champrond it was already quite dark, and without even the roughest of maps it was impossible to form any view about the nature of the surrounding country. The Bavarian official history remarked that 'the rapidity with which the war was carried on rendered it impossible to keep up the supply of the necessary maps.' In spite of the efforts of the Topographical Department of the Bavarian War Office, the maps often arrived after the troops had marched into another sheet.[34]

The threatened French movement at Illiers meant that it would not be until the following day that von der Tann would be in a position to attack, and it would be even later that the 22nd Division could come into action, while the 17th Division would have to cover 24 miles from Senonches. However, during the evening, news came that the French had retired.

The detachment was now operating in a country which offered particular advantages to the enemy:

> The irregular but continuous chains of hills, with more or less steep inclines, and often with precipitous ravines at the base, made it difficult to obtain any view of the situation, and hindered the movements of large forces in close formation, more especially of cavalry and artillery. The country was covered with thick woods and crossed by a number of small streams, both of which formed natural obstacles, well fitted for an obstinate resistance. There were comparatively few regular villages, but a number of isolated farms, the fields belonging to which were enclosed by hedges and walls, whereby the cavalry was restricted to absolute inactivity on the roads. The artillery could only obtain a sufficiently open range from certain conspicuous heights, which were not at all easy of access.[35]

It seemed evident that the French intended to make a serious stand at Nogent le Rotrou, and this appeared to be confirmed when, on 21 November, Wittich encountered stiff resistance on the heights of Le Colombier and around the railway station at Bretoncelles. This was finally overcome at about 1.00 p.m., and the French retreated in considerable disorder towards the Huisne Valley under the fire of the German artillery. Behind the 22nd Division, Tresckow met with opposition at La Madeleine, before driving the French back in a westerly direction. Wittich noted that on this day the enemy consisted of two battalions of marines, newly arrived via Cherbourg from Cochin China, together with a battalion of chasseurs, about 3,000 *gardes mobiles* and four guns.[36]

The Bavarians meanwhile were moving towards Nogent le Rotrou from the east. Stephan, with the 1st Division, met the enemy to the east of La Fourche in what appeared at first sight to be a strong position. He had, however, taken the precaution of posting his divisional artillery on a hill some two miles to the east, which overlooked the French position. He ordered Dietl's 1st Brigade to lead the assault, after learning that the 2nd Brigade, which had provided

34 Helvig, *Operations*, p.227n.
35 Helvig, *Operations*, p230.
36 Wittich, *Journal*, p 174.

the advance guard, had encountered strong resistance from prepared positions at the outskirts of La Fourche. Dietl, coming in from the west and north, soon caused the French to retreat in a southerly direction.

Since the French had proved capable of putting up resistance all along what had been a very wide front, it appeared probable to the Bavarians that they had come into collision with a considerable part of the Army of the Loire, the position of which had been their task to identify. In the conviction that this was indeed the case, and that at last there was an opportunity to inflict a decisive defeat on the enemy, the Grand Duke and Krenski on 22 November resolved to attack the place from two sides. Wittich was to move around and attack from the right bank of the Huisne, while von der Tann moved directly from the east. Tresckow was to be held in reserve.

During 21 November the headquarters of the detachment had received a telegram from Moltke reporting that Toury was now occupied by Second Army, and that the French were in position along a front of 35 miles between Orgères and Beaune-la-Rolande. The 4th Cavalry Division was given orders to establish contact with Second Army, and to reconnoitre the road from Chartres to Châteaudun. Hoenig severely criticised the Grand Duke for failing to draw the conclusion from the orders sent to the 4th Cavalry Division that a different view of the situation was now taken at Versailles, and that Moltke's telegram, 'was a weighty and clear strategical indication, and had been sent by wire in order that the detachment might, by proper preparations, be ready for other possibilities that might occur.' Hoenig did, though, concede that in order to recognise the somewhat enigmatic indication contained in Moltke's telegram, 'the penetration and intuition of a leader far seeing and of clear judgement were necessary.'[37] As it was, the Grand Duke and Krenski, evidently lacking these qualities, were quite unaffected by it. Since Moltke was already coming to a clear view of their limitations, it was perhaps a pity that he did not spell out his revised view of the situation in unambiguous terms.

At noon on 22 November the detachment advanced upon its prey in Nogent le Rotrou, only to find that during the night the bird had flown. The evacuation of the town had not been accomplished with any marked efficiency. Roger de Mauni, whose battalion had spent the whole of the day marching towards Nogent le Rotrou, described his arrival there:

> At Nogent we halted in the street; we sank down upon the doorsteps, and for a few minutes sat with our heads buried in our hands. Then, what we had foreseen, came to pass; a mounted adjutant rode up to say that we must make all haste to take the road to Bellesme, as the Prussians were on the point of entering the town. The counter order, which we were so astonished not to have received at Authon, had, it appears, been entrusted to a countryman, who had first thought proper to take his own time, and had ended by giving up the dispatch to a *gendarme*.[38]

It was the kind of experience that was frequently encountered among the poorly organised columns of the Army of the West. Cheated as he was of his prey at Nogent le Rotrou, the Grand Duke gave orders that the advance should be continued in a westerly and south-westerly direction; he had it in his mind that a decisive battle might be fought at Le Mans, 35 miles to the

37 Hale, *People's War*, p.128.
38 de Mauni, *Franco-Prussian-War*, p.62.

west. By nightfall the leading Bavarian unit, the 3rd Brigade, had reached La Ferté-Bernard, having marched some 30 miles during the day, which in all circumstances was a remarkable achievement. There, the only opposition encountered came from several hundred *gardes nationales* and *franc-tireurs*, most of whom appeared to be drunk. The detachment was now heading in a direction quite contrary to that which Moltke intended, but the Grand Duke must have thought that he was on the right lines when, early on that day, a letter had come from Frederick Charles to the effect that he expected to attack the enemy in his front in four or five days, and suggesting that the detachment should cooperate with this by advancing through Le Mans onto Tours. With evident satisfaction the Grand Duke responded by telegram: 'Cooperation in the direction of Le Mans, with the projected further advance on Tours, already prepared for by my departure from the Paris – Orléans road. Advance today for the concentrated attack on Nogent le Rotrou.'[39] That his plans for the detachment were not what was wanted, however, came in the form of a letter from Blumenthal on the same date as that from Frederick Charles.

It was, however, a surprisingly tentative letter, quite out of character for the ebullient Blumenthal. In this, he explained that he had not written previously, as 'our information is so indefinite that I have always been afraid of saying something that was incorrect. And even now things are so little clear that I must restrict my remarks to the following matters.' And after an inaccurate survey of the situation of Second Army, he went on to say that in view of the possible strength of the enemy in the detachment's front, 'it would be desirable not to advance too quickly on Le Mans, but rather to defer the attack for a few days, until you know with certainty about the advance of Prince Frederick Charles.'[40]

Diffident advice of this sort exerted no restraint on the Grand Duke, convinced as he was of the correctness of his own assessment, and on 23 November he issued orders for all units of the detachment to push forward in the direction of Le Mans. Tresckow was to march on St Cosme; Wittich, now to form the right flank, was to concentrate at Bellesme, and von der Tann was to concentrate his whole Corps at La Ferté-Bernard. The 6th Cavalry Division was to move south to Vibraye, and the 4th Cavalry Division to operate against the Châteaudun – Tours railway line. Fiereck and the Army of the West had been remarkably successful in luring the detachment so far away from where it should have been.

39 Hale, *People's War*, p.133.
40 Hale, *People's War*, pp.133–134.

5

d'Aurelle and Freycinet

While the detachment had been engaged in its energetic, but fruitless, tour of first the Beauce and then the Perche countryside, Second Army had been continuing its march westward from Metz. It provided Frederick Charles with an opportunity to see for himself the nature of the campaign on which his army was to embark, which had already been marked by a significant change in the attitude of the civilian population. For his troops, leaving behind them the boring monotony of the siege of Metz, the western movement was a welcome relief, but it made a marked impression on the mind of their commander. Riding towards Pithiviers on 20 November, which was the intended site of his headquarters, Frederick Charles was forcibly struck both by the civilian attitudes which he encountered, and also by the nature of the surrounding countryside, which would give the French a significant advantage:

> During the ride, the farms and villages were found deserted; in the fields bodies of armed men were visible; bullets fell all around irregularly; prisoners, some of them priests with gloomy faces, came before the Prince; the roads were in many places cut through and destroyed, the signposts carried away, and the bells of the churches signalled from church tower to church tower the march of the invaders. By this gloomy November picture the Prince was so deeply impressed that he repeatedly made remarks to those around him about the rising of the Spanish nation against Napoleon I.[1]

X Corps, marching from Chaumont by way of Châtillon sur Seine, had been ordered to make for Joigny, which it reached after a difficult journey, in the course of which it suffered 'much molestation on the way from freebooters, *gardes nationales* and armed inhabitants, who from their lurking places fired upon small detachments on the line of march or as they took up their quarters.'[2] On 19 November, Voigts-Rhetz belatedly received an order that he should reach Montargis by 20 November, but his leading troops only arrived there on 21 November.

Frederick Charles had, correctly, put in hand extensive reconnaissances, one of which he personally undertook, and these had established beyond doubt that the French were holding the 25-mile-long line between Orgères and Beaune-la-Rolande in considerable strength. In

1 Hale, *People's War*, p.124.
2 Official Account, vol. III, p.293.

particular, numerous watch fires were observed at Artenay, Creuzy and Chevilly which showed that there were larger concentrations of troops on the Orléans – Paris high road. On the evening of 20 November, Second Army was able to report to Moltke from Pithiviers that the main body of the Army of the Loire was in its front: 'Headquarters and III Corps have arrived here; the advanced parties today drove the enemy out of Nancray and Beaune-la-Rolande. No news of X Corps since the 17th but no ground for anxiety; its arrival at Montargis is awaited. Our impression is that after the fight at Coulmiers none of the enemy moved away to the north-west.'[3]

This, at last, provided Moltke with the positive intelligence for which he had been waiting. During 20 November he still felt uncertain about the whereabouts of the Army of the Loire, writing to Stiehle that it was still quite doubtful whether the Grand Duke had the Army of the Loire in front of him or whether this was at Châteaudun, or Orléans, or divided. At any rate, the reports reaching Moltke indicated that the enemy had troops of various kinds deployed in an arc from Verneuil to Bonneval. Moltke had, however, no concern about any threat to the investment lines from the south, since Manstein's IX Corps was posted at Angerville, and Alvensleben had now reached Pithiviers.

On 21 November, Stiehle wrote to Moltke with more precise information, it now having been possible to identify the 16th Corps south of Artenay and the 15th Corps at St Lye. Bearing in mind the presumed strength of these units, Stiehle felt that it would be unwise for Second Army to go over to the offensive before X Corps had joined it. He added that the plan was to drive the French back towards Tours, which he said would fit nicely with the advance proposed for the Grand Duke. This advance, it must be borne in mind, was the movement which Frederick Charles had suggested for the detachment, which would compel the French to detach troops from before Orléans to cover Tours, or so it was hoped…

In preparation for the advance on Orléans, the right wing of Second Army was on 22 November shifted to the west; Manstein moved to a position on the Toury-Allaines road, covered in his front by the 2nd Cavalry Division. III Corps, covered by the first cavalry division, also edged to the right, with the 6th Division at Bazoches les Gallerandes and the 5th Division between Pithiviers and Boynes. On the left of the Second Army, the X Corps closed up at Montargis; its patrols still reported enemy activity over a wide area. On the following day Voigts-Rhetz pushed forward outposts to Beaune-la-Rolande; his cavalry reported that the French were in strength at Bellegarde, six miles further south. Information gleaned from civilians suggested that as many as 80,000 troops were marching from Gien towards Montargis.

With the latest information before him, Moltke felt able to revise his strategy. The detachment's movement westwards must be halted immediately, and his line of advance switched back to a south-easterly direction to cooperate directly with the Second Army on its right flank. After gaining approval from the King, the necessary orders went to Blumenthal at 8.45 p.m. that night:

> As we have not succeeded at Nogent le Rotrou in inflicting a decisive defeat on the French Army of the West, the pursuit in the direction of Le Mans will only be carried out for the moment by cavalry reinforced by weak detachments of infantry, and His Majesty wishes that the Grand Duke, with the rest of his army, be put immediately en route towards the

3 Hale, *People's War*, p.125.

> Loire. The detachment must be able to reach Beaugency or Blois by 26 November or a little later.[4]

Even Blumenthal could see that Moltke had now had enough of the ineffectual operations of the detachment, and with good reason, and without a hint of shame he recorded in his diary:

> This is a most excellent move, and will effect a junction with Prince Frederick Charles on the 26th, about Orléans. Victory here will be certain, and the French will be not only cut off from a retreat to Tours, but also from a junction with the troops at Le Mans. The order will have to be telegraphed tonight.[5]

Blumenthal was evidently unaware that driving the French back towards Tours was exactly what Frederick Charles had in his mind.

Moltke naturally copied this order to Stiehle; Second Army was to 'postpone all hostilities until the arrival of the detachment. The slight opposition offered by the French on the Eure and Huisne sufficiently show that no serious danger threatens on that side; the enemy in that quarter need only be kept under observation by cavalry' [6] With the detachment and Second Army operating in unison, Moltke could see that he had an excellent chance to strike a decisive blow at the resurgent French armies, apparently now concentrating in front of Orléans. If the detachment duly arrived on the Loire between Beaugency and Blois, a stunning blow could be delivered at d'Aurelle's left flank.

The war against the Government of National Defence was now about to enter a decisive phase. In spite of all the demands on his time, on 23 November Moltke was able to write to his brother Adolph:

> When one is compelled to follow out but one idea day and night for months, it becomes almost a torture, and yet it is difficult to tear one's mind away from it. After Sedan and Metz, it appeared, no doubt, in Berlin as if all was at an end. We have had since, however, to pass through a most anxious time .... The only way, however, to bring about a final decision now is by the exercise of unmerciful strictness .... Nobody could wish for peace more heartily than I do, but never could I bring myself to vote for a peace which did not secure for Germany the existence which she has obtained through such great sacrifices.[7]

Outwardly, however, Moltke remained as calm and assured as ever. The Crown Prince noted in his diary for 23 November the reaction of different personalities at the Royal Headquarters to the developing situation:

> We are at a crisis of the most exciting and interesting strategical combinations. Day by day Count Moltke expounds the situation of affairs with the utmost clearness, nay, to some extent, with over much sobriety; he has always thought out and calculated everything and

4 Moltke, *Correspondance Militaire,* vol. II, pp.498–499.
5 Blumenthal, *Journals,* p.198.
6 Moltke, *Franco-German War,* pp.187–188.
7 Moltke, *Letters to his Wife et cetera,* vol. II, pp.232–234.

> invariably hits the nail on the head. War Minister von Roon, who has an asthmatic cough, spits copiously and is fond of shrugging his shoulders if any piece of news sounds strange; this sort of pantomime, joined to the Olympian calm and confidence that Lieutenant General von Podbielski shows under all circumstances, often makes more impression on the King's now highly nervous temperament than Count Moltke's admirable clarity.[8]

The Crown Prince's observations of events and discussions at the Royal Headquarters are of much more value than his comments on the operations of his own army, which are generally merely a recycling of the views of his sometimes overbearing chief of staff.

He was certainly right in noting the mounting anxiety of his father about the developing situation on the Loire. In spite of the meticulous and reassuring reports provided to him, the King decided as early as 23 November that he would send an emissary privately to the headquarters of Frederick Charles, to satisfy himself as to what exactly was going on. For this mission he chose his aide-de-camp Lieutenant Colonel Alfred von Waldersee, to whom he gave his instructions on 25 November. His mood, as he did so, was extremely downbeat, and it was apparent to Waldersee that he was not persuaded by those around him that all was well. The King told him: 'We are at a critical moment of the campaign. The French Army of the Loire has gradually become greatly strengthened. I saw that coming, but these gentlemen always know everything better than I and have been declaring that the war is at an end.' Referring in his diary to these comments, Waldersee noted: 'The King is referring principally to General Podbielski, who annoyed him by habitual overconfidence. As the King's tendency is towards pessimism, it is a good thing that there should be someone to take the opposite point of view.'

In reviewing the situation on the Loire, the King was looking on the black side, telling Waldersee that if Frederick Charles was beaten, the investment of Paris would have to be abandoned and the campaign would be lost. He entrusted Waldersee with a personal letter to the Prince, setting out his own views which he was to pass on to Frederick Charles, and he was to tell him that he had 'the fullest confidence in his command and in his experience of war.' Shaking Waldersee's hand, he told him not to be foolhardy; he wanted him to come back unhurt, as he had rendered excellent service and he wanted to make much more use of him.[9]

Waldersee accordingly made his way to Pithiviers, reflecting as he did so that Prince Frederick Charles might not be at all pleased to see him; he realised that he must be particularly tactful in his conversations with the Prince, whom he knew to be extremely touchy. He arrived at the headquarters of Second Army on 26 November, and handed over the King's letter, which Frederick Charles read 'extremely slowly.' Waldersee did not fail to make some flattering remarks to the Prince relating to his gifts as an army commander, which went down well; he wrote sardonically in his diary that he, 'knew that one could safely go to great lengths in this kind of thing.' He went on to assure Frederick Charles, quite untruthfully, that in his reports to the King he would write nothing but what the Prince wished. The King had chosen to send Waldersee on the basis of the latter's undoubted ability; but he was a mere Lieutenant Colonel and aide-de-camp, and it was a considerable responsibility. What was even more remarkable was that the King's decision to send him had been entirely unknown to Moltke. The latter, however, was soon to take a decision himself to get a real grip on the operations on the Loire.

8 Crown Prince, *War Diary*, p.199.
9 Waldersee, *Memoirs*, pp.81–82.

While awaiting the arrival of the detachment in accordance with Moltke's instructions, Frederick Charles had been continuing his efforts to establish the strength and dispositions of the Army of the Loire, ordering a number of reconnaissances in force. One of these was launched by III Corps, which on 24 November sent two squadrons, four battalions and two batteries under Colonel von Flatow through Teillay St Benoit southward towards the Forest of Orléans. The operation was not, however, altogether successful, as the official history recorded:

> They found St Germain, which on the previous day had been occupied by the enemy, now abandoned; detachments of French infantry, which showed themselves at daybreak in the farmsteads lying further to the south, were driven back as far as Neuville aux Bois by six companies supported by artillery. At this latter place fresh troops of all arms were in readiness to receive them in their retreat. The 6th Heavy Battery now came into action against the last named village, while the Prussian infantry, moving with difficulty over the rain sodden ground, and under a heavy musketry fire from the enemy, approached o within a hundred paces of it. But as the effect of the guns was, to all appearances, without result, and the enemy advanced with strong columns against the left flank of the Prussians, Colonel von Flatow broke off the action and commenced his retreat upon St Germain. After beating off an attack made by the French near Le Chêne, with united forces, the contending troops reoccupied their quarters towards noon. The losses on the Prussian side amounted to some 170 men; the French, according to report, lost less.[10]

Another reconnaissance led by Colonel von Falkenhausen was carried out further west with the 11th Regiment, with two batteries and the 9th Cavalry Brigade. His troops reached first Assas and then Artenay, with cavalry at La Croix Briquet before being obliged to fall back in the face of French infantry and artillery advancing from Chevilly. Neither of these reconnaissances had achieved much, prompting a derisive comment by Blumenthal in his diary that Frederick Charles, 'cannot dispense with that absurd reconnoitring in force, a form of tactics whereby the Austrians always spoil their battles. He forgets that one exposes one's own position just as much as one uncloaks that of the enemy.'[11] Blumenthal's low opinion of the utility of a reconnaissance in force was not, however, shared by a number of nineteenth century military commentators, who examined ways in which such an operation could and should be carried out.

On the left of the Second Army's front a number of rather more successful operations were being carried out, which taken together were in due course to provide Colonel von Caprivi, the astute chief of staff of X Corps, with enormously valuable information. Although two of the reconnaissance forces sent forward returned empty-handed, having encountered strong opposition and been able to take no prisoners, the third was more fortunate. Reconnoitring towards Boiscommun, the force under Major von Schöler was accompanied by Captain Seebeck, from Caprivi's staff, who emphasised the necessity of taking prisoners. Approaching Boiscommun, the leading cavalry unit met and drove back into the village some dismounted French Lancers; then, however, they rode into an ambush from which they only extricated themselves with some difficulty. As it happened, the commander of the lancers, Colonel de Brasserie, was just entering the south end of the village with the main body of

10 *Official Account*, vol. III, p.307.
11 Blumenthal, *Journals*, p.200.

his regiment. His leading squadron rode without orders in pursuit of the retreating German cavalry; de Brasserie went after them to recall them, but his horse bolted, and as he came up to his advancing troops they ran into the main body of the German cavalry coming south. In the ensuing engagement, the French were driven back, but the wounded de Brasserie was taken prisoner. Interrogated, he said that he was from 'Polignac's Corps' and had come from Besançon – which was only partially true; Polignac commanded a division of the 20th Corps, now commanded by Crouzat in succession to Michel. Seebeck was able thus to give Caprivi some extremely valuable information.[12]

Further crucial intelligence was gained on 24 November by a lucky chance. The 37th Brigade and 39th Brigade, both forming part of X Corps, were involved in fierce fighting at Ladon and Maizières as they moved up to join the rest of the corps at Beaune-la-Rolande. At Ladon, a trumpeter of the 9th Dragoons picked up a pocketbook belonging to an Englishman, a Captain Ogilvy, who was serving with the French army but who had been killed during the fighting. Three documents were found; one was an order of march of an unidentified army corps; another was a letter of introduction signed by Leon Gambetta, describing Ogilvy as being attached to the staff of 18th Corps but temporarily detached from it; in the letter Gambetta referred to Gien as being 'the key of our position on the Loire.' The third document was an order of battle of an army corps, which would have been of great value had it identified the formation in question. The information gathered in this way by X Corps was duly passed to the headquarters of Second Army, where it was interpreted as meaning that the right wing of the Army of the Loire was planning an advance from the direction of Gien. Von der Goltz described the conclusions drawn from this and the effect on Frederick Charles's strategy:

> If he [Gambetta] looked on Gien as the most important point on the Loire, while up to this time Orléans had been regarded as such, the intention was apparent that the attack was to be commenced with the right wing of the Army of the Loire. This emphasised that the often promised relief of Paris would not be carried out along the great road from Orléans to Paris, but down the Loing towards Fontainebleau. A number of advantages told in favour of this direction, and soon it acquired more and more probability.[13]

While the Germans were getting into position for their planned advance against the Army of the Loire, d'Aurelle was getting on with the task of creating the entrenched camp around Orléans. He wrote on 18 November to Freycinet to tell him of the progress that had been made: 'In spite of the bad weather, our works are going well. The emplacements are well advanced, above all those for the batteries. Today we will have two batteries armed with naval guns at Chevilly and Gidy.' He described the entrenchments on the line of advanced posts, and went on to explain that his principal line of defence ran along the edge of the forest, from St Lye to Chevilly and thence through Gidy, Boulay, Ormes and Ingre. This, he said, was a substantial set of defences, requiring numerous troops to man them, but it was also urgently necessary to complete the defensive works around the city of Orléans itself. Only when these had been completed would the Army of the Loire have freedom of action. He ended with an assurance:

12 Hale, *People's War*, pp.163–164.
13 Von der Goltz, *Gambetta*, p.99.

'In any case this slowness of the enemy in approaching us permits us to complete our defensive works and to make it extremely difficult for him to attack Orléans.'[14]

Reassurance of this kind was not what Freycinet wanted to hear. He and Gambetta were impatient to see the forces which they had created take offensive action. In addition, in Freycinet's mind was the threat posed by the westward march of the detachment to Tours, and he contemplated a diversion by the Army of the Loire in order to draw the Grand Duke away from his advance towards Le Mans. On 19 November he wrote to d'Aurelle to explain what he wanted him to do. After reviewing the forces which might be available, 20th Corps (Crouzat) and 17th Corps (Durrieu), he went on:

> I ask you to consider whether you could not substantially strengthen the forces available by gradually exchanging these units with those actually under your command. Thus perhaps it might be possible to replace Chanzy's corps with that of Durrieu, to which you will be able to apply your stern discipline, and a little later you could replace the former division of Pallières by Crouzat's Corps .... I would also ask you to study with your generals the best direction to give the whole force of 250,000 men which you will have under your command. We cannot remain forever at Orléans. Paris is hungry and calls for us. Study, then, the line of march to follow to join hands with Trochu, who will march to meet you with 150,000 men, at the same time launching a diversion towards the north.[15]

Freycinet added that they were studying their own ideas at Tours, and would meet d'Aurelle to discuss them either at Tiurs or at his headquarters.

D'Aurelle read this letter with dismay, commenting later, 'What contradictory ideas are muddled up in this letter, and what exaggeration there is in the calculation of our resources.' He had himself been in correspondence with Chanzy about the strategy to be followed. The latter had pointed out that Frederick Charles, free to move after the fall of Metz, was going to bring his army by forced marches towards Orléans, and he suggested that it would be better not to wait for him, but to seek out the Grand Duke's detachment and attack it. D'Aurelle, on the other hand, was entirely confident in the good defensive positions which had been constructed, and viewed without apprehension the approach of Frederick Charles and his junction with the Grand Duke. His view was that once the army had left its present positions it would find it impossible to return to them.[16]

Furthermore, to interrupt the construction of the defensive works was to waste valuable time in an operation of little importance. D'Aurelle recorded that he had not confided his own plan to anyone, since he knew, and each passing day confirmed this, that the secret of a planned operation was never secure. He had, he wrote, 'confidence in his army, knowing it well and having seen it in action; it was full of courage, but he was under no illusion that it possessed the aplomb and the solidity of experienced troops.'[17]

Though Chanzy's view of the right course to pursue was more in line with that of Freycinet than d'Aurelle, the latter had a good deal of respect for him, writing that 'this general officer

14 d'Aurelle, *Première Armée*, pp.169–172.
15 d'Aurelle, *Première Armée*. pp.179–181.
16 d'Aurelle, *Première Armée,* p.157.
17 d'Aurelle, *Première Armée*, p.159.

possessed to a marked degree the qualities of a real man of war.' He thought, though, that Chanzy was too prone to split up his troops when bivouacking, as well as immersing himself in too many details, with the result that his subordinates, lacking initiative, sometimes waited for orders which it was impossible to give. As the days passed, Chanzy was keeping a close eye on the movements of the detachment, and on 20 November he sent d'Aurelle a detailed analysis of what might be expected. He recommended that his corps be allowed to move forward as far as Patay, with his left wing along the line of the River Conie; in this way the high road from Châteaudun to Orléans would be covered, and contact established with 17th Corps.[18]

The apparent threat to Tours which so concerned Freycinet prompted Gambetta to go to Le Mans on 22 November to revitalise its defenders with his energy and optimism. He got there at much the same time that the Grand Duke received orders to terminate his advance to the west, and to turn back towards the Army of the Loire. Gambetta drew the conclusion that it was his arrival that had saved the day, writing, 'As a result of this journey the Prussians evidently thought there was a considerable concentration of troops on Le Mans and retreated .... I am convinced that I have saved Le Mans.'[19] While there, Gambetta relieved Fiereck of his command, complaining that 'he had compromised everything by his inertia .... Had not known how either to organise or to discipline his troops and had scattered them over too long a line.' This, having regard to what troops Fiereck actually had available to him, was scarcely fair.

In his memoir, Freycinet commented on the situation which had existed at Le Mans. Gambetta had found that 'the forces in the region were in a deplorable state. One had hoped previously, for some time, that they would be given some solidity, and had started to be reorganised into a 21st Corps. But this task had not been far advanced when the Duke of Mecklenburg attacked. It needed several days of rest to recover and to incorporate a number of battalions of the regular army, together with cavalry and artillery, which were indispensable to the formation of a new corps. Finally the new commander designate of the Corps, General Jaurès, had not yet arrived.'[20] Several thousand men had been cut off, and definitively lost to 21st Corps. The rest covered the roads in general disorder and were only collected at Le Mans with difficulty. However, once Jaurès, a naval officer, had arrived, he displayed a remarkable activity and, sustained by the presence of Gambetta, set about collecting the debris of the Army of the West and organising new regiments. In 36 hours this resulted in the assembly of 12,000 men from the regular army together with artillery. Several battalions of *gardes nationales* were concentrated in the camp at Conlie.

Meanwhile d'Aurelle had replied at once to Freycinet's letter of 19 November that had so annoyed him, writing on the next day with a report on the movements of Crouzat's 20th Corps. He went on to deal with Freycinet's suggestion of the exchange of corps intended to release 15th and 16th Corps for offensive operations:

> I think that this is not the time to do this in the face of the enemy who can himself make similar movements. I am obliged to reduce the estimate of 250,000 men which you indicate as being at my disposal. I will make every effort to get the best out of the troops given to

18 Chanzy, *Deuxième Armée*, pp.49–51.
19 Bury, *Gambetta*, p.187.
20 Freycinet, *Guerre*, pp.117–118.

> me, but it would be dangerous to trust in a deceptive mirage of numbers on paper and to take them for reality.[21]

He added that in order to prepare a plan to join hands with Trochu, it would be necessary to know what was going on in Paris, and actually what Trochu intended.

Aware of the failure of sympathy between Freycinet and d'Aurelle, Gambetta had, as has been seen, sat on 20 November to write his personal letter to the general in order to reinforce the instructions which been sent to him. In this, he had done his best to mend the relationship. He was glad, he said, to recognise that it was thanks to the general's vigilance and energy that the conduct and morale of the troops had been transformed. Orléans, he emphasised, must be the army's base of operations, as Salbris had been, from which to make the great movement towards Paris, for which d'Aurelle must plan.

This was a letter couched in much more sympathetic terms than those which d'Aurelle had been receiving from Freycinet, but it had sent effectively much the same message, and d'Aurelle noted that he had still not received a direct order to march on Paris. On the contrary, the only order he had received was to fortify an entrenched camp in front of Orléans. In making this observation in his memoirs, d'Aurelle was being disingenuous, he knew perfectly well what was wanted of his army, just as he knew, or thought he knew, of what it was capable.

Freycinet had been agitating for the Army of the Loire to make a diversion to relieve the presumed threat through Le Mans. This he suggested should take the form of an advance on Pithiviers. When the detachment turned away, and this threat had receded, he saw the possible movement as a first step on the march to Paris, and since d'Aurelle would not himself produce a plan for the operation, Freycinet issued his own orders. Pallières was to move to Chilleurs aux Bois on 24 November; Crouzat was to move at the same time and should reach a point between Beaune-la-Rolande and Juranville. D'Aurelle was told to pass these orders on. The commander-in-chief was also told to recommend his corps commanders to move circumspectly, particularly when they approached the edge of the forest.

At the same time Freycinet issued orders to 17th Corps to the effect that it must cover Châteaudun. The corps commander, General Durrieu, was not considered satisfactory, displaying little initiative or activity, and apparently was more concerned with his own well-being. Accordingly, he had to go; Freycinet contemplated replacing him with the redoubtable Admiral Jauréguiberry, but left it to d'Aurelle to choose between him and General de Sonis for the command. De Sonis had been an energetic colonel serving in Africa. D'Aurelle did not know him personally, but described him as young, active and renowned for his bravery, and was happy to appoint him, as he reported to Freycinet by telegram of 22 November.[22]

Although he had dutifully passed on Freycinet's instructions to Pallières and Crouzat, d'Aurelle did not approve of them, believing that in the prevailing bad weather the proposed movements should not be made, and he sent one of his staff to Tours to explain this. Freycinet replied with a letter of 23 November, to which d'Aurelle took particular exception:

> If you brought me a better plan than mine, or even any plan at all, I would give up mine and revoke my orders. But during the 12 days you have been at Orléans, you have not, in spite

21 d'Aurelle, *Première Armée*, pp.187–188.
22 d'Aurelle, *Première Armée*, p.214.

> of repeated invitations from M. Gambetta and myself, proposed any kind of plan. You have confined yourself to the fortifying of Orléans in accordance with our instructions, having begun by declaring that it would not be defensible. Your opinion on this, I am pleased to see, appears to have been largely modified, since you do not want to leave your lines. Unfortunately, this wish, which I understand, is not feasible. Of necessity we are obliged to do something, and this means leaving Orléans. As M. Gambetta and I have explained to you, Paris is hungry and requires your succour.[23]

Freycinet went on to tell d'Aurelle that he should already have left his defensive lines and taken the positions of Pithiviers and Montargis, and he sent him copies of the orders which he had issued direct to the various corps of the Army of the Loire. The lack of understanding between d'Aurelle and Freycinet meant that, with both issuing instructions to the various corps and divisions, there was no consistency of purpose or action in the movements which were ordered.

On 23 November Crouzat's 20th Corps had advanced from Gien to a point eight or nine miles south of Beaune-la-Rolande, while 18th Corps remained at Gien. 15th and 16th Corps were still more or less in their former positions between the Paris – Orléans high road and the River Conie. Pallières' large 1st Division of 15th Corps was to the east of the road, with the other two divisions to the west. Chanzy's 16th Corps prolonged the right as far as the Conie. To his left, the leading units of 17th Corps were as far north as Bonneval and Châteaudun on the Loir. The scattered troops of the Army of the West were still concentrating at Le Mans.

Freycinet's instructions to Pallières had required him to march on Chilleurs aux Bois, and on the following day to Pithiviers; in the face of d'Aurelle's protests this was amended to limit his movement to Chilleurs. Crouzat moved to Boiscommun and Bellegarde, and it was this which had led to the engagements at Ladon and Maizières.

The detachment, meanwhile, had begun to execute the change of direction which Moltke had ordered. The instruction to march on Beaugency, received at 11.00 a.m. on 23 November, had come too late to alter the march arrangements for that day, but next day the widely spread units of the detachment wearily got into position for their change of route. On receiving Moltke's order through Blumenthal, the Grand Duke had asked that 24 November be allowed as a rest day; but Blumenthal, on Moltke's instructions, firmly refused this, writing in his diary that, 'this cannot be dreamt of; every effort must be made to press forward, or the enemy will escape us, a contingency of which there is every possibility.'[24] This decision came as a serious disappointment to the detachment's various commanders, all of whom had warmly supported the request for a day's rest for their exhausted men:

> The troops, and more especially the infantry, were greatly fatigued by the last marches of from 21 to 24 English miles daily, in continuous rain, along bad roads and with irregular supplies. The troops frequently did not reach their quarters before nightfall, and were obliged to start again before daylight. Their equipment suffered considerably under these circumstances, as there was neither time nor daylight enough to clean it properly. The boots were the worst of all; in many battalions they were either in a lamentable condition or had been replaced by the sabots of the country stuffed with straw.[25]

23 Freycinet, *Guerre*, pp.122–123.
24 Blumenthal, *Journals*, p.199.
25 Helvig, *Operations*, pp.239–240.

The march was therefore continued on 25 November, and by nightfall the Bavarians had reached the area Mondoubleau – Savigny – St Calais. Behind them the 17th Division was on the road between Beaufoy and Vibraye; the 22nd Division was further to the rear at Authon. The 4th Cavalry Division had got as far as La Bazoche Gouet, having sent patrols towards Bonneval and Châteaudun. The detachment was spread out from the leading cavalry to the rearguard at Nogent le Rotrou; it had, during the day, accomplished a march of between 9 and 10 miles. This was not well-regarded at Versailles; Moltke and Blumenthal were extremely dissatisfied, the latter noting in his diary, 'The Grand Duke, unfortunately, marches very slowly, and Prince Frederick Charles will have to put off his attack until the 28th or 29th. That this pretty stroke is being carried out so haltingly is sad, but we must wait.'[26] In fact the orders for the day's march issued by Krenski had required no more than this, and it would seem that he and the Grand Duke, although refused their rest day, had decided not to ask more of their troops. That was, perhaps, understandable; but there was a development about to occur which once again would blow the detachment off course.

Before this, however, Moltke had decided that for the detachment to continue as part of and under the orders of Third Army was illogical, since it was on the Loire that it would be operating. At noon on 25 November he issued an order to the Grand Duke placing him in future under the orders of the Second Army, with which the detachment would be cooperating in its advance against the Army of the Loire. Moltke copied this to both Blumenthal and Stiehle. He hoped that the new arrangement would increase the control of the detachment's somewhat aberrant movements, but he was already turning over in his mind another possible step to address the problem.

Meanwhile the Grand Duke was alarmed to learn of a completely unexpected attack on the bridging train and ammunition column of I Bavarian Corps as they marched south from Authon and Brou. This attack appeared to have been mounted by a force advancing from Bonneval. Although the escort had moved ahead, the 10th Cavalry Brigade (von Krosigk) was at hand, and together with other units launched a counter-attack. Two Bavarian companies occupied Yevres and the bridge over the Ozanne, eight Prussian guns unlimbered on either side of the village. The French did not pursue their attack, and the Bavarian train continued its march, while the cavalry resumed their movement on La Bazoche Gouet, where they were joined in the evening by the 9th Cavalry Brigade. The remaining brigade of the 4th Cavalry Division remained on the road from Chartres to Bonneval. In the engagement the French suffered about a hundred casualties; the German losses were insignificant.[27]

The reports which reached the Grand Duke suggested that the French forces which had temporarily occupied Brou consisted of at least eight battalions. This posed a serious threat to the flank and rear of the detachment, stretched out as it was over 36 miles, from its advance guard just south of Savigny to its rearguard still around Nogent le Rotrou. The appearance of this French force came as a complete surprise, which should not have been so, since it had been known for the last two days that there was a substantial French force at Châteaudun.

This was 17th Corps, now under de Sonis, moving up the River Loir from Châteaudun and thus interposing between the detachment and Second Army. It presented a threat to the detachment's line of communications, and Blumenthal had warned the Grand Duke of the potential

26 Blumenthal, *Journals*, p.201.
27 *Official Account*, vol. III, p.304.

danger. Oddly, upon becoming aware of the French advance, the headquarters of the detachment had not reported it to Versailles. Hale speculated as to the reasons for this failure:

> It is possible that the morale of the Grand Duke may have been disturbed by the order to march on Beaugency. Hoenig suggests that in the order, the Grand Duke foresaw the possibility of the detachment ceasing to be an independent command, and of his being placed under the orders of the Prince; or even of the detachment ceasing to exist as a unit, and its corps being incorporated in Second Army; there may have therefore been no great excessive zeal on his part in contributing a share to the compulsory cooperation.[28]

It seemed evident to the Grand Duke that this threat to his communications required immediate action to retake Brou, and the orders issued for 26 November involved the line of march of the detachment being swung 90° to the north-east. The Grand Duke's intention was to concentrate the detachment in the position Brou – La Bazoche Gouet – Arville, but his orders required the employment of more of his troops than was reasonable. The situation of the detachment was unjustly described by the historian of I Bavarian Corps as 'to say the least of it very peculiar, and might be regarded as fatal even by those disposed to take a favourable view.'[29] As it was, von der Tann was ordered to concentrate the whole of his corps at Arville by 10.00 a.m., which was quite impossible, since only the 2nd Division in Mondoubleau could reach the rendezvous by the appointed time.

Nevertheless, the various units of the detachment marched off on 26 November towards their new positions. Von der Tann's corps had almost reached Arville by 3.00 p.m. when an order was received from the detachment's headquarters that cantonments were to be taken up, as the patrols sent forward had not found any traces of the enemy. What had happened was that de Sonis had become seriously alarmed by reports that the Germans were closing in on 17th Corps, and he had precipitately retired. When the Germans entered Brou, 'a report was current that the enemy, at a strength of 14,000 men and two batteries, had retired from there on the previous evening; it was said to Châteaudun.'[30]

In this way both the detachment and 17th Corps had each momentarily become alarmed by a threat to their communications, and each had reacted defensively to that threat. If the Grand Duke had been bolder, and had continued his march in a south-easterly direction, he might have found de Sonis in a very much exposed position; on the other hand, if the French commander had not abruptly lost his nerve, he might have imposed still further loss of time on the detachment. As it was, de Sonis had withdrawn his advanced troops to Marboue during the night of 25/26 November, and there received orders from Tours to move to Vendôme in order to protect the seat of government. However, German cavalry patrols had already been reported at Cloyes, Fréteval and Vendôme, and it seemed to de Sonis that his orders were impracticable. On the evening of 26 November, 17th Corps was withdrawn behind the Forest of Marchenoir. The movement proved extremely damaging to the corps: 'The continued night march had a demoralising effect on the cohesion of these loose, and but partially trained troops; masses of stragglers wandered about in the neighbourhood for days; a battalion and a battery wandered

28 Hale, *People's War*, pp.168–169.
29 Helvig, *Operations*, p.241.
30 *Official Account*, vol. III, p.305.

away to Tournoisis; some 2,000 dispersed troops could not be rallied until they had reached Beaugency.'[31]

By now Freycinet was issuing a stream of orders directly to the corps commanders of the Army of the Loire. Crouzat's 20th Corps had not been able to move to the positions ordered for it; the 18th Corps was now marching from Gien in the direction of the German left, with the object of creating a diversion, while Pallières was struggling along bad roads in the direction of an intended junction with Crouzat. The three were still a day's march apart. D'Aurelle, however, had for the moment practically given up his authority over the Army of the Loire; when Crouzat ended a dispatch to him on 24 November to say that he was awaiting d'Aurelle's orders, the latter simply forwarded it to Tours with the following comment:

> Since I do not fully know the object of the movements, it is difficult for me to give detailed orders; Generals Pallières and Crouzat are a long day's march apart, and could not therefore support each other. It is doubtful whether General Crouzat will be able to continue his movement tomorrow. Are the two corps to concentrate and where? For fear that General Crouzat may not receive his orders sufficiently early through me, I request that they be sent to him by telegraph direct to Bellegarde, and that I may know what they are.[32]

D'Aurelle told Crouzat that he had asked Freycinet to do this, warning him to be prudent in the meantime.

31 *Official Account*, vol. III, p.306.
32 d'Aurelle, *Premiere Armée*, pp.227–228.

Roon, Minister of War.

Moltke, Chief of the German General Staff.

Prince Frederick Charles of Prussia, commander of Second Army.

Friedrich Franz, Grand Duke of Mecklenburg, commander of an *Armee-Abteilung*.

Blumenthal, chief of staff of Third Army.

Konstantin Alvensleben, commander of German III Corps.

Manstein, commander of German IX Corps.

Voigts-Rhetz, commander of German X Corps.

Von der Tann, commander of Bavarian I Corps.

Tresckow, commander of German 17th Division.

Wittich, commander of German 22nd Division.

Leon Gambetta.

Freycinet, Minister of War in the Government of National Defence.

d'Aurelle de Paladines, commander of the French First Army of the Loire.

Chanzy, commander of the French Second Army of the Loire, by Henner.

Admiral Jauréguiberry, commander of French 16th Corps.

French troops from the Army of the Loire on reconnaissance, by Detaille.

Sonis, commander of French 17th Corps.

Bavarian troops on the march, by Zimmer.

Columb, commander of French 17th Corps.

Chanzy and his staff, 1870.

Billot, commander of French 18th Corps.

French artillery under fire, by Zimmer.

Bourbaki, commander of French 18th Corps.

Bavarian troops skirmishing, by Zimmer.

A general view of Orléans.

The entry of the Germans into Orléans, by von Braun.

French artillery in action at Orléans, October 1870, by Pallandre.

Artenay, 10 October 1870, by Pallandre.

The entry of the Bavarian I Corps into Orléans, 12 October 1870, by Zimmer.

The French defence of Châteaudun, October 1870, by Pallandre.

French artillery park, winter 1870–71, engraving by Lavée after Dupray.

Bavarian staff officers observe French movements, by Zimmer.

Bavarian firing line, winter 1870–71, by Zimmer.

French troops at Coulmiers, by Pallandre.

General von der Tann at Coulmiers, by Ernst Zimmer.

Lieutenant Colonel Ruck, chief of staff of the Bavarian 2nd Division, at Coulmiers, by Zimmer.

Staff of Bavarian I Corps under fire at Coulmiers, by Zimmer.

The Château at Coulmiers attacked by the French on 9 November.

A scene from the Battle of Beaune-la-Rolande, by Pallandre.

The *Légion Bretonne* in action at Beaune-la-Rolande, by Le Dru.

An episode from the sharp action at Huêtre, 1 December 1870, by Pallandre.

6

Albrecht von Stosch

In the 13 years since he assumed the duties of Chief of the Great General Staff, Moltke had steadily refined its structure and functions without departing from the general principles on which it was based. By 1870 it was the most effective military institution of its kind in the world. Moltke had been able to select the key officers upon whom he would come particularly to rely. The role of the chief of staff of an operational unit was one to which Moltke paid particular attention, and which steadily evolved. An American writer has described the relationship between a chief of staff and the field commander with which he worked as a partnership:

> During the time he was serving as chief of staff the peculiar status of that official to the commanding general was more firmly established. The General Staff officers serving in armies, corps and divisions tended more and more to represent the General Staff. The relationship of Moltke to the Crown was similar to the relationship of the lower chiefs of staff to their respective commanders.[1]

The role of chief of staff had been first defined by Gerhardt Johann von Scharnhorst. He provided in his first scheme for the organisation of the general staff that the duties of general staff officers were to be regulated by special instructions, which were not to be confined to the General Staff but were to be published to all the generals of the army. The purpose of this was explained in the document produced by Paul Bronsart von Schellendorff, who was one of the key General Staff officers on whom Moltke particularly relied, it was to ensure not only that General Staff officers should know what was expected of them, but also that their field commanders 'should be cognisant of the duties of a general staff officer, so that misunderstandings, overlapping, wrong expectations, or accusations might be avoided.'[2] Schellendorff regarded the independence of the General Staff as of the highest importance, which he believed, with some justice, was 'one of the most important causes of the splendid achievements of the General Staff in recent campaigns.' In particular, the direct access of the Chief of the Great General Staff to the King meant that

1 Hittle, *The Military Staff*, p.66.
2 General Paul Bronsart von Schellendorff, *The Duties of the General Staff* (London: HMSO, 1905), pp.23–24.

he was not subject to the control of a war minister, who might seek to assume the control of operations at a critical moment.

But the relationship of the chief of staff of an operational unit to his field commander was an extremely delicate one, the success of which depended to a great extent on the personalities involved and, in particular, the status and experience of the field commander. In the case of Third Army, for instance, there was never any question that, in the partnership between the Crown Prince and Blumenthal, it was the latter who was the dominant force. At the headquarters of Second Army, on the other hand, Prince Frederick Charles, as a career soldier, would certainly not be dictated to by Stiehle.

It was in their understanding of their powers and responsibilities that there existed among the officers of the General Staff a consistency of thought upon which Moltke could generally rely. Since it was understood that chiefs of staff had the right to take part in the evolution of operational decisions, it was essential that they thought and acted in the way in which Moltke expected of them, and this was a key objective of the immensely thorough training.

This being so, the question arises as to the reasons for the actions of the Grand Duke and Krenski, and their failure to act in accordance with what Moltke expected of the detachment. There are a number of possible explanations. One is that Krenski, in making a series of misjudgements, was able to impose his views upon a complacent Grand Duke. Another is that Krenski proved unable to stand up to the demands made by a wilful and wrong-headed Grand Duke, allowing him to dictate an entirely incorrect strategy. Put in that way, the latter explanation seems much the more likely. Of course, it may have been merely the interaction of the two personalities that led to wrong decisions being taken; but we will never know.

There is nothing in their previous careers which should have led Moltke to doubt the suitability of Krenski and the Grand Duke for the tasks that were assigned to them. Born in 1827, Paul von Krenski joined the Prussian Army as a second lieutenant. He saw service in the first Schleswig War as a battery commander, and rose steadily through the ranks. In 1863 he was serving on the staff of IV Corps in Magdeburg, and was promoted to major. In 1866 he had a particularly good war as General Staff officer of the 7th Infantry Division, commanded by Lieutenant General von Fransecky. He did well at the Battle of Munchengrätz, and at the Battle of Königgrätz, where his division was involved in the bitter struggle for the Swiepwald; he distinguished himself when rallying broken troops at a critical moment. For this, on Fransecky's recommendation, he was awarded the Pour le Mérite.

In 1870, by now a full colonel, Krenski was appointed to the staff of Frederick Francis II, Grand Duke of Mecklenburg-Schwerin, who had as Governor-General of Reims after the early battles of the war become the effective commander of those units not attached to any of the field armies, within the portfolio of his position as Governor-General; and he accompanied the Grand Duke when the latter was appointed to the command of the detachment.

Frederick Francis II was born in 1823. He was privately educated until 1838, when he attended the Blochmann Institute in Dresden and subsequently the University of Bonn. He succeeded to the title of Grand Duke in 1842. Joining the Prussian Army, at the outbreak of the second Schleswig-Holstein War he was offered a field command, which he refused, since he was a close friend of King Christian IX of Denmark. In the event he served on the staff of Field Marshal von Wrangel during the course of hostilities. During the closing stages of the Austro-Prussian War he was appointed to command II Reserve Corps mopping up resistance in southern Germany. Relatively inexperienced, his selection to command the detachment was perhaps surprising. Moltke may well not have wished to move one of his experienced corps commanders at a critical stage of the war. Or maybe the appointment of his Royal Highness was made to ensure that no difficult questions of seniority arose with von der Tann.

The decision to appoint the Grand Duke was, of course, effectively made by Moltke, although it will have been a matter discussed at his daily conference with the King. In the appendix to his history of the war, he described the conduct of these meetings:

> Excepting on the march and on days of battle, an audience was regularly held by His Majesty at 10 o'clock, at which I, accompanied by the quartermaster general, laid the latest reports and information before him, and made our suggestions on that basis. The Chief of the Military Cabinet and the Minister of War were also present, and while the headquarters of Third Army were at Versailles, the Crown Prince also; but all merely as listeners. The King occasionally required them to give him information on one point or another; but I do not remember that he ever asked for advice concerning the operations in the field or the suggestions I made. These, which I always discussed beforehand with my staff officers, were, on the contrary, generally maturely weighed by His Majesty himself. He always pointed out with a military eye and an invariably correct estimate of the situation, all the objections that might be raised to their execution; but as in war every step is beset with danger, the plans laid before him were invariably adopted.[3]

Moltke's doubts as to the leadership of the detachment came to a head on 25 November, when he raised the question of the possible replacement of Krenski as chief of staff. It was plainly necessary to send someone of sufficient authority to be able to take effective charge, regardless of what the Grand Duke might think. Sending one of his section heads, Bronsart, Verdy or Brandenstein, would not be suitable; each of them was a Lieutenant Colonel, and would have great difficulty in imposing his will on the Grand Duke. There were, Moltke thought, two possible candidates; the quartermaster general, Podbielski, his own deputy, and Lieutenant General Albrecht von Stosch, the intendant general. Walking back from the meeting, Stosch spoke to Verdy about the discussion of the leadership of the detachment, which he found deeply concerning, he added, 'I would be ready to assume this difficult post, and if the conversation returns to it, you can mention me as a candidate.' Next morning Verdy spoke to Moltke, and told him of Stosch's willingness to go; after checking with Stosch that he would be ready to leave at once, Moltke gratefully accepted his offer. Moltke next had a brief conversation with General Albrecht von Roon, who as War Minister was technically Stosch's superior, who consented to his release from his duties as intendant general, but stressed that it could only be for a short time. Moltke reassured him, saying that the future progress of the campaign could not be predicted with certainty, but that he hoped that the Army of the Loire would soon suffer 'an annihilating defeat,' whereupon Stosch could return to Versailles.[4]

The sending of Stosch to the Loire was a game changing decision. Fritz Hoenig wrote:

3 Moltke, *Franco-German War*, p.418.

4 Frederick B. M. Hollyday, *Bismarck's Rival* (Durham, North Carolina: Duke University Press, 1960), pp.73–74.

> The naming of General von Stosch as Chief of Staff of the Army Section was an important event, for, without a doubt, the general was one of the most outstanding men of that great time and had the reputation as a distinguished officer of the General Staff. Assured in his bearing, he combined a high degree of common sense with good judgement and a wide and inclusive point of view. The general, as a result of his high rank, could expect that more attention would be paid to his advice than that of Colonel von Krenski, and, moreover, he was in such close contact with Count von Moltke that professional relations between them were expected to be advantageous. He was completely informed of Moltke's ideas through his participation in the conversations which preceded the Chief of the General Staff's daily reports. Colonel von Krenski had previously served under Stosch, and could be expected to serve willingly under him again. They did not foresee in Versailles on 26 November that such important demands would later be made upon the Chief of Staff of the Army Section. Under the circumstances it was certainly good fortune that they decided to change the chief of staff at once, for without the penetrating clarity and energy of General von Stosch, the conduct of the war would not have taken its favourable course.[5]

Albrecht von Stosch was born at Koblenz on 20 April 1818. His father, Ferdinand von Stosch, had reached the rank of general in the Prussian Army, and his son followed the family tradition, being commissioned as a second lieutenant in the 29th Infantry Regiment at the age of 17. In 1839 he entered the general military school in Berlin, in 1843 he was posted to the Guard artillery, and following this served in the topographical bureau of the General Staff. He failed, however, to gain entry to the General Staff itself, apparently because he was said to be 'inclined to indiscipline,' which was a great disappointment to him. He was promoted to first lieutenant in 1849, and captain in 1852; and then at last achieved his ambition by being appointed to the General Staff. He was posted to VIII Corps at Koblenz, where he met the future King William I of Prussia, then serving as military governor of Rhineland-Westphalia; the latter was impressed by a lecture which Stosch gave on the needle gun, and later remarked that it was Stosch who first brought it to his attention.[6]

In 1856 Stosch was promoted to major, and served five years with the 10th Division at Posen. He had become interested in politics in his twenties, an interest which led to his being suspected of political unreliability by the reactionary leaders of the General Staff. He continued to serve at Posen, on the staff of V Corps, performing well in the manoeuvres of 1858; three years later, now a lieutenant colonel, he particularly impressed Moltke at the staff ride of 1861, who remarked that Stosch's insistence that his officers write a daily report was making too much work for him.[7]

Stosch was a firm supporter of army reform and of the military bill put forward in 1859. He had become chief of staff of IV Corps at Magdeburg, and was clearly an 'up and coming man'. The corps commander, General von Schack, reported him as, 'fit for every position and assignment;' Moltke, while approving his personal abilities and what he described as his amiable and promising character, felt that he lacked operational experience. Stosch was promoted to colonel in 1861; but his promising career was almost ended by a riding accident in November 1863, an

5 Hollyday, *Bismarck's Rival*, p.74.
6 Holliday, *Bismarck's Rival*, pp.8–16.
7 Holliday, *Bismarck's Rival*, p.18.

accident so serious that his life was endangered. He slowly recovered, though for the rest of his life he walked with a limp, and he was still unfit for service when war with Denmark broke out in 1864. However, he was making a number of influential friends, and in that year became acquainted with Crown Prince Frederick William and his wife, the Crown Princess Victoria, with whom he formed a close and enduring friendship. Since the Crown Prince held liberal views, this did Stosch no good in the eyes of the military cabinet.

When, in 1865, the Crown Prince asked that Stosch be appointed chief of staff of II Corps, of which he was in command, the military cabinet inferred his political unreliability from the mere fact that the Crown Prince had asked for him, and refused to appoint him. Frederick William then tried to get him as his adjutant. According to Stosch's biographer, when asked if she could cooperate with him, the Crown Princess replied that he was already indispensable to her, and that as a result his fate was sealed. The Crown Prince wrote angrily in his diary: 'Colonel von Stosch .... is now being persecuted by the military cabinet because I wanted him with me. Things have already reached these lengths! Furthermore, certain circles are furious that 'the Crown Prince dared to select his adjutant behind the back of the military cabinet.' *Signatura temporis*.'[8]

Apart from his friendship with the Crown Prince, Stosch was also associated with the liberal writer and publicist Gustav Freytag, and with the liberal Premier of Baden, Baron Franz von Roggenbach. In fact, many of Stosch's views would have been anathema to the liberal majority in Prussia, who would have seen him as an arch conservative, and this duality between his political reputation and his actual beliefs followed Stosch throughout his life.

With Bismarck's political objectives, however, Stosch was in warm agreement; he believed that the unification of Germany should be achieved on a *Kleinsdeutsch* basis, and that Austria would have to be excluded from German affairs. However, unlike the majority of nationalist liberals, he believed that it should be the Prussian Army that brought about unification.

In 1866, as the prospect of war between Prussia and Austria was becoming more likely, Stosch was appointed as Quartermaster General of Second Army, and hence number 2 to Blumenthal, its chief of staff; the Crown Prince was the army's commander. Visiting Berlin in May, Stosch met with Moltke, who told him that his principal responsibility would be to give effect to Blumenthal's inspirations.[9] It was evident to both men that working with Blumenthal would not be easy; Stosch was fortunate to have the very able, and very tactful Verdy as one of his assistants. The latter subsequently wrote of Stosch, looking back at 1866:

> He had a tall imposing figure, and always carries himself rigidly erect, even though he limped slightly .... He was also the picture of virile strength, which was expressed in indefatigable activity. His powerful frame was surmounted by an expressive head, out of which two shrewd eyes looked sharply into the world, and his candid features gave the impression that he grew more joyful the more difficult a situation became .... An unusual energy, which could attack details industriously, but which, in all emergencies, proved to be of the greatest profit for the whole, emanated from his entire being, his speech, and the mode and manner of his behaviour.[10]

8 Holliday, *Bismarck's Rival*, pp.28–29.
9 General and Admiral Albrecht von Stosch, *Denkwurdigkeiten* (Stuttgart: Deutsche Verlags Anstalt, 1904), pp.72–73.
10 Holliday, *Bismarck's Rival*, pp.32–33.

Stosch acquitted himself well during the campaign in northern Bohemia. Once war broke out, Second Army began its potentially hazardous advance through widely separated mountain passes, and was hence exposed to the risk of defeat in detail. On 27 June Stosch had his first experience of actual combat, when, riding with the Crown Prince and Blumenthal towards Nachod, they came under fire. He declined the request of the Crown Prince's adjutant that he should persuade him to withdraw; Stosch told him that he was under fire for the first time in his life, and that Blumenthal should do it. He rode on, ordering a retreating Prussian battery back into action, and then gave instructions that the road should be cleared to make way for promised reinforcements; these actions probably saved Steinmetz's hard pressed I Corps from defeat.

When on 2 July 1866 the crucial encounter at Königgrätz approached, Blumenthal was absent at the Royal Headquarters, and it fell to Stosch to draft the necessary orders to I Corps and the cavalry to advance towards a junction with First Army, orders which got Second Army moving forward sooner than might otherwise have been the case.

On 4 July, the day after the battle, Stosch accompanied the Crown Prince to the Royal Headquarters. He later described the battle as 'the best and greatest day in Prussia's history.'[11] He and the Crown Prince strongly urged that the terms of any armistice should be such as to not let the Austrians off the hook. In the following days relations between Second Army and the Royal Headquarters deteriorated, and on 15 July Stosch was sent there to put the Second Army's case, and was able to pour oil on troubled waters; Blumenthal, who had been particularly incensed at Moltke's suggestion that Second Army had not been moving fast enough, wrote in his diary, 'I was dead tired, but freshened up at once when Stosch returned and told me that General von Moltke had approved all that we had done.'[12]

Stosch had always taken a keen interest in politics, and his friendship with the Crown Prince and Crown Princess kept him close to the centre of power. He believed that the Crown Prince should work closely with the King and Bismarck. He had first met Bismarck in the aftermath of Königgrätz; he wrote in his memoirs:

> It was the first time that I encountered Bismarck personally, and I am glad to acknowledge that I was actually overpowered by the impression I received of him. The clarity and grandeur of his views gave me the greatest pleasure. He was assured and original in every direction, and each thought included a whole world. The fact that we ate and drank excellently besides did not injure the happy operation of Bismarck's process of enchantment.[13]

When the war ended Stosch took up the duties of Director of the Military Economics Department of the War Ministry. In this capacity he was responsible for supervision of the army administration and supply matters. Since the Department had not performed well during the war, Stosch was appointed to reorganise it, and was largely given a free hand to do so. He was subsequently heavily involved in the intricate negotiations with Saxony over the incorporation of the Saxon Army into that of the newly formed North German Confederation, and this brought him into conflict with Bismarck. The latter was discontented with some of the concessions which Stosch had made to achieve agreement with the Saxons, and made his feelings

11 Stosch, *Denkwurdigkeiten*, vol. I, p.106.
12 Blumenthal, *Journals*, p.51.
13 Stosch, *Denkwurdigkeiten*, vol. I, pp.97–98.

known in a painful interview between the two men. Subsequently, after the Saxon Convention was concluded, Stosch, as Director of the Military Economic Department, became involved in the tortuous negotiations over the Saxon military budget, which again brought friction with Bismarck.

This did not however affect his support for Bismarck's policy or his admiration for him as a politician, and he wrote to his friend Gustav Freytag in 1868:

> He is vigorous and bold in thought and clear in what he wants; he will never set a goal beyond his reach. He will ruthlessly destroy men and situations that stand in his way. But here his thoroughly monarchical conviction, which is innate in him, comes into consideration. Bismarck only uses liberalism and the constitution in order to lead and sway the King and the conservatives, but never as an assured element of power. Bismarck wants a united monarchical Germany.[14]

He continued to press the Crown Prince to support Bismarck's policies; this was not always easy, since the liberal Frederick William and Victoria were opposed to many aspects of Bismarck's domestic policy and personally disliked him. In addition, the Crown Prince was from time to time indifferent to public affairs and Stosch had difficulty in encouraging him to actively support Bismarck and his father.

In July 1870 Stosch, like many others at the head of Prussian affairs, was on holiday, until urgently summoned back to Berlin on 15 July as Franco-Prussian relations moved to a crisis. The prospect of war inspired him; he wrote in his memoirs: 'It is a joy to live in such times and immeasurable good fortune to participate actively in them. How many good and virtuous men must waste their powers in a petty age for petty goals without ever seeing one great moment.'[15]

He was, however, disappointed in the post selected for him. He and the Crown Prince had both hoped that he would be chief of staff to the army to be led by the Crown Prince, but Moltke insisted that this post must be held by Blumenthal. Instead, at Roon's urging, Stosch was appointed as intendant general, a decision which he had long feared, since it was a post which lay outside the mainstream of military direction. Nevertheless, it was a position of the first importance, and Roon insisted that Stosch was 'the only general who could direct the provisioning of the army in war.'

The huge increase in the numbers of men concerned in warfare meant a corresponding increase of the provisions required to feed and equip them. Once the war had begun, and the German armies advanced deep into France, the problems of supply were accentuated by the increasing length and complexity of the lines of communication, which became vulnerable to constant attacks by the franc-tireurs. The system that had been in force during the Austro-Prussian War had proved completely inadequate; Moltke insisted that, in future, provisioning should be combined rather than be dealt with by each separate unit. A military historian, Colonel George Furse, wrote in 1894:

> After the campaign of 1866, the Prussian staff, foreseeing all the advantages that could accrue in war by the employment of system of *etappen* carefully elaborated in all its details,

14 Holliday, *Bismarck's Rival,* p.60.
15 Stosch, *Denkwurdigkeiten*, vol. I, p.186.

> set themselves to work it out, and prepared an organisation which came into force when four years later the Franco-German war broke out. The results reaped from such judicious forethought are now matters of history, and the principal European armies have modelled their system on the German.[16]

From the moment mobilisation began on 16 July, the carefully prepared plans worked out by the Great General Staff swung into operation, as Moltke, in his history of the war, described:

> The mobilisation machinery of the North German Army had been elaborated from year to year, in accord with the changing conditions, by the combined exertions of the War Ministry and the General Staff. Every branch of the administration throughout the country had been kept informed of all it needed to know in this relation … This understanding enabled the preparations which it entailed to be proceeded with. The train and march tables were worked out for each body of troops, with the most minute directions as to the respective starting points, the day and hour of departure, the duration of the journey, the refreshment stations, and points of detainment …. And thus, when the stroke of war inevitably impended, there was required only the Royal signature to start the whole mighty movement in its smooth, swift course. Nothing needed to be changed in the directions originally given; it sufficed to follow the plans previously thought out and prepared.[17]

Stosch's biographer pointed to his effectiveness in ensuring that the system continued to work effectively, 'He was able to overcome the difficulties of Royal interference, blocked railways, opposition of subordinates, rapidly changing lines of supply, the provisioning not only of mass armies, but also of prisoners of war and of the French civilian population.'[18] After the war, The King told an old friend that the 'provisioning of the army exceeded anything previously heard of.' Martin van Creveld, has taken a somewhat different view, suggesting that the problems were greater than could be readily coped with, 'It is the fact that Moltke's forces could only live as long as they kept moving, and experienced the greatest difficulty in staying in one place for more than a few days at a time, that the supreme proof lies that the military instrument in his hands did not, after all, belong to the modern age.'[19]

This was a considerable overstatement. There is not much evidence that the German forces were obliged to move solely to gather supplies; and the largest component of the forces to be supplied was made up of the troops investing Paris. Colonel Furse quoted an estimate of what they required daily:

> 148,003 loaves of bread,
> 102,000lbs of rice,
> 595 oxen or 102,000lbs of bacon,
> 14,400lbs of salt,

16 Colonel G. A. Furse, *The Organisation and Administration of the Lines of Communication in War* (London: William Clowes & Sons, 1894), p.12.

17 Moltke *Franco-German War*, p.6.

18 Holliday, *Bismarck's Rival,* p.71.

19 Martin van Creveld, *Supplying War* (Cambridge: CUP, 1977), p.85.

> 960,000lbs of oats,
> 2,400,000lbs of hay,
> 28,000 quarts of spirits,
> A large supply of coffee and sugar, with many thousand cigars.[20]

The process of supplying the armies in the field depended to a large part on the use of railways, but the French railway system was, naturally, subject to many disruptions; and as Colonel Furse pointed out, '...with all the use the Germans made of railways, with all their large employment of the system of requisitions, there is no doubt that they could never have performed the feat of feeding their armies with regularity in 1870–1871 without the aid of their well-organised establishment of provision columns.'[21]

In November 1870 Stosch was delighted to have the opportunity now given to him to serve in the field, although he was perfectly aware of the difficulties he would face on the Loire, as a result of the discussions that had taken place at the Royal Headquarters. He set off the same day. On his way to the headquarters of the detachment at Châteaudun, he encountered the 22nd Division and the 4th Cavalry Division at Bonneval, and was struck by how low the morale of the detachment was:

> He found how widely different the actual condition of an army that had been struggling continuously for a fortnight against a people in arms, was from the idea formed of its conditions by high-ranking staff officers, including himself perhaps, who had been comfortably fed and lodged at Versailles all the time. The whole detachment, including its staff, was in a state of moral depression.[22]

He learned from the officers to whom he spoke that it was not merely the considerable physical trials and discomforts that had caused this; these they would have borne if there had been some tangible result, one big battle instead of a perpetual irritating skirmishing with guerrilla bands. He soon realised that a rest day was essential, and at once obtained permission for this from Versailles.

The Grand Duke had been told of Stosch's appointment by a brief letter from Moltke of 26 November, which he brought with him. He had of course had no warning that this was in contemplation and there had been no discussion with him. In the circumstances, when Stosch arrived on 27 November the Grand Duke received him frostily. It was customary for an army commander to approve the choice of his chief of staff, and this custom was still more respected when the commander was a reigning Prince. It called for all Stosch's tact to evolve a satisfactory working relationship with the Grand Duke, but this he managed to achieve by the confidence of his bearing and assurances of imminent victory, and by a careful willingness to remain in the background. Stosch wrote to his wife in December: 'It is not easy at all to work with the Grand Duke. Naturally everyone turns to me with their questions and he takes offence.'[23]

20 Furse, *Lines of Communication,* p.220.
21 Furse, *Lines of Communication,* p.210.
22 Hale, *People's War,* p.198.
23 Stosch, *Denkwurdigkeiten*, vol. I, p.216.

This was a problem which faced Stosch throughout his time on the Loire, since the Grand Duke was extremely touchy and was frequently offended. His biographer recorded instances of this:

> On 13 December, during a conference with Lieutenant General von Voigts-Rhetz, the very able commander of X Corps, and his staff, the Grand Duke suddenly interrupted Stosch in a loud voice: 'What are you doing there? That goes against the first rules of tactics.' Voigts-Rhetz countered with such disdainful remarks that Stosch was forced to pour oil on the troubled waters by altering the operations in the sense Frederick Francis desired. 'But from that hour on I have had a master who makes my task very difficult,' he wrote. Prince Albrecht of Prussia, brother of King William I and commander of the 4th Cavalry Division, looked upon the Grand Duke's pretensions as a general with a humorous eye. The day following the incident with Voigts-Rhetz, he entered the room where Frederick Francis and Stosch were discussing the course of operations and asked: 'Well then Stosch, what shall I do today?' Then the Grand Duke said curtly: 'I command here.' The Prince replied: 'We all know what the score is and don't need to inconvenience ourselves.... Stosch, what shall I do?'[24]

The presence of Stosch at the headquarters of the detachment materially changed the relationship of the detachment to Second Army, and affected the thinking not only of the Grand Duke, but also of Frederick Charles. As Hale wrote:

> Moltke knew that he had now on the Loire two obstinate personalities, over whom he had voluntarily given up control. Stosch was an excellent soldier, a large minded man, but in view of the situation he was a good deal more. Owing to his high position on the supreme staff of the German forces, and his close professional connection with Moltke, the chief staff officer of those forces, he was, on the Loire, little less than Moltke present by proxy. The Grand Duke must now be aware that if he rebelled against his new chief staff officer he would be rebelling against Moltke, while the Prince knew similarly, that although he might be determined to act in future in disregard of Moltke's expressed views and wishes, there was present only a few miles away from him in the theatre of war, Moltke's personal representative, endeavouring to hold him in check.[25]

Fortunately, Frederick Charles, who was entirely familiar with Stosch and understood his capabilities, regarded the change as greatly for the better.

During the course of 27 November the detachment had not had to concern itself with de Sonis, as a result of his precipitate and chaotic retreat. Accordingly, its various units had made good progress in reaching each of their objectives during the day: by nightfall the Bavarians were on the Loir between Marboue and Châteaudun, while the 17th Division was to the north of St Maurice and the 22nd Division was at Bonneval. The detachment was accordingly able to enjoy its rest day on 28 November.

24 Holliday, *Bismarck's Rival*, pp.75–76.
25 Hale, *People's War*, pp.186–187.

Stosch wasted no time in setting about the reorganisation of the staff of the detachment. He found to his surprise that there was no field bureau; the records were in a state of disorder; there was no précis of the information received; and there was no proper subdivision and allocation of staff duties. These shortcomings had no doubt derived in large part from the haste in which the detachment had been assembled and its staff structure brought into being, and they contributed to a considerable extent to the way in which the detachment had been led. Krenski must take a large part of the blame for failing to put this right, but as it was, Stosch's reorganisation soon put matters on a proper footing.

Meanwhile on 26 November there had been no movements of significance on the part of Second Army. As yet unaware, of course, of the imminent arrival of Stosch at the detachment, Frederick Charles issued an order to the Grand Duke at 11.16 a.m., 'Your Royal Highness is ordered, attacking the enemy by way of Chteaudun and Bonneval, to march without loss of time to unite with Second Army, of which the right flank is at Janville.'[26] This order was entirely at odds with the strategy which Moltke had been intending should be followed when he ordered the detachment to direct its march towards Beaugency. Instead of an attack on d'Aurelle's left flank, Frederick Charles had made up his mind to launch a direct attack on his front. It would be some time before the detachment could cooperate in such an operation; at the time the order was sent it was marching in the opposite direction in response to the perceived threat from de Sonis.

At midday on 26 November Stiehle sent Moltke a letter outlining his assessment of the current situation. The heavy rain had made movement extremely difficult, and as a result of this he anticipated that the French would not be able to advance to attack, but would instead wait and hope that Second Army would move forward to attack them in their well-prepared positions. Then, when this advance failed to make progress, Second Army would be obliged to turn back to meet the threat of French flanking movements made possible by their massive numerical superiority.

On the basis of this assessment of French thinking, Frederick Charles intended to not advance himself until the detachment was close enough to cooperate. Stiehle warned Moltke that the success of any such advance would depend on whether Voigts-Rhetz and X Corps could hold on against a French attack directed on Beaune-la-Rolande. Stiehle's understanding of what the French right wing consisted of was imperfect; 18th Corps, which was actually at Montargis, was, he thought, at Tours. On the basis of this, he regarded the reports that X Corps faced 60,000 men as being exaggerated.

On 26 November, too, Frederick Charles wrote to the King in response to the letter which Waldersee had brought with him. Notwithstanding the enemy's huge numerical advantage, he saw himself in no danger at the moment, thanks to the bad ground away from the main roads which would impede the progress of any French advance. He had begun to doubt whether the French now contemplated a march to the relief of the capital. It was always possible, though, that 'lawyers' orders decree that the Army of the Loire shall under any circumstances go to relieve Paris.' If so, he considered that the French would choose the direction by Pusieux to Fontainebleau; if they did, he said, it would give him much pleasure to deal with such an advance. More difficult, he felt, would be the problem of driving the French out of the Forest

26 Hale, *People's War*, p.185.

of Orléans, because of his lack of reliable information about the positions which they had taken up there. He went on:

> I hope that I shall know more about the enemy when the Grand Duke arrives, whom, under the existing circumstances, I must employ tactically, not strategically, against the Army of the Loire. I know nothing of the condition of the Grand Duke's troops, nor details of the length of their marches, but I have no great objection to their being given a rest day. The arrival of this detachment in front of Orléans, even without this rest day, is not concealed from the enemy, who must be in touch with it; and if I am compelled to make an attack, which I could not have carried out before today, but could carry out today, little is lost if I wait one day longer, and delay it to the 29th. The fight against Orléans will probably last many days and be very bloody; but I will undertake it unless I receive further orders.[27]

He ended his letter by saying that his troops were splendid, but that once the war was over the infantry must have a better rifle.

Hale is justly critical of the way in which Frederick Charles in this way abandoned Moltke's strategy, and substituted for it an operation of convergent tactics, observing: 'Moltke wished to take advantage of the weakness, the Prince ignored the weakness and preferred to attack under conditions most favourable to the enemy. Mechanically worked tactics were to be substituted for art like strategy.'[28]

27 Hale, *People's War*, pp.189–190.
28 Hale, *People's War*, p.194.

7

Beaune-la-Rolande

The next seven days would be decisive for the hopes of the Government of National Defence of relieving Paris, and possibly for the outcome of the war itself. If the Army of the Loire was able to inflict a defeat on the forces opposed to it in such a way that it could advance northwards to Paris, it was entirely possible that the Germans would be obliged to raise the investment of the capital, whether or not the breakout planned by Trochu was successful. If that happened, the war might be prolonged indefinitely unless the Germans succeeded in smashing each of the French armies in the field, or, on the other hand, were prepared substantially to moderate their terms for peace. Alternatively, if the Army of the Loire was to be decisively defeated, the prospect of the relief of Paris would effectively cease to exist. Once it was obliged to surrender, the release of the investing armies would mean that the forces available to Moltke would be unbeatable.

During 27 November the mood at the headquarters of Second Army began to change substantially. The situation now appeared to be a good deal less satisfactory than it had seemed when Stiehle and Frederick Charles had been writing their letters on the previous day. In particular, the confidence that his army was in no danger, which Frederick Charles had expressed in his letter to the King, began to fade rapidly over the morning. The reports now reaching him said that the enemy had gained some ground during the previous day. They also now indicated that the strength of the forces opposing X Corps in its position at Beaune-la-Rolande was not less than 55,000 men. Additionally it was suggested, based on statements from the inhabitants, that 25,000 French troops had occupied a camp to the south of Montargis on the previous night.[1]

It seemed to Frederick Charles that the French were embarking on a strategical advance, and that the direction that this would take would be up the valley of the Loing, through to Château Landon and Nemours. Accordingly, he planned that Second Army should move eastwards, fronting towards Montargis. In fact, the conclusion drawn by the Prince was entirely incorrect. Although 18th Corps (still under the command of Billot since Bourbaki had not yet arrived to take over) had been at Montargis on 26 November, it had subsequently moved west, and no advance up the Loing Valley was in contemplation.

Also during 27 November, Crouzat had been finalising his plans for an assault on the following day, in accordance with Freycinet's orders. He did have one considerable advantage

1 *Official Account*, vol. III, p.310.

over Voigts-Rhetz, upon whose corps the attack would fall, in that he knew fairly well the positions taken up by X Corps. His opponent, however, could only guess at the identity and movements of the French troops:

> The area over which X Corps was scattered in the neighbourhood of the battlefield is some 25 square miles in extent. There are a large number of villages and hamlets, plus roads and tracks in profusion; the line of German outposts was 10 miles in length, and, in front of Beaune, only 500 or 600 yards from that of the French. It was, therefore, impossible for the Germans to prevent the population collecting information over the whole area, and then transmitting it to the French outposts, from whence it went to Crouzat.[2]

Crouzat's orders were that by nightfall on 28 November he was to be in occupation of Beaune-la-Rolande, Juranville and Maizières, and then to dig in there and await further instructions. He considered that Beaune-la-Rolande was the key to the German position, and his plan was to envelop X Corps, cutting it off from the rest of Second Army, and then to crush it. His intention was that 18th Corps should advance from Ladon on the east side of Beaune-la-Rolande, after having driven in the German outposts, while 20th Corps simultaneously advanced against the front and west side of the village. In this way, both the German flanks would be threatened with envelopment, and their line of retreat menaced. If they retired, the village must be left to its fate; if they did not, they would be surrounded.

Crouzat's connection with the main body of the Army of the Loire to his left was covered by Cathelineau's *franc-tireurs* on the edge of the Forest of Orléans. To their west stood the first division of 15th Corps (Pallières), which on a wide front was guarding the entries to the forest east of the Paris road. This would deal with any German reinforcements sent forward from Pithiviers.

Over the course of 27 November both Crouzat and d'Aurelle, to the right and left of Pallières respectively, had told him that they expected to be attacked on the following day. For this reason, he considered that his task must be to remain in his current position, and to be ready to help in either direction, and to prevent the enemy breaking in between them. With orders coming in from both Freycinet and d'Aurelle, the generals fighting the battle were at times uncertain what was expected of them.

So far as support from Pallières was concerned, Crouzat might have been somewhat doubtful; the latter had, a few days earlier, hijacked a supply convoy carrying 25,000 rations intended for 20th Corps, and diverted them to his own troops. This prompted a strong intervention from d'Aurelle on Crouzat's behalf, telling Pallières that it was impossible to retain discipline if this sort of thing occurred.[3] D'Aurelle was thoroughly fed up with Freycinet, commenting at the time that it was in vain that the Delegate sent dispatches of encouragement and promises of rewards to lift the morale of his troops who were suffering from the weather while having to face an enemy superior in numbers: 'M. de Freycinet knew well what he had done, but his pride would not allow him to withdraw orders imprudently given, in spite of the representations and warnings of the commanding general.'[4] For the moment, therefore, all that d'Aurelle could do was to await the outcome of the offensive that was about to begin.

2 Hale, *People's War*, p.200.
3 d'Aurelle, *Première Armée*, p.291.
4 d'Aurelle, *Première Armée*, p.237.

Crouzat had 60,000 men and 138 guns at his disposal to attack the position occupied by Voigts-Rhetz. X Corps initially held the position with no more than 11,000 men and 70 guns. Its outpost line was nearly 10 miles long, with the main body of the corps established on the heights either side of Beaune-la-Rolande and on the Long Cour Ridge where it held a number of solidly built farmhouses:

> The main point of support to this position was Beaune, which was surrounded by the remains of a wall 12 feet high, and was arranged for defence; on the other hand, in the occupied district, the movement of artillery was hampered to a very considerable extent by the numerous farms, orchards and extensive brushwood.[5]

20th Corps advanced towards the right of the German position, the 1st Division (de Polignac) from Boiscommun and the 2nd Division (Thornton) from Montbarrois and St Loup directly on Beaune. The 3rd Division (Ségard) was held in reserve at St Loup.

Crouzat ordered Billot to advance through Maizières and Juranville. In Beaune-la-Rolande itself was the 38th Brigade (von Wedell) while to the east the position of the 39th Brigade (von Valentini) was based on Les Cotelles, south of the Long Cour Ridge. In support, the 37th Brigade (Lehmann) and the Corps artillery were moving up from Egny to Marcilly, partly because Voigts-Rhetz and Caprivi felt that the 39th Brigade was the more exposed, and partly because of continuing reports of French activity in the Loing Valley. Voigts-Rhetz could also look for support on his right from Stülpnagel's 5th Division from Alvensleben's III Corps in the event of a substantial French advance, which appeared highly probable. He also had Hartmann's 1st Cavalry Division in reserve around Boynes.

At 8.00 on the morning of 28 November a few shells fell into Beaune-la-Rolande from the south near St Loup, at a range of two miles. One of these hit the house in which Voigts-Rhetz had his headquarters, so that he was in no doubt that the battle had begun. All along the front line of X Corps the German outposts were driven back. On the extreme right of the French advance, Bonnet's brigade of 18th Corps pushed forward through Lorcy, its defenders falling back to the line of the railway embankment west of Corbeilles. On Bonnet's left, Robert's brigade advanced into Juranville; its garrison withdrew to the main position at Les Cotelles. In this sector the French were encountering stiffer resistance than they had expected. Crouzat had drawn up his plan on the basis of reports, correct at the time, that this part of the position was only lightly held. Voigts-Rhetz's decision to bring the 37th Brigade up to Marcilly meant that it was immediately available to support Valentini's troops around Les Cotelles; the latter launched a counter-attack around Juranville which, at around noon, he was able to reoccupy with the support of a battalion from Lehmann's brigade. He was, however, only able to hold the village for a short while before Bonnet's advance from Lorcy into Corbeille threatened to outflank him, and he fell back on Venouville and Long Cour.[6]

Voigts-Rhetz had concentrated the bulk of his troops on the Long Cour Ridge leaving Wedell to defend Beaune-la-Rolande with his brigade and the corps horse artillery. Billot prepared the main body of his troops for an immediate assault on the ridge, without waiting for artillery preparation. Advancing in dense columns over the open ground to the east of Les Cotelles,

5 *Official Account*, vol. III, p 314.
6 *Official Account*, vol. III, p.315.

the French infantry came under heavy fire from the German gun line north of the Moulin des Hommes Libres, and broke in disorder. In front of Les Cotelles, small detachments had moved forward to within 200 yards of the village, taking advantage of undulations in the ground. The first assault was repulsed at 2.00 p.m., but a further attack about half an hour later compelled the fusilier battalion holding the village to fall back towards the mill on the heights to the north. This, Billot realised, was as far as he could progress, and he dug in at Les Cotelles, while holding himself ready to support 20th Corps in its attacks on Beaune-la-Rolande.[7]

Crouzat's leading troops had encountered the German outposts at about 9.00 a.m. As these fell back, Crouzat ordered Thornton to advance with the 2nd Division against the south-eastern side of Beaune-la-Rolande, while Polignac's 1st Division endeavoured to work round Wedell's right flank by advancing eastwards from Batilly. This was broken up by heavy German artillery fire; it was only when Crouzat committed part of Ségard's division that the French were able to make any further headway to the west of Beaune-la-Rolande. By 12.30 p.m. the 1st Battalion of the 57th Regiment was compelled to retreat as far as the crossroads north-west of the village, and began to fall back along the Roman road known as the Chemin de César. This put Crouzat's leading troops well around the north-western edge of the town, in accordance with his plan to envelop it, while to the east his troops had begun to move up the heights of Les Roches, from which the two battalions holding that position fell back into the northern part of Beaune-la-Rolande at La Rue Boussier.

Voigts-Rhetz was able to counter the serious threat down the Roman road by bringing forward the 1st Cavalry Division, moving it at noon to the Butte de l'Ormeteau, from where its horse artillery opened fire on Polignac's troops as they moved eastward along the Roman road. The French halted, and deployed along the Fosse des Près. Hartmann sent forward two cuirassier regiments to charge the French infantry, but this failed to have any effect in the rain sodden ground, and the horse artillery fell back to the Butte de l'Ormeteau. Thus, by 1.00 p.m., Beaune was almost entirely surrounded by the French, who now concentrated all their efforts upon the village itself:

> The leader of the 16th Regiment, in command there, Lieutenant Colonel Sannow, had so distributed his three battalions, that to the 1st was assigned the duty of defending the south-west side and the cemetery, while the fusilier battalion occupied the south and the 2nd Battalion the east side of Beaune. Of the outposts which had retired to La Rue Boussier, two companies of Colonel von Cranach's 57th Regiment had in addition remained in Beaune-la-Rolande, and these, with some other available detachments, were dispatched to the north-west edge of the place, as the din of battle was more marked in that direction.[8]

A French assault on the village was beaten off at 1.00, as was a second assault, after which the French kept up a heavy rifle and artillery fire. Several houses caught fire, and breaches were made in the cemetery walls. Ammunition was beginning to run low, and it was starting to look as if the place could not be held. An erroneous report that the French were now in Beaune-la-Rolande led Voigts-Rhetz to give the order to retire, fearing that unless he pulled back his corps would be exposed to a heavy defeat. Caprivi, however, confident that reinforcements from the

7 *Official Account*, vol. III, p.316.
8 *Official Account*, vol. III, p.318.

5th Division would soon be at hand, prevailed upon him to suspend the order. This division had been assembled early in the day just outside Pithiviers, and had set off down the road to Boynes as the sound of gunfire reached Second Army headquarters. There Waldersee, who was engaged in writing his daily letter to the King, put down his pen and rode off towards Beaune-la-Rolande as fast as he could. On his way, it seemed to him that the local inhabitants were greatly aroused by what was seen to be the long-awaited battle:

> The firing had roused inhabitants of Pithiviers to a high pitch of excitement. At street corners, doors of houses, and in marketplaces and open spaces, they gathered discussing among themselves the course affairs were taking, and openly speaking of this firing as the commencement of the decisive battle. [9]

Frederick Charles remained at Pithiviers, monitoring reports as they came in. As well as reporting on the developing situation at Beaune-la-Rolande, there were other accounts, by no means all accurate, which appeared to confirm the earlier indications that the French might be preparing to advance up the Loing Valley. Early in the battle, at 8.30 a.m., he received a message from Voigts-Rhetz, sent at 7.04, to the effect that he had received during the night a report that the enemy had occupied Fontenay in the Loing Valley, about four miles south of Château Landon and eight miles north of Montargis. It was this that had led Voigts-Rhetz to strengthen his left wing, which had led to the ultimate failure of Billot's advance. Another, wholly erroneous, report which reached Frederick Charles was to the effect that French troops had reached Nemours, only eight miles south of Fontainebleau. Nothing of the sort, however, had come from the German troops in Château Landon, who could hardly have failed to be aware of such a move on the part of the French.

As a result, Frederick Charles paid more attention to the threat that he supposed to be developing on the left of his army, than to the desperate fight of X Corps in Beaune-la-Rolande. He sent an order to Voigts-Rhetz to move a brigade into the Loing Valley to counter what he supposed to be a move northwards from Montargis by 18th Corps. At 11.00 Stiehle sent Moltke a report on the situation as it was then seen at Second Army headquarters, telling him that it was intended to deploy X Corps between the Loing and the Yonne, while III Corps took up a position on the line Beaumont – Château Landon and IX Corps concentrated at Pithiviers. He continued: 'obviously, this state of affairs upsets, for the time, all plans for crossing the Loire below Orléans …. I suggest to your Excellency whether, from the troops before Paris, a strong occupation of Fontainebleau and Moret could not be carried out. The fight on the left flank of X Corps is extending; we go there.'[10] The plans which he thus described demonstrate how complete was the belief of Frederick Charles that it was in the Loing Valley that he must prepare to meet the enemy advancing towards Paris; the suggestion that troops might be detached from the investment and sent to Fontainebleau suggests that his anxieties had increased still further.

Voigts-Rhetz, notwithstanding the powerful attacks that he was facing at Beaune-la-Rolande and on the Long Cour Ridge, was also still unsure whether the French did intend to advance up the Loing Valley. In a report which he sent to Frederick Charles at 11.45 a.m. he described the situation of his corps and the enemy attacks; commenting on the fact that he had no news

9 Hale, *People's War*, p.206.
10 Hale, *People's War*, pp.209–210.

from his left flank, he added, '...but I regard it as not impossible that the enemy is masking by the engagement his march north.'[11] Frederick Charles left Pithiviers at noon; if he had read this message before setting off, it will have confirmed his fears about the Loing Valley.

His progress towards the battlefield was slow, as he preferred to only ride at a trot. He had reached a point south of Boynes, about halfway to Beaune-la-Rolande, when the leading troops of the 5th Division arrived there, and he ordered them to march south-east towards the fighting. He also sent orders to Alvensleben that the 6th Division and the Corps artillery should follow. Continuing his journey, he reached the right flank of X Corps, but neither he nor Stiehle appears to have yet grasped the extent of the battle in which Voigts-Rhetz was engaged, making no attempt to contact him on the Long Cour Ridge from where he was continuing to direct the defence of his hard pressed position.

The advance guard of the 5th Division, under Colonel von Wulffen, had deployed on the south side of the Butte de l'Ormeteau and towards Arconville; thereafter the French made no very determined advance in this sector. When the main body of the 5th Division came up it deployed in support of the 1st Cavalry Division and drove the French out of the woods at La Pierre Percée, while Wulffen, crossing the Roman road, occupied the Bois de la Leu.[12] The 12th Regiment, coming up in support of the advance guard, then dispersed the last stragglers of the retreating enemy on the south-west of Beaune-la-Rolande.

Around the battered walls of Beaune-la-Rolande itself a fierce struggle continued. All day Crouzat had been waiting for units from the 18th Corps to come up and join in the assaults on the village. It was, however, only as night was beginning to fall that Billot's troops came forward to support the attack on the eastern side of Beaune-la-Rolande. In spite of the heavy odds against which Sannow's troops were fighting there at close range, they continued to hold out. In desperation, Crouzat ordered the bugles to be sounded, and led his troops to a final charge in the gathering gloom, as he later described:

> We reached the first houses, and were greeted there by a most intense fire at point-blank range. Our horses startled at the red flames from rifles; revolvers cracked .... it was futile.... The street was blocked by a burning timber barricade, and by now only a few officers were following me. We had to return to our point of departure, which we did at a walk. The road was covered with my poor dead or wounded *gardes mobiles* and Zouaves.[13]

As the French fell back, they were pounded by the eight batteries which the Germans brought up on either side of Beaune-la-Rolande. Crouzat led his corps back to the positions which it had occupied at Bellegarde and Boiscommun before the battle, while Billot continued in possession of Venouville, Juranville and Maizières. To the left of 20th Corps, Cathelineau's *franc-tireurs* disappeared into the Forest of Orléans. Behind them the 1st Division of 15th Corps, which had made no move to support Crouzat, remained at Chambron. On the German side, X Corps remained in Beaune-la-Rolande and along the Long Cour Ridge in the positions which it had defended so well. The 5th Division bivouacked for the night at La Pierre Percée and Marcilly. During the day the 6th Division had come up to Boynes.

11 Hale, *People's War*, p.209.
12 *Official Account*, vol. III, p.320.
13 Fermer, *France at Bay 1870–71*, p.90.

The battle had cost the Germans 898 men killed and wounded; the bulk of these, naturally, had come from X Corps which had suffered a loss of 758 men. Crouzat lost a total of about 3,100 men, of whom 1,800 were taken prisoner. It had been a hugely important victory for the Germans, inflicting what might be a fatal check on the advance on Paris of the Army of the Loire. Frederick Charles, however, appears not to have realised at first either the extent of the battle or of the victory which had been won. He had arrived at Barville, north-east of Beaune between 1.00 and 2.00 p.m., at a time when 20th Corps had reached the limit of its advance against the German right, and he remained there for the rest of the battle, concerning himself only with the operations on the right flank.

Unusually, the official history was prepared to draw attention to the failure of Second Army to appreciate the extent of the victory, although of course making no reference to Frederick Charles personally. It observed: 'The headquarters staff of Second Army was unable, on the evening of 28 November, to grasp to its full extent the importance of the victory which had been gained.' The history went on to record the cautious instructions issued that night to the units of Second Army in anticipation that on the following day the enemy would renew his attack.[14]

Colonel Hale reviewed the far reaching effects of the victory:

> Rarely has an attacking force been so completely overthrown and rendered so thoroughly incapable of either defence or offence; rarely has the demoralisation resulting from a single defeat in one theatre of war so greatly influenced the course of a subsequent renewal of the struggle in another theatre of war. Beaune-la-Rolande made itself felt on the Lisaine. Usually after a battle the victor knows he has won, but here, strangely enough, while the losers fully realised the completeness of their own defeat, the victor not only did not realise his victory, but he completely misunderstood what had happened; he believed that his victory was only a narrow escape from actual defeat, and that he would have to undergo a similar ordeal next day. So the fruits of victory remained ungarnered.[15]

Not everyone on the German side, though, was in doubt as to what had been achieved. Waldersee had been on the battlefield all day, and he came up to Frederick Charles at 5:30 just as the latter was preparing to ride back to Pithiviers. He had been in touch with both Voigts-Rhetz and Alvensleben. He said to the Prince, 'A complete victory has been won, it will be a Rossbach for the French if there is a vigorous pursuit.' His reference to Frederick the Great's victory was made to emphasise the importance of what he was saying. He was aware that Hartmann had been urged to launch his cavalry in pursuit of the beaten French, but that he had received no orders to do so from a senior officer, and had ignored the suggestion on the basis that the ground was too heavy for his cavalry to operate effectively. Frederick Charles did ask Waldersee if the 1st Cavalry Division had moved to the attack; tactfully, Waldersee replied only that there might be difficulties in the way. The Prince did not follow up the matter with Waldersee, but instead turned to Stiehle and said, 'According to the report by Count von Waldersee, X Corps cannot be employed in pursuit. One of its brigades must, however, move off today for the Loing. But a vigorous pursuit in several directions by the 5th Division and the 1st Cavalry Division

14 *Official Account*, vol. III, p.321.
15 Hale, *People's War*, pp.203–204.

promises a great success. Be so good as to convey my wishes to Generals von Alvensleben and von Voigts-Rhetz.'[16]

Stiehle went off to give the necessary orders, but by now, it was really too late for Hartmann to launch an effective pursuit. Frederick Charles then rode back to Pithiviers, accompanied by Waldersee. The latter, drawing on his personal knowledge of the battle, did his best to make the Prince aware of what had transpired, since he had not seen more of the battlefield than the sector in which the 5th Division had been engaged; he had not been near Beaune-la-Rolande nor seen for himself the extent of the casualties that had been suffered. Waldersee was entirely certain that the battle had been far more than a mere demonstration to mask a strategic movement on the part of the French. He tried hard to make Frederick Charles understand that two French corps had been engaged, and that the decisive nature of the victory meant that there was no longer any reason to fear a French advance down the Loing Valley. To his intense frustration, Frederick Charles remained convinced that the strength of the enemy had been overestimated and that he must still take action to strengthen the forces on his left flank.

On his way, the Prince stopped at Boynes to send a telegram to the King with a laconic report of the battle, in which he said it, 'was to a certain extent severe.' This did scant justice to the defenders of Beaune-la-Rolande, or to the completeness of the victory which they had won. The complete misconception which Frederick Charles had of the battle was due to his failure to go on to Voigts-Rhetz and see for himself the true extent of the fighting. This failure left him still convinced that a French advance in the Loing Valley was a serious possibility.

Stiehle, meanwhile, had found Alvensleben, and appears to have accepted from him that he had no forces available for a pursuit. He then went on to seek Voigts-Rhetz; not finding him, he left a written order about the transfer of an infantry brigade to the Loing Valley, in accordance with the instructions given by Frederick Charles. Voigts-Rhetz, when he came to read the order, properly refused to comply with it; he was certainly not going to send off one of his exhausted brigades that night. He made his position entirely clear in his reply:

> The sending a brigade tonight to Château Landon is impossible. All three brigades have been engaged today, and all three have put out outposts. All three are short of ammunition and none have finished cooking. As soon as possible tomorrow morning I will move a brigade to Château Landon, but I would remark that it is impossible for only one brigade to hold the position of Long Cour, and that if I am to take a brigade away from it, that can only be on the assumption that, meanwhile, it is replaced by a brigade of III Corps.[17]

Voigts-Rhetz was a capable and experienced corps commander, and Frederick Charles could only accept what he had told him. Fortunately, on the following day, a report came in from a detachment at Château Landon that the enemy had quitted his advanced position in the Loing Valley.

Crouzat himself was under no illusion as to the outcome of the battle, reporting to d'Aurelle that night his retreat to his previous positions, and noting with relief that he had not been followed. Three days later he sent a comprehensive report of the current state of his corps following the battle. He listed their urgent needs: 'Twenty thousand haversacks, ten thousand

16 Hale, *People's War*, pp.211–212.
17 Hale, *People's War*, pp.213–214.

pairs of shoes, ten thousand pairs of gaiters, and tents for ten thousand men. Let me have several days of rest for me to recover. The morale of my men is good, but they lack too much for the cold and wet weather.'[18]

This greatly annoyed Freycinet, and he immediately sent to Crouzat a response which d'Aurelle fairly described as 'hard, brutal, unjust':

> It seems to me that you are very quickly discouraged, and you do not face the enemy with the solidity without which success is impossible .... It is necessary to march and to march quickly .... If the attitude of this corps continues to appear so uncertain, I will consider you as personally responsible, and you will have to account to the government for the consequences of the situation.[19]

When he read this, d'Aurelle was understandably outraged, saying to his chief of staff, General Borel, that he refused to transmit such a message, which he described as 'a moral assassination.' Borel, however, pointed out to him with some sadness that the copy had come to d'Aurelle for information only, and that the original message had been sent to Crouzat direct. For his part, Crouzat was understandably hurt and bewildered by Freycinet's inexcusably harsh letter; he had considered that it was no more than his simple duty to give a candid assessment of the state of his troops. For the moment, they enjoyed a brief respite, since on receipt of his report on the Battle of Beaune-la-Rolande he had not been ordered to pursue any further attack, so he pulled back those units of 18th Corps that had remained in position around Venouville and Juranville in the direction of Ladon.

On considering the reports of the battle, Freycinet issued a decree particularly commending the troops of 18th Corps, and confirming the promotion of Billot to the rank of *général de brigade*. This also seriously annoyed d'Aurelle, who noted that Billot was qualified to be a chief of staff, but not a corps commander. In fact, he said, Freycinet had been in effect the commander of 18th Corps, and by his decree took the credit for the command. D'Aurelle also commented on Freycinet's suggestion of an advance to Pithiviers, conceived as a diversion to deal with the threat perceived to Blois and Tours, a diversion which had completely failed in its effect.[20] What baffled d'Aurelle particularly about the way in which Crouzat had been treated was that on the morning after the battle Freycinet had gone out of his way to send a message to Crouzat and Billot expressing satisfaction with their vigorous attack, which he said had achieved its object by halting the enemy movements towards Le Mans and Vendôme. It was obvious to d'Aurelle that it had done nothing of the sort, and in his own memoir he published this correspondence in order that the reader could form their own conclusion about the way in which Freycinet had dealt with the situation.

Freycinet, in the account which he published in 1872, was still disposed to claim, against all the evidence, that the Battle of Beaune-la-Rolande could in some way be regarded as a success. In asserting this, he was still disposed to give the credit to Billot and 18th Corps, evidently still not having forgiven Crouzat. He also offered the fanciful suggestion that Frederick Charles believed that he could not hold the position at Beaune-la-Rolande after the battle, and had ordered a

18 d'Aurelle, *Premère Armée*, pp.245–246.
19 d'Aurelle, *Première Armée*, pp.246–247.
20 d'Aurelle, *Première Armee*, pp.243–244.

retreat after burning the houses which provided the most solid *points d'appui*. He then went on to make the even more ludicrous observation that if Pallières had been launched towards Pithiviers, it would probably have resulted in the capture of the place, thereby cutting off the retreat of the troops in Beaune-la-Rolande.[21] Freycinet was an able and energetic man, and had access to all the known facts of the battle; it is impossible that, when writing this nonsense, he could have believed it to be true. It must be said that his account of the operations of the Army of the Loire is useful only in the text of the messages sent to and from d'Aurelle; Freycinet's own descriptions of the events which were occurring were generally written without any regard for accuracy.

In the days immediately preceding the Battle of Beaune-la-Rolande, d'Aurelle had been concerning himself particularly with the left wing of his army, and especially the movements of de Sonis and 17th Corps; he had ordered the latter to retreat into the Forest of Marchenoir since, as he reported to Freycinet, Chanzy could not cover this retreat without uncovering Orléans. It was therefore essential, he said, that Chanzy should remain where he was. D'Aurelle had a lively apprehension that an attack might be pending from the detachment. This led him to warn Chanzy and Pallières of the probability of an attack from the direction of Châteaudun on the following day, and he issued a number of orders to prepare for this.[22] In particular, he ordered Pallières to march to the sound of the guns should such an attack materialise.

Meanwhile, on 28 November the detachment had been making the most of its well-earned rest day. It was urgently needed. The official history of I Bavarian Corps recorded its condition after the punishing marches of the preceding weeks:

> The troops were much exhausted, their clothing and equipment were very defective, the horses were tired and in poor condition, and the general tone was far from cheerful. The incessant and forced marches of the last fortnight, under most unfortunate conditions of weather and ground, as well as the fatiguing outpost and patrol duty in face of an enemy we could never grasp, and yet whose existence continually made itself felt, had exhausted the physical strength of the soldiers.[23]

While his troops recruited their strength, Stosch pondered how best to execute the general spirit of Moltke's instructions. Looking at the opportunities presented by what was known of the position of the French, he prepared and sent to Second Army a message outlining a plan for the detachment to move next day in an arrowhead formation, the point being aimed at Villamblain on the main road from Châteaudun, 17 miles from Orléans. However, Stosch was obliged to abandon this scheme, which would have given the detachment the chance to operate strategically against d'Aurelle's left flank. During the day Stosch received instructions from Stiehle to move towards Janville-Toury, to take up the duty of covering the Orléans – Paris road so that Second Army would be free to move to its left to deal with the, imaginary, threat in the Loing Valley. Accordingly, Stosch sent a revised march plan which would next day put the detachment in a position facing south and standing immediately to the right of Second Army. It was not what he wanted, nor did he suppose that it would be what Moltke wanted, and he was careful to report it all by telegram to Versailles.[24]

21 Freycinet, *Guerre*, p.122.
22 d'Aurelle, *Première Armée*, pp.260–264.
23 Helvig, *Operations*, p.245.
24 Hale, *People's War*, p.214.

It was only on the day after the Battle of Beaune-la-Rolande, when staff officers from the headquarters of Second Army visited the battlefield, that the extent of the success of X Corps began to be appreciated. Kretschmann, writing to his wife that day, recorded his impressions of the heavy losses that the attackers had suffered:

> X Corps has sent back 700 [wounded] prisoners; we have nearly 900 more, unwounded. Most of them are soldiers of the line and Zouaves. The French brought against us their best troops. The 1st Zouaves has been particularly hard-hit; around Beaune-la-Rolande alone, among the dead, there are nearly 300 Zouaves. The men fought extremely well; in fact there were corpses all round a position within 2 yards; in one place three officers together.[25]

Frederick Charles himself did not leave Pithiviers, which was a pity, because he might have felt more disposed to follow up the victory by launching an attack on the beaten French. As it was, the Germans spent 29 November dug in around Beaune-la-Rolande and on the Long Cour Ridge, awaiting an attack that Crouzat had seen clearly was out of the question. When he pulled back during the day, the Germans were able to stand down and go into quarters.

At Pithiviers, Stiehle on the morning of 29 November had received Moltke's letter of two days earlier, reporting on the imminence of the expected sortie from Paris, and confirming Stosch's departure to take over as chief of staff of the detachment. In his letter, Moltke also analysed the overall position of the German armies. He drew attention to the threat to communications from the south, where Werder did not have sufficient resources to cover the whole of the line between Montbéliard and Châtillon, as a result of which he was moving the 13th Division by rail to Troyes. But the main point of his letter was to emphasise the crucial role of Second Army:

> It is the struggle which you are going to engage in against the only real army that France can put into the field that has a truly decisive importance. If (and I sincerely hope to the contrary) you lose the battle, my plan will be to raise the blockade of Paris without regard to the loss of our siege equipment. The Crown Prince of Saxony would operate with General Manteuffel against the concentrations in the north, and the Crown Prince of Prussia with you against the Army of the Loire. In this way our decisive superiority will bring us victory, and we shall return to Paris which because of the broken rail lines will not have been able to be revictualled, and after the surrender of which we will recover our guns.[26]

Reviewing the frankness of this letter, Hale noted that 'it hardly seems to admit of misunderstanding .... It was almost a counsel of despair, and had the Grand Duke been in command, with Stosch at his elbow, of the offensive, it is well-nigh certain would have been taken on the Loire immediately after the Battle of Beaune-la-Rolande; but on the Prince and Stiehle, Moltke's letter had not the slightest effect.'[27]

It was an emphatic statement of the need to take the offensive at once, but Stiehle and Frederick Charles had got themselves into a mind-set that meant that Moltke's encouragement had little effect on their conviction that Second Army must await the expected attack from

25 Kretschmann, *Lettres*, p.300.
26 Moltke, *Correspondance Militaire*, pp.513–515
27 Hale, *People's War*, p.216

an enemy that hugely outnumbered it. Stiehle was, however, sufficiently struck by the obvious difference of view between Moltke and Second Army to fix a meeting for the following day with Stosch at Bazoches les Gallerandes, evidently feeling that he had better hear at first hand from the detachment's new chief of staff about the current state of opinion at Versailles.

8

Villepion

For the moment, the orders from Second Army issued at noon on 29 November merely provided for a concentration against a French advance. Voigts-Rhetz was relieved from any further responsibility for the Loing Valley, since the arrival of the 40th Brigade (von Kraatz) would enable that part of the front to be covered, and he was ordered to concentrate east of Beaune. III Corps would stand on his right, while IX Corps remained behind Pithiviers. Meanwhile the detachment had been making good progress in its eastward move. The troops, back in the Beauce country, were not sorry to be on familiar ground again:

> After nearly three weeks of exhausting marches, the monotonous and undulating plain appeared like an old acquaintance, whom we did not exactly regard with affection, but whose good qualities absence had taught us to esteem. The cavalry and artillery felt a sense of security, when they debouched from the valley of the Loir brook on to the wide open plain of La Beauce, leaving behind them the ground so ill adapted to their arms.[1]

The march of the detachment, however, was not without incident. Its path, from which de Sonis had so abruptly removed himself when he retreated from Châteaudun on 26 November, took it into the flank of Chanzy's 16th Corps, and this led to a sharp encounter at Varize, on the River Conie, where a force of Lipowski's *franc-tireurs* had been posted to hold up the detachment's advance from the main road from Châteaudun to Orgères on 29 November.

Early that morning, Von der Tann's scouts had located French troops occupying Nobleville and Civy on the flank of the Bavarians. The batteries of Rudolph von der Tann's 4th Brigade, which formed the advance guard, at once came into action; and a brisk advance by seven companies of infantry sufficed to clear the villages of the French troops. These now retreated to a strong position in a park to the west of Varize. This had been well prepared for defence, and there was a stiff fight before two companies of the 10th Regiment, advancing from Civy, forced their way into the park. The French troops remaining there now found themselves attacked on all sides, and at 11.00 a.m. surrendered. The Bavarian official history records that the prisoners

1 Helvig, *Operations*, p.248.

were extremely indignant about Lipowski's bad leadership in leaving them in the lurch and asked von der Tann to publicise his cowardice: he declined to do so however.[2]

Meanwhile, to the south the 6th Cavalry Brigade had been active in clearing the right flank of the detachment's advance by driving back Digard's cavalry brigade which it encountered near Tournoisis on the road to Orléans. Further north, the 6th Cavalry Division had by the end of the day reached the Paris – Orléans high road at Toury, while the 22nd Division was at Allaines and Ymonville, and the 17th Division's advance guard was at Bazoches les Hautes. The 1st Bavarian Division had stopped short of its intended destination around Terminiers, as reports indicated that the place was still occupied. Finally, the 2nd Bavarian Division took up a position south of Orgères. Von der Tann had suggested hopefully that in order to give his corps some rest it might take up a position in which it was covered by one of the cavalry divisions, and thus not have to bivouac in direct contact with the enemy; but the request was firmly denied.

Therefore, although the detachment intended to make no move southwards from Varize, being concerned only with their march eastwards towards a junction with Second Army, d'Aurelle was exceedingly anxious about the threat which he perceived to his left flank. A report from Chanzy outlining what had happened at Varize confirmed him in his belief that there would be an attack on the following day. He reported this to Freycinet at 9.00 p.m. and then spent the next three hours issuing a stream of orders to each of the corps of the Army of the Loire in preparation for the expected attack.[3]

D'Aurelle need not have worried. At Second Army headquarters, Frederick Charles and Stiehle had no intention of moving forward; they were still concerned about what they believed to be in imminent advance by the French. Frederick Charles remained at Pithiviers throughout 29 November, and so did not add anything to his personal understanding of the outcome of the battle on the previous day, though receiving reports from those of his staff officers who had gone down from his headquarters to Beaune-la-Rolande to report on the situation. This second-hand information was not enough however to change his view of the situation.

Kretschmann was one of Second Army's staff officers who rode down from Pithiviers to Beaune and he wrote to his wife on the evening of 29 November after spending 12 hours in the saddle:

> The French are in part very old, in part very young; we have already taken those of an intermediate age. The inhabitants are profoundly depressed; all of them had believed in a victory; it is only today, seeing the interminable columns of prisoners, that they have changed their opinions.[4]

Thus both commanders, rather than planning offensive operations for 30 November, were concerned only with making preparations to meet an imminent enemy assault.

Stosch and the Grand Duke established the detachment's headquarters at Viabon, about five miles north of Orgères, and there received Frederick Charles's orders for the following day's operations, which were for the detachment to take up a position extending from Orgères to Bazoches les Gallerandes, a front of over 16 miles. Second Army was similarly extended so that

2 Helvig, *Operations,* p.250.
3 d'Aurelle, *Première Armée*, pp.260–266.
4 Kretschmann, *Lettres*, p.300.

in all Frederick Charles's forces were spread over 40 miles. The defensive nature of his intentions was unmistakable. That evening, the report from Second Army to the Royal Headquarters was still extremely cautious. Advance guards were to follow up the retreating French towards Montargis and Bellegarde. In taking such a limited view of what was practicable, Frederick Charles appears to have been swayed by Alvensleben, whose reception of a tentative suggestion that III Corps should advance on its own towards Orléans had been unenthusiastic.

Next morning telegrams came with news that the sortie from Paris had finally begun, which supported the expectation that the French would now be advancing to the attack. Frederick Charles rode south from Pithiviers to watch the advance of the units which had gone forward to reconnoitre the French positions. All along the line to the south of Beaune-la-Rolande the advancing Germans encountered resistance, a further confirmation of the view that the French were getting ready to advance. This was partly correct; orders sent direct by Freycinet to Crouzat were to the effect that 18th and 20th Corps should shift to their left behind the cover of some modest advances northwards and it was this which had produced the series of collisions with the German reconnaissances. One of these led to an attack at daybreak on the German outposts in some farmhouses on the northern edge of Montbarrois; by noon, however, the French had been cleared from the village with a loss of 100 prisoners. Another advance, north from St Loup, was soon abandoned when it encountered a company of German infantry supported by artillery. The orders given by Voigts-Rhetz for the operations of his corps pushed the 39th Brigade towards St Loup, Maizières and Lorcy, while the 38th Brigade remained on the Long Cour Ridge. The 37th Brigade was to advance on Montargis.

The 39th Brigade was the first to come into action, advancing to the attack of Maizières, which was found to be strongly held by French infantry, supported by artillery. Even after a half hour bombardment of the village by 10 guns, the German infantry could make no headway, and Valentini, commanding the brigade's advance guard, broke off the action and fell back. These signs of the enemy strength in his immediate front led Voigts-Rhetz to conclude that a general attack might be imminent, and he halted the march of the 37th Brigade to Montargis, pulling it back to the Long Cour Ridge to await the assault.

The 39th Brigade had asked for support from the 5th Division and Stülpnagel sent forward the 52nd Regiment together with a squadron of cavalry and an artillery battery. When they arrived in front of Maizières, at about 4.00, the 39th Brigade had already broken off the action; but seeing that the enemy were resuming their advance, the German artillery opened a heavy fire on the French infantry and silenced their artillery, as a result of which they fell back and the Germans returned to Beaune-la-Rolande.

All of this had led Frederick Charles to believe that he must reinforce his front line, and he ordered Manstein to advance to Boynes in support; when the leading troops of IX Corps arrived there, they were pushed forward to Courcelles. By nightfall the fighting had died down and Manstein's troops went back to Pithiviers. Meanwhile Kraatz and the 40th Brigade had reached the valley of the Loing. Little had been learned from an inconclusive day in which no significant damage had been inflicted on the enemy. Something of this seems to have communicated itself to Frederick Charles, who encountered Waldersee as he was preparing to return to Pithiviers. Inviting him to travel back with him in his carriage, the Prince mused on the outcome of the battle of 28 November: 'The battlefield reminds me of St Privat. Yesterday great results might have been obtained, for this corps [Crouzat's 20th Corps] could not possibly be fit for a fight, and also is not now. Today a strong offensive might have reaped its reward, but

…' At this point he broke off and changed the subject, but he later returned to it: 'The favourable moment for an offensive is gone; the information leads to the conclusion that the French had been reinforced on the line Boiscommun – Bellegarde; what is going on behind the Forest of Orléans is out of sight …. Now I am reduced to awaiting attitude.' He went on to speculate gloomily that, 'a soldier's good fortune seldom comes back to him with the same favour;' and he put his situation down to the difficulty of collecting intelligence in the face of a hostile population in difficult terrain. Evidently, whatever excuses he might make, he was now aware of the opportunity which he had missed.[5]

Some idea of the continuing discontent at Versailles can be gained from the Crown Prince's diary. He was not, of course, an entirely dispassionate observer, missing few chances to criticise his royal cousin; on 29 November he noted: 'today our prospects are once again quite favourable, and if only Prince Frederick Charles could make up his mind to face Orléans, the Parisians would have to abandon for good their hopes of relief.'[6] Next day, however, and more significantly, he recorded Moltke's own feelings about the lack of progress of Second Army: 'Every day come reports from the 'Prince Field Marshal,' as he calls himself, with fresh reasons why the attack cannot be made, so that General Count Moltke is by this time quite beside himself at the dilatoriness displayed there.'[7]

Meanwhile the conference between Stosch and Stiehle took place on 30 November. Stiehle had asked for the meeting for two reasons; first, he wanted to hear from Stosch the views held by Moltke about the campaign on the Loire; and second, to justify the actions of Frederick Charles, both those in the immediate past and in the present, as well as his proposed actions in the future. It was only at Versailles that the relative importance of the various theatres of war could be judged, and from Stosch, newly arrived from there, Stiehle could learn the importance attached to the Loire campaign. On the other hand, he considered that it was the view of the commanders on the spot that ought to form the basis of future action. The two men discussed the best way of covering the road to Paris, whether direct or indirect, and when the time would come for taking the offensive. Stosch came to the meeting with a clear understanding of what Moltke had in mind, and stressed both the need to move forward at once, and the advantage to be gained by turning the left flank of the Army of the Loire. Stiehle, as was to be expected, described the opinion held by Frederick Charles as to the forces opposed to him, and argued that for the moment Second Army should stand on the defensive; when it came, the advance should be directly on Orléans. The two men parted without being agreed on any of the questions discussed.

When Stiehle got back to Pithiviers and reported to Frederick Charles, it seemed to them both that Stosch's offensive propensity was such that the situation should be spelled out in a formal order to the detachment. This was accordingly done; the instructions went out that night. In this communication, Frederick Charles maintained that, 'besides 18th Corps there was another corps in his front. Since this did not take part in the battle of the 28th, I believe that for the protection of his right wing, the 15th or the 16th Corps has been drawn in this direction.' This was at odds with the telegram that Frederick Charles had sent to the King on the previous evening to the effect that the whole of 20th Corps and troops from 18th, 15th and 16th Corps

5 Hale, *People's War*, pp.222–223.
6 Crown Prince, *War Diary*, p.206.
7 Crown Prince, *War Diary*, p.207.

had taken part in the battle. He went on to say that he intended to remain on the defensive in anticipation of another enemy attack, and that the 22nd Division should relieve the brigade of IX Corps standing at Pithiviers and Bazoches les Gallerandes, his intention being that it should, if necessary, serve as a reserve to Second Army. After adding some inaccurate information about the enemy units in front of the detachment, and Dietling arrangements for the exchange of the 4th and 6th Cavalry Divisions, he ended his message with a pompous assertion of his own authority: 'Until the situation on the enemy's side is clearer, I must reserve to myself the communication to your Royal Highness of my further plans for driving the enemy out of Orléans.'[8] Reading this, Stosch was left in no doubt that Frederick Charles and Stiehle had, as he would have supposed from his meeting at Bazoches les Gallerandes, lost sight completely of what Moltke required should be the principal objective of Second Army, which was the destruction of the Army of the Loire and not merely the recapture of Orléans.

Hans von Kretschmann had accompanied Frederick Charles in his visit to the battlefield of Beaune-la-Rolande. It had made a profound impression on him, as he again wrote to his wife:

> Our battlefield of the 28th has a terrible aspect. There are still Frenchmen who have not yet been buried; thus today I have remained with the Prince for half an hour in the middle of a hundred bodies. Happily, I got my way; it is really absurd to leave without a grave masses of men for no reason at all. The Prince was very nice to me; that was not always the case for the last few days.[9]

Kretschmann's visit to Beaune-la-Rolande was still much on his mind on the following day, when he reflected on the number of wounded men who had still not been treated.

Meanwhile at Tours, Gambetta and Freycinet were becoming extremely agitated as a result of d'Aurelle's failure to take the offensive. They had been further provoked by the dispatches which had reached them from Favre to the effect that the deadline for the relief of Paris was now 15 December, three weeks earlier than had been supposed. This was much in their mind when, during 30 November, they finally received the much travelled and long delayed message from Trochu announcing that the operation to break out from Paris would commence on 29 November. Freycinet sent a message at once to d'Aurelle ordering him to continue his preparations for an advance by the road to Étampes and the road to Pithiviers, by Chanzy's 16th Corps and two divisions of 15th Corps; 17th Corps was to remain in front of Orléans. He went on to say that he would come to d'Aurelle's headquarters, suggesting that, if they could do so without impairing the situation of their troops, Chanzy and Pallières should also attend. The government's discontent with d'Aurelle was such that Freycinet took with him a signed order which provided for the commander-in-chief's dismissal if he refused to carry out the instructions for an immediate advance.[10] Meanwhile d'Aurelle had been made fully aware of the condition of Crouzat's 20th Corps; Pallières had visited it, and reported that it was in a 'miserable condition.'

Freycinet arrived at d'Aurelle's headquarters at 9.00 p.m., he was accompanied by Auguste de Serres the ablest of his assistants, who brought a collection of maps for the use of the staff. The

8 Hale, *People's War*, p.205.
9 Kretschmann, *Lettres*, p.303.
10 Official Account, vol. III, p.327.

meeting lasted for two and a half hours. Present were d'Aurelle, Chanzy and Borel; Pallières sent a message that it was necessary that he remain at his post. Freycinet recorded that the generals reacted strongly to the news from Paris: 'With a patriotism that did them honour, they did not hesitate for a moment about the need to advance to meet General Ducrot. They did not, however, conceal the unfavourable situation resulting from so precipitate an advance.' They accepted the need to advance on Fontainebleau through Pithiviers and Beaune-la-Rolande.[11]

D'Aurelle's own account of the discussions differed somewhat from that of Freycinet; according to him, he, Chanzy and Borel pointed out the dangers arising from an advance before the junction of 15th and 16th Corps, and pointed out the danger of advancing while there were strong enemy forces on their left flank. Freycinet rejected this, as d'Aurelle recorded: 'M. de Freycinet obstinately maintained that Chanzy's Corps was more than sufficient to defeat the Grand Duke, and he finished by saying that the plan which he had described had been irrevocably approved by the government at Tours.' D'Aurelle bluntly told him that if Chanzy advanced on his own, his Corps would be exposed to being crushed. Freycinet was adamant; in spite of d'Aurelle's protests, the plan was adopted. It involved a change of front to the right, with the advance of Chanzy's Corps pivoting on Pallières's 1st Division at Chilleurs. 17th Corps would remain in front of Orléans, while 18th and 20th Corps, which would receive Freycinet's orders direct, would move on Pithiviers via Beaune-la-Rolande in order to rejoin the main body of the army.[12]

After the conference ended, and Freycinet was on his way back to Tours, the generals went off to issue their orders for the following day. When Chanzy reached his headquarters, it became even clearer to him that before the general advance he must first do something about the detachment which was poised on his left flank. He sought and was granted permission by d'Aurelle to advance on the following day to clear it out of his way, and if necessary he would be supported by 17th Corps. In the first instance his immediate target must be von der Tann's Corps, which now stood between Orgères and Pithiviers. D'Aurelle ordered the 2nd Division of 15th Corps (Martineau) and the 3rd Division (Peytavin) not to leave their present positions on 1 December but to ensure that the men were promptly fed and that arrangements be made to bring up further supplies. D'Aurelle was later to record his profound disagreement with Freycinet's claim that 'the generals accepted as good, the principles of the operation.'[13] They did not; but Freycinet would brook no dissent with his orders for an immediate advance.

The role of 18th and 20th Corps in this forward movement was not properly clarified. Colmar von der Goltz pointed out that 'officially these corps were under the direct control of the War Ministry. It was an error for there to be considered as significant factors these two corps, which following the Battle of Beaune-la-Rolande, were scarcely capable of remaining in the field. The doubt which remained over the question of their command was fatal to the army.'[14] These corps were restored to d'Aurelle's direct command by Gambetta during the night of 1/2 December, but d'Aurelle was not made aware of this at the time; it was only on 3 December that he was notified.

11 Freycinet, *Guerre*, pp136–137.
12 d'Aurelle, *Première Armée*, pp.273–276.
13 d'Aurelle, *Première Armée*, p.277.
14 Colmar von der Goltz, *Gambetta et ses Armées* (Paris: Librairie Sandoz, 1877) p.115.

Stosch intended no significant movement for the I Bavarian Corps on 1 December, although he stressed in the order that he issued that, 'the general situation of the war necessitates great activity in patrolling, in order to maintain the touch of the enemy, and to make him believe that an attack is pending.'[15] Stosch was, however, suffering from a quite unnecessary handicap which resulted from the insistence by Frederick Charles that the 6th Cavalry Division (von Schmidt) should become part of Second Army, and be replaced at the detachment by the 4th Cavalry Division. He had justified this unfortunate request to Moltke on 25 November by saying that to evaluate reports correctly a thorough knowledge of the individuals from whom the reports came was necessary, and the 6th Cavalry Division was well known to him. He had originally proposed to replace the 6th Cavalry Division by transferring to the detachment the 2nd Cavalry Division (Stolberg) which had been watching the Army of the Loire, but since it was still engaged on this task it was the 4th Cavalry Division that was to be transferred.

Stosch's ability to conduct offensive reconnaissance operations had thereby been diminished by the exchange, which had begun on 30 November when the leading units of the 6th Cavalry Division set off on a long ride for the night around the rear of the detachment in order to join Second Army; the 4th Cavalry Division had arrived to take its place, but was a poor substitute, being extremely worn out and far less familiar with the terrain. Schmidt rode into Stosch's headquarters at Janville at 1.30 p.m. on 1 December to take his leave of the Grand Duke before having a final conference with Stosch. The latter remarked that it was very unfortunate that he should be leaving the detachment at this time. 'And I also lament it,' Schmidt said. 'I do not grudge to any of my comrades the laurels which undoubtedly are immediately at hand for them but after I have gone through the Perche country without any satisfaction, I am obliged at this very moment to ride in rear of the army, when I could reap all the fruit of my previous hard work.' He added that the enemy was on the point of attacking, and that what Stosch needed just then was an enterprising body of cavalry. Stosch asked him if he thought that part of the Army of the Loire had moved eastwards with a view to an advance on Fontaine. 'Certainly not,' replied Schmidt: 'The whole lot are still round the salient point, Orléans, but if you do not look out they will be on top of you here.' And he went on at Stosch's request to give chapter and verse for his belief that the detachment was threatened by at least 50,000 men; even when told that Stiehle believed that both 15th and 16th Corps were on the line Boiscommun – Bellegarde, Schmidt stuck to his opinion.[16]

All of this left Stosch convinced that it was going to be the detachment and not Second Army that would strike the decisive blow, and he wasted no time in sitting down with the Grand Duke to get him to agree that on the following day steps should be taken to concentrate the detachment with a view to taking the offensive. One problem was the fact that Frederick Charles had earmarked the 22nd Division as a reserve for the Second Army, so that it was vital to regain control of that division at once. It was essential, explained Stosch, that the detachment should not be tied to a position astride the Orléans – Paris road: the detachment would accomplish the duty assigned to it if at the right time it brought up all its troops, even to the very last man, and beat the enemy. That would be the best protection of the roads. He added '…that in any case they would have freedom of choice for the concentration in the favourable position from Loigny to

15 Helvig, *Operations,* p.255.
16 Hale, *People's War*, pp.229–230.

Lumeau, which answered best for the attack and the defence according to the circumstances.'[17] The Grand Duke was immediately convinced and told Stosch that he should give orders for an attack next day, which went a bit further than Stosch had intended. Even after getting the Grand Duke's agreement, he still had his problems; what he was proposing was not only to overturn the strategy of Stiehle and Frederick Charles, but take control of the decisive operations out of their hands. Although he might be Moltke's representative in this theatre, he needed to carry Stiehle with him, and at 6.00 p.m. he sent a carefully worded letter to the headquarters of Second Army explaining what he intended to do, adding that, although on 2 December he could manage with only the 17th Division, on the following day at any rate he would need to employ the 22nd Division. Not surprisingly, the Prince, when he came to read the letter, was not best pleased, and at first not inclined to agree. News, however, that the French had pulled out of Boiscommun reassured him as to his left flank, and at 9.37 p.m. Stiehle was able to send a telegram giving Stosch the necessary permission, although this did not arrive until midnight. Stosch had written his letter without having received up-to-date reports from von der Tann; he was soon to discover, however, that a lot had been happening to the south of Orgères.

On 1 December, after the occupation of Terminiers, the 1st Bavarian Brigade had taken up a position to the west of the village fronting south along the line Guillonville – Gommiers. In posting Dietl's brigade there, von der Tann wished to cover the concentration of the rest of his corps around La Maladerie, at the important crossroads a mile to the east of Orgères. At the time, he did not feel undue concern about the forward position of the 1st Brigade, because as late as 1.00 p.m. cavalry patrols were reporting, incorrectly, that the enemy had not moved beyond Patay. Dietl's flanks were covered by cavalry; on the left the Bavarian Cuirassier Brigade stood near Tourette Farm, while the right flank was covered by the 9th Prussian Cavalry Brigade. As the day wore on, however, strong French columns were seen moving forward, covered by cavalry on both flanks. Chanzy had launched his 2nd and 3rd Divisions towards Sougy and Jauréguiberry's 1st Division towards Guillonville and Gommiers.[18] The French left was covered by Michel's strong cavalry division and the advance of this force soon compelled the heavily outnumbered 9th Cavalry Brigade to fall back on Cormainville, uncovering Dietl's right flank. In his very exposed position, he had no option but to retreat, and at 3.00 p.m. he fell back to Villepion. The park walls, which had not been prepared for defence, were too high, so he put two battalions into the château and the other buildings on the east side of the park, with another battalion on the west of it, supported by one battery. On his left, on the road to Faverolles, he posted one battalion and a rifle company with two batteries; and he covered his right with two companies in the open country south-west of Nonneville.

News of the French advance brought reinforcements pell-mell southwards; the first to arrive was Orff with the 2nd Brigade, who deployed his troops under very heavy fire to the west of Nonneville. They were opposed by Deplanque's brigade, which moved forward to the attack under the cover of an intensive artillery barrage. The Bavarian batteries, moving with difficulty in the heavy ground, responded; one of them was compelled to retreat almost at once, abandoning one gun when all the horses were killed. Gallant attempts by two companies of infantry failed to rescue it, and it was only when Lieutenant von Stengel brought up a gun limber and, under heavy fire, harnessed it, that it could be brought to safety. All along the front

17 Hale, *People's War*, pp.231–232.
18 *Official Account*, vol. III, p.327.

the Bavarians were taking heavy casualties, and von der Tann gave orders to commit the rest of the corps. The 3rd Brigade, however, was in cantonments well to the rear while the 4th Brigade, which was much closer at Loigny, had heard nothing of the battle. When it moved, it came up on the left of the position on the Faverolles road.

One of the casualties was Stephan, the commander of the 1st Division, who was seriously wounded when he was hit simultaneously by a shell splinter and bullet while with the front line of the 2nd Brigade. In spite of his vigorous protests, he was carried to the rear, and the command devolved upon Dietl. The 1st Brigade was by now coming under increasing pressure on the east side of Villepion, where as dusk fell Jauréguiberry personally led three battalions of Bourdillon's Brigade in an attack which succeeded, in fierce hand-to-hand fighting, in forcing its way into the farm buildings around the château. Dietl realised that the position was no longer defensible, and pulled his own brigade out towards Loigny. On the right, Orff was able to hold his position until the French ceased firing, and he then retreated to Orgères, where he was joined by the 3rd Brigade. The 4th Brigade had also retreated to Loigny, while to the west the 4th Cavalry Division went into quarters to the north of the River Conie. Chanzy remained where he was at the end of the engagement, holding Villepion, Terminiers and Sougy; de Sonis was well behind him at St Péravy and Patay. It was a success for the French, accomplished largely as a result of substantial numerical superiority; but the success was limited by the inability of the victors to pursue. Total German casualties amounted to 939, while the French losses were about 1,100.[19] That night was bitterly cold and the Bavarian official history recorded: 'The troops had no shelter, and, being compelled to bivouac on account of the vicinity of the enemy's outposts, suffered greatly. In addition, the commissariat waggons were unable to find several detachments in the darkness; and the latter, being thrown upon the small contents of their haversacks, passed the cold night in hunger upon the frozen ground.'[20]

Information about the fighting at Villepion only reached Stosch at about 9.00 p.m.; half an hour later he sent a telegram reporting on these events to Stiehle, which he amplified about three hours later. The news confirmed the opinion which Stosch had expressed as to the whereabouts of the French, so that at Pithiviers the doubts that may have been held there about the imminent attack of the French were entirely dispelled. Stosch, reviewing his situation, decided that he must draw the 22nd Division into his own fighting line, even though Frederick Charles had intended it to serve as a reserve for the Second Army.

News of the success at Villepion reached Gambetta and Freycinet soon after the arrival of the latest news from Paris. The balloon bringing the dispatch had been swept across France, finally and luckily coming to earth at Belle Isle, and the news it brought seemed stunning. Describing the events of the first day's fighting during the great sortie from Paris, the dispatch announced the capture of Épinay. Gambetta jumped to the conclusion that, rather than the village of Épinay sur Seine, which had been taken in the diversionary attack to the northwest of the capital, the attackers had reached Épinay sur Orge, 12 miles south of Paris.

This being so, it was concluded that the lines of investment must have been broken through at Longjumeau, although the dispatch made no mention of that place. Dazzled by the prospect which this imagined success brought, Gambetta issued a proclamation couched in characteristically extravagant terms, which he was very soon to regret:

19 *Official Account*, vol. III, p.329.
20 Helvig, *Operations*, p.265

> The genius of France, for the moment veiled, is appearing anew! The Prussians can now judge the difference between a despot who fights to satisfy his whims and a people in arms determined not to perish .... France and the universe will never forget that Paris first set the example, taught this policy and thus founded its moral supremacy in remaining faithful to the heroic spirit of the revolution. Long live Paris! Long live France! Long live the one, indivisible Republic.[21]

Inevitably, the orders now given to d'Aurelle for the Army of the Loire's advance on 2 December were appropriately ambitious. At 5.30 p.m. on 1 December Freycinet sent d'Aurelle the following message:

> Paris has made a sublime effort. The lines of investment have been broken, tumbled over with an admirable heroism. General Ducrot advances towards us with his army resolved to conquer or die. Today he occupies the positions of Champigny, Bry sur Marne, Villiers sur Marne, on this side of the Marne. General, this heroism determines what we must do. Fly to the support of Ducrot, without losing a moment, by the roads which we discussed yesterday. Accelerate in every way this movement to commence in the morning. Redouble your strength and energy. Appeal to the patriotism of your generals. Their great heart will respond to yours. But this elan must not affect your sangfroid; continue your operations with the same prudence, just carry them out with lightning speed.[22]

Freycinet went on to tell d'Aurelle to give orders to 17th, 18th and 20th Corps so that nothing should stand in the way of a combined offensive of the whole army; as d'Aurelle pointed out, here was proof positive that they were therefore under his command, contrary to the suggestion in Freycinet's account to the contrary. This message was written in terms to make it clear to d'Aurelle just how far short of the determination shown by Trochu and Ducrot had been his conduct of the campaign so far, and d'Aurelle cannot have failed to have been profoundly offended by this. It was, though, typical of the way in which Freycinet addressed him.

Chanzy was to advance to Allaines, Janville and Toury, with 17th Corps in support, while 15th Corps was to move on Santilly. Even discounting the momentary euphoria engendered by the misreading of Trochu's dispatch, it was clear to all that the coming encounter was likely to be extremely significant; as it turned out, the events of 2 December were to prove the decisive point of the entire Loire campaign.

21 Howard, *Franco-Prussian War,* p.310.
22 d'Aurelle, *Première Armée*, p.290.

9

Loigny-Poupry

D'Aurelle recorded that the night of 1/2 December was bitterly cold, the temperature falling to between 3° and 4° below zero: 'The French army and the Prussian Army bivouacked only a little apart from each other .... One could see the fires of the enemy which the Prussians made no attempt to conceal, unlike their usual practice.'[1] To Chanzy, seeing the enemy camp fires which stretched from Orgères to Baigneaux, it appeared that he was in the presence of very substantial enemy forces. Nevertheless, heartened by his success at Villepion, he was in a confident frame of mind as he rode out at 7.00 a.m. on 2 December to survey the terrain over which his troops would advance; he had, he wrote later, the certainty that behind him there was support on which he could count.[2]

He had on the previous evening issued minutely detailed orders for the advance of his troops. It would be Barry's 2nd Division which would be the first to come into action, with the objective of taking Loigny. Jauréguiberry, with the 1st Division, on the left, would form a reserve, moving on Château Goury once Loigny had fallen. Meanwhile Maurandy's 3rd Division would move on Lumeau, occupying the villages of Neuvilliers and Ecuillon.

At his headquarters at Janville, Stosch was preparing for the coming battle in the knowledge that the day's fighting would prove crucial for the campaign on the Loire. He had grasped, as Frederick Charles and Stiehle had not, that it was on the left flank of the French advance to the relief of Paris that the decisive battle would be fought.

However, at the headquarters of Second Army, serious misconceptions still prevailed. Indeed, ever since he had arrived to conduct the campaign on the Loire, Frederick Charles had not distinguished himself in his analysis of the situation which he faced. It was not just due to the uncertainty of some of the reconnaissance reports which he received. He had formed his own view of the position, and even after members of his staff had reported the true nature of the outcome of the Battle of Beaune-la-Rolande, confirming Waldersee's assessment of the scale and significance of the victory, he doggedly persisted in his opinion.

On 2 December, at his headquarters at Pithiviers, Frederick Charles spent the morning anxiously awaiting news from the detachment. At dawn on 2 December, the main body of IX Corps was quartered around Pithiviers, with one of its brigades well to the west at Bazoches

1 d'Aurelle, *Première Armée*, pp.365–366.
2 Chanzy, *Deuxième Armée*, p.70.

les Gallerandes. Both III Corps and X Corps were still reconnoitring towards Montargis and Bellegarde. The first news to arrive came in the form of a message from Stosch, timed at 8.10 a.m., reporting that the whole of the detachment was now concentrated for its advance on the line Tanon – Baigneaux, with I Bavarian Corps and the 4th Cavalry Division on the right, and the 17th and 22nd Divisions on the left. At this point there had so far been received at Pithiviers no indication of any serious enemy activity; Kretschmann, that morning, began a letter to his wife telling her that he had enjoyed an undisturbed sleep for the first time for several days, and that there had been merely some insignificant artillery exchanges near Montigny, to the north of Bellegarde. He was, however, to add momentous news when he completed his letter that evening.[3]

Frederick Charles had received no report from any of the three corps of the Second Army, but in response to the report from the detachment, he resolved to move Manstein's Corps to the west to its support. However, since the corps would have to cover a distance of some 15 miles, the effect of its march would not be felt until about 4.00 a.m. Soon after this came an extremely alarming telegram from Waldersee. Convinced that there would be a crucially important battle that day, he had set off early to the Paris – Orléans high road. What he found there led him to write a telegram at about 9.00 am, which was apparently handed in at Leon en Beauce an hour or so later, and which reached Pithiviers at 10.35. Referring to the movements of the divisions of Martineau and Peytavin from 15th Corps, Waldersee stated that east of the road the enemy had deployed a very substantial force, estimated at 8 squadrons and 15 battalions, with supporting artillery, and that an advance of all arms on Bazoches was reported. The reports which Second Army was receiving from III Corps and IX Corps did not make the situation any clearer. At 11.30 Frederick Charles ordered Manstein to march, after his men had eaten, towards the Paris road for its protection. He also sent orders to the 6th Cavalry Division, at that time making its way from the west, to halt on the Paris road. Manstein, before he set off, had a meeting with Stiehle, whose imperfect understanding of the situation led him to jeer at the Grand Duke, saying that he was behaving somewhat in the same way as, '...at a *Kriegspiel* in peacetime.'[4]

Loigny today is still, as it was in 1870, a quiet little town at the junction of a number of roads, lying in a plain so flat that the town's church spire can be taken as a point of reference for some distance in all directions. Surrounding it were a number of walled farms that, not surprisingly in that open countryside, were to become key strong points during the battle. For Chanzy, marching north-east in what he intended as an advance directly towards Pithiviers, it was essential to get through Loigny and on towards Bazoches les Hautes with as little delay as possible. For Stosch, intent on marching south to attack what was, incorrectly, believed to be the whole of the left wing of the Army of the Loire, Loigny served as the first point to be seized, and was the line to be taken by the right wing of the detachment.

It had been Stosch's original intention that I Bavarian Corps, which, in the vicinity of Loigny, was the force nearest to the advancing French, should stand to at 8.00 a.m. on 2 December. As the full position became clear after the fighting at Villepion, he revised this to provide for von der Tann to concentrate his entire Corps at La Maladerie at 6.30 a.m. It was evident to Stosch that he must be ready to encounter a French advance early in the morning, and that he must unite his whole force to meet them. For this reason, he included Wittich's 22nd Division in the orders which he issued for the concentration of the detachment. Von der Tann was to

3 Kretschmann, *Lettres*, p.301.
4 Hale, *People's War*, pp.238–239.

move eastwards to take up a position to the north-east of Loigny between Beauvilliers Farm and Château Goury, and to be prepared to hold it against Chanzy's advance until the 17th and 22nd Divisions arrived, which he expected would be about 11.00 a.m. Tresckow, with the 17th Division was directed to move at once to Lumeau, while Wittich, with the 22nd Division and the 3rd Cavalry Brigade, was to advance to Baigneaux. The only units that Stosch directly assigned to cover the Orléans – Paris road were the remaining two brigades of Stolberg's 2nd Cavalry Division. Finally, the 4th Cavalry Division was, as on the previous day, to be responsible for covering the right flank.[5] With these orders duly issued, Stosch was able to send his report to Second Army at 8.10 a.m. that the detachment was concentrating for its advance. He also reported to Moltke telling him of the events of 1 December and of his intention to advance against the Army of the Loire, which, when Moltke compared it to Second Army's failure to move, exercised a considerable effect on his mind.[6]

The intense cold was accentuated by the severe wind chill factor caused by a biting north-east wind; but the day was fine, and movement was easier over the frozen ground.[7] The ground over which the battle was to be fought was generally level, broken only by gentle undulations. Although highly cultivated, it was generally unfenced, and offered little cover. The Bavarians moved off soon after receiving Stosch's orders at around 8.00 a.m.; as they did, French infantry and cavalry were already able to be seen to the south towards Villerand and Loigny. These skirmishers were followed by strong columns directed upon Loigny and towards Lumeau, where they came into contact with an advance guard of the 4th Bavarian Brigade which had passed the night there. The brigade was composed of the 3rd Battalion of the 10th Regiment, commanded by Captain Wetzger, with three squadrons of light cavalry and a 4-pdr battery; it was at once clear to Rudolf von der Tann, the 4th Brigade commander, that Château Goury was of crucial importance to the Bavarian position, and must be held at all costs. He ordered Wetzger to break off the action and move at once to occupy the château. It was as well that he did; Wetzger got there just before the French leading troops reached it. Wetzger deployed one company in the building of the château, with two in the grounds surrounding it, and one in reserve, and he succeeded in repulsing the first assaults upon the position. The remainder of the 4th Brigade soon came up. One battalion was left to hold Beauvilliers Farm, while another took up a position on the crest of the gentle ridge that ran from the farm towards Château Goury. The remaining troops were moved into the grounds of the château to reinforce Wetzger's garrison, one battalion going into the château with the rest in reserve behind the park.[8]

Behind the 4th Brigade, the 3rd Brigade, now commanded by Colonel Roth, reached Beauvilliers at about 9.00, with orders to occupy the farm and surrounding buildings, and to extend its position along the long ridge to link with Rudolf von der Tann in Château Goury. Its artillery almost at once came into action against strong French columns which were seen advancing from Loigny and along the whole line. The terrain was open, offering little cover for both attackers and defenders, and as the day wore on this had a telling effect as the casualties on both sides steadily mounted. The French were advancing down the slope of the low ridge from Loigny to Ecuillon, which was very similar to that occupied by the Bavarians, and the

5 *Official Account*, vol. III, p.331.
6 Moltke, *Correspondance Militaire*, vol. II, p.593.
7 Helvig, *Operations*, p.266.
8 *Official Account*, vol. III, p.331.

heavy columns presented an easy target for both artillery and rifle fire. The Bavarians' position, however, presented one disadvantage, as the official historian noted:

> Beauvilliers and Goury were exactly on the crest of the height, the north-east slope of which was sufficiently wooded to prevent our batteries from taking up a position on it. They were therefore obliged to take up positions in front of the line Beauvilliers-Goury, on the slope towards Loigny, completely exposed to the enemy's fire. The advanced position of the artillery necessitated a corresponding advance in the position of the infantry, during which we suffered greatly, owing to the long range of the enemy's firearms.[9]

Meanwhile, as the 2nd Bavarian Division got into position along the ridge, the 1st Division assembled behind it at Le Prevost, with the Corps artillery.

The French attack through Loigny was made by Barry's 2nd Division of the 16th Corps, while Maurandy's 3rd Division advanced on Lumeau. Jauréguiberry's 1st Division followed closely behind the 2nd Division. By 9.00 Barry's leading units had got close up to Beauvilliers when they were suddenly assailed by a Bavarian counter-attack down the slope from the farm by three battalions of the 3rd Regiment, without waiting for any preparation by artillery. The attack succeeded in driving back the French, who fell back quickly upon their main body:

> Our troops were not satisfied with having repulsed the enemy's attack by an offensive movement, but, as soon as the enemy began to waver, they pressed forward with loud cheers, in spite of their heavy losses, until they came within close range of the 1st Division of the 16th Corps, which had just deployed at the centre of the enemy's position, and were forced to halt and commence a stationary musketry engagement. This decided the result of the attack, which, although very gallant, was unprepared, and therefore premature.[10]

By 10.30 the pressure of the heavy French numerical superiority was beginning to tell, and the Bavarians were gradually forced back up the slope to the position from which they had advanced, suffering heavy losses as they did so. Their sudden counter-attack had, however, disrupted Barry's advance on the Beauvilliers position, and Chanzy was effectively on the back foot for the rest of the day. Meanwhile, Deplanque's Brigade had begun a fierce struggle in and around Morâle Farm with the 1st Bavarian Division, of which von der Tann had deployed two battalions of Orff's 2nd Brigade in front of Tanon and the leading troops of the 1st Brigade (Tauffenbach) in front of Le Prevost, with its left in contact with the 3rd Brigade at Beauvilliers. Gradually the remaining units of the 1st Brigade were drawn into the action, battalions being fed into the firing line on either side of Beauvilliers, while the five batteries of Corps artillery under Colonel Bronzetti moved up in close support. The French advance was stopped, and a hard fought struggle ensued, with neither side able to get the upper hand, although two companies of the Leib-Infanterie succeeded in re-entering the woods north of Morâle farm, which had been occupied by Deplanque's leading battalions.

At 11.30, however, the stalemate was broken by the advance on the extreme right of the 4th Cavalry Division, and by the rest of Orff's 2nd Brigade. The latter's artillery had been pounding

9 Helvig, *Operations*, p.268.
10 Helvig, *Operations*, p.270.

Deplanque's troops from the edge of the Tanon Heights; the French now found themselves at risk of being outflanked when Prince Albrecht's cavalry, supported by the Bavarian Cuirassier Brigade, swung around the French left through Orgères and La Frileuse. The 4th Cavalry Division had something to prove after its rather ineffectual showing as a flank guard during the previous day's fighting; now, Prince Albrecht's troopers rode down the French infantry on the road south to Villevé. The French troops scattered and broke, leaving 300 prisoners in German hands. Another party of uhlans had a similar success near Villerand, and Jauréguiberry's flank was in danger of complete collapse, since Michel's Cavalry Division, which was supposed to be covering it, had gone all the way back to Muzelles, four miles to the south. To meet this threat, he posted a *garde mobile* regiment midway between Villerand and the Villepion Mill.[11]

Orff launched a vigorous attack with all five battalions of the 2nd Brigade. Held up at first by French artillery fire and by the rifle fire of the defenders of the Morâle farm, he was soon aided by the artillery of the 4th Cavalry Division which, coming into action south-west of La Maladerie, took the French artillery in flank and set fire to the buildings of Morâle farm. After a long struggle, first the stables north of the farm, and then the farm itself, were taken at the point of the bayonet, and Deplanque's Brigade was driven back off the road from La Maladerie to Loigny. Orff's men held their ground in spite of a series of French attempts to regain the lost position, and their success soon began to affect the fighting on their left.

Colonel Tauffenbach's 1st Brigade, which had come up piecemeal to join the battle line, was mainly in position between Orff's left and the Beauvilliers Farm. When the second French attack on the centre of the Bavarian position came in a little before noon, Tauffenbach countered it by advancing southwards. This movement, however, did not produce any prolonged effect, in part because the individual battalions attacked independently, in part because ammunition was running low, but principally because of the continued French assaults around Beauvilliers Farm which threatened Tauffenbach's left. The struggle for Beauvilliers, which formed the centre of the Bavarian position, had continued all morning; by 12.30, however, in spite of the heavy bombardment, the Bavarians had gained ground towards Morâle Farm, compelling the French to fall back a little way, and enabling the battalion that occupied Beauvilliers to be relieved, it having exhausted its ammunition.

Throughout the morning the fire of the Bavarian artillery had proved crucially effective. Firing from a range that was at times less than 400 yards, and completely exposed to the enemy rifle fire, the gunners had held their ground. So close were the enemy that at times various batteries had to fire in several directions at once. They sustained heavy casualties, not least among the horses; at times, the threat of losing guns to the enemy infantry was only narrowly averted. During the morning, von der Tann had been able to deploy a total of 12 batteries, of which 7 were in position between Morâle Farm and Beauvilliers Farm, while 5 were posted between Beauvilliers and Château Goury.[12]

Having failed to take Beauvilliers, Chanzy now concentrated on Château Goury, whose defenders were running short of ammunition. The château is surrounded by high walls and every loophole and window was manned. At about 1.00 p.m. Bourdillon's Brigade, under cover of a heavy artillery barrage, advanced over the snow-covered plain to the attack. A correspondent of *The Times* was present in Château Goury:

11 *Official Account*, vol. III, p.334.
12 Helvig, *Operations,* p.276.

> Ascending one of the towers of the old château, I found myself in an admirable position for seeing the battle. The room was full of soldiers, who had loopholed the walls; but the enemy were not within range, or were not thought to be so, until suddenly a large body of infantry, which was supposed to be German for the first moment or so, unexpectedly opened a hot fire upon a regiment drawn up beneath the walls of the château. Then from every loophole and crevice in the towers and walls rolled an incessant fire of rifles, and the chassepot balls seemed to rain upon the roofs and walls in reply, until by degrees the old castle became the centre of the fight, and, as it seemed to me, with every possible chance of being taken.[13]

The garrison had had orders to hold their fire until the last moment; when the signal was given, an annihilating file fire inflicted heavy losses. As the French wavered, the garrison charged out of the buildings in a counter-attack. For a short while the issue was in the balance, then, suddenly, the French were attacked in their flank and fell back in disorder. The new arrivals were the leading troops of Tresckow's 17th Division, who had been marching from Santilly through Bazoches les Hautes to take up their position on the left of the Bavarians at Lumeau. Chanzy later commented on the arrival of these reinforcements: 'The heroic efforts of the 3rd Chasseur Battalion, the 39th *Régiment de Marche* and the 75th *Gardes Mobiles* had in the end completely failed to take the position, and they made a fighting retreat to Loigny, where they established themselves.'[14]

Earlier that morning, on hearing the gunfire from the south-west, Tresckow had sent ahead two batteries of horse artillery, escorted by three squadrons of dragoons, and since mid-morning these had taken part in the defence of Château Goury. Their contribution had been invaluable; they had arrived in time to help the battered 3rd Brigade disengage itself and fall back, and throughout the day they were constantly in action; the two batteries, which had 10 guns between them, firing a total of 1,196 shells.[15] As he moved first west. and then south with his main body, Tresckow learned that strong enemy columns were advancing towards Lumeau and Baigneaux. He left a rifle battalion to hold Baigneaux until Wittich arrived with the 22 Division, and himself hurried on to Lumeau. As his troops began to arrive there, they found that the leading units of Maurandy's division had already entered the village; but an immediate assault by a battalion of the 90th Regiment ejected them, and the French fell back towards Neuvilliers and Domainville. They also abandoned their advance on Baigneaux, and for the moment confined themselves to a prolonged bombardment of Lumeau.[16]

After about half an hour of this Maurandy made another attempt on Lumeau, throwing forward strong columns of infantry, preceded by skirmishers, who got close to the village before, under a hail of rifle and artillery fire, they were thrown back towards Domainville. By now Tresckow was being supported by the six leading batteries of Wittich's Division which had been sent on ahead to take up a position north-east of Lumeau. Behind them, marching fast, was the leading infantry unit of the 22nd Division, the 44th Brigade under Colonel Marschall von Bieberstein, with orders to follow up the retreating French by advancing through Anneux. Close

13 Quoted; E. Rich, *A History of the Franco-German War* (London: Swan Sonnenschein & Co, 1884) p.309.
14 Chanzy, *Deuxième Armee*, p.73.
15 E. S. May, *Field Artillery with the Other Arms* (London: Sampson Low Marston & Co, 1898).
16 *Official Account*, vol. III, pp.335–336.

range artillery fire accelerated the French retreat, in addition to which they were harried by the German cavalry, and they soon disappeared behind the hills south of Domainville, falling back towards Echelles and Terminiers in disorder.

In one remarkable exploit, Captain von Marschalck with a squadron of the 11th Uhlans had observed what he thought at first was a waggon train near Neuvillers. It was, in fact, a 12-pdr battery of Chanzy's Corps. Marschalck, who had ridden on ahead of his squadron, prepared an ambush; when he realised it was a battery preparing to fire, 'The squadron rushed out suddenly upon their flank just as they were coming into action. So quickly and skilfully was the surprise effected, that not one single round was fired by the battery and the whole of it was captured .... 1 officer, 76 men, 77 horses, 6 guns and 8 waggons fell into the hands of the Germans without a shot being fired in self-defence.'[17]

It was after ejecting the French from Lumeau that Tresckow had been able to swing to his right and deliver the decisive blow at Bourdillon's flank. The attack was delivered by two Hanseatic regiments of the 33rd Brigade under von Kottwitz, and fell upon Bourdillon's infantry as they were launched forward to the assault of Châteaux Goury. Taken completely by surprise, the French panicked and fell back in great disorder towards Loigny; they tried to make a stand on the gravel pits just to the east of the town, but were driven out at bayonet point by a battalion of the 76th Regiment. Another battalion of the regiment forced its way into Loigny, while further companies charged onwards to Fougeux and took the village. An attempt to push on towards Villepion was however checked. The Bavarians, who had defended Château Goury all morning under continuous shellfire and against repeated infantry assaults, could not help some mixed feelings about the success of the Prussians, as their official historian recorded: 'We were of course delighted that the reinforcement was so effective; but, to prevent misconception, we must state that the defenders of Château Goury had no idea at that time of giving up.'[18]

Von der Tann together with his staff remained on the road from Beaugency to Morâle, from where he conducted the battle. Two Prussian officers, who were bringing reports, were severely wounded close to him; but for some time he and his staff remained uninjured. In the evening however, near to Loigny, he was struck on the boot by a bullet. His particular concern at this time was that the defensive position he had taken up was costing him heavy losses and he asked that the 17th Division might attack as soon as possible in order that he might take the offensive in conjunction with it.

Although Tresckow's men had succeeded in gaining a footing in Loigny, Bourdillon still held the bulk of the village. Tresckow brought up four battalions from the 34th Brigade, which were in Lumeau, in an assault on the eastern side of Loigny, while a Bavarian battalion advancing from Château Goury swung around the north of the town. With the Germans gaining ground on all sides, Bourdillon had no choice but to retreat, falling back to Villepion. There remained, however, a small party which obstinately held on to possession of the churchyard on high ground at the western edge of the town. Loigny had in this way fallen to sustained infantry assaults and for once the German artillery had played little part in the action, watching in frustration from close range as the infantry battled for possession of the town. As the artillery waited about a mile outside Loigny, an enterprising group of French skirmishers moved forward to threaten

17 May, *Field Artillery*, p.250.
18 Helvig, *Operations*, p.277n.

them before they were ridden down by a squadron of the 17th Regiment. Other squadrons of this regiment rode forward to Villepion, but were driven back by French artillery fire.

Villepion, the scene of such fierce fighting on the previous day, was now the key point in Chanzy's line as he strove to prevent the complete disintegration of his corps. Quite apart from the defeat of the attacks by Deplanque and Bourdillon, he was becoming increasingly fearful about his left flank. The sight of strong German columns, supported by large numbers of cavalry, moving down from Tanon through La Maladerie told its own story: 'As soon as the enemy saw that our right wing was no longer to be feared, he embarked on a manoeuvre so often successful, and switching his order of battle, he moved en masse on our left with the intention of turning it.'[19] To meet this threat, Chanzy swung round part of Deplanque's brigade to take up a position south of Villerand, fronting the road to Nonneville, where it was supported by a battery of mitrailleuses. It seemed to Chanzy that he was facing an enemy that was considerably superior in numbers, an erroneous belief that reflected considerable credit on the efforts of the detachment during the battle.

Summing up his situation, at about 2.00 p.m. Chanzy wrote that his right was disorganised, his centre scarcely solid and composed of troops suffering from their ordeal of the morning. His 1st Division on the left, was heavily engaged and facing the principal thrust of the enemy; 'On the side of the 3rd Division the disorder was becoming even more serious; two guns from a battery of 12 pounders, sent there, had been taken by the enemy, because the troops charged with protecting this battery had abandoned it.'[20]

With Bourdillon's retreat from Loigny, the German artillery moved forward from the defensive line which it had occupied all day, and formed a gun line to the north of the town. From here it pounded the positions held by Deplanque and Bourdillon north and east of Villepion. By 2.30 von der Tann felt able to move to the attack of Villepion, and he ordered Dietl with the 1st Division to advance directly south from Villerand, with the right wing opposite Nonneville and the left opposite the Château and Park of Villepion. Under cover of a heavy bombardment of the French by around 80 guns of 12 batteries, Dietl's leading troops occupied a wood on the Loigny-Villepion road before themselves being pinned down by heavy French rifle and mitrailleuse fire. On the right, Prince Albrecht's cavalry were continuing to advance, moving through Villevé towards Villepion; this advance in its turn was halted by the fire of the artillery of de Sonis' 17th Corps, which was now arriving on the battlefield, its leading brigade having moved at Chanzy's request to prop up his right flank at Faverolles. Three batteries of German horse artillery, however, remained around Nonneville, less than a mile from the Park of Villepion, and continued to fire on Deplanque's Brigade. In the meantime Michel's Cavalry Division had moved rather diffidently forward again from Muzelles through Guillonville; but when Prince Albrecht switched his artillery in that direction, the French cavalry again abruptly left the field, falling back to the south until they were well out of harm's way.[21] 'So headlong was their flight that the 10 German cuirassier squadrons which had advanced to charge them could never catch up to them. Finally, the French squadrons rallied behind their infantry at Gommiers, and the pursuing German horsemen had to let their prey escape.'[22]

19 Chanzy, *Deuxième Armée*, p.73.
20 Chanzy, *Deuxième Armée*, p.74.
21 *Official Account*, vol. III, p.339.
22 May, *Field Artillery*, p.254

De Sonis had begun his march forward as early as 4.00 am, although he hoped that his support would not immediately be required by Chanzy, due to the exhaustion of his troops. At 11.30, however, he received a message from Chanzy seeking his immediate help, and it was in response to this that he had sent a brigade on ahead to Faverolles, together with his Corps artillery. It was clear to him that 16th Corps was beginning to fall apart, and this made him fearful for his detached force, and he hurried on with reinforcements. When he reached the front it was apparent that unless action was taken immediately, the advancing Germans would indeed destroy Chanzy's corps, and with it 17th Corps as well. De Sonis ordered an immediate advance on Loigny, but as darkness began to fall the two leading regiments of *gardes mobiles* crumbled under the fierce fire of the German infantry. Riding through them, de Sonis cried 'Forward! Are you afraid? Miserable men! You will be our destruction!' But in spite of all he could do, the *gardes mobiles* fell back in disorder. In a last attempt to rally them, de Sonis personally led a charge of some 300 Papal Zouaves, with 500 other troops, in the direction of Villours. He had the satisfaction of seeing the German defenders pull back from that village, and he pressed on. Outside Villours, however, his charge was halted with heavy losses when it encountered Tresckow's last reserve, which consisted of two battalions of the 75th Regiment. Hundreds of Frenchmen went down in the face of withering rifle fire; among them were de Sonis himself and the commander of the Zouaves, Colonel Charette, both of whom were badly wounded.[23]

Tresckow's men, retaking Villours, pushed on southwards towards Faverolles; the units of 17th Corps which opposed them here were scattered, and retreated in great disorder, leaving many prisoners and a mitrailleuse battery in the hands of the Germans. On the edge of Loigny, the beleaguered defenders of the churchyard finally laid down their arms. In front of Villepion, von der Tann reckoned that the fierce defence being put up by Jauréguiberry made it imprudent to attack again that night; he calculated, correctly, that the French would abandon the position during the night.[24]

Against very heavy odds, Stosch had now fought off two of the French corps opposed to him. He had won the battle for Loigny, but it was the appearance of a third French corps on his left flank that now presented the greatest threat of all to the detachment. While Marschall, with the 44th Brigade was engaged at about 1.00 in clearing Anneux, on the left flank of the 17th Division, Wittich, his divisional commander, received an alarming message from Major General von Colomb, whose 3rd Cavalry Brigade was covering the left of the detachment at Dambron. The news that von Colomb sent was to the effect that large French columns appeared to be moving north through Artenay in the direction of Allaines and Toury. At this time the only German units covering the main road were the 4th and 5th Cavalry Brigades and one of these, the 4th, was to the south of Pithiviers leaving only von Baumbach's 5th Cavalry Brigade at Toury to hold up the French advance.

The advance consisted of the 2nd and 3rd Divisions of 15th Corps. On the left wing of the advance, Peytavin's 3rd Division had marched off with the intention of moving on Santilly. On its right, Martineau's 2nd Division was moving towards Ruan and Aschères. The 1st Division of 15th Corps was further to the east. At about noon, Peytavin's leading units had encountered Colomb's troopers at Dambron; under heavy artillery fire, and greatly outnumbered, Colomb was obliged to retire. He was responsible for covering the detachment's left, and mindful of this

23 Baunard, *Le Général de Sonis* (Paris: Librairie Ch Pourrielgue, 1903), p.336.
24 Helvig, *Operations,* p.279.

he moved down the road towards Poupry, and reported the position to Wittich. It was as well that he did; Peytavin, alerted by the sound of gunfire to the west, had abandoned his advance on Santilly and was turning to take the detachment in flank.[25]

Wittich at once appreciated the danger. Although, as it happened, Stosch was at that moment sending orders to him that he should move on Loigny, he at once swung his division round to face the new threat:

> At the same moment, I learned positively that the enemy were threatening Poupry. There was no time to reflect; the Grand Duke was advised of the situation by an ordnance officer and that I was not able to conform to the order to follow the 17th Division into Loigny but that I would march with all my division on Poupry and Artenay. The division had already reached the road from Lumeau to Poupry.[26]

The troops nearest to the advancing French were the men of Colonel von Kontzki's 43rd Brigade, and Wittich ordered Kontzki to lead the advance of the division from Anneux to Milhouard followed by the divisional artillery and then Marschall's 44th Brigade. The right flank of the advance was covered by the 13th Hussars. Peytavin by now was moving westwards across the Chartres-Orléans road towards Poupry, and he and Kontzki sighted each other's troops as the latter advanced to Milhouard. Realising that above all it was essential to prevent the French from gaining possession of Poupry, Kontzki led forward his leading unit, the 95th Regiment, at the double. He collided with the first troops of Peytavin's Division in the middle of the village before driving them back and gaining control of the eastern edge of Poupry.[27] The village lies at the centre of a network of small roads; its loss would expose the left flank of the detachment, but without it, Peytavin could make no progress in his march to the relief of Chanzy's Corps. For both sides, therefore, the struggle that ensued for possession of the village was of crucial importance.

D'Aurelle had arrived at Chevilly, which he had designated as the location of his headquarters for the day, at about 10.30 am. Anxiously awaiting news of Chanzy, he was surprised to hear no gunfire; after a little while he ordered his staff to move forward to Artenay where they would be nearer to 15th Corps as well as to 16th Corps:

> He arrived there about midday, and a certain agitation reigned in the town. On the left, towards Loigny or Villepion, there was fighting; the guns could be heard, but the sound did not indicate an engagement that was a serious as was actually the case. The 3rd Division (Peytavin) of 15th Corps was heavily engaged in front of Poupry with the part of the Prussian Army that had beaten and forced the retreat of the 3rd Division (Maurandy) of 16th Corps. If this general had been able to rally his division and resume the battle, the Prussians would find themselves taken between two fires: their destruction at this point appeared certain. A prompt and bold decision could have turned our fortunes and powerfully influenced the result of the day.[28]

25 *Official Account*, vol. III, p.340.
26 Wittich, *Journal*, pp.223–224.
27 *Official Account*, vol. III, p.340.
28 d'Aurelle, *Première Armée*, p.312.

The advance by the two divisions of 15th Corps had effectively initiated a separate battle. To protect the left flank of the detachment, Wittich had to face a numerically far superior enemy. Clearly Poupry was the key point of the 22nd Division's defensive position, and the engagement here was increasing in ferocity:

> In order to reach Poupry before the enemy, Colonel von Kontzki led forward the 95th Regiment at the double. The 1st Battalion met with some French detachments in the middle of the village, drove them back after a brief struggle, and posted itself firmly at the eastern edge. The 2nd Battalion pressed forward in the copse lying to the north as far as the road to Eards, and that brought to a standstill the enemy's skirmishers and columns, which were endeavouring to outflank the German left wing. During the struggle now raging in the copse, and in front of Poupry, the six batteries of the 22nd Division came into action to the south of the village; the three next available battalions of the 32nd Regiment were also gradually pushed forward into the fighting line, in order to ward off their adversary's constant attacks.[29]

Behind them, Marschall had succeeded in disengaging the 44th Brigade and this too had set off on the road towards Poupry. As his battalions arrived to join the battle line, Wittich sent the 94th Regiment into the copse to the north of the village, while the 83rd Regiment joined the 32nd Regiment in defence of the eastern edge of Poupry.

These reinforcements emboldened Wittich to make a forward move himself and he ordered the two regiments to advance against the French skirmish line. Although initially successful the advance stalled when French reserves came up; as the Prussians retreated towards their original position around Poupry, they suffered heavy casualties. One of these was Kontzki, who was mortally wounded. The French did not, however, follow up their success, and Wittich took the opportunity to sort out the battalions of various regiments which had become thoroughly intermingled. In particular, he was concerned with his left wing, which was heavily involved in trying to clear the larger copse north of Poupry of French troops. By about 3.00 the 94th Regiment, together with part of the 95th Regiment, had reached the eastern edge of the copse when it was suddenly confronted by a large body of fresh troops advancing from the two smaller copses to the east, with the support of a battery which had unlimbered in the open ground between them. The French infantry charged forward to within 200 yards of the German infantry in position along the edge of the large copse:

> ...but at this moment the case shot from the 5th Light Battery, unlimbered in front line, fell with such effect amid the ranks of the French, that the latter hurried back under cover of the woods, while for the same reason the guns posted in the intermediate space were also compelled to retire. About this time General von Colomb, with six squadrons of the 3rd Cavalry Brigade, had moved forward along the north-east border of the wood in the direction of some infantry columns, which were endeavouring to cross the open ground on the German left flank, but now retired hastily before the cavalry attack, followed by the shells of the 3rd Light Battery, which had just reached the border of the wood.'[30]

29 *Official Account*, vol. III, p.340.
30 *Official Account*, vol. III, p.341.

Both on the north and south of Poupry the French had now deployed a powerful gun line. D'Aurelle watched his artillery, which included 10 mitrailleuses, in action on the south side of the village:

> Some Prussian batteries, rapidly brought up from Milhouard and Mamerant, replied to our fire, and a terrible artillery duel ensued. The superiority of our batteries of 12 pounders, and especially our mitrailleuses, inflicted heavy damage on the enemy; in less than three-quarters of an hour the Prussian guns were dismounted and reduced to silence.[31]

Having gained the upper hand in this artillery duel, Peytavin launched an attack by four battalions, supported by the mitrailleuses, and advanced from La Villeneuve and Haut Roche towards Wittich's right flank. All that Wittich had available to meet this attack were the five companies of infantry which had been assigned to protect the German artillery, which had been drawn up along the road leading south from Poupry. These companies deployed to the north of Morâle, supported by two pioneer companies, which were all that could be spared from the garrison of Poupry. Somehow, in spite of the heavy odds against them, the German infantry held on to their position; casualties were high, however, and included Major von Lengerke, a battalion commander in the 83rd Regiment, who was killed as the French swept forward against the position at Morâle.[32]

Wittich was now fighting in a very exposed position, with his back towards the troops of 16th and 17th Corps. Fortunately for him, these were more concerned with getting away from the battlefield of Loigny than with any adventurous move eastward, where Wittich might have been caught between two enemy corps, as d'Aurelle had seen.

By 4.00 d'Aurelle had the whole of Martineau's 2nd Division in hand, and a fresh attack was launched all along the line. Preceded by dense clouds of skirmishers, French columns again advanced towards Morâle; this attack was broken up by the rifle fire of the defenders. Other columns were launched against Poupry village, but these too were repulsed with heavy losses. On the German left, however, the French made more progress, pushing into the northern edge of the copse, and moving southwards, driving the Germans back towards Poupry. Fresh French troops came up to reinforce the success; a counter-attack by a battalion of the 95th Regiment from Poupry failed to halt the French advance, and the Germans fell back into the village, giving up all but a narrow strip of woodland. Both sides sustained heavy losses during this fierce fighting; another senior German officer died fighting in his front line when Pallmenstein, the commander of the 94th Regiment was killed in the struggle for the copse.

Inside the village, Colonel Marschall decided to commit his last reserve, the 83rd Regiment. Supported by detachments of the 94th and 95th Regiments, they charged northwards into the copse. The French recoiled, and as darkness fell they were driven out of the copse altogether, and back across the open ground to the shelter of the two small copses to the east. In an attempt to capitalise on the situation, Colomb again moved forward to pursue the retreating French infantry, but quickly broke off an attempt to charge them in the face of vigorous chassepot fire from the copses. It was too dark for either side to do more. Wittich's men at first settled down for the night in the positions that they had so strenuously defended; later they pulled back

31 d'Aurelle, *Première Armée,* p.313.
32 *Official Account*, vol. III, p.342n.

to Anneux and Domainville, leaving only a line of outposts facing the French. Behind them Tresckow's 17th Division was quartered at Lumeau, with its outposts at Loigny and Fougeux, where part of I Bavarian Corps was quartered. The rest of von der Tann's men were spread out between Villerand, Orgères, La Maladerie and Tanon. The cavalry screen to the south and west covered the exhausted troops, who 'either moved into enclosed cantonments, which they were often obliged to share with wounded friends and foes, or else bivouacked in the frozen fields. In the latter case, the bitter cold, the want of straw, and the very scanty nourishment prevented the soldiers from deriving much benefit from the repose.'[33]

The fighting had been extremely fierce and consequently casualties on both sides had been high. The Germans had lost 771 men killed, 2,829 wounded and 544 missing, while French losses exceeded 6,500, of whom some 2,500 were unwounded prisoners. Although dearly bought, it was a stunning victory; and Stosch and the Grand Duke were entirely aware of it, as that night they prepared to exploit their situation on the following day, by a thrust towards the Loire in furtherance of Moltke's strategic objective of the destruction of d'Aurelle's army. It seemed to Stosch that the wisest course for the French would be to fall back to the west, and in preparing his orders for the detachment for the following day, he intended to cut off this escape route, and drive the enemy back into Orléans. Reporting laconically at the end of the battle to tell Frederick Charles of its outcome, he wrote, '...if the enemy is to be pursued tomorrow, it is absolutely necessary that Second Army should attack Artenay, and undertake the protection of the Orléans – Paris road.'[34]

33 Helvig, *Operations,* p.281.
34 Hale, *People's War,* p.237.

10

Impatience at Versailles, Delusions at Tours

The hopes that Stosch and the Grand Duke entertained on 3 December of being able to carry out a movement consistent with Moltke's strategic objectives were soon to be seriously disappointed, when at 10.00 p.m. they received an explicit order from the headquarters of the Second Army which was entirely at odds with their plans.

At Versailles, Moltke's anxiety about the course of events on the Loire had been deepening. None of the advice which he had been giving seemed to have had any effect on Frederick Charles, whose failure to pursue an energetic offensive was causing great dissatisfaction. With the defeat of Ducrot's attempted breakout, matters on the lines of investment around Paris were more or less under control, and Moltke felt able to turn his attention to getting some prompt action on the Loire. He had received no further news from Stiehle, and on the morning of 2 December he resolved to do something about it. He chose not to any longer attempt to get an effective response from the Second Army to the instructions which he had been giving which were intended to lead to the destruction of the Army of the Loire; instead he proposed to give a direct order to Frederick Charles to move forward to attack the French and take Orléans. Only in this way did it appear possible to bring about a decisive engagement with the Army of the Loire. However, when he went to the King to obtain permission for this, he found him uneasy. On the basis of the information which he had received from Waldersee, it seemed to him that the bulk of the French army was directly in front of the Second Army. Owing to the numbering of the four French corps said to have been engaged at Beaune-la-Rolande, it was the King's view that there were no substantial forces in front of the detachment, and if this was so, practically the whole of the Army of the Loire stood in the path of Frederick Charles. The King raised with Moltke the risk of the French attempting a turning movement between the Rivers Loing and Yonne. This was something that had featured in Stiehle's reports to Moltke, but he had never mentioned it to the King, and he was therefore surprised when at his audience the King brought forward this suggestion in almost the very same words that Stiehle had used.

Confronted with the King's serious anxiety on the point, Moltke was able to reassure him by pointing out that there was no longer any risk that the army in Paris could undertake a serious offensive following the comprehensive defeat of Ducrot's attempted breakout. He reviewed the overall situation in some detail, and succeeded in persuading the King that it would be appropriate to issue the direct order to Second Army which he had proposed.

However, the King, who was perpetually nervous about sometimes real, but more often imaginary threats, soon afterwards learned of the report from X Corps that on the night of 30 November/1 December 'according to the assertions of the inhabitants, 20,000 men are in Montargis.' This had already been shown to be incorrect, but Second Army had not passed this on. The King now had second thoughts about the proposed order to Frederick Charles, and he dashed off a note to Moltke:

> From the annexed you will see that my opinion that the great Forest of Orléans keeps us in doubt as to what the enemy is doing (is correct) [*sic*], so that moving into the Forest of Orléans which is some 28 miles long involves at least two days fighting during which time Second Army can be marched around on the flank and rear if there are 20,000 men in Montargis. I am doubtful whether our order of today is still advisable.[1]

It was not unusual for Moltke to have to go to considerable trouble to calm his sovereign's fears. The King was perpetually anxious, even when things seemed to be going right. On this occasion Moltke sent Verdy to the King to reassure him that the dangers which he had identified were entirely illusory. The report about Montargis, Verdy explained, was based only on hearsay; it referred to a past situation, and in any case no corroboration of it had been received. The King accepted this, and duly authorised the sending of the order.

This was at 12.30 p.m. At this time the Battle of Loigny-Poupry was still raging. Had Moltke known the current situation, and had he felt able to await its outcome, he might well have amended his order to take advantage of the detachment's victory in the way that Stosch and the Grand Duke contemplated. The opportunity to cut off d'Aurelle's retreat was something that Moltke had kept constantly in mind. However, further delay in attacking the Army of the Loire was completely unacceptable, and if the only way of bringing this about promptly was to issue an order for a direct advance on Orléans, then that was what must be done.

The order was couched in simple terms that left no room for misunderstanding:

> According to a report, the bulk of the Army of the Loire is now south of Artenay. The Grand Duke, on his own, is not in a state to meet an offensive from there upon Toury. His Majesty regards it as absolutely necessary that Second Army moves without delay directly on Orléans for a decisive attack. This morning several advanced posts on the outpost line before Paris, which were lost yesterday, have been recovered.[2]

This order arrived at the headquarters of Second Army at 1.10 p.m.

Colonel Hale, in his detailed analysis of the circumstances which led up to the sending of this order, is critical of Moltke, describing his telegram to Second Army as 'extraordinary.' It was, he wrote, unsuited to the needs and requirements of the situation, pointing out that at the moment that it was sent the detachment was engaged with the real attack of the Army of the Loire, while the left wing of Second Army, extended and widely scattered, was engaged in reconnoitring, and the centre was so destitute of troops that the direct line of an advance on Paris lay almost open to the enemy. This is not entirely correct. Both IX and III Corps were in

1 Hale, *People's Army*, p.240.
2 Moltke, *Correspondance Militaire*, vol. II, pp.539–540.

position to resist any advance of this nature, but at the time when Moltke issued his order the current state of the information before him was extremely sketchy, although he did know that the detachment would be engaging the enemy on that day. What had prompted his reference to d'Aurelle's main body being south of Artenay is unclear, but it is evident that he had for the moment abandoned his plan of operating on the enemy's flank and rear, and was hoping instead that a frontal assault would not only result in the taking of Orléans, but also in breaking up the Army of the Loire in the process.

Hale went on to speculate about the source of the report that had prompted Moltke's order, noting that Hoenig believed it came from the intelligence branch. In fact, the source would have mattered little to Moltke at that moment; his impatience with Frederick Charles had reached a point where a direct instruction seemed to him to be the only way to get Second Army moving forward. Hale regarded it as 'extraordinary' that when Moltke issued the order he was not aware of the battle then raging at Loigny-Poupry:

> From midnight of 1/2 December, there was no longer any doubt at Pithiviers as to the critical state of affairs to the west of the road, there does not appear to have been any intimation to this effect to Versailles, although Stiehle himself had on the evening of 1 December told Waldersee he believed that there would be a fight at the detachment next day. And all this is even more strange because the battlefield was little more than 50 miles from Versailles. Toury, the German telegraph station on the Paris road, was only six or seven miles from the left of the battlefield. The battle commenced at about 8.00 a.m. and lasted until dark, yet nobody seems to have sent any news whatsoever to Versailles during the day about what was taking place, but between 5.00 and 6.00 p.m. Waldersee wired the King a short but very clear summary of the successful encounter. The inappropriateness of Moltke's order was clearly due to the absence of knowledge of the military situation.[3]

At Versailles, the dissatisfaction felt by Moltke with the failure of Second Army to go forward had been widely understood, and there was a general feeling of relief that Moltke had now given a direct instruction to Frederick Charles to take the offensive. Blumenthal, in his journal, recorded that the Crown Prince had told him at midday of the intention to send such an order, which news, he wrote, came to him, 'as a ray of sunshine, that the King had positively commanded Prince Frederick Charles to march and attack the Army of the Loire. It is impossible that he (Fabius Cunctator) can ignore such an order. He will have to go forwards at once.'[4]

In his diary the Crown Prince reflected on the strategic demands of the situation and how Moltke was facing them:

> In these times our military experiences from day-to-day are for all the world as they are laid down in the books. Combinations have to be made for three armies, quite separate and distinct, but still working in cooperation; successes alternate with reverses and surprises – in a word the higher strategy and tactics are the order of the day. General Count Moltke in

3 Hale, *People's War*, pp.242–243.
4 Blumenthal, *Journals*, p.212.

> all this remains always his own calm, clear headed, matter-of-fact self – a veritable worker of miracles; for me, it is a pleasure of the rarest sort to hear him make his daily report.[5]

The reaction of Frederick Charles to the order was sulky in the extreme. He sent back no fresh information to Moltke, even when he had received reports that might bear upon Moltke's decision. At the time that the order was issued he knew no more than Stosch's report that he was concentrating preparatory to a southward advance. Later in the day the King did get the telegram from Waldersee announcing the victory at Loigny-Poupry. As to this, he later recorded that he had 'telegraphed The King that a complete victory had been won' adding that the order to Frederick Charles of 2 December was given before Moltke was aware of this.[6]

Frederick Charles resolved to carry out the instructions to the letter. Although the order was peremptory, he could easily have assured himself that the King and Moltke were fully informed about the situation on the Loire when the order was issued. He could thereby have removed all possibility of a misunderstanding of the situation at Versailles; and then, if notwithstanding this further information the order was confirmed, all responsibility for the consequences rested on the right shoulders. It was also open to Frederick Charles to construe the order liberally, as merely requiring him to give up his defensive attitude and to go over to the offensive. The making of the capture of Orléans as the principal objective chimed with the view, reported by Hoenig, which was apparently held by the King, by Frederick Charles, and by the Grand Duke, that this would bring the war to an end. In fact, the importance attached by both sides to its possession was largely fictitious, occasioned perhaps by the events of the immediate past. Its capture by von der Tann was a success in terms of public relations, if not of any real strategic significance. Its recapture by the Army of the Loire was seen by the French as a huge achievement, and had a powerful effect on public morale, however, as Hale pointed out, its real value to the French was doubtful:

> Save in its proximity to Bourges, the chief arsenal, Orléans had little to recommend it in connection with offensive operations on a large scale. The Germans had originally taken it in order to keep the country between it and Paris clear of the annoyances inflicted on them by the half-trained troops and the bands of irregulars, and also on the erroneous supposition that it would serve as a sort of halfway house to Bourges and Tours.[7]

For the Germans, driving the French out of Orléans was also useful, because the position there did provide a screen behind which the French could concentrate very large forces ready to take the offensive suddenly and without warning. For each side, therefore the possession of the city had taken on a symbolic value out of all proportion to its military significance, but Moltke may well have felt that, because of this, d'Aurelle would feel compelled to risk his army in fighting for its retention.

In deciding how to execute Moltke's instructions, Frederick Charles had the benefit of regular information from Stosch as to the progress of the Battle at Loigny-Poupry. At 3.00 p.m. came

5 Crown Prince, *Diary,* p.210.
6 Hale, *People's War,* pp.242–243n.
7 Hale, *People's War,* pp.244–245.

news that the 17th and 22nd Divisions were advancing on Terminiers, while on the right the Bavarians were holding their position. At 5.00 p.m. another telegram arrived, reporting the capture of Loigny, and the advance of the 17th Division supported by I Bavarian Corps in the direction of Nonneville-Orgères. This telegram also gave important news from Poupry: '22nd Division advancing successfully on Artenay. Apparently 15th Corps in front of it.'[8] Second Army headquarters should have been in no doubt as to the extent of the victory.

Later in the evening, but still before the issue of operational orders for the following day, Frederick Charles heard from Waldersee, who was by now at the headquarters of the detachment at Janville, with an outline of the events of the day. Waldersee added that he regarded the battle as having been a brilliant victory. Then, just before the orders were distributed, there came a report from Stosch with the proposal that Second Army should attack Artenay, and cover the main road to enable the detachment to strike south-west and then south. The mood at Pithiviers was decidedly upbeat, as Kretschmann recorded in the postscript which he added to his letter to his wife: 'The Grand Duke has won a brilliant victory. The telegraph will already have carried this news before this letter. I must still go to find the Prince to take him the news and to obtain his orders.'[9]

None of this information made any impression on Frederick Charles or on Stiehle. Still sulking, and resolved to do literally what they had been told, their orders began: 'The Second Army and the Detachment of HRH the Grand Duke of Mecklenburg are to advance tomorrow to a concentrated attack against Orléans.' Manstein was to move on Artenay, Alvensleben on a wide front towards Chilleurs aux Bois and Voigts-Rhetz to a line between Villereau and Chilleurs aux Bois. The detachment would 'according to its own dispositions, advance tomorrow west of the Artenay-Orléans road for a corresponding attack,'[10] Perhaps significantly, since Second Army had not been very good at keeping Moltke informed, the order expressly required that 'All important incidents, especially any possible advance of the enemy, are to be reported direct to General Count Moltke at Versailles by telegraph, and also by means of orderly officers.'

Hale was sharply critical of this order which he considered remarkable for its terseness and incompleteness. He went on to observe:

> In this plan and scheme there is no strategy, notwithstanding the fact that on this long front of 40 miles there is plenty of scope for its employment. It is all tactics, tactics of a kind almost barbaric – those of weight and brute force. The influence of ground tactics and the selection of the ground most suitable for a force weak in infantry but strong in the other arms are alike ignored. III Corps with its numerous artillery is to be plunged, isolated, into the densest woodland, a theatre most favourable for its half-trained defenders; what becomes of the enemy is a matter of indifference, so long as the pressure on the main road suffices to force him back; and it is precisely on this line of advance that will be found, in all probability, numerous localities well prepared for defence.[11]

8 Hale, *People's War*, p.248.
9 Kretschmann, *Lettres*, p.306.
10 Hale, *People's War*, pp.246–247.
11 Hale, *People's War*, pp.247–248.

The order was sent out at 10.00 p.m., but before receiving it, Stosch had transmitted to Stiehle the plans which he had made for the detachment's operations on the following day. He then subsequently confirmed that both 16th and 17th Corps had opposed the detachment on 2 December. Still hoping that all this would lead to some modification in the orders from Frederick Charles, he waited until 4.00 a.m. the next day before issuing orders to his units; but no modification came, and he reluctantly acquiesced in what was required of him. Stiehle, in reporting to Moltke that night, unctuously offered an explanation of the orders issued for a concentric advance on Orléans:

> The offensive movement of the detachment of HRH the Grand Duke had been so arranged with General von Stosch that an endeavour should be made to secure a crossing over the Loire below Orléans, but as today's telegram seems to make great haste necessary, the endeavour will be made to reach the objective of Orléans by the direct road.[12]

D'Aurelle had been able to watch at first hand the defeat of the divisions of Martineau and Peytavin, but for a long while he had no official news from Chanzy of the fighting around Loigny. He did have a report from an ordnance officer who had seen the position at about 2.00 p.m. which did give rise to grave concerns as to the outcome. For the rest of the afternoon therefore he awaited further news from the 16th Corps with deepening anxiety. Such information as he received did nothing to relieve his mind. He sent several dispatches to Chanzy calling for a report, because he did not feel able to issue orders for the following day without knowing what had happened to his left wing.

At 11.30 he sent a message to Freycinet to the effect that they had been fighting until nightfall, but that was all that could be said of Peytavin's Division, while Maurandy had been obliged to retreat as far as Huêtre. It seemed that the enemy losses had been considerable but it was impossible to know what should be done on the following day pending news from Chanzy.

That came towards midnight when Captain Bois, from Chanzy's staff, arrived at d'Aurelle's headquarters after a journey of great difficulty; it was freezing cold and the falling snow covered the roads and made communication almost impossible during the night. He brought the sad details of the results of the day's fighting. Chanzy told him that he expected a further attack that night or the following morning, and that it was vital that 15th Corps support him.[13]

At 4.00 am on the following morning Chanzy sent a further report:

> The generals of the 17th Corps have just left here. They declared that their troops are in such a condition that it will be impossible for them to make any movement tomorrow. Many men are without shoes, no supplies have been distributed, all are exhausted. Not yet knowing your instructions, and wishing to be in the best position to carry out your wishes, I told General Guépratte, commanding 17th Corps in the absence of General de Sonis who is wounded and has disappeared, to take steps to distribute provisions and to be ready in the morning[14]

12 Hale, *People's War*, pp.249–250.
13 d'Aurelle, *Première Armée,* pp.317–318.
14 d'Aurelle, *Première Armée,* p.320.

Chanzy's first report had made up d'Aurelle's mind that he had no alternative but to retreat. At 3:40 am he wrote to Chanzy: 'In the situation in which yesterday's battle puts us, it is impossible to carry out a march on Pithiviers, or any forward movement, and we must retreat to our former positions. I am too far from you to give you effective support, and I believe that the enemy have, during the night, been concentrating artillery on my right.'[15] To Pallières, he sent instructions that the 1st Division of 15th Corps was to retreat early in the morning to Orléans to take up a position to defend the enceinte, leaving only a strong rearguard to cover the retreat. These instructions were entirely at odds with an order that Freycinet had issued over Gambetta's signature the previous afternoon at 4.00, but which d'Aurelle did not receive until the morning of 3 December:

> From today, and during the current operations, you will give your strategic orders directly to 15th, 16th, 17th, 18th and 20th Corps. Until yesterday I have directed 18th and 20th and for some time the 17th. From now on I leave this duty to you. From all the information received I do not believe that you will find, at Pithiviers or elsewhere, prolonged resistance. In my opinion the enemy is only attempting to mask his movement to the north-east, to meet Ducrot. The column which you encountered yesterday and perhaps today is no doubt an isolated detachment which seeks to delay us. But the main body must be, I repeat, making off towards Corbeil. At this moment we have reoccupied Châteaudun.[16]

This absurd communication demonstrated just how completely Freycinet and Gambetta were living in a fool's paradise. Corbeil is on the Seine, 15 miles from Paris; the ludicrous suggestion that the detachment was engaged in a rearguard action while Second Army was slinking away northward demonstrates that the ignorance of German movements prevailing at Tours was even greater than that at Versailles with regards to the precise whereabouts of the Army of the Loire. In terms of command structures there had been one other event that day; Bourbaki had finally arrived, and taken over command of 18th Corps from Billot.

At 3.45 a.m. on 3 December d'Aurelle had reported the situation to Freycinet. He began by passing on the information which he had received from Chanzy as to the extent of the defeat of 16th and 17th Corps, and went on:

> In this situation a movement on Pithiviers across the plain is no longer possible. 16th and 17th Corps need to recover after two days' efforts the latter without enjoying any success. I would add that the 3rd Division of 15th Corps has suffered to a considerable extent. The march on Pithiviers is not possible in the face of considerable enemy forces who control the plain. Not only must I give up any forward movement, but I consider that I must withdraw the two divisions at Chevilly. I have therefore given the order to General Chanzy to return to his former positions and I shall myself return to Chevilly at 10.00 a.m..[17]

Faced with the events of 2 December, d'Aurelle could see that he had no choice whatsoever but to fall back on the positions which had been prepared for the defence of Orléans. Even Freycinet

15 d'Aurelle, *Premiere Armée*, p.322.
16 d'Aurelle, *Premiere Armée*, p.321.
17 Freycinet, *Guerre*, pp.155–156.

in his later account was not prepared to dispute the wisdom of this directly, merely posing the question: 'Could the position at Artenay still have been defended? It is impossible for me to say.' He did though seize on a quotation from an English correspondent who had been at the Prussian headquarters, and who later wrote that he regarded it as mysterious, '…that General de Paladines retreated from Artenay on 3 December, in place of defending the position for a further day, having an army almost twice the size of his adversaries.'[18]

18 Freycinet, *Guerre*, p.156.

11

The Second Battle of Orléans: 3 December

Whether, in considering Moltke's order for 3 December, Frederick Charles had simply taken his duty to be to carry them out without further consideration, or whether, irritated by the implied censure, 'he determined to give vent to his resentment by interpreting it according to its exact wording' is a question which Colonel Hale raised, but did not answer. Moltke's order was clear enough; if Frederick Charles did not feel able to check with Moltke that the order held good in the light of the Battle of Loigny-Poupry, then he could understandably feel that his own orders must comply with Moltke's instructions to the letter, and it is therefore hardly necessary to consider whether he did so in a spirit of petulance.[1]

Frederick Charles and Stiehle were of course perfectly aware that the information available to Moltke was extremely limited, as indeed was their own. Second Army had reported to Versailles only the sketchiest outline of the positions occupied by the Army of the Loire, and had not passed on any news of the detachment's battle. Apart, therefore, from a brief report by Waldersee to the King to the effect that a complete victory had been won, Versailles was in the dark about the situation. And neither Moltke nor Frederick Charles had much information about the defensive works that the French had been building to defend Orléans, although they were aware of the problems presented by the forest that lay before Second Army.

In considering the overall situation as it appeared to them on the evening of 2 December Frederick Charles and Stiehle had not had to take account of any significant activity directly in their front during the day. Neither the 1st Division of 15th Corps, nor 18th and 20th Corps, had made any important movement, and the French still had only a token presence at Montargis and in the Loing Valley, rather than the large force which had so alarmed the King. During the day Manstein had moved off with IX Corps in response to his instructions to take over from the detachment the responsibility for covering the Orléans – Paris high road, and by nightfall he was concentrated to the east of the road, well placed to advance on the following morning to the attack by way of Artenay. Alvensleben, with III Corps, was in position around Pithiviers ready to advance, and Voigts-Rhetz, whose X Corps was to act as a reserve, was concentrated around Boynes and Beaune-la-Rolande. Schmidt, with the 6th Cavalry Division, would follow the right wing of Second Army from Châtillon le Roi, while the army's left flank would be

1 Hale, *People's War*, p.245.

protected by the 1st Cavalry Division, reinforced by four infantry battalions and a battery taken from X Corps, which would operate in the country between the Yonne and the Loing.

Having decided simply to carry out Moltke's order to the letter, it may have seemed immaterial to Frederick Charles that he had little intelligence on which to base his own orders, but he was certainly not well informed:

> Rarely has any leader entered so completely blindfolded into a battle as did Prince Frederick Charles enter the second Battle of Orléans. Of even the general disposition of the enemy, he knew very little; of the position of even the larger hostile units, such as the Army Corps, he was equally in ignorance, and he refused to accept as right the approximately correct information furnished to him by the detachment. He was aware that, for at least a fortnight, a vast amount of labour had been expended in putting the position he was about to attack into a state of defence, and that in it were heavy guns; but of the system of works, he could see only the fringe.[2]

Nor was he in any hurry to find out things for himself; there was no reason why he should not have paid a visit to the headquarters of the detachment, but 'possibly the prospect of an interview with a Royal Prince he personally disliked, and with a chief staff officer who held views opposite to his own, was not especially attractive.'[3]

The advance of Second Army would be led by Alvensleben, whose task for 3 December would be to advance down the road which led from Pithiviers to Orléans, marching through Chilleurs aux Bois, aiming to reach Loury by the end of the day. Once it had passed through Chilleurs, III Corps would plunge into the Forest of Orléans. Although Second Army did not have much information about the enemy positions, it was the continuing belief at the headquarters that a large part of the Army of the Loire was still to be found in position between Chilleurs and Bellegarde, which if correct meant that Alvensleben's mission was going to be extremely hazardous. The actual positions of the troops which he would immediately face were, however, spread wide. The 1st Division of 15th Corps was covering a front of nearly a dozen miles in order to protect the various entrances to the Forest of Orléans. On the left, 1,850 men and 8 guns were posted at Villereau; Minot, with 8,400 infantry and 12 guns stood at Neuville aux Bois; the main body of 8,500 men and 38 guns, which was accompanied by Pallières, was at Chilleurs aux Bois fronting towards Santeau. Finally, on the right of the division, 2,070 men with 6 guns covered the next road at Courcy aux Bois. Three and a half miles to the east, also on a road, was the left flank of 20th Corps, which, with 18th Corps beyond it, faced north-east towards Beaune and Montargis.

Hale commented on the orders given to Alvensleben:

> As the Prince, when dispatching III Corps on its mission, believed that the French were in very strong force on its left, with troops also in strength at Chilleurs, the course he adopted was certainly a departure from his usual caution. In fact, his whole leading during the two days was that of a man who, forced by superior authority to adopt a line of action he regarded as both dangerous and hazardous, went recklessly ahead, regardless of possible consequences.[4]

2 Hale, *People's War*, p.251.
3 Hale, *People's War*, p.252.
4 Hale, *People's War*, pp.253–254.

Alvensleben himself was under no illusions about the difficulties of his task, which would increase the further south he went. It was clear to him that once he was in the forest, he would be severely hampered in the use of his artillery, while if the advance of the rest of Second Army was checked, he might find himself isolated in front of the fortifications of Orléans. He had with him 84 guns. Taking all these through the forest roads, which were certain to be obstructed, would be a difficult task, while the artillery teams could easily be crippled by a few sharpshooters concealed in the trees. To leave them behind would require the detachment of a strong escort. He explained his position:

> We are ordered to beat the enemy, so we will beat him; the position of the general is not usually with the outposts, at least not in wooded country of this kind, but since we cannot command unless we are at the outposts, we will go there. The general in command should not be under the fire of the enemy, and I shall only go there if necessary, but if I find myself there by chance it will not be proper for me to ride away.[5]

Alvensleben assessed that he faced one enemy division on the Loury road and one and a half corps to the east of it which was a very close estimate. He later reflected on the situation which confronted his corps:

> I went, I was fully aware, into a den, of which the door closed of itself after my last man had passed Chilleurs. With every step forward diminished any chance of support, and also the possibility of withdrawing or of sending any news about myself, or of receiving news; and if I did fortunately succeed in arriving at the southern edge the situation of my corps before the city could become very unpleasant. No use was there in previous calculations and speculations. I knew nothing as to the state of affairs south of the forest: of only one thing was I sure, the impossibility of employing all my guns. And was it quite out of the question that the Prince's attack might be repulsed, that I should be for one or two days in front of the bridgehead and with the enemy on my line of retreat? In this case we should certainly hold out, but my corps could hardly escape a catastrophe.[6]

III Corps set off before dawn from its positions around Pithiviers, and by 9.30 a.m. was pushing south down the road to Santeau. Pallières sent forward his main body to try to hold the enemy there, 2 miles north of the entrance to the forest. Alvensleben's advance was led by Buddenbrock's 6th Division; as soon as the French were encountered at 10.30 a.m., the divisional artillery, which was moving just behind the leading infantry battalions, deployed on either side of the road, with the 12th Brigade on its right. It was hard going for the gunners. The ground had frozen during the night and some snow had fallen. With the divisional artillery posted between the road and the railway embankment, there was no room for the corps artillery. Colonel von Dresky, its commander, described his situation:

> A reconnaissance that was made from the top of a windmill informed us that on the south-west of the village of La Brosse there was a more excellent position, whence that which

5 Hale, *People's War*, pp.254–255.
6 Hale, *People's War*, p.255.

> the enemy occupied at Santeau could be taken in the flank, and from which it was also possible to sweep all the ground which extended to the Forest of Orléans. In order to get to this position, it was necessary to cross the embankment of the railway (which was not yet completed) from Pithiviers to Orléans .... A little to the south of La Brosse there is a small wood. I had ordered the horse brigade [of artillery] to take up its position between the wood and La Brosse, while the field brigade [of artillery] was to stand to the south of them. By this arrangement I covered the front of my batteries with an excellent protection, the embankment of the railway. The 2nd Regiment of Dragoons formed up to protect our left flank, while the railway embankment and the small wood were occupied by some detachments of infantry belonging to the 6th Division .... As soon as the field brigade opened fire the enemy's artillery, which was posted at Santeau, abandoned the fight and retired, under an ample escort, to a position situated between Moulin de l'Épine and Chilleurs, whence it renewed the action against the core artillery with three batteries of guns and one of mitrailleuses; this did not continue long, for it soon retired farther yet.[7]

By noon the Prussians had 78 guns in action. In the artillery duel that ensued the French were heavily outgunned, and their artillery was so knocked about that Pallières withdrew his guns, ordering them back to Orléans down the Loury road while their retreat was covered by the infantry. Buddenbrock followed them, advancing to the west of La Brosse, over the line of the unfinished Orléans-Pithiviers railway, while on his left the 5th Division moved through Santeau down the main road, closely supported by the artillery. Alvensleben's men continued to push the French southwards, and soon Chilleurs was abandoned, and Pallières fell back to the edge of the forest where he intended to make a stand; but the speed of the advance was such that he was quite unable to do so, and he fell back down the road into the forest. The retreating infantry were sped on their way by Dresky's artillery:

> When I saw the French infantry leave Chilleurs, I rode, after having given a general order that the fire was to be directed on them, up to the 4th Light Battery, whose leader, Captain Muller, had been through a course of instruction at the School of Gunnery, and had learned to shoot on a good principle. I turned to his men and said, 'For every shot which you throw directly into the enemy's infantry, I will give you three thalers.' A gunner replied, 'That will cost you a lot of money, Colonel; we shoot pretty well in this battery.' The first shot went over, the second was short, then seven hit directly, which was, without doubt, the principal reason that the column broke up. I paid my 21 thalers in the midst of the cheers of the battery.[8]

It was a striking example of the effectiveness of the German artillery, which was demonstrated time and again during the course of the Franco-Prussian War. If Frederick Charles was, as Hale wrote, conducting the current battle without strategy, but employing only tactics of the most brutal kind; it was his artillery which enabled him to do so successfully. By using their artillery so effectively, the Germans had kept their casualties to the minimum, as the official history pointed out: 'On nearly every occasion the enemy had abandoned the field directly after

7 Prince Kraft zu Hohenlohe, *Letters on Artillery* (London: Edward Stanford, 1890) pp.104–106.
8 Hohenlohe, *Letters on Artillery*, p.107.

the deployment of the German artillery, and it was only at St Lye and Neuville aux Bois that he held out until evening.'[9]

At 1.00 p.m. Alvensleben sent a message to the headquarters of the Second Army:

> The enemy has had in action 15th Corps' 1st Division in front of Santeau in a strongly fortified position, and has shown three batteries and two mitrailleuse batteries. He has been driven back from Santeau, and he retired to the position of Chilleurs, and has also abandoned this. The wood is being attacked. One gun taken, 200 prisoners. Our loss small up to the present.[10]

However, this message did not reach Frederick Charles until 7.00 p.m.

Alvensleben gave his troops a short breathing space, while he reorganised the corps for its advance into the forest. Recognising the limited effectiveness of artillery there, he left outside the forest the six batteries of the corps artillery, and the four batteries of the 5th Division; these were protected by the 48th Regiment and two battalions of the 24th Regiment. With the rest of his force, which included the 24 guns of the 6th Division, Alvensleben resumed his advance at about 3.00 p.m. The 5th Division moved along the unfinished railway leading due south from La Rive du Bois, at the entrance to the forest. At the same time, to the west, the 6th Division marched down the road to Loury. The French had made the road impassable in several places and as a result the advanced parties of the 6th Division did not reach the southern edge of the extensive clearing near Loury until 6.00 p.m., by which time darkness had fallen. The German troops were in high spirits, buoyed up by the events of the morning. At the time the rattle of rifle fire had been heard from the direction of Neuville aux Bois, outside the forest. Alvensleben considered it unwise to halt until the meaning of the firing could be ascertained, as it was evidently not merely an outpost affair, so he sent his cavalry to investigate while covering his flank and rear with infantry. As the rifle fire increased in intensity, guns could also be heard. By the time that Loury was reached, darkness had fallen. There was not a light to be seen and all that could be done was to place outposts on the approaches around the village from the west, south, and east. That done, the rest of Alvensleben's troops settled down for the night in and around the town.[11]

It had become apparent to Alvensleben almost immediately that he could not hope to exercise effective control of the operation unless he was on the spot when a crisis developed, and accordingly he rode with the leading units of the 6th Division. He was very conscious of the dangers of his position, but it was only to his chief staff officer, Colonel von Voigts-Rhetz, that he spoke of his fears. By 6.15 p.m. the sound of firing from the north-west had died out but some enemy troops had been reported to the east. A little later there was a brief engagement between the outposts fronting towards Neuville and parties of French troops, but the French were soon driven off, and the rest of the night passed quietly.

When Pallières found it impossible to make a stand on the edge of the forest he fell back in accordance with d'Aurelle's orders as far south as the Avenue de Nibelle, one of the roads which criss-crossed the forest and which ran east–west. There, he turned off with his infantry in a

9 *Official Account*, vol. III, p.354.
10 Hale, *People's War*, p.266.
11 *Official Account*, vol. III, p.347.

westerly direction; he sent the artillery on down the road through Loury to Orléans. D'Aurelle had directed Pallières to retreat on St Lye and Chevilly. Although there was a field telegraph station at Neuville in contact with d'Aurelle, Pallières does not appear to have informed d'Aurelle of the advance of III Corps. Had he done so, d'Aurelle would no doubt have given instructions that the German advance should be halted, if possible, at Loury. As it was, Pallières's movement to the west left this sector entirely unprotected. It was a decision which, since he was aware of the line of advance of Alvensleben's leading troops, was surprising.

On the right of III Corps, Manstein had assembled the troops of IX Corps at Château Gaillard on the morning of 3 December and had dispatched a detachment under Colonel von Winckler in the direction of St Lye. This consisted of a squadron of cavalry, an infantry regiment, a rifle battalion, and a heavy battery. As he approached the farm of La Tour, Winckler ran into strong columns of French infantry advancing between the farm and the village of Mauregard. Winckler deployed one battalion across the line of the old Roman road supported by the battery. At first these were unable to check the French advance, but the attempt to outflank the German left from Mauregard failed as a result of the strong resistance of the German troops there followed by a counter-attack of three companies. By 4.00 p.m. the French had had enough and fell back to St Germain, closely pursued by Winckler's men. Darkness however had begun to fall and there was a heavy snowstorm, and Winckler prudently retreated to a position behind La Tour.[12] The French troops which he had encountered were those of Minot, whose orders had been to hold Neuville as long as he could and then to fall back on St Lye. By this movement Pallières hoped to be able to cover his own march westward along the Avenue de Nibelle.

Winckler's retreat for the night, however did not mark the end of Minot's difficulties. In the plan for the advance of Second Army, X Corps had been designated as the army reserve, and its operations for the day had involved it in a move westwards to a position in which it could support the advances of both III and IX Corps. Voigts-Rhetz's main body had reached Chilleurs aux Bois; when, however, Kraatz, with the advance guard, heard of the engagement at La Tour, he decided to push on to Neuville, at which he launched a battalion in an attack which, deprived of artillery support by the fall of night, was unable to force its way into the village. Kraatz, therefore, postponed any further assault until the following day. Meanwhile by about 4.00 p.m. Pallières had reached a point due south of Neuville, and, through a peasant, he sent a message to Minot that instead of taking the road to St Lye, which he knew to be a bad one, and on which Minot might be attacked in flank, he could instead take the road to Rebrechien, by which he might gain the Loury-Orléans road before the Germans got there. It is unclear whether the message was ever received; but Minot had already decided on this course, and set off on a night march through the forest. At this point he was not aware that the Germans had penetrated into the forest. Reaching a fork in the road not far south of Neuville, in the darkness and in a heavy snowstorm, his column, led by his 12 guns, chose the wrong road; the one which led to Loury, rather than that to Rebrechien. As a result, at about 8.00 p.m. they ran into the outposts that Alvensleben had posted around his bivouacs at Loury. The sudden appearance of the French gave Kretschmann, who had been sent by Frederick Charles to accompany III Corps, a nasty shock when he was seeking quarters for the night:

12 *Official Account*, vol. III, p.347.

> I was just in the process of finding a stable, when a salvo of shells bursting in the village so close to me that I jumped into a house .... French troops had suddenly appeared close to our village; they ran into our outposts and there was a scattering of fire. The night gave me an ominous feeling; one could only hear the whistling of bullets and the crackle of rifle fire.[13]

Not surprisingly there was confusion on both sides, but the better disciplined German troops soon recovered, while the French column disintegrated, the infantry fleeing in the direction of Orléans. The French gunners struggled heroically to save their artillery, but only managed to get seven of the guns away. On the following morning the patrols sent out by III Corps found the other five guns abandoned close to their positions.

Meanwhile, Manstein's task for 3 December was altogether more straightforward. His advance guard moved off early from Château Gaillard down the main road in the direction of Artenay, and soon encountered enemy resistance there and also at Assas to the east of the road – this came from troops of Martineau's Division of 15th Corps. Manstein deployed, sending the 85th Regiment west of the road towards Dambron and the 84th Regiment, with a horse artillery battery, to the east of the road to outflank the French at Assas, where a powerful force of artillery was firing on the high road at the main body of IX Corps as it moved south. The German artillery clattered down the road and, deploying on either side of it, came into action causing the French to pull out of Assas. The German artillery moved on south, and soon found fresh targets in the form of the rest of Martineau's artillery, which had been posted to the north-west of Artenay. Manstein's artillery was quickly assisted by seven batteries of the 22nd Division and the 2nd Cavalry Division which opened fire at about 10.00 a.m. from a position south-east of Poupry. The outposts of the 22nd Division had, before dawn that morning, fallen back towards Baigneaux in the face of a strong French reconnaissance towards the copse north of Poupry, but returned to the village before 9.00 a.m. and were joined there by the 2nd Cavalry Division.[14]

With 90 German guns pounding his troops in and around Artenay, Martineau could not be expected to hold on for very long; and he soon withdrew first his artillery and then his 1st Brigade down the road to La Croix Briquet; his 2nd Brigade retreated to Arblay Farm. They were closely pursued by the 11th Regiment, which occupied Artenay after a brief engagement, capturing numerous French stragglers in the streets of the village. Further on the right the 85th Regiment took possession of Autroches, while other detachments advanced on Arblay Farm.

Frederick Charles had been present to witness the fighting around Artenay. It seemed to him that the slowly retreating French forces would put up a stiff resistance at the Forest of Orléans and he sent a summons to the detachment to push forward the 22nd Division upon Chevilly village, while the 17th Division advanced on Château Chevilly which lies to the west. What Frederick Charles wanted from the detachment was support for IX Corps particularly with artillery. Meanwhile the 2nd and 6th Cavalry Divisions advanced to Autroches. The German advance meant that they were approaching the first of the prepared positions which formed part of the fortified camp of Orléans. D'Aurelle had intended to meet the German advance in this position, but the speed of Manstein's movements southwards meant that Martineau could not avoid becoming engaged with the Germans further north.

13 Kretschmann, *Letters*. p.309.
14 *Official Account*, vol. III, p.348.

After half an hour's rest, X Corps resumed its advance southwards at approximately 12.30. The 36th Brigade, which was joined by the batteries at Artenay, marched with the 11th Regiment along the high road and railway and the 85th Regiment from Autroches, in the direction of La Croix Briquet; the rest of the corps, with the 35th Brigade on the left wing, followed in reserve. Meanwhile to the west of the high road the brigades of the 22nd Division, led by the 13th Hussars, advanced in a southerly direction past Murville and Lille farm, while the batteries which left their positions at Poupry somewhat later together with the 2nd Cavalry Division, accompanied the advance of the infantry on the left. As the leading infantry columns of the 22nd Division approached La Croix Briquet, a heavy artillery barrage fell on them from the artillery of 15th Corps, which had taken a position on the heights to the north of the village. Martineau held both the Bavilliers Mill to the west of the road and Arblay Farm on the east, and the position was strong enough to warrant the postponement of any infantry assault until the German artillery had done its work.

Manstein deployed his guns on the slope south of Artenay, firing down the main road, on either side of which infantry units moved forward to La Grange Farm and the Château of Auvilliers. For a time, a stalemate developed, as the respective gun lines sought to gain the upper hand in a prolonged artillery duel. Manstein's artillery commander, Major General von Puttkamer, was frustrated by the cover enjoyed by the French artillery firing behind trees in their front, until he brought four batteries around the south-west of the château. There they were joined by batteries from the 2nd Cavalry Division and soon after were also supported by the artillery of the 22nd Division firing from Lille Farm. Taken in enfilade, and overwhelmed by the now usual concentration of German artillery fire, the French gunners ceased firing at about 2.00. Without the protection afforded by their gunners, the French infantry were unable to resist the ensuing assault by the 85th Regiment which stormed the d'Auvilliers Mill and by the 84th Regiment which forced its way into the burning buildings of Arblay Farm.[15]

With the capture of d'Auvilliers Mill, Manstein was able to deploy five batteries there, and under their outflanking barrage the French defenders of La Croix Briquet fell back before the assault of the 11th Regiment. On their right flank the French infantry took up a strong position under the cover of some naval guns posted at Andeglou. The French infantry were briefly emboldened to counter-attack, before the arrival of four batteries of German artillery on the heights between Arblay Farm and the high road compelled them to retreat behind their own gun line, which for the time being prevented any further German advance. La Croix Briquet had fallen soon after 3.00; by then Frederick Charles had already laid down final objectives for IX Corps at 2.45, issuing an order that called for a substantial further advance:

> I shall consider today's work finished when, after a thorough preparation by artillery, the village of Chevilly and the angle of the forest east of it are in possession of IX Corps, and are, under all circumstances, held by them. The 17th and 22nd Infantry divisions will similarly, after a bombardment, capture the Chevilly Château and the angle of the forest south of the village, and hold firmly onto them. If the day is not long enough the attacks must be continued after dark.[16]

15 *Official Account*, vol. III, pp.349–350.
16 Hale, *People's War*, p.260.

This was a hugely ambitious requirement. The French positions were strongly fortified and in the most favourable circumstances were always going to be a tough nut to crack. The order called for a night attack through forest upon prepared positions some two miles away. Wittich received the order from Frederick Charles with great concern. His division was to take part in the attack on the village while the 17th Division moved on the château. Wittich sent Lieutenant von Kleist to Manstein's headquarters in order to attack in concert with the IX Corps attack on the village, and he also notified Tresckow of his plans. The latter's 17th Division had driven back a forward movement by the enemy without needing any support and was now ready to attack the château.[17]

With daylight on the short December day coming to an end it soon became clear that a night attack was going to be unavoidable if Frederick Charles's order was to be complied with. In spite of a heavy bombardment by the German artillery, the French heavy artillery at Andeglou remained in action until after darkness had fallen. The German infantry had however succeeded in taking two farms to the east and south-east of La Croix Briquet.

On the western flank of the German advance, von der Tann had had the least demanding task for the day. His principal objective was to cover the right against any attempt by Chanzy to renew his offensive of the previous day, although after the hammering taken by 16th and 17th Corps this was unlikely. The French had hung on to Villepion overnight, but only to cover their retreat towards Patay. Bavarian patrols probed towards Faverolles and Echelles while the main body of the corps moved down to Lumeau to await further orders. At 11.00 von der Tann was instructed that his 2nd division should follow the 17th Division as a general reserve, while the rest of the corps was to march to Sougy to guard against any flank attack by Chanzy.[18]

In accordance with these instructions the Bavarians moved forward but had no contact with the enemy until after 3.00, when the advanced patrols of the 1st Brigade found a substantial concentration of French troops in position north of Trogny. These were, however, forced to retire by heavy artillery fire from the batteries of the 1st Division and the 17th Division. Although the French halted and put up a stiffer resistance in a prepared position to the south of Trogny, it was not long before they were forced out of the entrenchments there. There was also a short lived advance from l'Encormes towards Sougy. The French troops which the Bavarians were facing here came from Barry's Division of 16th Corps, and their movement was intended to cover the southwards retreat of the main body and offer some support to 15th Corps on the high road. Chanzy's intention was that Barry should, by the effective use of his artillery, hold up any further German advance until nightfall.[19]

Frederick Charles had not taken the trouble to let the headquarters of the detachment know where he was to be found during 3 December, other than to say that he would go to Chilleurs aux Bois after the fighting ended. Until 1.00 p.m. he was unaware of the orders given by Stosch to the detachment, and the extent to which these orders departed from those which he had himself given. For a long time, he devoted little attention to the movements of the detachment. At the time his headquarters was little more than a mile from those of the Grand Duke, but he made no effort to arrange a meeting. It was at about 1.00 p.m. that Frederick Charles sent Stosch an order setting out the way in which the 17th and 22nd Divisions should be employed.

17 Wittich, *Journal de Guerre*, pp.233–234.
18 Helvig, *Operations*, p.284.
19 Chanzy, *Deuxième Armée*, p.82.

He still had firmly in his mind the notion that the detachment was making far too much of the resistance of the enemy; in particular, he did not believe that it had been engaged with the main body of d'Aurelles left wing at Loigny-Poupry. 'Believe me,' Frederick Charles said, 'the Grand Duke has nothing of any importance in front of him.'[20]

Meanwhile Stosch and the Grand Duke had been considering the way in which Second Army was setting about the advance on Orléans, and in particular the orders issued to the 17th and 22nd Divisions for the proposed night attack on Chevilly. Stosch decided that the situation called for a personal meeting with Frederick Charles, and obtained the Grand Duke's approval that he should ride over to the headquarters of Second Army. This he found at the village of Creuzy, some 3 miles from Chevilly. Stosch told the Prince of the current position of the forces of the detachment, and of the movements of the French left wing under Chanzy, reporting that enemy forces of at least the strength of one division were threatening his right flank, as a result of which the 1st Bavarian Division was now engaged with it.

In an effort to make Frederick Charles realise the true extent of the forces which had been opposed to the detachment on the previous day, he told him that they had faced not only 16th and 17th Corps, but also a large part of 15th Corps. By now I Bavarian Corps had, he said, been reduced to the strength of a weak division, while the 17th Division was still engaged with the 3rd Division of 15th Corps. Frederick Charles listened carefully to Stosches exposition, but at the end of it said:

> Many prisoners of many regiments of the 3rd Division of 15th Corps have been captured in Artenay; the Grand Duke has made a mistake, this division cannot be opposite to him; he has nothing much opposed to him, and has been deceived by a demonstration, and again allowed himself to be drawn away from the real point of attack.[21]

Stosch, of course, knew this to be absolute nonsense, but he could see that there was little point in getting into an argument with an individual as stubborn as Frederick Charles. He might have been forgiven for doing so; as a man who had just so successfully fought the Battle of Loigny-Poupry, he was entitled to be seriously offended. But time was of the essence, so Stosch went on to warn the Prince that it was impossible in the light of the existing situation of the detachment to tell whether it would be possible to continue on the following day with the convergent advance on Orléans, which must depend on von der Tann's ability to see off the threat from the strong hostile forces advancing from l'Encorme.

Frederick Charles dismissed this, saying pointedly: 'They are only *franc-tireurs* and *gardes mobiles*; Orléans is the parole; the detachment will advance against it tomorrow with all its forces.' Stosch was again careful not to argue directly with the Prince, though he was perfectly aware that the Bavarians were at that time facing Barry's division of Chanzy's Corps, which included more troops from *régiments de marche* than *gardes mobiles*, and that the 3rd Division of 15th Corps was indeed in action against his left. Instead, he turned to the question of the proposed night attack on Chevilly which was, he pointed out, extremely dangerous. He must have put his point with considerable emphasis, for Frederick Charles, without making any further comment, turned to Stiehle and countermanded his orders for the attack. He then,

20 Hale, *People's War*, p.261.
21 Hale, *People's War*, p.262.

perhaps feeling that he had been behaving discourteously, turned back to Stosch, 'Night attacks are always bad, they should only be undertaken when success is certain: I may not run any risk. Under the present circumstances I am not certain of success. I had relied on the flanking movement of the whole of the detachment. The Grand Duke will remain for the night in his present position.' Stosch had won his point; satisfied, he swung into his saddle, and was already riding away when Frederick Charles called after him: 'But tomorrow we must be in Orléans.' To this, Stosch replied only: 'It will not be our fault if we are not,' and made his way back to his headquarters. He was certainly entitled to congratulate himself on his restraint during the discussion, as a result of which he had obtained the cancellation of the night attack.

This account of the conversation was expressly confirmed by Stosch himself.[22] Colmar von der Goltz, however, in his account of the Loire campaign, offered a rather different description of the interview, which could only have been based on what he learned from either Frederick Charles or Stiehle:

> After it had already begun to get dark, General von Stosch, the chief of staff of the detachment, came to the commander-in-chief and represented to him that the Grand Duke's troops, exhausted by the severe fight of the previous day, and tired out by today's marching with fighting, were hardly able to take part in a determined attack on the Chevilly position. The Field Marshal felt himself compelled to postpone to the next day the capture of Chevilly and the edge of the forest.[23]

Given the surrounding circumstances and the detailed description of the interview provided by Stosch, and expressly confirmed by him to Hoenig, it is not difficult to accept his account as being the more accurate.

The counter order for the attack on Chevilly came as a profound relief to Wittich and Tresckow, whose troops were already preparing for the assault, which was within 15 minutes of being launched. The order read only: 'Discontinue the attack on Chevilly today. The troops will take shelter in their present position.'[24] As it so happened, however, the French pulled out of Chevilly just as the counter order reached Wittich. He was certainly not prepared to comply with the suggestion that his troops remained where they were:

> There was nothing for my men but the bare plain covered with wet snow, a bivouac without straw, wood, water or food. My troops had been fighting throughout the whole of 2 December; the leading troops had arrived at 10.00 p.m. that night, the last at one in the morning, in the icy bivouac at Anneux, where they had little to eat; they had fallen in before daybreak and had been in fighting formation all day, without taking into account the duty that must now fall to the advance guard; so I had determined to go back to Poupry [5 miles] for the night and come back next morning. I waited, however, for the receipt of information from my cavalry regiment, which I had ordered to reconnoitre towards

22 Stosch, *Denkwurdigkeiten*, pp.213–216.
23 Hale, *People's War*, p.262.
24 Wittich, *Journal*, p.234.

> Chevilly and the château after the artillery fire had ceased. Reports came in from it that the enemy had evacuated both the village and the château.[25]

As a result, both his division and the 17th Division were able to pass the night in shelter there.

D'Aurelle had finally left Chevilly at about 5.30, but it was not until 3.00 on the following morning that he established his headquarters at Saran, some 5 miles north of Orléans; and there, he and Borel, his chief of staff, reviewed the situation. On the road, he had passed large numbers of Martineau's troops falling back in disorder to Orléans, and when he got to Saran he finally received news of Pallières and of his retreat from his position at Chilleurs aux Bois. His right wing, consisting of the 18th and 20th Corps had, he knew, been badly shaken by its defeat at Beaune-la-Rolande and from which it had not recovered; Bourbaki, who was now in command of both corps, had at 7.00 p.m. received orders to concentrate to his left to support Pallières, but so far as d'Aurelle knew these corps had not yet been able to take any part in the Battle of Orléans. As for his left wing under Chanzy, he was aware that 16th and 17th Corps had been badly beaten the day before at Loigny-Poupry, and was in retreat; and he had seen with his own eyes the collapse of his centre on the high road. In the absence of any news of Pallières it seemed to d'Aurelle that he had no choice but to abandon Orléans, and to put the Loire between himself and his enemy. Borel emphatically agreed, telling him: 'Your troops will not hold, the demoralisation is too great, and, if you wait too long to order the evacuation of Orléans, you will expose yourself to a disaster much greater than the loss of this town.'[26] D'Aurelle believed that it was, above all, necessary to take a prompt decision, and there still being no information as to Pallières's Division, at 4.00 am he telegraphed Tours, announcing 'the sad and cruel necessity' of evacuating Orléans.' After recounting the events of the last three days, he stated bluntly that he regarded the defence of Orléans as impossible. 'If we had time before as to reorganise and pull ourselves together, this could be attempted; but the enemy will be on us tomorrow and I must, sadly, but with a profound conviction, repeat to you that our troops, sorely tried and demoralised by the last two days, will not hold.' He went on to inform Gambetta that Chanzy's two corps would retreat by Beaugency and Blois and 18th and 20th Corps by Gien, while 15th Corps would cross the Loire at Orléans; the army would thus retreat into the Sologne.[27]

Predictably, Gambetta and Freycinet were appalled to receive d'Aurelle's telegram. Freycinet dispatched at 5.00 a.m. an immediate response which d'Aurelle later justly described as haughty and angry in tone:

> Your dispatch of tonight has caused me a painful stupefaction. I can see, in the facts you recount, nothing which seems to justify the resolution of despair which you report .... You still have 200,000 men ready to fight if their leaders knew how, through their own example and the firmness of their attitude, to strengthen their courage and their patriotism. The evacuation of which you speak will be both for itself and beyond its military consequences an immense disaster.

25 Wittich, *Journal*, p.234.
26 D'Aurelle, *Première Armée,* p.333.
27 D'Aurelle, *Première Armée,* pp.334–345.

Freycinet suggested that d'Aurelle should draw in the 18th and 20th Corps, while the other three corps closed up.[28]

D'Aurelle was not going to put up with lectures of this kind, replying crisply at 8.00 a.m.: 'I am on the spot and better able to judge the situation. It is with no less pain than yours that I decided to take this extreme step.' He went on to add, in an echo of the advice given by Borel: 'In spite of all the efforts that we have been able to make, Orléans will inevitably fall into the enemy's hands tonight or tomorrow. It will be a great misfortune; but the only means of avoiding a still greater catastrophe is to have the courage to make a sacrifice while there is still time.' Then, satisfying himself that his orders were being carried out, d'Aurelle left Saran and made his way to Orléans.[29]

At around 10.00 a.m. he learned of the arrival of Pallières with 1st Division. He was still unaware of the chaotic nature of the retreat from Chilleurs during the previous evening, and in the presence of Pallières and the strongest division of the army, his spirits rose. At 11.55 he telegraphed Gambetta again: 'I am changing my plans; directing 16th and 17th Corps on Orléans, calling in 18th and 20th, organising resistance, on the spot in Orléans.'[30] This had crossed with a telegram from Freycinet grudgingly acknowledging d'Aurelle's decision to evacuate the city; when he got the news of d'Aurelle's change of heart, Freycinet sent a joyful response at 1.35 p.m. 'Expressing complete faith that you will be able to put up an effective resistance behind your naval batteries,' and announcing that Gambetta would himself leave for Orléans in 30 minutes.

28 d'Aurelle, *Première Armée*, pp.339–340; Freycinet, *Guerre*, pp165–166.
29 d'Aurelle, *Première Armée*, pp.341–342.
30 d'Aurelle, *Première Armée*, p.344; Freycinet, *Guerre*, p.168.

Fierce fighting at the Château at Villepoin, 1 December 1870, by Pallandre.

General Rousseau and his troops before the heights of Morée, 1 December 1870, by Pallandre.

Charette's troops at Patay, by André.

The Pontifical Zouaves charge at Loigny, 2 December 1870, by Pallandre.

An episode from the Battle of Loigny-Poupry, by Grolleron.

Prince Frederick Charles at Orléans, by Hünten.

French troops attack the Bavarian 3rd Brigade at Loigny, by Zimmer.

The Grand Duke of Mecklenburg at Orléans, by Zimmer.

Peytavin's Division at Loigny-Poupry, by Pallandre.

Bavarian troops gather around a fire on the night of 3/4 December 1870, by Zimmer.

The band of the 3rd Bavarian Infantry Regiment under fire at Loigny, by Zimmer.

Von der Tann in Orléans, December 1870, by Birkmeyer.

The Bavarian 4th Chevaulegers charge at Loigny, by Zimmer.

The Archduke of Mecklenburg and his staff at Orléans, 4 December 1870, by Zimmer.

The French evacuation of Orléans, 4 December 1870, by Pallandre.

The retreat of the French 15th Corps on the morning of 6 December 1870, by Pallandre.

Bavarian staff officers discuss orders, 7–8 December 1870, by Zimmer.

The bridge over the Loire at Beaugency.

The combat at Changé, 11 December 1870, by Pallandre.

The charge of the Algerian éclaireurs at Vancé, 15 December 1870, by Pallandre.

The combat at Alençon, 15 December 1870, by Pallandre.

The French delaying action at Vendôme, 15 December 1870, by Pallandre.

A Bavarian firing line, December 1870, by Zimmer.

A view of Le Mans, 1870.

French prisoners of war in Orléans, December 1870, by Zimmer.

Combat in the streets of Le Mans, elements of the French 16th and 17th Corps, by Pallandre.

French mitrailleuses in action at Illiers, Le Mans, 1870, by Pallandre.

French *Mobiles* at Le Mans, by Pallandre.

The combat at Yvré-l'Évéque, 11 January 1871, by Pallandre.

12

The Second Battle of Orléans: 4 December

When, on the evening of 3 December, Frederick Charles and Stiehle considered their orders for the following day, they could feel reasonably satisfied with the first day's operations, on the basis of such information as they had. They were aware of the events that concerned Manstein's IX Corps, and the positions taken up by X Corps, and following the occupation of Chevilly knew that the detachment was in a position to follow this up. On the other hand, they knew little of the movements of III Corps, the only information available being Alvensleben's message of 1.00 p.m. which reached them only at 7.00 p.m.

Frederick Charles was entirely clear about the objective for the next day; as he had told Stosch, he was determined to be in Orléans by nightfall. Accordingly, IX Corps was ordered to advance through Chevilly and in the woods to the east in order to cooperate later with the detachment in an enveloping attack on Cercottes, where it was expected that the Army of the Loire would make a stand. The left flank Detachment of IX Corps was to advance through St Lye. X Corps, still acting as a reserve, was to march towards Chevilly and take up a position immediately to the north. The 6th Cavalry Division was to remain south of Artenay behind the right wing of Manstein's Corps.[1]

But it was in framing the orders for III Corps that Frederick Charles and Stiehle had the most difficulty:

> III Corps will advance along the Chilleurs-Loury Road towards Orléans, covering itself on its left flank against any forces perhaps coming from Bellegarde, and has, as objective, to bring into action as much artillery as possible against the town of Orléans. The corps will move off at 7.00 a.m.[2]

These orders were necessarily based on guesswork, but reflected the Prince's wish to be in Orléans that day.

Unfortunately, the staff officer bearing the orders for 4 December lost his way during the night in a heavy snowstorm and it was not until 8.00 a.m. that he reached Alvensleben's headquarters. However, preparations for the march had already been made, and III Corps was able to move off

1 *Official Account*, vol. III, p.354.
2 Hale, *People's War*, p.265.

an hour later. The 6th Division, followed by the Corps artillery, took the main road south-west from Loury, putting out a flanking detachment through Rebrechien to cover the right wing of the corps. It had been necessary to first bring up the Corps artillery from Chilleurs, where it had spent the night; the long line of 60 guns was extremely vulnerable to sudden attacks from the parties of French troops that remained in the forest. The 5th Division took a side road a little to the east, by Vennecy. The left wing of the corps was covered by a detachment from the 5th Division.

Alvensleben was unimpressed with these orders, remarking that they were 'armchair strategy,' and he did not regard them as practicable. One feature of the orders was that only those directed to III Corps expressly gave Orléans as the objective for the day, and the suggestion that artillery should be brought into action against Orléans seemed to Alvensleben to be still more ridiculous. He did not need the warning about his left flank; the presence of both 18th and 20th Corps within striking distance of his line of march meant that, if necessary, the left flanking detachment could act as a rearguard.

The infantry divisions arrived at and near Boigny, after a march of 5 or 6 miles from Loury, and halted there for a short break before continuing their march. The 6th Division remained on the main road, while the 5th Division marched by Bourgneuf towards Chécy, on the Loire. When the 6th Division had reached Vaumainbert, 2½ miles from Orléans, at about 2.00 p.m., it encountered the first serious resistance of the day. This came from troops from the 1st Division of 15th Corps who had taken up positions in farm buildings covering the village, from which they opened a heavy rifle fire on the advancing German troops.[3]

Kretschmann described the encounter:

> At Vaumainbert, in an area planted with vines, inaccessible to artillery and cavalry, covered with isolated farms, we were met with rifle fire, and there followed a fierce infantry combat. The French – Marine infantry and Zouaves – fought like lions: but I saw the way in which our men overwhelmed their adversaries. It was a combat of man against man, delivered with the most violent fury. At the same time our left wing encountered an enemy corps coming from Boiscommun, and there also followed a fierce infantry engagement, which ended with the total collapse of the enemy.[4]

Once Vaumainbert had been taken, the German infantry advanced to the edge of the heights immediately north of St Loup, and by now darkness was falling. Mindful of his instructions to shell Orléans, but with the more practical motive of announcing his progress to the other two corps, which he supposed to also be closing in on the city, Alvensleben ordered his artillery to find some way to send shells into the city:

> The sound of the guns would thus signal to the troops on the main road his arrival. So close was the country, that only with difficulty was found a place for a whole battery to come into action. At last, a grass plot in front of a villa was discovered; a heavy battery was unlimbered and 12 shells were fired, and then the battery limbered up just in time, for hardly had it gone, than 11 heavy shells, fired from Orléans, fell on the lawn.[5]

3 *Official Account*, vol. III, p.355.
4 Kretschmann, *Lettres*, p.310.
5 Hale, *People's War*, p.268.

Kretschmann and others on the staff of III Corps were keen to push on in the darkness, believing that the French would not stand and fight, but Alvensleben refused to allow this. It was clear to him that it would be foolhardy to run considerable risks merely to be able to be the first German units to enter the city. The stubborn resistance put up by the French at Vaumainbert and St Loup suggested that a still more resolute defence might be made on the outskirts of Orléans itself. Additionally, Alvensleben had no news of the progress of the German advance elsewhere. The 6th Division and the Corps artillery went into quarters between Vaumainbert and Boigny, and the 5th Division at St Jean de Braye. Outposts were placed on the roads leading into Orléans.[6]

Meanwhile the expected threat from the east had materialised. The advance guard of the 5th Division, under Lieutenant Colonel von l'Estocq, had reached the Loire at Chécy at about 2.00 p.m., in accordance with its objective for the day, when patrols reported French troops advancing in a westerly direction over the Orléans Canal at Pont aux Moines, about two miles to the east. By 2.30 parties of skirmishers had appeared, followed by strong infantry columns. At this time the main body of the 5th Division had reached Bourgneuf, about a mile to the north. L'Estocq deployed two companies somewhat in front of Chécy; these, as the French attacks developed, were obliged to fall back on the village itself. At about 3.00 p.m. he was reinforced by a battalion and a battery from the main body, and when these came into action the French began to break off the engagement and to fall back towards Pont aux Moines. Another regiment joined l'Estocq and he advanced in pursuit of the retreating enemy. The French barricaded the further portion of Pont aux Moines as well as the bridge over the canal, which they recrossed, holding the line of the canal for a while before disappearing eastwards.

L'Estocq's boldness had been well rewarded; the troops opposed to him consisted of the whole of 20th Corps under Crouzat, which had advanced from Chambon in accordance with orders received from Freycinet at 4.00 a.m. Together with 18th Corps under Billot, Crouzat was now under the command of Bourbaki, who was ordered to put all his troops in motion along roads to Orléans almost parallel to the line of advance of III Corps. After this march had begun, Bourbaki received a message from d'Aurelle:

> We have been fighting for three days in succession against large forces. Our losses in 15th, 16th and 17th Corps are very heavy. We have gone back to our line in front of Orléans. The enemy has captured one of the most important points. I am afraid now that it will be impossible for the Army of the Loire to hold on to the right bank of the Loire. There is no bridge between Orléans and Gien. 18th and 20th Corps under your command must, if they are to cross the river, do so at the last named place. Give your orders, therefore, for the eventuality that the retreat by Gien may be necessary.[7]

D'Aurelle was wrong about the bridges; there was one at Sully, but as it happened this made no difference.

Crouzat had been the unfortunate recipient of a stream of orders and counter orders from Freycinet and d'Aurelle throughout the preceding day. He was well informed of the progress of III Corps, which he had followed from reports from his scouts. At about 11.00 a.m. an orderly

6 *Official Account*, vol. III, p.356.
7 Hale, *People's War*, p.269.

officer came to him and told him: 'We are in the midst of the Prussian Army,' and gave him a report from a local mayor which said that the enemy was already around Orléans.

Crouzat arrived at Fay aux Loges, four to five miles east of Pont aux Moines, at about 2.00 p.m. From there a road led direct to Jargeau, where there was a bridge over the Loire. He called a hasty council of war with his commanders, after which he decided to march with his infantry by the right bank to Orléans, while prudently sending his trains and artillery across the river at Jargeau. Crouzat sent an officer to check on the condition of the bridge; he found that it had been destroyed, but the local inhabitants had repaired it and rendered it practicable. When his leading Brigade encountered l'Estocq's two companies in front of Chécy, he reached the correct conclusion that the Germans had got to the river and he accordingly ordered his infantry back to Jargeau, where they crossed to the left bank on the following morning.[8] L'Estocq's boldness had enabled III Corps to have a narrow escape. Meanwhile Billot, with the 18th Corps, had followed a road further to the east before turning south. He reached the Loire higher up, and crossed on the night of 5/6 December.

Frederick Charles expected that the decisive blow against the Army of the Loire would be struck down the main road by IX Corps. Here, unlike the dense forest through which Alvensleben was advancing, the terrain would enable the German artillery to dominate operations, as it had done so far in the campaign. Manstein's advance was led by the 18th Division, which marched out of La Croix Briquet at 8.30 am. His patrols reported that the French were in force at Cercottes, as well as being active in the forest immediately to the north, so he directed the 36th Brigade and the corps artillery to advance by the high road, while the 35th Brigade moved along the line of the railway and through the forest against the French right flank.[9]

At this point the road and the railway run parallel to each other at a distance of 200 or 300 yards apart. To the south of Chevilly they entered a wooded area, where the angle of the forest projected to the west, the woods being close with dense undergrowth. It was only when the Germans reached the woods, where the French had deployed a line of skirmishers, that any resistance was encountered. This, after the 4th Light Battery had opened fire from Chevilly, was soon cleared away by the 85th Regiment, and by 11.00 a.m. the advance had reached the edge of the woods. To the east, a battalion of the 36th Regiment advanced towards Cercottes, while further still to the left the 9th Rifle Battalion pushed through the forest and drove the French back into the village.

This lay about half a mile south of the wooded area. It had been strongly fortified, with gun emplacements and shelter trenches, and was connected by entrenchments with Gidy, two miles to the west, which had also been fortified. In front of this line outposts covered the exits from the wood. It was a strong position, and formed the right of the principal fortifications which had been erected west of the Paris – Orléans road, and was strongly held by the 2nd Division of 15th Corps. The key to the position was a height just to the west of Cercottes, and on this Manstein directed the fire from the southern and western edges of the woods of seven batteries, after the 85th Regiment had occupied La Borde and l'Epinette farms. Even before this, eight companies of infantry had charged into the village, partly towards its north-east angle and partly through the railway station, and the French precipitately retreated, ultimately into the vineyards in front of Orléans.[10]

8 Hale, *People's War*, p.276.
9 *Official Account*, vol. III, p.356.
10 *Official Account*, vol. III, p.357.

The Corps artillery pushed on along the main road. The 35th Brigade to the east, and the 36th Brigade to the west, continued their advance. At first the infantry was supported by the artillery, which pounded the retreating French:

> But in this country intersected by hedges, walls, and ditches, and covered with orchards and farmsteads, the infantry of the 18th Division had now to carry on the further struggle unassisted. Although the French skirmishers held out at almost every point capable of defence, the Germans at first made comparatively rapid progress, and did not meet with any resolute resistance until they reached the railway station north of Orléans, where, at the deeply sunken road, troops of 15th Corps had ensconced themselves in sheltered trenches and behind barricades, while several naval guns brought into position effectively swept the ground in front.[11]

Fighting continued throughout the afternoon. As the German advance continued, the 2nd Heavy Battery came up in support of the infantry. By 5:30 p.m. it was completely dark and the French artillery ceased firing; at this point two Prussian companies had occupied the railway station at Les Aubrais close to the walls of the city. Behind these the French still resisted, and threw back an attack by the 11th Regiment which had assaulted a strongly held barricade. Manstein was not prepared to undertake a night engagement in the suburbs of Orléans, with an enemy evidently still capable of strong resistance, and notwithstanding the wish of Frederick Charles to be in the city that day, decided to break off the attack until the following morning; his troops went into quarters in the larger farms near the high road. However, at 10.00 p.m. the defenders of the railway station had to beat off a determined French attack on their position.

Meanwhile Voigts-Rhetz, with X Corps, had followed Manstein south, reaching Cercottes at 4.00, where he halted, his troops being echeloned as far back as Artenay. Held in reserve, Voigts-Rhetz was not called on to undertake any operations during the day, which appeared to be ending with the failure of the Second Army to take Orléans as its commander had wished.

To the west, the detachment was to advance in support of IX Corps, and to cover the right flank. It was led by Tresckow's 17th Division, marching south from Château Chevilly and Chameul in the direction of Gidy. This was followed by the 22nd Division and the 2nd Cavalry Division, while von der Tann marched towards Janvry. The 4th Cavalry Division was to move through Huêtre and Boulay towards the Châteaudun Road; patrols reported that strong columns of French troops had moved off southwards from l'Encormes, and that Huêtre had been evacuated, but that Gidy was still occupied.[12]

Tresckow moved out at 7.30 a.m., driving some French detachments out of the village of Cuny. Gidy was indeed held by strong bodies of the enemy, with heavy guns located behind earthworks on the old road to Chartres. Since an attack might cost heavy casualties, Tresckow resolved to await the advance of the Bavarians and of IX Corps before launching an assault.

During the night of 3/4 December there had been increasing signs that the enemy's morale was deteriorating: 'During the bitterly cold night a number of deserters arrived at the outposts and reported that the enemy was in retreat and had had enough fighting.'[13] In the next few

11 *Official Account*, vol. III, p.357.
12 *Official Account*, vol. III, p.358.
13 Helvig, *Operations*. p.287.

days however the troops under Chanzy were to recover sufficiently to put up a very determined resistance.

The suggestion that French morale was collapsing appeared to be confirmed when, at 7.00 a.m., the eight naval guns at Gidy fired only half a dozen rounds before being abandoned by their gunners later in the morning. The French retreated from Gidy without the necessity for Tresckow to order an assault, and the 17th Division was ordered to continue its advance towards Janvry.

At 9.00 a.m., to the Grand Duke's considerable surprise, Frederick Charles paid an unexpected visit to the headquarters of the detachment, then located at Château Chevilly. The interview was brief, frigid and uninformative. The Prince found it difficult to conceal his personal dislike of the Grand Duke, and merely confirmed, in a distant manner, the orders which had previously been given to the detachment:

> The Grand Duke expressed his belief that the enemy was retreating over the Loire. The Prince held a contrary opinion, that the retreat was on Orléans. Both seem to have regarded the surrounding of the Army of the Loire as the end to be attained, but, unfortunately, the orders of the Prince, which involved the whole detachment in the struggle on the Paris to Orléans road, rendered the envelopment of the French left wing very improbable. Before the brief interview came to a close, the Prince repeated to the Grand Duke the words of the previous evening that Orléans must, under all circumstances, be occupied this day.[14]

Regrettably Frederick Charles had allowed his feelings towards the Grand Duke to mean that he made no proper enquiries as to the fighting of the detachment on the previous day or about the view held there of the overall position, and he rode slowly back to his own headquarters not much better informed.

In front of I Bavarian Corps there were signs that the French were intending to make a stand at Boulay. Von der Tann's left column had encountered resistance at Bricy, but this was soon overcome by the German artillery, which brought no less than eight batteries into action. Following this, at about 9.30 a.m. the 2nd Bavarian Brigade advanced towards Janvry. Once there, preparations were made for an attack on Boulay; the leading troops of the 17th Division also arrived there some two hours later. Wittich, with the 22nd Division, came up on the left to support the attack, and to maintain contact with IX Corps.

The Bavarian gunners opened a heavy fire on the French position at Boulay, soon overpowering the French artillery, and the infantry moved forward to the attack. As soon as they did so, the French fell back southwards, once again abandoning their guns. Although the French had the opportunity to make a stand in each of the positions that had been prepared in the path of the German advance, so that at every step they could find shelter in which to delay their pursuers, their poorly trained and indifferent troops were nearly worn out by hard marching, fighting, lack of food and rest, and by the bitter weather. The stream of orders and counter orders which reached these French units further rattled their commanders, and panic set in easily. The Grand Duke, positioned with his leading troops, did not hesitate to take advantage of the opportunity before him, ordering Stolberg's 2nd Cavalry Division to press the retreating enemy closely, and it trotted forward past the west side of Gidy through the open space near Montaigu farm.

14 Hale, *People's War*, p.271.

As they emerged from the woods, a squadron of the 4th Hussars charged the escort of a French battery just as it was unlimbering on the Châteaudun Road, while another squadron took the battery in front, flank and rear and captured the guns. Other French artillery began to open fire from a position to the west of Ormes, but the hussars cleared the front to make way for the horse artillery batteries of the 2nd Cavalry Division, which unlimbered at Bois Girard. As soon as the German gunners opened fire, the French resumed their retreat.[15]

The hussars, only 65 sabres strong, had captured 9 guns and 4 waggons, along with 4 officers, 75 men and their horses. Soon after this striking success, three more squadrons of the 5th Hussars advanced on another French battery but as they approached the Châteaudun Road came upon three French squadrons, which they completely routed, taking a large number of prisoners, and pursuing the rest towards the Loire, until stopped by rifle fire at Ingre.

Meanwhile, earlier in the morning, to the north, patrols of the 4th Cavalry Division had, for some time, been watching the concentration of large numbers of French troops at Coinces, and also the movement of waggon trains down the road towards Orléans. Two squadrons of the 2nd *Leib* Hussars charged the escort of the waggon trains, seizing 11 waggons and taking 250 men prisoner. The French forces at Coinces were part of Barry's Division of 16th Corps, and in conjunction with 17th Corps, in front of St Sigismund and Gemigny, to the rear, were intended by Chanzy to launch an attack on the right flank of the German advance.[16]

To meet this threat, von der Tann moved the 3rd Bavarian Brigade, the Cuirassier Brigade and the artillery reserve, north of Bricy, to face west. At the same time the 9th Cavalry Brigade with the horse artillery of the 4th Cavalry Division advanced from Huêtre towards Coinces. Prince Albrecht assured von der Tann that his two cavalry brigades were sufficient to check any French advance; Major Will, the commander of the reserve artillery, was of the same opinion.[17]

Accordingly, von der Tann decided to continue his advance with his main body towards Ormes, leaving the 3rd Brigade and the artillery reserve at Bricy; his troops were exhilarated as they pushed forward over familiar roads:

> The towers of the cathedral of Orléans once more rose in the distance, and the houses of Ormes glittered in the sunshine, as they had done two months ago. Our goal was the same as on 11 October, and neither officers nor men could restrain a feeling of proud satisfaction, when the trenches were once more stormed amid loud cheers, and the enemy was again seen in full flight. Since the Battle of Coulmiers, how many thousands had contributed towards the recapture of Orléans by the sacrifice of their lives![18]

Stolberg's advance had ripped a hole in the centre of the French defences, causing panic to spread in all directions. The French attempted to delay his advance by bringing up several batteries, but these were soon driven off by his horse artillery. In the chaotic French retreat two *gardes mobiles* regiments, a *Régiment du Marche* and a battery completely disintegrated. Pierre Lehautcourt wrote:

15 *Official Account*, vol. III, p.360.
16 Chanzy, *Deuxieme Armee*, p.89.
17 Helvig, *Operations*, p.292.
18 Helvig, *Operations*, pp.293–294.

> The retreat which commenced in great disaster is continued in the midst of ever increasing confusion. Demoralisation quickly assumes terrible proportions. There is no longer any command, any direction; isolated parties of infantry and entire bodies of troops are mixed up with trains and batteries. Some make for Orléans, most gain Meung, Beaugency, Mer or even Blois.[19]

A considerable way to the north-west, the French had remained, in the early part of the day, in occupation of Patay, upon which the 8th Cavalry Brigade, supported by some Bavarian infantry, had made an unsuccessful attack early in the morning. Now, however, coming under fire from a Bavarian battery, the French abandoned the place and were pursued by the German cavalry, which captured some more ammunition waggons. Chanzy, in the light of this, gave up his plan for an assault on the German right wing, and pulled back 17th Corps under the cover of Jauréguiberry's Division. Another striking success was recorded by the German cavalry, when the lancers of the 9th Cavalry Brigade came upon, between Patay and St Péravy, the column of retreating French infantry, which was being covered by a strong detachment of cavalry:

> Against the latter, General von Bernhardi, clearing a broad shelter trench in full career, led four squadrons to the attack, which the enemy, after delivering a volley from their carbines, evaded by a retreat to St Péravy. The 1st Squadron of the 6th Lancers had meanwhile ridden down the French skirmishers, and had charged the left flank of the cavalry, while at the same moment the 3rd Squadron of the 1st Lancers broke into it from the opposite side.[20]

Chanzy had done his best to delay the German advance, but had been under no illusions about the possibility that Orléans might be successfully defended, as he later wrote: 'All our positions in the centre had been abandoned; it was no longer possible to think of retreating upon Orléans, the enemy already being masters of a large part of the works covering the city.'[21] D'Aurelle had been doing his best, later writing a description of the efforts which he had made to put some backbone into his troops:

> The commanding general had tried hard, but without success, to rally his senior officers; he urged them to use their authority to lead their troops into the trenches. He appealed to their honour, to their patriotism; a small number responded to his appeal, the others fell back, saying, 'Our troops can hold out no longer.'[22]

He had sent an officer to Chanzy with orders, but he could not get through, and returned to d'Aurelle's headquarters to say that the enemy had passed Les Barres and were on the march to Ormes, and that the uhlans were covering the country in all directions. Communications with Chanzy and 16th and 17th Corps had been interrupted since noon.

The German advance towards Orléans continued with little opposition; since the earlier successes of Stolberg's cavalry, there were no longer any organised bodies of French infantry

19 Hale, *People's War*, p.273.
20 *Official Account*, vol. III, p.361.
21 Chanzy, *Deuxième Armée,* p.92.
22 d'Aurelle, *Première Armée,* p.346.

on the Châteaudun Road. But night was already beginning to fall and the short December day ended with the leading Bavarian troops having turned off the road to Ingre, while the 17th Division moved on to the Châteaudun Road and marched down towards the gates of Orléans. After dislodging some French troops who tried to make a stand at St Jean de Ruelle, Tresckow's leading troops reached the walls of the city at 6.00 p.m.[23] The Grand Duke, who had spent most of the day with Tresckow, was of much the same opinion as Alvensleben and Manstein about the wisdom of launching a night attack on what might be a stubbornly defended city, and he too ordered a halt for the night. The main body of the 17th Division took up a position at the railway embankment about a mile from the city; Colonel von Manteuffel with the advance guard pressed on and by 6.00 p.m. he was outside the entrance gate.

At the headquarters of Second Army, Frederick Charles was becoming gloomily aware that his hope of taking Orléans that day was now gone, and at 6.45 he issued orders that all forces should cease fire and remain where they were, with a view to renewing the attack next day. Inside Orléans, however, the situation had steadily deteriorated throughout the day, as demoralised French troops streamed back into the city. D'Aurelle's brief hope that he might after all be able to mount an effective defence flickered briefly but, as the afternoon wore on, it soon died. As d'Aurelle graphically described it: 'The illusion did not last long; the soldiers of the 1st Division of the 15th Corps were scattered over the various quarters of the town, in pubs, in private houses, or lying drunk in public places and beside the houses. The officers had abandoned their troops, and filled the hotels and cafes.'[24] By 4.00 it was abundantly clear to him that his situation was militarily impossible, and that he must revert to his previous decision to abandon the city at once if he was to save even a part of the troops still remaining within its defences. He was expecting Gambetta's arrival, but the latter's train ran into the leading units of German cavalry that had pressed on to the river. A horse artillery battery opened fire and it was only by the speed with which the drivers put the engine into reverse that it avoided falling into the enemy's hands. Had he got there, d'Aurelle wrote, Gambetta 'would have seen for himself …. the unavailing efforts made to restore a feeling of honour to the soldiers, for the moment distraught as a result of their suffering, exhaustion and demoralisation, and who refused to fight to their last bullet. All hope was lost.'[25]

While he was awaiting the arrival of Gambetta, accompanied by the *Préfet*, M. Pereira, d'Aurelle expressed himself bitterly about the position in which had been put by the government at Tours. Pereira tried to cheer him up, telling him that their misfortune was not his fault, and that all France knew his energy and his courage; it was a reassurance that d'Aurelle particularly valued, since Pereira, whose health had been failing, died a few days later.

At the city gate Manteuffel could see French soldiers in the streets; when the guard refused his demand that the gate be opened, he insisted that the commanding officer be sent for, and he notified this to Tresckow before riding back to report to the Grand Duke. Pallières, given by d'Aurelle the task of covering the retreat, received Manteuffel's message at 7.00. By then he was already aware that the French troops behind the walls of Orléans immediately facing the line of advance of the 17th Division had practically melted away, so he sent Captain Pendezec of his staff to find out what Manteuffel wanted, and moved up a battalion of infantry to frustrate any German attempt to seize the gate by a *coup de main*. Pendezec was taken to Tresckow, who told

23 *Official Account*, vol. III, p.362.
24 d'Aurelle, *Première Armée*, p.344.
25 d'Aurelle, *Première Armée*, p.347.

him that he had occupied the suburb of St Jean, while Second Army was at the railway gate in the suburb of Bannier. He was firm, saying:

> If you wish I will have you taken there to convince yourself. I intend to occupy Orléans today, but would like to avoid a street fight, which will injure much both the city and the inhabitants; so for that reason I have halted here. Be so good as to convey to your commanding officer my summons that he evacuates the city by 11.30. I shall then occupy the city as far as the Artenay road. If the commandant refuses, my batteries, which are now in position, will immediately open fire.

To emphasise his point Tresckow asked that they synchronise watches.

Tresckow was, of course, bluffing, but what Pallières knew, and he did not, was that there were scarcely any French troops left to resist a further German advance, and he sent Pendezec back to accept the terms. However, soon after this Pallières received an order from d'Aurelle to delay the evacuation and he was obliged to send General d'Aries to Tresckow to ask for more time. They met on foot in the street outside the gate, and Tresckow extended the deadline by an hour; d'Aries accepted this and went back to d'Aurelle with the news. The Grand Duke, meanwhile, had deferred reporting to Frederick Charles until the situation had been clarified, but at 10.30 he was able to report that he would occupy the city in an hour's time. At 1.00 a.m. on the following morning he had the considerable satisfaction of riding into Orléans at the head of the 17th Division and the 2nd Bavarian Brigade. The news was not at all well-received by Frederick Charles, as Waldersee recorded: 'It was a thunderbolt, the Prince was beside himself. He had intended to make a formal entry into Orléans; his joy had vanished, and all owing to the Grand Duke, of whom he had an enduring dislike.'[26]

For Frederick Charles's injured feelings there would have been little sympathy at Versailles. There was, however, profound relief that Orléans had been recaptured. The King, to whom the news came first in a telegram from the Grand Duke, responded promptly by awarding to him the Pour le Mérite with oak leaves, and to Tresckow and Wittich the same decoration without oak leaves. The Crown Prince was overjoyed by the news, but confided sombrely to his diary that in spite of the victories at Paris and Orléans the war was far from over:

> In a few weeks we shall have to fight again just the same, for in this war no single event is any longer decisive, in the same way as we have always hitherto found to be the case .... One cannot but think highly of the obstinate power of resistance shown by the French, for from it we clearly see what a united people can do when swayed by a great national ideal.

On the other hand, it did seem to him that the completeness of the collapse of French morale was not entirely unexpected: 'It is typical of the French how, so long as the struggle lasts, even when they are in the field against their will, they always fight bravely, but directly it is all over they throw to the winds, so to speak, all that is generally expected of soldiers.' He did however draw particular satisfaction from Stosch's influence on the outcome; 'From the moment he arrived, all became clear and orderly, and we must thank him for the successes already reported.'[27]

26 Hale, *People's War*, p.280.
27 Crown Prince, *War Diary*, pp.214–217.

Moltke was immediately concerned to exploit the victory to the greatest possible extent. With an eye to the effect on the morale of the Paris army, he sent a courteous note to Trochu to tell him of the defeat of the Army of the Loire and the occupation of Orléans. He offered a safe conduct to one of Trochu's officers to enable him to check the position for himself, a proposition which was politely declined. More importantly he responded to the news with a telegram to Frederick Charles, to ensure that no time was lost in following up the victory: 'It is necessary to vigorously pursue the beaten enemy with the main body of Second Army, without regard to events here.'[28]

The immediate decision taken by Frederick Charles may not have been inconsistent with Moltke's view of the immediate situation, but it was nevertheless a mistake. The Prince ordered that the pursuit down the right bank of the Loire should be carried out by the detachment, rather than the relatively fresh units of Second Army which he had at his disposal. When Stosch pointed out the exhausted state of his troops, the Prince granted him a rest day, but still did not change his orders that it should be the detachment which was to march on Beaugency.

Overall, Frederick Charles could at least claim that the forces under his command had won a considerable victory. He had defeated an army far larger than his own and split it into two parts, and done so at the expense of relatively low casualties. His total losses amounted to 1,747 men, of whom 353 were killed. French casualties exceeded 20,000 men, of whom 18,000 were prisoners. The French had also lost 74 guns, and 4 gunboats left behind on the Loire. The moral effect of the loss of Orléans was quite as bad as Gambetta and Freycinet had feared would be the case; not only was the morale of the French troops badly damaged, but that of their opponents had been greatly strengthened. The military effect of the campaign which culminated in the second capture of Orléans fell short of Moltke's hopes for the complete destruction of the Army of the Loire; but its offensive power had been materially weakened, and there was no longer any realistic possibility of either part of the army mounting a direct attempt to relieve Paris. Although Moltke knew that he must continue to keep Frederick Charles up to the mark, he could at least turn to deal with French activity at other points of the compass in the knowledge that the most dangerous point of the war was almost certainly now past.

28 Moltke, *Correspondance Militaire,* vol. II, p.543.

13

Meung

It was obvious to Moltke that everything possible should be done to pursue the retreating elements of the Army of the Loire, and he followed up his telegram to this effect by writing a lengthy letter to Stiehle on 6 December to reinforce this message:

> As I have already telegraphed you, it is absolutely necessary to pursue the Army of the Loire vigorously, without a pause, since otherwise it will be able in a few days to reassemble behind the river Yevre, and by the size of its forces, create a fresh embarrassment. If the pursuit is continued with sufficient strength, at least as far as Vierzon, this army, without cadres and without cohesion, will perhaps be completely dispersed; it will certainly abandon a large part of its materiel. It is essential, come definite peace negotiations, that France is not able to point to an army of more than a hundred thousand men still in the field.
>
> In truth, if the future does not appear very clear, it seems that you can now give Second Army as the direction of its operation the line Bourges – Nevers – Châlons sur Sâone, in which it can support in turn the corps of Generals von Zastrow and von Werder. The army of his Royal Highness the Prince Field Marshal has an effective strength to cover against the south all our lines of communication, Alsace and the siege of Belfort and even to undertake, if necessary, an offensive towards Lyon.[1]

Moltke went on to reflect that it was scarcely possible that d'Aurelle and the Army of the Loire would, after his defeat, be able to mount an isolated offensive towards Paris. On the contrary, it was more likely, he thought, that d'Aurelle would retreat with his whole force. If he did not, it would be reasonable to operate along the right bank of the Loire towards Gien with a view to reuniting with the rest of Second Army, perhaps at Bourges or perhaps at Nevera. In all this Moltke seems to have discounted the possibility of any serious threat from the forces under Chanzy; after having chased the French government out of Tours, the Grand Duke could, he thought, turn towards Le Mans, and he now restored the independence of the detachment from Second Army. Moltke did add, however, a warning that it would not do to underestimate the significance of a *levée en masse* of the whole of a nation such as France; the only way to overcome it was to march on the points where the largest masses were concentrated.

1 Moltke, *Correspondance Militaire*, vol. II, p.543.

On the other side of the hill, the defeat at Orléans led to entirely predictable results. Freycinet and Gambetta had been prepared to leave the command of the Army of the Loire in d'Aurelle's hands all the time it remained undefeated, albeit with a considerable reluctance, which was not concealed in their communications with him. Now, though, they saw no reason to leave him in his post. A curt note from Freycinet informed him that the command structure of the Army of the Loire was altered with immediate effect. The command would be divided to reflect what had happened on the ground. 16th and 17th Corps, supported by the newly formed 21st Corps which was now coming up from Le Mans, would comprise 2nd Army of the Loire, which would be commanded by Chanzy. The rest of the army, 15th, 18th and 20th Corps, would be designated as 1st Army of the Loire, and would be commanded by Bourbaki.

As for d'Aurelle, who was now at Salbris, he was ordered to hand over his command, passing it for the moment to Pallières, and to report for duty to take command of the strategic lines of Cherbourg. This insulting proposal was certainly made in the knowledge that it would be declined, as of course it was. D'Aurelle duly passed the command to Pallières; this then prompted a rather more courteous letter from Freycinet. As d'Aurelle remarked, it offered a striking contrast with Freycinet's previous dispatch; it suggested that his experience at Salbris, to which a large part of the army was retreating, would be useful to Pallières and Crouzat, and proposed that he give advice to the former and orders to the latter. D'Aurelle was having none of this; he replied at once that he could not give advice to Pallières without wounding the latter's *amour propre* and depriving him of the moral authority and prestige necessary to command. As for Crouzat, he would himself have no authority to give him orders. His presence, he wrote, was of no use, and he asked leave to retire as soon as possible.[2]

D'Aurelle took leave of his command at 2.00 p.m. on 7 December. As he bade farewell, his staff, his generals and his service commanders all expressed their warmest sympathy for him. With profound sadness he left an army which he had 'created, trained, inspired, disciplined and led to victory.'[3]

In his account of the war in the provinces Freycinet suggested that the army was originally to be split into three parts, 15th Corps under Pallières being independent. But this was not what he had directed, and 15th Corps duly formed part of First Army of the Loire. Meanwhile he sent orders to Chanzy to take up positions between Vendôme, the Forest of Marchenoir and the Loire, an area with which he was already very familiar. In addition to 21st Corps, which was led by Jaurès, the independent division commanded by Camô was being sent from Tours to Beaugency to take up positions there pending Chanzy's arrival.[4]

Freycinet and Gambetta soon demonstrated that they had learned nothing from the events of the last few days. Unaware of the defeat of Ducrot's attempted breakout from Paris until 6 December, they remained determined to take the offensive. On 5 December, orders went to Bourbaki and Pallières to concentrate at Gien and launch an advance northward towards Fontainebleau, while Chanzy embarked on the recapture of Orléans. These ludicrous orders not surprisingly caused absolute dismay among the generals who were seeking to get their battered units safely out of the way of the Germans; on this occasion, their vehement protests were accepted. When Gambetta visited 15th Corps at Salbris he saw for himself the state of the

2 d'Aurelle, *Première Armée*, p.356.
3 d'Aurelle, *Première Armée*, p.356.
4 Freycinet, *Guerre*, p.190.

troops; he told Freycinet that they were in a deplorable state of disorganisation and presented 'the saddest sight.' When news of Ducrot's defeat finally arrived, the urgency of a northward march disappeared, and Gambetta authorised Bourbaki to fall back on Bourges. Pallières, once he had brought the 15th Corps to safety there, had had quite enough, and resigned his command, saying that nothing would induce him to remain any longer 'at the disposal of the military fantasies of the telegraph from Tours.'[5]

The first orders issued by Frederick Charles after he received the news of the entry into Orléans went out early on the morning of 5 December. The detachment was to extend down the right bank of the Loire as far as Beaugency, while III Corps was to advance on the right bank upstream in the opposite direction as far as St Denis de l'Hôtel. IX Corps was to push its advance guard along the left bank as far as the river Loiret.[6]

During the day the split of the Army of the Loire became apparent. At 7.00 p.m. Frederick Charles, intending that the detachment should continue its march westwards to Tours, directed III Corps to Châteauneuf, while IX Corps was to send cavalry patrols into the Sologne. The 25th Division, which was on the south side of the river, was assigned to support the detachment, together with a brigade of the 2nd Cavalry Division. The order to the detachment to push westwards brought an immediate protest from Stosch, who pointed out the exhausted state of his troops, and in response to this Frederick Charles agreed a rest day for 6 December.

Meanwhile, the pursuit of the French units retreating southwards was conducted by the 6th Cavalry Division, supported by some battalions of IX Corps, with orders to press forward as rapidly as possible to Vierzon, where it was to break up the railroads. III Corps was to ascertain whether there were any movements in the neighbourhood of Gien and Montargis. Meanwhile X Corps for the moment remained in Orléans. One immediate problem for the Germans there was to deal with the large number of prisoners which had been taken during the battle for the city. Kretschmann, greatly moved by the plight of these captives, wrote to his wife on 6 December to describe the scene in the cathedral where a large number were temporarily housed:

> Picture for yourself, shut in a space double the size of Halberstadt Cathedral, some 9,000 French prisoners. The poor devils, half frozen and half dead with hunger, left one with an unforgettable impression. Thick clouds of steam made it almost impossible to make out the form of the columns. Black *turcos*, their legs folded underneath them, were squatting down around a fire with an air of stupefaction.[7]

On the Loire, the 18th and 20th Corps had crossed to the left bank, having destroyed the bridges at Jargeau, Châteauneuf and Sully. There appeared to be only a small French force holding the road to Gien. Meanwhile in the Loing Valley the 1st Cavalry Division, which had advanced as far as Lorris, had found no substantial enemy forces save some *franc-tireurs*. South of the river the German cavalry, supported by infantry, followed up the retreating units of 15th Corps, picking up a substantial number of prisoners. The 6th Cavalry Division reached Nouan le Fuzelier on 7 December, but its leading units were obliged to retreat when met by heavy rifle fire, suffering heavy losses. The French infantry that had inflicted this check followed up the

5 Howard, *Franco-Prussian War,* p.382.
6 *Official Account*, vol. IV, p34.
7 Kretschmann, *Lettres*, pp.311–312.

success but were in their turn driven back into Nouan where they took up a strong defensive position. Next day the cavalry continued their movement on Vierzon in accordance with their orders, at Vierzon they duly wrecked the railway.[8]

Although the second Battle of Orléans had not resulted in the complete destruction of the Army of the Loire, as his original strategy had intended, the victory did allow Moltke to hope once again for an immediate advance on Bourges. This, he still considered, was the most important point at which Second Army should be aimed, and the directions which he had given Stiehle reflected this. By the capture of Bourges, he reckoned he would effectively destroy any chance of the Government of National Defence assembling, to the south and west, a force realistically capable of threatening the investment of Paris. In the event, however, his hopes were to be again disappointed. The 6th Cavalry Division, having destroyed the railways at Vierzon, was ordered to hold the town, but to go no further. Events on the Loire almost immediately meant that Bourges must, for the moment at any rate, cease to be regarded as a priority objective. The region between Orléans and Bourges remained an area in which movement was extremely difficult, and the weather made it even worse.

Moltke, looking back at the operations which immediately followed the occupation of Orléans, remained convinced that a significant opportunity had been missed, writing, 'It can scarcely be doubted that if the 18th Division had followed the advance of the 6th Cavalry Division, possession would have been obtained of Bourges and of the vast military establishments there.'[9]

During the battles of 2–4 December, the achievements of Wittich's Division had been considerable, and they did not go unnoticed; on 5 December Stosch sent the general a message:

> I am charged by his Royal Highness the Grand Duke of Mecklenburg to express to the 22nd Division his particular satisfaction with the energy and endurance displayed in the recent battles. The Grand Duke adds that the victory of 2 December and its consequences, both present and future, are in large part due to the 22nd Division. On that day, the division fought against enemy forces four times more numerous. In winning the victory, it enabled the advance of the other corps. Accordingly I express my thanks to all the troops of the division .... I shall not fail to bring their glorious conduct to the notice of the King.'[10]

Chanzy had already demonstrated more ability, and more determination, than any of the other generals in the Army of the Loire. Years later, looking back at the war, Moltke was to describe him as, '...probably the most capable of all the leaders whom the Germans had to encounter on the battlefield...' and this was certainly correct; only Faidherbe could be said to stand comparison with him.[11] Michael Howard wrote of him:

> Unlike his colleagues he was not discouraged by the material he had to command. He neither tried to fit his untrained citizen-soldiers into the mould of the regular army nor gave them up in despair. He knew what could be expected from them, and how to extract it; where other commanders overstrained their forces till they collapsed into an unmilitary rabble, Chanzy kept his in hand and knew when he could stand and fight. Alone perhaps among the

8 *Official Account*, vol. IV, p.41.
9 Moltke, *Franco-German War*, p.235.
10 Wittich, *Journal*, p.241.
11 Moltke, *Franco-German War*, p.236.

> generals, he never allowed himself to doubt the possibility of ultimate success. Until the very end of the war he was fertile in devising plans and enthusiastic in urging them.[12]

Although the troops under his command had suffered a serious defeat in the battles for Orléans, Chantzy had been careful to disengage and give them a breather before asking them to fight again. When they did, they surprised the Germans by putting up a stout resistance. Chanzy now had under his command three corps: 16th Corps commanded by Admiral Jauréguiberry, 17th by General de Colomb in succession to de Sonis, and 21st by General Jaurès, another former naval officer. In addition, he had now been joined by the independent division under General Camô. As a result, the forces under Chanzy's command enjoyed a very substantial numerical superiority over the German units that would oppose him.

In the account which he subsequently wrote of his campaigns, Chanzy described the area in which his troops were operating, and in particular identified the only strong position which he could occupy:

> The vast plain between the Loir and the Loire, which comprises the Beauce, the Orleanais and the Blaisois, including the woods which surround Orléans and the Forest of Marchenoir, offer only very few defensive positions. The only really serious position is that given by the latter forest, which extends from Morée as far as Poisly, some 20 kilometres in length. From Lorges to Beaugency, the terrain is more broken than in other parts of the plain, the villages and farms being closer together; it is the gap through which an enemy can pass coming from the direction of Orléans and marching on Tours. By occupying this area strongly, which is only about 11 kilometres, and the Forest of Marchenoir, one holds all the country from the Loir to the Loire, and covers the lower reaches of that river.[13]

Accordingly, Chanzy resolved to make a stand there, which had the additional advantage of being the only position which was remotely feasible for launching a subsequent advance on Orléans or Paris. On the right of the position, behind Meung, he posted Camô's Division; behind which was 16th Corps. 17th Corps was on the left at Cravant and 21st Corps was on the extreme left of the line at St Laurent, on the edge of the forest.

Reviewing the situation on the Loire, Moltke came to the conclusion that there would be much to be said for removing the detachment from the command of Second Army. By restoring its independence, he would more effectively be able to manage its operations as it advanced down the river towards Tours. Accordingly, he notified Frederick Charles and the Grand Duke of this decision; he wrote to the latter:

> It is important to compel the enemy government to abandon this location, which it has occupied up till now, and to disperse the troops which have been concentrated there, as well as those which would be able to reach Le Mans. Second Army has received the order to pursue to Vierzon the Army of the Loire which it has defeated. First Army has occupied Rouen, and is pursuing towards Le Havre the troops of General Briant.[14]

12 Howard, *Franco-Prussian War*, pp.382–283.
13 Chanzy, *Deuxième Armée*, p.103.
14 Moltke, *Correspondance Militaire*, Vol. II, p.547.

Moltke added that the detachment should maintain a close liaison with Second Army and asked that he should be kept informed of the progress of operations.

As he was very soon to discover, Moltke was, in the directions which he was giving to Frederick Charles and the Grand Duke, seriously overestimating the ability of the detachment to brush aside 2nd Army of the Loire. He was not alone in this; Frederick Charles and Stiehle appear to have been of much the same opinion. There was perhaps more than one reason for Moltke's misjudgement. Certainly the intelligence reaching him as to the French Army was inadequate. In addition to this, though, he had for so long seen Bourges as the key strategic target that he was still making this the centre of his thinking, and this perhaps led him to accord less significance to the army that Chanzy was so rapidly restoring as a serious military threat.

A disposition to regard the elements of the Army of the Loire as having been so badly beaten as not to constitute a serious adversary was widely held. Colonel Adolf von Heinleth was von der Tann's chief of staff; after the war he wrote an essay on the first part of the Loire campaign. In this he described the frame of mind of the German forces after the recapture of Orléans:

> The events of the last few days had inspired officers and men with the utmost confidence of victory; they all felt convinced that the whole French Army of the Loire was broken into fragments; thousands of prisoners were in the hands of the Germans; compact bodies of men had surrendered without a struggle; all the enemies encountered on the 4th and on the 5th were broken down, disheartened and filled with deep hatred of their own commanders, or were in mute, apathetic despair. The detachment looked forward to an easy pursuit, and hoped soon to reach rich districts and cities as yet little visited by the war, and affording good shelter and abundant supplies. No one anticipated the necessity of fighting more bloody, obstinate battles.[15]

During the rest day of 6 December, it had only been the Départment's cavalry that moved west. The 4th Cavalry Division (Prince Albrecht) rode as far as Ouzouer le Marché, and the 2nd Cavalry Division (Stolberg) reinforced by the Bavarian Cuirassier Brigade, towards Beaugency. On the following day, the 17th and 22nd Divisions were to follow the cavalry, while I Bavarian Corps moved into the space between Villermain and Beaumont. The 25th Division, which had been assigned to support the detachment by advancing on the left bank of the river, would push forward as far as Lailly, sending its cavalry brigade to Muides.

Stolberg's troopers had a brief engagement to the east of Meung, into which the French were driven. However, advancing patrols were soon reporting substantial enemy forces between Baulle and La Bruère, and as Stolberg had only one infantry battalion supporting him, which was insufficient on its own to occupy the whole of Meung, he retreated to St Ay, sending the Bavarian cavalry to Huisseau sur Mauve. Further north, Prince Albrecht had, likewise, reached his objective without difficulty, but the appearance of strong French infantry columns led him to fall back on Baccon and Charsonville.[16]

The troops which Stolberg's patrols had encountered came from Camô's Division. On the following morning Stolberg assembled his division at St Ay, with the Cuirassier Brigade to

15 General A. von Heinleth, 'Orléans' in J. F. Maurice (ed.), *The Franco-German War* (London: Swan Sonnenschein & Co., 1900) p.430.

16 *Official Account*, vol. IV, p.41.

the west, where he awaited the advance of the 17th Division and the 1st Bavarian Division. The advance guard of the former pushed along the river road into Meung, which it was able to occupy without difficulty, while the Bavarians came up on its right through La Challerie against what was taken to be Camô's left flank. To the west the Mecklenburg Dragoons rode forward to reconnoitre, but soon encountered serious resistance. The 1st Battalion of the 90th Regiment attempted to outflank the position which the French appeared to have taken up, but the enemy slipped away to Foinard and La Bruère. Supported by the batteries of the 17th Division, the German infantry pushed forward towards La Bruère against a stubborn defence, in a terrain which was covered with vineyards. Soon, however, a further French column threatened them, advancing from Langlochère, and barring any advance towards Beaugency.[17]

Tresckow deployed the whole of his division and moved forward against Baulle and Langlochère, pushing a detachment northward to block a threatening advance from La Bourie. Although both Baulle and Langlochère were taken, albeit not without considerable loss, the enemy advance from La Bourie succeeded in driving back the flanking detachment into Langlochère. Units of the 1st Division of Jauréguiberry's 16th Corps were now moving up to take part in the engagement. The French units, with Le Mée as their objective, were in considerable force, and engaged the 1st Bavarian Brigade there and at Grand Châtre; after a stiff fight the Bavarians captured the latter as night fell.

Further French columns, from the 1st Division of the 17th Corps, now appeared, and they threatened the right wing and the rear of the Bavarians. The 1st Bavarian Brigade now faced west instead of south, while the 2nd Brigade continued to push towards La Bourie in support of Tresckow's right. While the 1st Brigade was engaged in changing front in this way, it was attacked by a battery of 10 guns firing from La Bourie; a bayonet charge resulted in the whole of the battery being captured, but unfortunately there were not the horses available to carry off the guns, and as night fell Camô brought up a rifle battalion and his divisional reserve, and was able to retake the guns.

Meanwhile the 2nd Bavarian Division had advanced from its assembly point at Huisseau sur Mauve and it took up a position near Baccon, from where the advance guard of the 3rd Brigade marched on Vilocry, while a 6-pdr battery opened fire on the French units falling back to Cravant. The 22nd Division had reached Ouzouer le Marché following behind the 4th Cavalry Division, and at noon it assembled at Binas. During the afternoon the division became engaged with strong enemy columns; it soon appeared, however, that in addition there were considerable French forces at the northern edge of the Forest of Marchenoir, and Wittich drew back and occupied quarters for the night to the north of the road to La Morée.[18]

Towards 5.00 p.m., as darkness was falling, a dense fog settled over the battlefield, reducing visibility to less than 100 yards; at this time the struggle for Grand Châtre was still continuing, although elsewhere fighting had ceased. The detachment had been engaged on a front of some 14 miles; its advance down the right bank of the Loire had been matched by the 25th Division, on the opposite bank, which had by nightfall got as far as Cléry. During the day total German casualties had amounted to 332 killed and wounded; French losses were substantially higher.

But the engagement had not been at all what the Germans had expected, as Heinleth wrote:

17 *Official Account*, vol. IV, p.42.
18 *Official Account*, vol. IV, p.44.

> The joyous hopefulness with which they set out on their westward march had by the evening of 7 December given way to grave anxiety. From Baulle on the Loire, as far as west of Binas, that is, over a range of more than 12 miles, the feeble detachment had encountered superior forces of the enemy who so far from beating a hasty retreat had at times, as at Langlochère, fought very energetically and even assumed the offensive.[19]

It was clear to Stosch that, on the following day, he must take steps to shorten the detachment's line. Chanzy, meanwhile, was also taking stock of his position:

> The fighting at Meung had led Chanzy to suppose that the enemy was going to direct his principal effort on his right, with a view to cutting him off from Tours and the centre of France. With the aim of meeting this purely hypothetical danger, he ordered Jauréguiberry to, before dawn, establish his 1st Division at Grand Bonnevalet and Villorceau, in touch with 17th Corps and Camô's division.[20]

Meanwhile Barry's Division would take up a position on the right and act as a reserve.

19 Heinleth, 'Orléans,' pp.431–432.
20 Pierre Lehautcourt, *Campagne de la Loire* (Paris: Berger Levrault et Cie, 1895) p.9.

14

Beaugency

Stosch issued his orders for the following day at 10.15 p.m. In these, he noted that the French seemed to attach particular importance to the defence of Tours, and had concentrated substantial forces between the Forest of Marchenoir and the Loire with this in mind. His intention was to press forward along a shortened front: the 17th Division would advance on the left through Baulle; I Bavarian Corps, concentrated at Grand Châtre, would move on Beaumont; and the 22nd Division would advance through Villermain on Cravant. Across the river, the 25th Division would march in parallel to the detachment. As a result of the losses which they had suffered, the 2nd and 4th Cavalry Divisions were ordered to each requisition 600 horses and, if possible, four wheeled transport.[1]

It would be a demanding day:

> During the night of 8 December an icy wind had changed the dense winter fogs into driving snowstorms. The morning dawned gloomily. The bare vineyards lay like dark shadows scattered over the snowclad landscape. From the valley of the Loire a brown mist rose, which lay heaped up spectrally over the eddying flood, and then, seized by the wind, flew in rags and strips beyond the banks, now veiling a village, and again in wide gaps revealing the outlines of the Forest of Marchenoir.[2]

Although Stosch had decided that he must shorten his line in the face of the enemy resistance on 7 December, he still began the following day on a wide front, with the 22nd Division starting from as far north as Ouzouer le Marché before marching south towards Cravant. If this suggested that the French would not put up a stout resistance, it was a miscalculation; but Wittich's presence so far north may have discouraged Chanzy from making use of his huge numerical superiority by attempting to turn the detachment's right.

It is also true that the French did not appreciate just how great was their superiority. Freycinet was, as usual, wide of the mark when he put the total of German infantry facing Chanzy on 7 December at 50,000 men, 'exclusive of a strong reserve .... of fresh troops.'[3] In actual fact the

1 Wittich, *Journal*, p.247.
2 Heinleth, 'Orléans,' p.242.
3 Freycinet, *Guerre*, p.191.

total infantry strength of the detachment was about 27,000. The strength of I Bavarian Corps had been steadily eroded, and the 22 battalions available to von der Tann totalled no more than 9,994 infantry. Both Wittich and Tresckow had also seen their available numbers fall during the intense fighting that had preceded the capture of Orléans. In addition, the Bavarian troops were almost completely exhausted. Their official historian remarked that although, 'their courage and discipline had as yet not suffered from their continuous fatigues, battles and losses, they were nonetheless coming to the end of their tether:'

> Under fire, and during the active operations of the day, the feeling of military honour, the example of the officers, and a certain unquenchable lust of battle, all contributed to support the weary soldiers. Away from the field of battle, behind the scenes as it were, there were unmistakable signs of such a considerable falling off of physical strength, as must inevitably be followed by a loss of morale.[4]

On the morning of 8 December, Wittich's Division marched southwards from Ouzouer le Marché; the left column, the 44th Brigade, on Château Coudray, and the right column, the 43rd Brigade, through Mézières. South of this place it encountered heavy enemy fire from the direction of Poisly. In response, two battalions of the 95th Regiment advanced rapidly through Villermain, and supported by three batteries of the right column and the 8th Cavalry Brigade, drove back the enemy. Meanwhile the 44th Brigade pressed on to reach the wood of Montsouris.

Cravant lies on the road from Beaugency to Châteaudun. The road runs in a shallow valley, and this would mark the battle lines taken up at the start of the day, running north-west/south-east. To the east, behind the German lines, the country was mainly arable; to the west, behind the French position, the country was densely covered with vineyards. The weather continued to be appalling. During the bitterly cold night of 7/8 December it had snowed again, and there was a thin covering of snow upon the frozen ground. There was also a dense fog.

At 11.00 a.m. Wittich was ordered to close up on Cravant and to establish contact with the right wing of von der Tann's Corps, which he achieved by 1.00 p.m. In this way Stosch had greatly reduced the length of his front, and the detachment now moved to the attack. On its left Tresckow with the 17th Division advanced on Beaugency; in the centre the 2nd Bavarian Division had Villechaumont as its objective. The 1st Division and the 2nd Cavalry Division remained for the moment in reserve.[5]

The French columns encountered by the 43rd Brigade at Poisly came from Colin's 2nd Division of 21st Corps, and these fell back towards Loynes in the first instance, before subsequently moving forward again to their original position in the angle of the Forest of Marchenoir. Meanwhile, to the right of 21st Corps, 17th Corps had come into action against the Bavarians. Advancing from Villechaumont, Rocquebrune's 1st Division of 17th Corps, supported by Deplanque's 1st Division of 16th Corps, drove back the Bavarians by weight of numbers towards Beaumont, although one battalion managed to hold on at Le Mée.

The French advance was not successful for long, however, and once again it was the German artillery which brought it to a halt. Stosch deployed five batteries of his reserve artillery before Cravant and Beaumont, firing on the advancing French at close range:

4 Helvig, *Operations*, p.344.
5 *Official Account*, vol. IV, p.48.

> The onward surging masses of the adversary were not proof against the serious onset of the swiftly moving infantry or the heavy fire of the guns; pursued by the three Bavarian brigades they retired again across the high road on which the Germans establish themselves anew.[6]

While the Bavarians occupied Cravant, Wittich brought up behind it the whole of his artillery to form a powerful gun line at Beaumont, covered by the 8th Cavalry Brigade. This was just as well, since at approaching 3.00 p.m. the French launched a powerful attack on Cravant with the whole of 17th Corps, pressing forward to take Loynes, only half a mile from Wittich's guns, before a counter-attack by the 43rd Brigade drove them back again. The various Bavarian units had become seriously intermingled, and had been suffering serious losses during the course of the fighting during the afternoon. Chanzy was able to throw forward large numbers of infantry against the Bavarian positions, in the face of which they were forced back:

> The exceptionally heavy fire of the enemy caused us enormous losses in a very short space of time, while ammunition again began to fail. Officers and men alike felt that their present position, in the total absence of any kind of reserve, was absolutely untenable, unless fresh supplies of ammunition could be at once procured. Before this could be done, some of our detachments gave way before the presence of the enemy, and at last a general retreat began towards the road, in which our troops, exposed to the rapid fire of the enemy's infantry, sustained still further losses.[7]

The Bavarian artillery had also suffered considerably; but in answer to von der Tann's call for reinforcements Stosch sent forward three further batteries which took up a position on the left of the Bavarian guns. At about 4.00 p.m. the 1st Bavarian Brigade joined the line along the high road, and advanced to storm the rising ground to the west. It was an unwise move; a French counter-attack compelled the Bavarians to fall back to Beaumont under the cover of a sustained barrage from the German gun line.

On the German left, Tresckow had spent the morning consolidating his position opposite Beaugency, pushing forward outposts towards Les Vallées and Villeneuve. At 12.30 Stosch ordered him to advance on Beaugency; his advance guard moved down the main road, while two battalions of the 75th Regiment launched an attack towards Messas. Two batteries of artillery shelled the village for a considerable time before the infantry stormed into the place. Bitter house-to-house fighting ensued all afternoon before the village was finally taken and the French retreated, leaving behind 150 prisoners. An abortive counter-attack as darkness fell was driven off.

The advance into Beaugency also encountered fierce resistance. A battalion of the 90th Regiment succeeded in occupying a height north-east of the town, while at the same time the 14th Rifle Battalion pushed forward along the riverside. The French resisted the advance along the line of the railway embankment, and it took the arrival of two further battalions to finally secure the town. In the confusion, a retreating French battery, unaware that the town had fallen, drove into Beaugency and was captured. North of the town, the 75th Regiment took the village of Vernon, and took 200 prisoners.[8] Meanwhile ferries had been established in both Meung and

6 *Official Account*, vol. IV, pp.48–49.
7 Helvig, *Operations*, p.325.
8 *Official Account*, vol. IV, pp.50–51.

Beaugency enabling contact to be made with IX Corps, which was continuing to advance along the left bank toward Lailly; eight batteries of the corps came into action in support of the 17th Division's attack on Beaugency.

Thus, as night fell the French had been unsuccessful all along the line. The German official history notes that the Grand Duke, whose headquarters during the day had been at Grand Châtre, had become convinced that on the following day Chanzy would retreat, and the orders for the detachment reflected this belief. Tresckow was ordered to advance with the 17th Division on Tours, while Wittich, with the 22nd Division relieved von der Tann's battered corps. Meanwhile the orders issued by Second Army for III Corps for 9 December were based on the belief that three or four French corps had taken the direction of Bourges and Vierzon.[9] These orders were for the corps to pursue the French eastwards towards Gien while IX Corps kept pace with the detachment, on the left bank of the Loire as far as Blois. X Corps was to concentrate at Orléans before itself advancing to Blois along the right bank. Frederick Charles, by these orders, offered little support to the detachment, which in his opinion faced no substantial opposition, though he did provide for Voigts-Rhetz to hold his 20th Division at Orléans in case support was necessary.[10]

However, Stosch, having from the fighting on 7 December correctly deduced that Chanzy was in much greater strength than had been supposed, had sent by letter and telegram a full report to Moltke, making clear that as things stood he could not guarantee a successful advance on Tours. Moltke took this warning extremely seriously; he acted promptly and at 10.00 a.m. on 9 December his peremptory telegram reached the headquarters of 2nd Army:

> From a report from the Grand Duke, it appears that the bulk of the enemy are in his front. His Majesty orders that, in order to allow the particularly important operation against Tours to continue energetically, as quickly as possible the detachment must be supported on the right bank of the Loire by at least one division; in addition, you are free to bring effective strength to bear on the left bank. His Royal Highness the Prince Field Marshal will have the overall direction of all the operations on the Loire.[11]

Frederick Charles continued to be sceptical about the opposition which the detachment was facing. He had a poor opinion of the Grand Duke's ability, and as has been seen he personally disliked him. This no doubt led him to question the information reaching him from the detachment, to the extent that he was recorded by Waldersee at one point as having remarked: 'the Grand Duke is a very brave gentleman but no commander. Believe me, there's nothing in front of him. He simply has not the energy to attack.'[12] Quite apart from this, Frederick Charles was extremely sensitive to what he imagined to be a serious threat from the forces of Bourbaki at Bourges, and this had inhibited him from reinforcing the detachment at the outset of its advance down the right bank of the Loire.

In the face of Moltke's explicit orders, Frederick Charles accepted that this meant that he must, for the moment at least, give up all thought of an advance into the Sologne. Orders were

9 *Official Account*, vol. IV, p.51.
10 *Official Account*, vol. IV, pp.51–52.
11 Moltke, *Correspondence Militaire*, vol. II, pp.561–562.
12 Howard, *Franco-Prussian War*, p 385.

at once sent to Voigts-Rhetz to bring up in support of the detachment all of his forces in and around Orléans, and to Alvensleben to suspend his movement upriver and to return to Orléans with III Corps and the 1st Cavalry Division. The 6th Cavalry Division was ordered to return from Vierzon and join X Corps on the left bank.

It was extremely fortunate that Moltke had intervened; Chanzy had no intention of retreating on 9 December, but had resolved to stand and fight, as Stosch and the Grand Duke discovered from documents that fell into their hands during the night. A courier was captured carrying copies of various orders showing that the 2nd Army of the Loire was to hold its present positions. Accordingly, at 7.00 a.m. on 9 December orders went to the 17th Division to concentrate at Messas, and the 22nd Division at Beaumont, with the 4th Cavalry Division to the north-east. The Bavarian Corps and the 2nd Cavalry Division were to remain in reserve at Grand Châtre. However, as Lehautcourt noted, it was already impossible for these orders to be carried out. [13]

One problem which the pugnacious Chanzy had to face on 9 December had however been created by the retreat of Camô's Division from Beaugency in breach, as he told Freycinet, of his direct orders; Camô had, apparently, claimed that he withdrew in accordance with orders received direct from the War Ministry. As it was, Barry, who was at Mer, had reported to Chanzy that, '...the column Camô is in complete collapse. I have not a man, I have not a Division. In order not to be taken by the enemy, I am retiring on Blois.'[14] Camô, who was suffering from a fall from his horse, and was completely exhausted, had also retired and was replaced in command of the Division by General Tripart.

The support for the detachment which Moltke had ordered could not be of any effect for some considerable time, so Stosch and the Grand Duke must continue to fight alone on 9 December. Before, however, the orders given at 7.00 a.m. could be brought into effect, the detachment faced a dense cloud of skirmishers advancing on Vernon:

> They were received with a vigorous file fire by the 2nd Battalion, 75th Regiment, and after a forward movement by the latter were forced to retreat, while the hostile artillery, which had at the same time deployed, found itself shortly after reduced to silence by the 5th Heavy Battery, which had come into action to the north of Messas, and by four other batteries arriving by degrees.[15]

At Le Mée, von der Tann's Corps was attacked by strong columns of French infantry, but again the advance was broken up, on this occasion by the concentrated rifle fire of the two battalions of the 3rd Brigade in the front line, as well as, as ever, by the artillery. When the French fell back, the Bavarians counter-attacked and by 10.30 a.m. were in possession of Villorceau. At Cravant, meanwhile, another heavy attack was launched on the 44th Brigade, and the French gained an advantage when the 83rd Regiment by mistake evacuated the farms of Beauvert and Layes. Wittich, when he heard of this, gave orders that the positions should be retaken immediately; supported by Orff's 2nd Brigade, the 83rd Regiment was able to do this. Wittich strengthened the position, which he regarded as of the greatest importance, by bringing up a strong force of artillery.[16]

13 Lehautcourt, *Campagne*, p.36.
14 Chanzy, *Deuxième Armée*, p.130.
15 *Official Account*, vol. IV, p.53.
16 Wittich, *Journal*, pp.255–256.

As the morning wore on, the 2nd Battalion of the 95th Regiment with men from the 83rd Regiment took Cernay by storm. To strengthen his position at Cravant, Stosch ordered Tresckow to advance with the 17th Division to Villevert and Villorceau. Tresckow moved with almost the whole of his division from Messas to Grand Bonvalet, leaving only a small detachment in Beaugency. As the 76th Regiment moved to relieve the Bavarians holding Loyness and Villorceau, it faced a fresh assault from the direction of Villejouan. This, thanks to the tireless German artillery, was broken up with heavy loss. At the same time other units of the 17th Division pushed forward on the de Feularde farm, a move which seriously threatened Chanzy's right flank.[17] The French made desperate attempts to retake the position, supported by artillery and mitrailleuse fire, but were ultimately unable to drive the Germans back.

During the early part of the afternoon the fighting at Cravant had died down, and Stosch was able to pull out of the front line various units of the 22nd Division and of 2nd Bavarian Division in order to assemble a reserve. Towards 3.00 p.m., however, he sent forward a force of six squadrons, three battalions and 14 guns to support Tresckow's advance, and this succeeded in taking Villejouan before nightfall. The French retreated on Josnes, and the Germans went into quarters for the night, covered by outposts between Beaugency and Cernay.

Meanwhile X Corps had been making its best way forward to support the detachment. By evening its leading infantry had reached Meung, and Voigts-Rhetz sent ahead a cavalry regiment and eight batteries, which arrived at Grand Châtre in mid-afternoon.[18] On the other side of the Loire, IX Corps had continued its advance, encountering little opposition and reaching Muides before nightfall; the bridge over the river there had been destroyed. The enemy took up a position at St Die, but when the advance guard of the 25th Division arrived the enemy was soon driven back and pursued as far as Montlivault.

Chanzy's headquarters was close to the front line, at Josnes, and it was here that Gambetta arrived at 6.00, and where he stayed the night. Chanzy took advantage of the meeting to make Gambetta aware of the needs of his army, and in particular described the extent of the losses suffered in the fighting since 30 November. The troops, he told Gambetta, were still holding on, but had been weakened by fatigue, and the limit of their endurance was approaching. He discussed with Gambetta the alternatives open to his army; he had based his determination to hold Beaugency on the hope that relief might come from Bourbaki's forces in the Sologne, but it was now clear that this would not happen. Retreat, therefore, was going to be inevitable.[19] Gambetta was, though, cheered by the meeting, and sent an upbeat message to Freycinet:

> I have found everything perfectly in order here, thanks to the strength of will and indomitable energy of General Chanzy. Not only has he held his position for three days, but he has repelled the advancing masses of Prince Frederick Charles, and inflicted cruel losses on them.[20]

Gambetta told Chanzy of the decision to transfer the seat of government to Bordeaux. The two men discussed what direction 2nd Army of the Loire should take in its retreat, and agreed that

17 *Official Account*, vol. IV, p57.
18 *Official Account*, vol. IV, p.57.
19 Chanzy, *Deuxième Armée*, pp.142–143.
20 Freycinet, *Guerre*, p.95.

it should be in the direction of Vendôme and the valley of the Loir. As Chanzy remarked in his memoirs, the conduct of the retreat was necessarily going to be a very delicate operation if his army was not to fall to pieces in the process. It would be necessary to conduct the operations on 10 December in such a way as to enable the army to be disengaged. A particular concern was the fact that the Germans had taken Villejouan and then Origny, and he ordered Guépratte with the 2nd Division of 17th Corps to launch a surprise attack on Origny before daybreak.

The village was, with Villejouan and Villorceau, held by the 32nd Regiment from Wittich's Division. However, before dawn on 9 December part of the garrison of Origny had been withdrawn to join the main body of the 43rd Brigade. Guépratte's attack, launched at 6.00 a.m., took the garrison of Origny by surprise, and he captured the village, taking 150 prisoners; the rest of the defenders fell back in the first instance to Villejouan, but were unable to hold on there, and Wittich took up a position with his division near Villechaumont Mill. It seemed to him that these assaults would be followed up, and he applied to Stosch for reinforcements. To check any immediate advance, six German batteries came into action from Villechaumont, Cernay and Beauvert.

Stosch had only the units of von der Tann's corps on which to draw to reinforce Wittich; they had been intended to have a rest day, but needs must… and Orff's 2nd Brigade moved up to Beaumont and Loynes on Wittich's right, followed by four batteries of the corps artillery of X Corps. Together with the batteries already in action there were now no less than 19 German batteries engaged and these, by 3.00 p.m., had succeeded in mastering the French artillery, most of which had been withdrawn.

Further south, Tresckow was concerned that the French capture of Villejouan had exposed his right, and at about noon he launched a fierce attack in an effort to retake it. Prince Kraft, in *Letters on Infantry*, gave a detailed account of the way in which this action was carried out. Two batteries were directed to fire continuously on Villejouan, bombarding the village for about an hour before the attack was launched:

> Under this fire a part of the defenders appeared to have drawn back into the interior of the village. The infantry (the 76th Fusiliers) had orders to approach the place in such a manner so as not to mask the fire of the guns. They thus advanced without firing until they were about 200 paces from it; the enemy then opened fire. They at once rushed with a cheer into the village. The few defenders who remained at the edge were overwhelmed, but the greater part of the garrison must have fallen back, since the battalion in the action, including street fighting from noon until the evening, lost only 4 officers and 88 men. The surprise of the defenders much facilitated the victory of the Fusiliers.[21]

The official account painted a rather more severe picture of the action, noting that the defenders, 'offered a desperate resistance to the 76th, which had been reinforced by their first battalion, and it was not until between 3.00 and 4.00 p.m. that they were completely overpowered after a sanguinary house-to-house engagement.'[22] The French made a vigorous attempt to recapture the village, launching a fierce assault from the direction of Origny.

21 Prince Kraft zu Hohenlohe-Ingelfingen, *Letters on Infantry* (London: Edward Stanford, 1892), p.138.
22 *Official Account*, vol. IV p.61.

Heinleth records the grave anxiety felt by the Germans at the strength of the forces the French were assembling for their counter-attack on the village:

> With imminent danger a cart laden with cartridges needed for the supply of the men was dragged into the burning village, and now again the needle guns were in full activity. But dense bodies of the French kept continually assembling in the neighbourhood of Josnes, distinctly visible like a thundercloud, from the heights of Villemorceau. Suddenly a horseman at full speed galloped up onto the flat hill of Villemorceau; it was Major von Körber, the enterprising indefatigable commander of the horse artillery field division of X Corps. At a swinging trot his batteries followed, and now the guns of the 17th Division also came up, and speedily a well-directed hail of iron was discharged from the concentrated batteries upon the minatory cloud at Josnes. It was dissipated and scattered like the mists of the Loire before the howling east wind. There is nothing more to be feared here today.[23]

There had of course been no sign of any support from Bourbaki's troops far away to the south in the Sologne, and Chanzy recognised that without it the time had come to go, and on the evening of 10 December he spelled out his view of the position in a telegram to Gambetta, a copy of which went also to Bourbaki:

> The movement which is possible and indispensable to enable us, whatever the cost, to restore our situation is as follows: march from Bourges on Vierzon; push the bulk of the 1st Army through Romorantin on Blois; take post between the Loire and the Cher to intercept enemy communications between Orléans and his army advancing on Tours, in this way cutting the latter off from its base.[24]

A helping hand from Bourbaki was obviously essential, but he was quite unable to provide it. After the arrival of 1st Army of the Loire at Bourges, Freycinet and Gambetta had been ceaselessly urging him to make a move northwards, but he insisted that his troops were unfit to fight, reporting that, 'the men are in a state of misery and demoralisation of which you cannot form any conception.' Gambetta had decided to go straight from his visit to Chanzy at Josnes to do what he could to get Bourbaki to move immediately towards Blois, but immediately on his arrival was forced to accept that Bourbaki's account of the state of his troops was by no means exaggerated. He wrote to Freycinet that his forces were, 'in veritable dissolution; it is the saddest sight I have ever seen.' Even Gambetta's fiery optimism could not blind him to the fact that Chanzy's proposals were completely impossible, and in these circumstances Chanzy had no option but to put into effect his planned retreat.[25] This was to begin on the following day, when the army would fall back to Vendôme.

Meanwhile on 12 December Bourbaki, under the accumulated pressure which he had been receiving, reluctantly made a limited advance in the direction of Vierzon, as a result of which a detachment of German cavalry posted there fell back on the main body of the 14th Cavalry Brigade at Salbris. So far so good; but it was too little too late. Bourbaki concluded that he was

23 Heinleth, 'Orléans,' p.440.
24 Chanzy, *Deuxième Armée*, pp.150–151.
25 Lehautcourt, *Campagne*, p.60.

opposed by the greater part of Frederick Charles's army, which he supposed to be coming at him rather than at Chanzy, and that as a consequence there was a real doubt whether he would be able even to remain at Bourges. In any case his position was menaced by Manstein's progress along the left bank; the latter had on 9 December occupied Vienne, opposite Blois.

Chanzy had done all that he could, fighting both skilfully and energetically, and he had brought the best out of his troops, whose performance had come as a considerable surprise to the Germans, Helvig observed:

> Although the French had the advantage of superior numbers and a better firearm, it cannot be denied that at some points they also fought with remarkable bravery and great devotion. It must at any rate be allowed that the tenacity and endurance with which the enemy's troops made their stand for four days, is a proof of the conspicuous energy and inspiring activity of their leader, General Chanzy.[26]

Chanzy had, of course, the benefit of a fourfold numerical advantage in men, and for this reason the victory of the detachment reflected particular credit on Stosch. In the course of the three days' Battle of Beaugency he had made a skilful use of his limited resources. Hoenig attributed his success to Stosch's: 'strong will and iron firmness. Up to this point he had only proved himself to be an excellent chief of staff; from then on he showed himself a hero in his bearing, thoughts and actions.' In his obituary of Stosch, Hoenig later described his conduct of the Battle of Beaugency as 'perhaps the greatest performance with insufficient resources in the entire history of modern warfare.'[27]

The firmness which Hoenig described was particularly important during the Battle of Beaugency. At one point the Grand Duke began to lose his nerve, and suggested that it would be necessary to retreat, and Stosch had to call on all his tact and energy to encourage the Grand Duke to hold firm.[28] Stosch's achievements during the time he spent on the Loire was well understood at Versailles. Moltke, on reading his reports of Beaugency, was generous in his praise of the German soldiers who had fought so well against heavy odds: 'Victory after victory: our brave troops have only to be led to the right spot and then you can sleep in peace! You can't help taking off your hat even to the very drivers of the transport.'[29]

During the three days of battle the total German casualties amounted to 578 killed, 2,033 wounded and 780 missing. The heaviest losses, totalling 1,986, had been sustained by I Bavarian Corps, upon which the bulk of the fighting had fallen. In his report of the battle, Chanzy referred to his army as having sustained significant losses, but an accurate total of French casualties is difficult to arrive at. They must, however, have been at least three times as great as the losses of their antagonists. During the course of the battle the French infantry had been committed to a series of assaults which were broken up with heavy losses, while the Germans took over 5,000 prisoners in the course of the three days.

26 Helvig, *Operations*, p.352.
27 Hollyday, *Bismarck's Rival*, pp.77–78.
28 Howard, *Franco-Prussian War*, p.385.
29 Verdy, *Royal Headquarters*, p.225.

15

Chanzy's Retreat

Chanzy was entirely aware of the limitations of his troops, facing as they were an experienced and well-disciplined enemy, themselves insufficiently trained and operating in bitter weather conditions. He had decreed that during the fighting at Meung and Beaugency his men should not go into quarters, but should bivouac in the open, without shelter and often unable to light a fire. This was because, he believed, if he had allowed them to go into quarters his undisciplined units would dissolve. For this, he was severely criticised by Pierre Lehautcourt, who wrote that, 'for no adequate reason his troops in this way suffered a loss of bodily strength, and lost the spirit of resistance.'[1]

But Chanzy knew and understood his men; and he also knew that undertaking a retreat from the battlefield of Beaugency was going to have the gravest effect on the discipline and stability of his army. It would, he wrote, be an extremely risky operation if the enemy took up a bold pursuit. He would be retreating across an open plain, upon which his movements could not be concealed, and there was no readily defensible position available.[2]

Nevertheless, following his defeat over the three days of the Battle of Beaugency, Chanzy realised that he now had no choice but to retreat, whatever the cost might be. Lehautcourt graphically described the ordeal of his army:

> The 2nd Army of the Loire on 12 December executed the movements which Chanzy had prescribed. But the temperature had entirely changed, and a torrential rain fell during the first hours of the day. The roads, covered with deep snow and ice, became impracticable. As for the countryside, rendered completely impracticable by the thaw, it changed rapidly into potholes. Chanzy had adopted according to precedent an order of march by which the artillery and the trains alone followed the roads while the infantry marched in line of columns across the fields. The result was that the movement of the army was painfully slow. With the greatest difficulty, in the end it managed to make two kilometres per hour. As a result of this hard winter campaign shoes and clothes were already in a deplorable state; the beanpoles of the vineyards which were crossed ripped the men's uniforms to shreds and they were soaked to the skin.[3]

1 Lehautcourt, *Campagne,* p.69.
2 Chanzy, *Deuxième Armée*, pp.162–163.
3 Lehautcourt, *Campagne,* pp.68–69.

To make matters worse for Chanzy's exhausted and dispirited army, the local population was indifferent to their suffering. By now the peasants were losing support for a struggle which they believed was being needlessly prolonged by a government for which they felt little sympathy, and it appears that of the two armies they preferred the Germans, who could pay for what they took. Desertion became rife; thousands of men threw away their arms and left their ranks. As the Germans advanced the extent of the disintegration of 2nd Army of the Loire became more apparent:

> As the previous bitterly cold weather had been succeeded by thaw and rain, the troops on the march had to overcome considerable difficulties, which however affected the enemy in a much more marked degree. For instance, in the country to the south of Marchenoir Forest several thousand stragglers were picked up by the Germans; the roads were strewn with quantities of firearms which had been thrown away, and a mass of abandoned waggons; in the fields lay the unburied corpses of men and horses, in the villages were thousands of untended wounded. All these indications of serious disorganisation in the French ranks were as yet unknown on the 12th at the headquarters of Second Army which had been moved to Beaugency; on the contrary, the opinion prevailed that the enemy would again assume the defensive provided the positions were favourable. No definite reports as to the principal line of retreat of 2nd Army of the Loire had yet been received.[4]

Chanzy was, however, able to benefit from the fact that the bold pursuit of his retreating army which he feared did not materialise. At first it was not even immediately apparent to the Germans that the French had begun to retreat, and when the German cavalry pursued them they moved with extreme caution. Chanzy had directed 16th Corps on Vendôme, while 17th Corps took the road to Oucques and 21st Corps that to Fréteval. Giving orders for the pursuit, Frederick Charles wisely directed that it be led by the relatively fresh troops of X Corps, and Voigts-Rhetz pushed his 19th Division towards Josnes, while the 20th Division moved forward to the south.

By the morning of 13 December the full extent of the French disorganisation had become clear. Cavalry patrols reported the abandonment of Blois and that, to the north of the Forest of Marchenoir, Chanzy was in full retreat towards the Loir:

> The doubts hitherto prevailing against any movement to the right towards the line of the Loir were thus set aside; Prince Frederick Charles consequently gave orders, about noon, to the detachment to advance on the following day with the right wing to Morée, with the left to Fréteval. A communication from IX Corps that arrived shortly after stated that the Germans had entered Blois and that isolated detachments had penetrated to the Cher without coming into conflict with formed bodies of the enemy.[5]

Voigts-Rhetz was accordingly ordered to send forward an advance guard to the Cisse brook, and Cavalry patrols towards Herbault and Tours, while Alvensleben with III Corps and the 1st

4 *Official Account*, vol. IV, p.65.
5 *Official Account*, vol. IV, p.66.

Cavalry Division was directed to advance towards Maves. Manstein, with IX Corps and the 6th Cavalry Division was for the moment to remain on the left bank of the Loire.

Moltke, meanwhile, had written a lengthy letter to Stiehle on 12 December, reviewing the overall situation of the various German armies. So far as Second Army was concerned, Moltke was at pains to stress the continuing need for activity on its part:

> In the last days of November and at the beginning of December, we have succeeded in repulsing the attacks which the enemy made in different directions to raise the siege of Paris; it is now necessary, by an energetic pursuit, to put out of action for a long time the disorganised masses which the enemy have had in the field. This requirement still exists, in my opinion, in respect of the enemy corps which have in recent days been engaged with the Grand Duke's detachment; it is necessary that they are pursued with sufficient force and, as far as possible, dispersed.[6]

Moltke did not, though, wish to see the Second Army set off in a chase across France. The troops needed rest, and until Paris should fall he prescribed as a limit to Second Army's advance a line through Tours, Bourges and Nevers, with the main body based on Orléans. He suggested that the detachment could cover any threat from the west by taking up a position at Chartres. There was, of course, the potential threat posed by Bourbaki and 1st Army of the Loire, as he pointed out:

> It is necessary to pay particular attention to a careful and permanent watch on the enemy Corps (18th and 20th) which, under the orders of General Bourbaki have retired through Gien et cetera in the direction of Bourges and Nevers. In the event of these corps making an advance, you may count on the cooperation of General von Zastrow who, leaving tomorrow, will be at Châtillon sur Seine and will be reinforced by the 60th and 72nd infantry regiments.[7]

As for Bourbaki, Moltke was preaching to the converted; Frederick Charles still had it in mind that 1st Army of the Loire represented a continuing and serious threat. Moltke also suggested that the 5th Cavalry Division, presently at Chartres, should threaten Chanzy's left and rear by moving on Nogent le Rotrou and La Ferté-Bernard.

To Frederick Charles it had appeared after Beaugency that while no further offensive action from Chanzy was immediately to be expected, the French commander would stubbornly defend the positions which he occupied. Accordingly, he ordered III Corps into his front line and planned to send the detachment around the north of the Forest of Marchenoir in order to prevent the enemy heading for Chartres. IX Corps with the 15th Cavalry Brigade opposite Blois were, for the moment, to desist from attacking the enemy to their front until the troops moving along the right bank of the Loire should have come abreast. Once it was clear that the French were indeed retreating, the question that needed answering was the direction which they would take, and to resolve this X Corps was ordered to advance on Mer, while the detachment

6 Moltke, *Correspondance Militaire,* vol. II, p.566.
7 Moltke, *Correspondance Militaire,* vol. II, p.567.

was not to pass around the north of the forest, but was instead to endeavour to turn the enemy's left to the south of it.

The advance guard of the 22nd Division reached a point east of Maves by nightfall on 12 December, while the 17th Division was at La Madeleine Villefrouin. The German advance was still, for the moment, very cautious. Most of von der Tann's Corps had been withdrawn to Orléans; only the 4th Brigade remained at Josnes. Any doubts that the French were indeed in full retreat were dispelled by the reports reaching Second Army headquarters on 13 December. An indication of the disorganisation of the French came with the abandonment of Blois on 12 December – a decision taken by General Barry apparently in breach of the instructions he had received from Chanzy; the Germans had intended to launch an attack on the place on 13 December, but as it was, units of Manstein's X Corps entered the town and sent patrols forward to the Cter without meeting any opposition.

The French were pulling back as fast as the weather conditions allowed, heading for Vendôme and Fréteval. It was in Chanzy's mind that the Loir would provide him with a point at which he could halt his retreat, in order to give his troops some rest and to reorganise the units of his army that had become intermingled during the Battle of Beaugency. The right bank of the Loir would, he reckoned, give him useful positions from which to resist any attempt to cross the river. The heights were variable, but could present serious obstacles to an attacker. In establishing himself on the Loir, Chanzy calculated that he could threaten the flank of any advance from Orléans towards Tours, while covering his own line of retreat towards Le Mans.[8] Always combative, Chanzy may also have been emboldened by the cautious response of the Germans in following up his retreat.

On 14 December the German advance continued. The detachment moved somewhat to its right, heading for Fréteval and Morée on the Loir. At both places strong resistance was encountered, and in each case it was necessary for the artillery to come into action before the day's objectives could be reached.

At Fréteval, Jaurès, recognising the importance of the place, launched an attempt to recapture it from the Bavarian units that had occupied it, sending forward the 2nd Brigade of Guillon's 1st Division. The brigade was commanded by former naval captain du Temple. Unfortunately, this counter-attack was badly mismanaged, only a small force of marines went forward, and although they briefly entered the village, were soon driven back.[9] Roger de Mauni's battalion formed part of du Temple's brigade, and he recounted the dismal failure to organise the attack; as it was, his battalion took no part. He described the impossible weather conditions in which the French were endeavouring to fight:

> Two more days of fighting, of which we have been inactive spectators. We thought we should have rested on Wednesday. Our hopes were doomed to be disappointed; at 12.00 we had to put on our knapsacks and take up fighting positions along the road to Paris. The mud, swelled by the deluge of rain that had fallen, was greasy and deep; we sank slowly into it, hardly able to maintain our balance; there was not a single dry spot in the field on which we could sit down or even lay our knapsacks. We had to be incessantly changing from one foot to the other to keep ourselves from sinking up to our knees.[10]

8 Chanzy, *Deuxième Armée,* pp.173–174.
9 Chanzy, *Deuxième Armée*, pp.184–185.
10 de Mauni, *The Franco-Prussian War*, p.93.

On 15 December, in accordance with orders from Frederick Charles, the Bavarians pulled back from Fréteval, re-crossing the river; the French took advantage of this to destroy the bridge over the Loir.

To the north, cavalry patrols indicated that the French were in position in strength at Cloyes, while along the Loir, Voigts-Rhetz's leading units reported that there appeared to be a substantial concentration of the enemy at Vendôme. Information from the local population suggested that there were now few troops at Tours, and that the government had departed to Bordeaux. Frederick Charles issued orders for a concentration of all his available troops:

> The reports which were transmitted during the 14th to army headquarters placed beyond doubt that General Chanzy would once more offer resistance with his whole army on the Loir. For the decisive struggle thereby in prospect Prince Frederick Charles could not bring III Army Corps forward on the following day, it still extended to the rear as far as Mer and urgently needed a day's rest after its continuing marches since the 9th, nor could he draw forward X Corps in sufficient time to support, to any effect, an engagement commenced by the Grand Duke's detachment. Moreover, the detachment had had to make extraordinary efforts during the last fortnight. After the Grand Duke had at noon received a written communication of the contents of General Count von Moltke's dispatch of the 13th and also of the inferences drawn from it, he received orders in the evening to avoid any serious collision with the enemy on the 15th, as on that day X Corps and the advance guard of III Corps were in the first place to move up to the positions of the French right wing.[11]

On the morning of 15 December the advance guard of X Corps, moving along the main road to Vendôme, encountered opposition from French infantry and artillery at Crucheray. In a protracted engagement with what was evidently a very substantial enemy force, Voigts-Rhetz brought up the 40th Brigade in an effort to turn the French right flank; this attack was supported by three batteries, and was successful in occupying the villages of Orgie and Le Grand Puteaux, but it was clear that the French were in such strength on the Vendôme road that for the moment no further progress could be made. Meanwhile, III Corps was hurrying to fill the gap between the right of X Corps and the detachment. Its movement was, however, impeded by the state of the road, necessitating frequent diversions. Manstein, having had the bridge at Blois repaired, was now able to move his corps across the Loire, leaving only a mixed brigade south of the river.

It was now clear to Frederick Charles and Stiehle that in order to deal with Chanzy's position on the Loir it would be necessary to concentrate their whole force, and they decided to postpone the assault until 17 December, which would enable the bulk of their troops to get some much-needed rest. On 16 December, however, the situation changed dramatically. An intelligent telegraph clerk at Blois succeeded in intercepting dispatches passing from Le Mans via Vendôme to Tours, from which it was learned that 2nd Army of the Loire was now in retreat towards Le Mans and the Camp of Conlie. Confirmation of this came with news that Vendôme had been evacuated.

Meanwhile, further north, it had become apparent to Stosch that the exhausted condition of the 17th Division was such that it had to be pulled out of line and replaced by the 22nd Division. From his position close to Fréteval, Stosch issued orders that Wittich's Division should move

11 *Official Account*, vol. IV, pp.69–70.

forward to relieve the 17th Division in its position to the south of the Forest of Marchenoir, while Rauch's detachment at Morée should be replaced by the Bavarian combined brigade. All the units of the detachment along the Loir were ordered to keep a minutely careful watch on the enemy positions on the river. At Fréteval, the relief of the 17th Division was at first carried out without difficulty.[12]

The process was however delayed by an attack launched by 21st Corps led by Rousseau with part of his 1st Division on Rauch's troops at Morée. Several French battalions advanced from St Hilaire under the cover of artillery firing from the west bank of the Loir. In severe fighting, the 89th Regiment, now reinforced by the Bavarian brigade, was able to throw them back.

Chanzy's hope of making a prolonged stand on the Loir had begun to fade during 15 December as it became increasingly clear that the morale of his troops was crumbling; without shelter or campfires, bivouacked in the mud and snow, and drenched in the pouring rain so graphically described by de Mauni, they had suffered terribly. He wrote, sadly: 'It was evident that they were so exhausted that it would prevent them responding vigorously, if the struggle commenced again that day; the corps commanders did not conceal their apprehensions on the point.'[13] From each of his generals came seriously pessimistic assessments of the morale of the troops. It was in the end, however, the opinion of Jauréguiberry that was finally decisive. Chanzy had come to count on the determination and tenacity of the admiral, and when he declared that he did not believe that any serious resistance was possible, he reluctantly accepted the inevitable, and gave the necessary orders to prepare to retreat. Lehautcourt, observing that the retreat could not be avoided, noted that if the Germans had pushed their advance more vigorously, 2nd Army of the Loire must have suffered to an even greater extent.[14]

While Frederick Charles was setting off in pursuit of Chanzy's army, Moltke had been giving further thought to the overall position on the Loire. He remained anxious not to see Second Army overextended, although still prepared to leave operational decisions to the man on the spot. Accordingly, he wrote again to Stiehle on 14 December: How far, he wanted to know, was it necessary for III Corps to follow the enemy, and for how long?

> It is for you to decide in the light of the resistance you encounter. For me, I do not believe that it is necessary, either for forcing General Chanzy to continue his retreat or of occupying Tours. Even today this city must doubtless have been occupied by a division of IX Corps, which has followed the left bank of the Loire, and is fully sufficient to ensure possession of this area. One must also imagine that the other half of the Army of the Loire has had time to assemble around Bourges; under the leadership of a general as able as Bourbaki it would easily be able within a few days to take the offensive on the left bank against Orléans or on the right bank through Gien. In these two cases, the Bavarian Corps would scarcely be able to hold this attack; particularly in the second case it will not be strong enough, even with the support of Hartmann's Division, of which we do not know the exact position.[15]

12 Wittich, *Journal,* pp.284–285.
13 Chanzy, *Deuxième Armée*, p.203.
14 Lehautcourt, *Campagne*, p.108.
15 Moltke, *Correspondance Militaire*, vol. II pp.591–592.

While this letter was in transit to Second Army headquarters, Frederick Charles received a message from von der Tann in Orléans which rekindled his anxiety about the threat from Bourbaki. On 15 December von der Tann reported that von der Groeben with the 14th Cavalry Brigade had been obliged to retreat from Vierzon to Salbris upon the appearance of large bodies of infantry advancing from the south and east. On the evening of the following day Frederick Charles received a message that the body of troops at Gien, consisting of three squadrons and two battalions, had been attacked on the afternoon of 15 December by superior forces from Briare.[16]

To Frederick Charles this seemed very much to indicate that Bourbaki was preparing a substantial advance on Montargis and Fontainebleau, a possibility which had never left his mind. At that moment the only forces available to resist such an advance were three under-strength brigades of von der Tann's Corps at Orléans; but the information that Chanzy was again retreating meant that it was no longer necessary to engage in a major struggle on the Loir, so it would only be for a short time that von der Tann would have to take up a defensive position on the Orléans Canal while awaiting the arrival of units of Second Army. On 15 December, before Moltke's letter had reached Stiehle, the latter's report of the position on 14 December had arrived at Versailles, followed by another report recording the advance of X Corps on Vendôme. In these, he did not mention Tours, and at 5:30 p.m. on 15 December Moltke sent off a sharply worded telegram:

> Is Tours occupied? It is very desirable that all railway bridges in and around Tours, three on the Loire and one on the Cher, be totally destroyed. The bridge at Cher and that at Cinq-Mars on the Loire, are of no use to us; the Loire bridges in the direction of Le Mans will not be useful if we have occupied Tours. Where is the 1st Cavalry Division?[17]

Moltke was evidently coming to the conclusion that, whatever might be his desire not to interfere, it was still sometimes necessary to give operational instructions.

Stiehle, meanwhile, was sufficiently uncomfortable about the threat from Bourbaki to send an enquiry to Moltke on 16 December as to the situation of Zastrow's VII Corps. Moltke was able to respond once with a reassuring telegram:

> General von Rheinbaben was yesterday, with the brigade Barby at Courtalain. Today, the heads of the columns of the 5th Cavalry Division reached Montmirail and Mondoubleau, where they will receive instructions for 17 December. Yesterday General von Zastrow received orders to march on Auxerre.[18]

During 16 December Frederick Charles made his way to La Chapelle Vendômoise, where he arrived at noon; there was no sound of artillery, from which he deduced that Chanzy had already begun to retreat, which meant that he could turn his attention to doing something about the threat from Bourbaki. Immediately, IX Corps, having crossed to the right bank of the Loire, was ordered to march eastwards to Beaugency, and to proceed to Orléans on

16 *Official Account*, vol. IV p.75.
17 Moltke, *Correspondance Militaire*, vol. II, p.593.
18 Moltke, *Correspondance Militaire*, vol. II, pp.593–594.

17 December. Confirmation of Chanzy's retreat reached Frederick Charles later that afternoon and at 4.00, III Corps was ordered to move eastwards as far as possible, aiming to reach Mer on 17 December and Beaugency next day. The 6th Cavalry Division was to set off towards Coulmiers. The task of following up Chanzy's retreating army was left to X Corps, and to the detachment.[19] Voigts-Rhetz was to occupy Tours, while holding Blois, and breaking up the railways to the south; and the detachment, its independence from Second Army now restored, was to move to Châteaudun.

It was, therefore, only Voigts-Rhetz and X Corps that were seriously engaged once Chanzy had begun his retreat. He posted Kraatz, with the 20th Division, at Vendôme to watch for indications that the French were contemplating any aggressive action, and with the rest of his force set out to advance on Tours, in accordance with his orders. An advance guard under Major General von Lüderitz, consisting of the 9th Lancers, the 78th Infantry Regiment, and 2nd Heavy Battery reached St Amand on 18 December, and the neighbourhood of Villedomer on the following day, when the main body reached Châteaurenault. Information from prisoners suggested that a substantial French force of at least 15,000 infantry had been concentrated at Monnaie, near Tours, and as X Corps advanced it began to encounter increasing resistance. This was, however, overcome, although not without cost, and the French resumed their retreat.[20]

Voigts-Rhetz, unclear as to the position and intentions of the French, the next day ordered von Woyna, with six squadrons, six battalions, and two batteries to advance along the Tours road. He was ordered to only occupy Tours if it could be done without serious action. As it was, he encountered some resistance, sufficient to lead Voigts-Rhetz to conclude that he had not sufficient strength both to occupy Tours and to move to destroy the railway bridges over the Loire above and below the city, and he put his troops into quarters. In the following days he sent out patrols to monitor the French, who were encountered at St Calais and Montrois.

Frederick Charles got back to Orléans on 18 December, where he found the troops of IX Corps, which had arrived on the previous day after marching about 50 miles in 24 hours. It stood ready to operate against any enemy advance from Gien or up the Loing Valley, while III Corps and the 6th Cavalry Division were also making their way towards Orléans. But the concern which had been caused by the French activity at Gien turned out to be a false alarm; it was merely a roving column which occupied the town briefly before withdrawing. The units of Second Army at Orléans, therefore, could look forward to a well-earned rest.

Moltke, though, pondering the overall situation of those of his armies charged with preventing a relief of Paris, thought it was time to spell out to Frederick Charles, and to Manteuffel in the north, the strategy that was hereafter to be pursued, and the reasons for it. He wrote his letter on 15 December, although it was not sent until the evening of 17 December:

> The general situation requires that after a victory the enemy is pursued only as far as it is necessary to disperse the bulk of his forces and thus render it impossible for them to concentrate again for a considerable time. We cannot follow the French all the way to their last strongholds such as Lille, Le Havre and Bourges; we do not wish to permanently occupy distant provinces such as Normandy, Brittany and the Vendée; we must resolve to

19 *Official Account*, vol. IV, p.76.
20 *Official Account*, vol. IV, p.86.

> abandon certain points which we have taken, such as Dieppe and eventually Tours, in order to concentrate our principal forces at a small number of important points.[21]

While the principal German forces should remain concentrated until the opportunity arose to deliver a short sharp blow to the enemy, flying columns should, he recommended, be organised to chase *franc-tireurs* away from the immediate vicinity of the key points. Moltke went on to outline the strategy to be pursued in the north, in the west and in the south. In the north, First Army was to concentrate at Beauvais; Rouen, Amiens and Saint Quentin should continue to be occupied, while the army was to evacuate the left bank of the Seine, continuing to observe the river as far as Vernon.

In the west, the detachment, after it ended its pursuit of Chanzy's army, would concentrate at Chartres, with a strong detachment at Dreux. Facing south, Second Army should concentrate at Orléans, evacuating the left bank of the Loire but observing the enemy in the direction of the river Cher. On the other hand, Gien should be occupied, as should Blois if Tours was not. If Bourbaki did advance, it would be important to maintain the bulk of the army on the right bank. Meanwhile Zastrow with VII Corps was to advance on Auxerre. It was a clear and well considered strategy, but Moltke knew that he must keep a close watch on both Manteuffel and Frederick Charles to ensure that they had the necessary self-restraint to execute it. It was his intention to keep in his own hands the decision to go on the offensive; it would be for him to decide whether the enemy had concentrated sufficiently to justify an attack. For the moment I Bavarian Corps was to remain attached to Second Army, although a week later it was decided that it should be concentrated at Étampes, and would serve as a general reserve, being placed again under the orders of Third Army.[22]

The retreat of Chanzy's army was by no means straightforward:

> All the movements, carried out at dead of night, almost always along narrow and difficult roads, affected the troops profoundly, perhaps as much as a battle lost. Their morale, already badly weakened on the Loir, could not fail to be gravely affected. This was particularly regrettable since the Germans were not pursuing closely.[23]

A further difficulty, as Chanzy found when he arrived at Epuisay, was that while the army was falling back along the roads towards Le Mans, columns of reinforcements, munitions and supplies, which had been sent to the army by the War Ministry were attempting to move in the opposite direction. As a result, only short marches were possible during 17 December. As the retreat continued, the weather changed again, becoming bitterly cold, and the rain was replaced by snowstorms. Fortunately for Chanzy, the pursuit was still being carried out very circumspectly, partly because of the exhaustion of the German infantry, and partly because Frederick Charles remained uncomfortable about the possible threat from Bourbaki. Nevertheless, as his army struggled westwards across close and hilly country along the narrow twisting roads, Chanzy's fears about the steady disintegration of his army were proved altogether justified, and it ultimately reached Le Mans in a state of total exhaustion. His personal energy and

21 Moltke, *Correspondance Militaire*, vol. II, pp.594–595.
22 Helvig, *Operations*, p.362
23 Lehautcourt, *Campagne,* p.110.

determination, however, was unaffected, and he immediately set about reorganising his army – he still did not accept that all was lost.

Meanwhile Stosch's eventful stint as chief of staff of the detachment was coming to an end. With Chanzy's retreat, it was judged that he should now return to the Royal Headquarters. Waldersee, to his great delight, was nominated to succeed him as the Grand Duke's chief of staff. At Versailles, Stosch was left in no doubt how well-regarded was his time on the Loire. He wrote in his memoirs: 'I emerge from the campaign as a soldier and not without recognition. I thank God for that.'[24] The King was particularly grateful, telling him that he had fulfilled all his expectations and had done exactly what he wished; he had already conferred on him the Iron Cross First Class. Moltke, never one to wear his heart on his sleeve, warmly welcomed him, and reportedly said: 'We have always felt your strong hand there.' Verdy wrote in his journal for 21 December that Stosch had done brilliantly with the detachment, '…and a considerable part of the successes gained is due to him.'[25]

Stosch was certainly appreciative of the recognition of his achievements by those in a position to really understand all of the circumstances. But he would not have been human if he had not felt a lingering resentment that convention dictated that the public credit for his victories should be accorded to the Grand Duke and to Frederick Charles. The King, though, always profoundly loyal to those that served him well, never forgot Stosch's achievements in a difficult situation, and Stosch was able to count upon his personal support for his lifetime.[26]

As he took up his duties as intendant general at Versailles again, Stosch hoped that another opportunity might arise for him to be sent into the field, observing in his memoirs that he had 'acquired a taste for blood.'[27] However, in this he was to be disappointed, and he continued in his post for the rest of the war. The continuing ill-health of War Minister von Roon led to rumours that Stosch would be appointed in his place. Waldersee, in his diary, was inclined to believe that this was possible; he wrote that Bismarck had been trying to establish contacts with officers on the General Staff, but that certain generals had not fallen entirely into his net: 'It is different with Stosch. For a long time, he has been the secret adviser of Bismarck. It is calculated that Roon will soon die or resign. Then Stosch will become his successor through Bismarck's friendship.'[28] Stosch, though, told his wife not to believe a word of such rumours.

24 Stosch, *Denkwurdigkeiten,* p.217.
25 Verdy, *Royal Headquarters*, p.227.
26 Hollyday, *Bismarck's Rival*, p.79.
27 Stosch, *Denkwurdigkeiten*, p.218.
28 Hollyday, *Bismarck's Rival,* p.84.

16

Vendôme

The precipitate and disorderly retreat of Chanzy's army from the Loir to Le Mans might have suggested that no significant activity was to be expected from the French for a considerable time. Certainly, Chanzy was obliged to accept the fact that many of his units were for the moment quite incapable of advancing against the enemy. Barry's Division, for instance, had been gravely weakened by the events of the past few weeks, and he told Chanzy that he could not think of taking the offensive. The situation of his division was, he said, aggravated by the indifference being displayed by the local authorities to the extreme distress of his troops, and the inhabitants preferred to sell their produce to the enemy.[1]

Not all of Chanzy's forces were, however in a totally enfeebled condition. German cavalry patrols were soon reporting the presence of substantial bodies of enemy troops to the west and north-west of Vendôme in pursuance of the indomitable Chanzy's wish to resume offensive operations as soon as possible. The main body of his army established itself around Le Mans, a process which was completed by the morning of 21 December. Chanzy was able to feel satisfaction that his entire force had moved into the exact positions which he had prescribed. There was, however, no improvement in the weather. It was bitterly cold; a light covering of snow lay on the ground and had rendered movement painfully slow along difficult roads, and there were few inhabited areas offering cantonments for the troops, most of whom thus continued to camp in tents and as a result suffered severely from the cold.[2]

Nevertheless, a number of the units of 2nd Army of the Loire were able to send forward continuous reconnaissances, backed in many cases by larger detachments. Kraatz, the commander of the 19th Division decided, on 26 December, to send forward a force under Lieutenant Colonel von Boltenstern in order to establish exactly what the enemy were up to. His detachment comprised a squadron of lancers, two battalions of the 79th Regiment, and two guns. It was not a large force; the two battalions together totalled only 931 men.[3] However, Boltenstern was about to, unknowingly, march into a trap.

Chanzy had been able to form two mobile columns. One of these, commanded by General Rousseau, who had impressed him with his conduct during the operations on the Loir,

1 Lehautcourt, *Campagne*, pp.136–137.
2 Chanzy, *Deuxiéme Armée*, p.231.
3 *Official Account*, vol. II, p.89.

comprised 2,000 infantry drawn from the 21st Corps, later reinforced by two battalions of the 56th *Régiment de Marche* under Lieutenant Colonel Villain. Rousseau also had two squadrons of light cavalry, a battery of four pounders, and a section of mitrailleuses. He was ordered to push forward to Nogent le Rotrou, retreating along the Huisne or through Bonnétable if he encountered considerable opposition.[4]

The other column was much larger, consisting of the 3rd Division of 17th Corps under General Jouffroy. This column was to reconnoitre the country between the Loir and the Loire as far as the railway from Le Mans to Tours, which it was to endeavour to restore if possible. This division had taken up a position on the right bank of the Sarthe, and it was from here that it moved out on 24 December. The movement of this column was facilitated by a diversionary march to the south-west undertaken by a force under General Ferri-Pisani advancing from Saumur. In accordance with Chanzy's instructions Jouffroy reached La Boutinière on 24 December, Courdemanche on the following day, and Bessé by 26 December. From here, Jouffroy was in a position to threaten both St Calais and Montoire; having got there, he applied to Chanzy for fresh instructions as to his further movements, and in response was directed to continue his march on Montoire.[5]

While these movements were getting under way, Chanzy had been in receipt of important information from Trochu in Paris. One of the latter's staff, Commandant Boisdeffre, had escaped from the capital by balloon on 22 December, and had made his way to the headquarters of the 2nd Army of the Loire. What he had to say profoundly impressed Chanzy, who on the following day sent a detailed appreciation of the situation as he saw it, based on what he had been told, calling for an immediate and coordinated advance towards Paris. The spirit of the population of the capital was, he wrote, ready to make all the sacrifices necessary. The dissident party of Blanqui, Pyat, Flourens and others had been crushed by the resistance of the people en masse. He reviewed the state of the forces available to Trochu; the troops of the line, notwithstanding heavy losses, were well disposed, well organised, well led and ready to march; the *gardes mobiles*, on the other hand, lacked solidity. In terms of resources, Paris should be able to hold out until the end of January. Boisdeffre had also told him that the army there was intended to recommence operations on 21 December. It could not lift the siege by itself; it could only be lifted by the simultaneous action of an immediate and energetic relieving army. This must involve not only Chanzy's own forces, but also those of Bourbaki and Faidherbe.[6]

This passionate appeal for united and vigorous action should have prompted a detailed reply from Gambetta or Freycinet. What Chanzy received, however, was the kind of highly coloured and imprecise response from Gambetta to which he was unfortunately now becoming accustomed. Gambetta, who was at Lyon, did not reply until 27 December. He complemented Chanzy on the care with which he was restoring his men, who he said had proved themselves in glorious struggles. He counted on Chanzy being ready soon, and that he should produce a plan of operations, which he would pursue with his habitual vigour. Gambetta ended his letter with a typical flourish: 'You have decimated the Mecklenburgers; the Bavarians have ceased to exist; the rest of the army is already overcome by anxiety and lethargy. Persevere, and we shall drive these hordes from our soil with empty hands.'[7]

4 Lehautcourt, *Campagne*, p.140.
5 Lehautcourt, *Campagne*, pp.141–142.
6 Chanzy, *Deuxiéme Armée*, pp.235–239.
7 Chanzy, *Deuxiéme Armée*, pp.240–242.

Chanzy was unimpressed by this sort of empty rhetoric, observing caustically: 'This letter did not appear to contain sufficient information or appreciation as to enable the situation to be defined.' He dispatched an urgent reply on 30 December insisting on properly coordinated action:

> Our best chance of success must reside in the combination of our movements, in the simultaneous cooperation of three armies towards the same end, in the same effort at the same moment. Without this, we expose ourselves to seeing our forces beaten in detail, when properly directed they would have been able to triumph.

He went on to set out the role of his own army as he saw it, which was, he said, clearly defined by the situation.[8]

He followed this up with another letter, dated 2 January, which he sent by hand with Boisdeffre to Bordeaux, reiterating the urgency of the situation. The final crisis had, he said, arrived; and it was necessary that all the forces available should be employed in an effort to relieve Paris. In a wide ranging review of the overall situation (hampered, as he not unreasonably pointed out, by the lack of clear information from the centre), he put forward a plan for the immediate advance towards Paris by all the various armies; his own advance, 120,000 strong, would be on a broad front from the Loir and the Huisne.[9]

While engaged on this correspondence, which he must have been coming to regard as increasingly futile, Chanzy's troops had been in action around Vendôme. The infantry had pushed forward to Montoire, and had only evacuated St Calais on 25 December, following some shells fired into the place by the Germans, whose pursuing cavalry subsequently met superior forces at Bouloire.[10]

Boltenstern's force reached Montoire on the afternoon of 26 December, and on the following morning, after leaving two companies at Montoire as a garrison, marched towards Sougé. En route, however, as the head of the column reached Troo, it was met with fire from the village; two more companies were detached to search the place, and the rest continued to Sougé. Here, however, it ran into stiff resistance and, fired at on all sides, was forced to retreat. Passing through Troo, it picked up the two companies left there and continued its march. East of St Quentin, the column found its way barred by dense crowds of skirmishers, supported by substantial columns of infantry and, to the north, a battery which opened fire on the Germans. Boltenstern's force now found itself completely surrounded; if it could not cut its way out, it faced either surrender or annihilation.

Boltenstern ordered his guns to fire independently for a short time, and then launched his five companies in a charge without firing a shot:

> After a bitter hand-to-hand struggle, on which the French artillery poured in shell fire regardless, they succeeded in forcing back the enemy's right wing to the heights and through the gap thus created effected their retreat. In the rear of the infantry Lieutenant Bachmann with both guns dashed at full gallop towards Montoire, to each gun he had rapidly hooked

8 Chanzy, *Deuxiéme Armée*, pp.243–244.
9 Chanzy, *Deuxième Armée*, pp.243–249.
10 *Official Account*, vol. IV, p.88.

> up four untouched horses from a farmstead; he fortunately reached the village, although during the retreat under the heaviest artillery and musketry fire, he had to unharness two wounded horses. The squadron also reached the same village without appreciable loss, after breaking through two lines of hostile skirmishers and, dismounted, leading their horses over several ditches.[11]

While this was going on the two companies left in Montoire had been fired upon since 2.00 p.m. but had not been attacked in strength. When the French did subsequently launch an assault at about 4.00 these companies drove it back and also successfully repulsed further attacks. The remaining German detachments reached the other bank of the Loir and took the road through Lavardin, followed by the garrison of Montoire; they were only followed for a short distance by the enemy.

In this action the Germans lost a total of about 150 men, of whom 70, some of them wounded, were taken prisoner. French losses were about 450, of whom nearly 250 had been captured and were brought away by Boltenstern's force. The success was hailed with great enthusiasm at Versailles, where the Crown Prince wrote in his diary on 29 December:

> We received today the glorious news how Lieutenant Colonel von Boltenstern of the 3rd Hanoverian Infantry Regiment Nr.79, with six companies, a squadron of horse and two guns, had at Montoire-la-Chartre, after a courageous defence against superior forces, which had actually surrounded him, triumphantly fought his way through and with the loss on his side of some hundred men had brought in 10 officers and 230 men as prisoners. A noble example for the army, over which General Count Moltke, altogether against his wont, came very near to breaking down.[12]

The resistance which Boltenstern had encountered suggested to the Germans that, somewhat surprisingly, the French were preparing an attack on Vendôme. This was indeed the case; it was a tribute to Chanzy's ability to restore at least some elements of his army to the status of an effective fighting organisation. This was in spite of the fact that the weather had continued to be appalling, and that the troops had mostly still been obliged to bivouac in the open. In spite of his defeat at Beaugency, and his subsequent chaotic withdrawal from the Loir, Chanzy had not given up hope that Paris could yet be relieved, as his correspondence with Gambetta demonstrated. For the moment he planned a characteristically bold movement by Jouffroy on Vendôme. At Montoire on 28 December the latter received orders to continue his march on Vendôme, calling to him all the reinforcements which Barry had available. The brigade of General Marty, consisting of four battalions and six guns had reached Lunay; the other two brigades of Barry's Division, those of Thierry (seven battalions and four guns) and Baille (six battalions and six guns) were to remain in support, as was the column of General Cleret which had reached Mattray.[13] Jouffroy received the reinforcements from Barry on 30 December and prepared his move on Vendôme.

11 *Official Account*, vol. IV, pp.89–90.
12 Crown Prince, *War Diary*, p.237.
13 Lehautcourt, *Campagne*, p.148.

Meanwhile Kraatz, on receiving news of Boltenstern's engagement, had occupied Varennes, and sent forward patrols to assess French intentions. These found that substantial bodies of the enemy were assembling on the far side of Azay. On 29 December he was reinforced by the detachment which had been at Herbault, while the 1st Cavalry Brigade (Lüderitz) took over responsibility for covering the bridge at Fréteval, releasing the detachments which had been posted there. This gave Kraatz, at Vendôme, a total of 3 cavalry regiments, 11 battalions of infantry, and 6 batteries, and he resolved to move forward on Epuisay; at the same time Lüderitz was to advance in the same direction from Fréteval.[14]

On 31 December, Kraatz's advance guard under von Diringhofen moved forward on the road to Azay, with flanking detachments in the Vendôme Forest and towards La Gué du Loir. He had 2 squadrons, 4 battalions and 10 guns. Approaching Azay, his leading troops were fired on from the village and also from La Merillière. At 10.00, Diringhofen ordered his troops to attack the French positions, but soon found that his left was threatened by six French battalions advancing from Le Briand. At the same time Kraatz received reports from his cavalry patrols that considerable bodies of the enemy were moving round the north of Azay towards Espéreuse and from thence in the direction of Vendôme, and he realised that the French were undertaking a substantial advance. In view of this he ordered Diringhofen back to Vendôme.

Diringhofen's right flanking detachment, at Bel-Air Château, had advanced to Les Petites Belzéveries, where it beat off a French advance before, hearing the distant thunder of artillery from the direction of Vendôme, retreating to the suburb of Tuileries. The French troops advancing from Espéreuse occupied the Château of Bel-Air, but were then driven back by a battalion of the 56th Regiment which Kraatz sent forward. In its turn however this unit was forced back when its left flank was threatened, and it then took up a position along the railway embankment. By 2.00 p.m. the German artillery had got into position on the heights south of Vendôme, from where six batteries opened on the French right wing, which then withdrew in disorder.[15]

Jouffroy had advanced on Vendôme with a total of 11 squadrons, 24 battalions, and 34 guns. He had received intelligence that the Germans were now in considerable strength around the town, but he believed that he was obliged to persist in his planned attack. His advance was in two principal columns, one moving through Azay and Espéreuse and the other through Courtiras. Meanwhile another detachment crossed the Loir at Lisle and moved to the south of Vendôme. Further west, a force of Algerian *éclaireurs* crossed the Loir at Montoire, and headed eastwards to cut the roads to Oucques and Blois.[16] It was Jouffroy's hope that these movements together would enable him to occupy Vendôme on the following day. If all went well he might even be able to cut off the German line of retreat, and he appealed to Chanzy for all of the available reinforcements. However, the strength of Kraatz's Division proved too much for him, and during the night of 31 December/1 January he withdrew to the positions he had occupied on 25 December.

While the combat at Vendôme was taking place, there had also been a sharp action at Danzé when Lüderitz's Brigade, advancing from Fréteval, encountered a strong force of enemy infantry. After a brisk struggle the French were driven back to Epuisay, abandoning three guns in their

14 *Official Account*, vol. IV, p.91.
15 *Official Account*, vol. IV, p.93.
16 Lehautcourt, *Campagne*, p.151.

retreat. Three squadrons of hussars followed the enemy, and these then threw back an attempt to turn the flank of Lüderitz's Brigade. Thereafter, he withdrew, as intended, to Fréteval, carrying off the captured guns and also 53 prisoners.[17]

Chanzy's launch of these operations around Vendôme was certainly bold, but not, in all the circumstances, altogether wise. It appears that there was a difference of opinion between Chanzy and Jouffroy as to how the operation was to be developed. According to Lehautcourt, Chanzy saw it as intended to harass the enemy, and clear the country between the Loir and the Loire with a view to further operations; Jouffroy was to recapture Vendôme, and if this was possible, then to reoccupy Blois. Jouffroy, on the other hand, appears to have seen it as having a more ambitions aim, believing that after taking Vendôme, the whole army would not delay in following him there.[18] The only chance of a successful outcome was, in Lehautcourt's opinion, if it was carried out with precision and, especially, if the Germans did not bring up all their available forces. Since it was altogether unlikely that they would fail to do this, in all the circumstances the operation was imprudent. Apart from anything else, this evidence that 2nd Army of the Loire was still a force capable of offensive action contributed substantially to the decision that Moltke was about to make.

Conscious that the attack had failed to achieve its object, Chanzy tried to put the best face on it in his memoirs, writing:

> This demonstration at Vendôme, carried out most vigorously by our troops, had forced the enemy to concentrate at this point. His losses, according to the inhabitants, had been considerable; ours were less serious, thanks to the elan of our troops. We took 200 prisoners, and this operation proved to the Germans that 2nd Army was able still to disconcert them.[19]

Whatever had been hoped from the advance, it had nevertheless failed; obliging the Germans to concentrate at Vendôme was hardly in itself capable of being regarded as a satisfactory outcome. In fact, actual German losses in the combat at Vendôme on 31 December amounted to a total of 34 killed, 94 wounded and 100 missing; the extent of French casualties is unclear, but was probably rather greater.

At Versailles, as the war went on, the pressure on Moltke was unrelenting. Not only had he to manage the siege of Paris; he was, as the year drew to a close, obliged to deal also with three disparate campaigns in the north, the west and the south-east, each of which represented a determined attempt by the French to mount a relief of the capital. At the Royal Headquarters, his difficulties were compounded by the increasingly bitter dispute which had developed with Bismarck over the latter's insistence on the bombardment of the city. In spite of all this, Moltke remained calm, and unwaveringly confident of ultimate success. A glimpse of him appears in Verdy's journal for 9 January:

> Concerning Moltke, he lives entirely with his staff, and is as kind as ever to every one of us. No one has ever heard a single harsh word from him during the whole campaign.

17 *Official Account*, vol. IV, p.94.
18 Lehautcourt, *Campagne*, pp.159–160.
19 Chanzy, *Deuxiéme Armée*, p.267.

> With us, he is even merry, in his simple, cheerful and modest way. We all feel happy in his company, and absolutely love and worship him. But outside of our small circle, also, there is only one feeling, and that is admiration towards him; everyone says that he is a truly ideal character.[20]

Chanzy's abortive attempt to take Vendôme was much in Moltke's mind when he came to review the efforts of the Government of National Defence to launch an offensive for the relief of Paris. He concluded that Chanzy was the nearest and most imminently dangerous enemy. On 1 January 1871 the following order went to Stiehle:

> The intelligence received from various quarters shows that Bourbaki's army, if not in its entirety, at any rate in its bulk, was still at Bourges a few days ago. The immediate advance of these forces may also be expected as soon as the hostile offensive movement upon Vendôme and Courtalin from the west has commenced. It would be hazardous to await the approach to each other of these two groups, which are as yet separated by a considerable interval; it rather appears necessary to assume the offensive with superior forces as rapidly as possible against the nearest group, so as to defeat that ere the other can arrive sufficiently close to cooperate. His Majesty the King therefore orders Second Army to take the offensive forthwith against the forces advancing from the west. In order to give Second Army sufficient strength, not only will XIII Army Corps (17th Division and 22nd Division under the command of HRH the Grand Duke of Mecklenburg-Schwerin), but also the 2nd and 4th Cavalry Divisions pass under the direct orders of HRH Prince Frederick Charles… His Majesty, therefore, expects Second Army to assume the offensive without delay in the strength of three and a half Army Corps and three Cavalry Divisions. As a preparatory step thereto it would be well to order the concentration on the Loir between Vendôme and Illiers, and cause it to be completed within two days.[21]

20 Verdy, *Royal Headquarters*, p.239.
21 Moltke, *Correspondance Militaire*, vol. II, pp.637–638; *Official Account*, vol. IV, Appendix CXX.

17

Le Mans: The Approach

When reviewing the orders for Second Army to take the offensive, Frederick Charles and Stiehle had to take into account Jouffroy's failed attempt to take Vendôme. They reached the conclusion that its purpose had merely been to secure a breathing space while the rest of Chanzy's army made its way to new positions around Le Mans:

> It was not improbable that the French would await the abatement of the cold weather, which affected them so terribly, before renewing their operations, and it was to be hoped, that if the German advance was kept secret, the enemy might be surprised in his quarters.[1]

Accordingly, when the orders for a forward move for the various units of Second Army were issued on 5 January, the need for secrecy was impressed on them. For Hans von Kretschmann, this was perfectly absurd; in a letter to his wife written from Meung on 3 January he mockingly questioned just how it was supposed that 30,000 men could begin to march without anyone noticing. Perhaps, he suggested, an accommodating fairy might provide them with a cloak of invisibility.[2]

At all events, Kraatz, in Vendôme, was ordered, 'to maintain an expectant attitude.' He was to act on the defensive so as not to give any indication to the French that a forward move was imminent.

The coming battle, which would mark the climax of the campaign on the Loire, reflected the fundamental differences between the two armies, their composition and their military situation. In the second, exhausting and long drawn out phase of the Franco-Prussian War, for which no one had been prepared after the crushing German victories in the summer and autumn of 1870, the French were compelled always to seek the strategic offensive, for it was incumbent on them to attempt to relieve Paris. On the other hand, for Moltke, the task was strategically defensive, although in pursuing the aim of thwarting any advance towards the capital, it was necessary from time to time to go over to the attack.

The German armies had, therefore, fought their way across France, usually against a heavy numerical supremacy. Their leadership, ethos and training had enabled them almost invariably

1 *Official Account*, vol. IV, p.189.
2 Kretschmann, *Lettres*, p.363.

to overcome these odds. By the turn of the year, their superior military qualities had over and over again been demonstrated. At the same time, however, it had become very apparent that, in the chassepot, the French had by far the best infantry weapon. It was a practical advantage that was, fortunately for the Germans, effectively cancelled out by their peerless artillery, which almost always proved decisive.

Frederick Charles now prepared to advance on a broad front with his three and a half corps and four and a half cavalry divisions. All told, the total forces available to him amounted to 16,360 cavalry, 58,097 infantry, and 324 guns. The southern end of his advance was composed of X Corps, with the 1st and 6th Cavalry Divisions. Its commander was the extremely capable General Konstantin von Voigts-Rhetz, who had demonstrated his ability many times already during the war; his chief of staff continued to be the shrewd Colonel Leo von Caprivi. The 19th Division was commanded by Major General von Woyna; the 20th Division was led by Major General von Kraatz-Koschlau. Together, the two divisions comprised 15,716 infantry. The 1st Cavalry Division was commanded by Lieutenant General von Hartmann and the 6th Cavalry Division by Duke William of Mecklenburg-Schwerin. Voigts-Rhetz was ordered to assemble on the line Vendôme-St Amand, and to advance on 6 January to Montoire.

On the right of the X Corps, General Konstantin von Alvensleben, who had particularly distinguished himself at Mars-la-Tour in August and during the second Battle of Orléans in December, was ordered to move with III Corps south of the Forest of Marchenoir, taking the road to Vendôme, which he was to reach by 6 January. Thereafter, his leading units were to reach the line of the Azay. The 5th Division was led by Lieutenant General von Stülpnagel and the 6th Division by Lieutenant General von Buddenbrock. The corps was 17,235 men strong.

IX Corps, under General von Manstein, was lacking its 25th Infantry Division (Lieutenant General Prince Louis of Hesse) which was posted at Orléans, where it watched for any sign of forward movement by Bourbaki from Bourges. Its advance units were at Gien. The rest of the IX Corps (8,996 men strong), to which the 2nd Cavalry Division (Lieutenant General zu Stolberg) was attached, was to advance to Morée on the Loir on 6 January.

Finally, the newly constituted XIII Corps, under the command of the Grand Duke of Mecklenburg-Schwerin, with Waldersee as its chief of staff, consisted of the 17th Division (Lieutenant General von Tresckow) and the 22nd Division (Major General von Wittich), together with the 4th Cavalry Division (commanded by General von Bernhardi in the absence sick of General Prince Albrecht senior). The divisions of Tresckow and Wittich had, as part of the detachment under the Grand Duke, endured a particularly tough campaign in the battles that culminated in the recapture of Orléans. They had been reinforced by fresh drafts, and had a total combined strength of 16,150 infantry. This corps was ordered to march on 6 January from Chartres to Brou, sending a strong detachment to Nogent le Rotrou. Finally, the 12th Cavalry Brigade was responsible for covering the extreme right flank of the army as it moved forward. In spite of the fresh drafts which arrived from Germany to make good some of the numbers lost in the punishing winter battles, each of Frederick Charles's seven infantry divisions was at roughly half its full establishment, and the loss of so many experienced and battle-hardened troops had inevitably diminished their fighting efficiency. Nevertheless, as the forthcoming Battle for Le Mans would show, those that remained lived up to their well-deserved reputation for discipline, professionalism and bravery.

Frederick Charles had, on 2 January, taken the trouble to write a personal letter to Wittich. He had, he wrote, been intending for some time to tell Wittich of the satisfaction he felt at the performance of the brave troops under his command, but had been prevented from doing so by the exigencies of the service. He now sent his warmest wishes and congratulations on the subject of the brilliant feats of arms, 'which assure your division and yourself of a memorable page in the history of the campaign.'[3]

The Second Army, in its advance towards Le Mans, would be entering an area which seriously impeded its progress. The official history described the difficulties which it would have to overcome:

> The whole army now passed into the district between the Loir and Sarthe, which consists partly of small plateaux, partly of a labyrinth of ridges, which not infrequently attain a relative height of 200 feet or more. Well filled rivers flow with rapid course through valleys which are generally broad and with steep sides. The entire country is covered with the densest cultivation of long-standing growth, with vineyards, orchards and vegetable gardens. The villages consist mostly of a number of isolated and solidly constructed farmsteads, among which are interspersed châteaux, surrounded with extensive park enclosures and copses. Owing to the extensive subdivision of the land, customary in the country, every property is surrounded by hedges, ditches and walls. There are consequently numerous positions and isolated points at which even moderate troops could defend themselves behind good cover. Although the superior effect of the Chassepot here ceased to avail, the mitrailleuses were in their true element, and became a dangerous weapon in the narrow passes.[4]

Given the difficulties of the country, and the appalling weather conditions which his army had experienced for so long, Frederick Charles decided to stick to the main roads for his advance; the side roads would, he expected, almost certainly be found to be impassable, and he preferred to confine each of his corps to one major road, so that there should be as little delay as possible in getting to grips with Chanzy's army. In fact, a spell of relatively clear frosty weather enabled the army to move towards its jumping off points along the line of the Loir with little difficulty.

Moltke, having given Second Army a clear and simple objective, was quite content to leave Frederick Charles to determine how he should carry it out. Significantly, he sent no further messages to Second Army until after the battle had begun, and then only to tell Stiehle of the creation of the *Südarmee*. He did send a telegram to Rantzau, in command at Gien, on 7 January instructing him to send daily reports to Versailles, and push forward reconnaissance patrols in the direction of Nevers and Clamecy.[5] He was no longer worried that Bourbaki might make a northward move from Bourges, having already assigned to II Corps the duty of leaving the lines of investment around Paris to take up a position at Montargis. In fact, as it was, Bourbaki was already committed to the eastward move which Gambetta and Freycinet had emphatically preferred to Chanzy's proposal for a united advance towards Paris.

Chanzy had already done enough to convince Moltke that he was not only the nearest but also the most dangerous of the French armies endeavouring to mount an advance to the relief of Paris. Although he had suffered very heavy losses in the fighting around Orléans, and in the course of his subsequent retreats, ultimately to Le Mans, Chanzy still enjoyed a huge superiority

3 Wittich, *Journal*, p.340
4 *Official Account*, vol. IV, p.159.
5 Moltke, *Correspondance Militaire*, vol. II, p.635.

in numbers over Frederick Charles. Fresh troops had joined the army, and he had been substantially reinforced by 22 battalions of Breton *gardes nationales* sent from the camp of Conlie; 15 miles north of Le Mans, this camp had been established as a base at which to concentrate new units as they were formed.

Unfortunately, although the concept of creating an assembly area for new troops joining the army was perfectly sensible, the camp proved to be an administrative disaster. Established by Count de Kératry, the former Chief of Police of Paris who had escaped from the capital by balloon, it had been seen as a centre for the building up of a new 'Army of Brittany,' but it had been brought into existence without proper preparation, and inflicted considerable suffering on those troops unfortunate enough to be billeted there. In this way it typified the hurried and ill-considered planning of so many of the projects of the War Ministry. In defence of its officials, though, they were working against a clock which they knew was ticking against them. The numbers at Conlie had grown to a peak of 48,712 officers and men, housed in tents and barrack huts with a completely inadequate water supply.[6] Its occupants had had to endure the prolonged spell of bad weather that afflicted France during the autumn and winter of 1870, and suffered appallingly from sickness. General Gougeard remarked of the camp: 'Many reproaches were made regarding Conlie Camp, all deserved in my opinion.'[7] The special correspondent of the *Daily News* reported from Rennes on 30 December:

> At the present moment the Camp of Conlie exists only in name. Ever changing, modifying, suppressing, and creating, the Delegation of Bordeaux, by the mouth of its effervescent Minister of War, has thought proper to raise the camp, after allowing several millions of francs to be spent upon it for defensive works. The troops who are now daily evacuating Conlie are to be dispersed, we hear, among various encampments, to be formed principally in Ille-et-Vilaine and Mayenne .... Such of the *mobiles* and *mobilises* of Conlie who were armed, have been sent to Le Mans to join the army of General Chanzy, which, it would appear, is growing more and more formidable every day.[8]

The 22 battalions of *gardes nationales* which joined Chanzy's army were of doubtful military value. Their commander, former naval captain Marivaux, protested that they were neither trained nor armed. Many of them were equipped with obsolete American muzzleloaders discarded after the American Civil War and they had not been trained to use even these weapons. All told, these unfortunate troops had been equipped with no less than 11 different models of rifle. The ammunition issued to them was frequently of the wrong calibre, ruined by rain and snow. In spite of this, they took their place in the army preparing to defend Le Mans.[9]

Numerically, it was certainly true that 2nd Army of the Loire was continuing to grow in strength. It was still organised in three corps. Chanzy was fortunate in his corps commanders. Outstanding among these was Admiral Jean Bernard Jauréguiberry. Born in 1815, he had reached the rank of captain by 1860, having served in Crimea and China. After a spell as Governor of Senegal, he was promoted admiral in 1869. With the failure of the

6 Lehautcourt, *Campagne*, p.181n.
7 Fermer, *France at Bay*, p.168.
8 War Correspondence of the *Daily News*, p.482.
9 Lehautcourt, *Campagne*, pp.179–182.

French navy to achieve anything during the early part of the war, he was one of a number of naval officers that were appointed by the Government of National Defence to senior posts in the army, and he quickly justified the confidence placed in him. As commander of 16th Corps, he was a tower of strength, and Chanzy soon came to rely completely upon him. After the war, returning to the navy, Jauréguiberry was to enjoy an illustrious career before becoming Minister of Marine in 1879. 16th Corps consisted of three infantry divisions, commanded respectively by Generals Deplanque, Barry and De Curten; and a cavalry division commanded by General Michel.

Benjamin Jaurès, the commander of 21st Corps, also came from the navy. He was born in 1823, and served successfully in a number of overseas postings prior to the outbreak of the Franco-Prussian War. As with Jauréguiberry, he too proved a competent corps commander upon whom Chanzy could depend. After the war he returned to the navy and, again like Jauréguiberry, in due course became Minister of Marine. Jean Jaurès, the famous socialist politician who was assassinated at the outbreak of the First World War, was his nephew. 21st Corps consisted of four divisions: 1st (General Rousseau) 2nd (General Colin) 3rd (General Villeneuve) and 4th (General Gougeard), together with a cavalry division under General Guillon.

The third of Chanzy's Corps commanders was General Louis Joseph de Colomb. Born in 1823 he had served most of his career in Algeria. He had reached the rank of *general de brigade* before he was called by Chanzy to the command of a division of the 17th Corps, in which he served in the battles around Orléans. He subsequently succeeded General Guépratte in command of the corps, and also proved a reliable leader. 17th Corps comprised: 1st Division (General de Roquebrune), 2nd Division (General Paris), 3rd Division (General Jouffroy) and a cavalry division commanded by General d'Espeuilles.

Chanzy had not been idle since the bulk of his army had reached Le Mans. It is not altogether correct to say, as Michael Howard observed, that the security of Chanzy's base there 'depended not on geographical or artificial defences of its own but solely on the difficulty which the Germans found in supplying troops fighting so far to the west – difficulties which their staff found means to overcome.'[10] In fact, in the last two weeks of December most of Chanzy's army had been put to work in fortifying a line of defence running across a wooded plateau along the River Huisne; the flank and rear of this position were covered by the River Sarthe. Lehautcourt described the huge effort which Chanzy had made to strengthen these lines of defence: 'epaulments, shelter trenches, barricades and abatis had been prepared at many points; the corps remaining around Le Mans after the advance of the mobile columns received food, supplies and munitions which they had lacked. Batteries of seven pounders and mitrailleuses reinforced the army; remounts were supplied for the artillery and the cavalry.'[11] The correspondent of the *Daily News* wrote, 'The ground in front of Le Mans is of such a conformation that it has been declared impossible for any general to take up a bad position there. General Chanzy's army held a series of wooded heights, which he had had plenty of time to fortify.'[12]

The city of Le Mans had been less badly affected by the war than might have been expected. Roger de Mauni, whose unit had endured such severe privations as it was shuttled from place to place during November and December, found it a refreshing change from rain sodden campsites:

10 Howard, *Franco-Prussian War*, p.397.
11 Lehautcourt, *Campagne*, p.247.
12 War Correspondence of the *Daily News*, p.481.

> The capital of Maine has become a general rendezvous, not only for the army, but for all who have friends or relations under our flag; they avail themselves of these few days' respite to come and see them. The shopkeepers are all agreed in asking double price for everything one cannot do without, and thanks to the misfortunes of their country, are making very substantial gains; but it must not be forgotten that the billeting of the troops upon them is a very serious evil. And yet how far more are the country people to be pitied, they lose everything and sell hardly anything. For anyone passing down the high street of Le Mans or the Place des Halles, the town would appear as gay, as animated, and as glittering with gold and pleasure as any country town could be. There are no indications here of the misery and suffering which prevail in the more distant quarters.[13]

It was a picture which was about to undergo a spectacular change.

If Second Army was to take the offensive to the west, Le Mans was the obvious target:

> By the size of its population as much as by its geographical situation, Le Mans is one of the most important points in western France. Located between Brittany, Normandy and the central provinces, in other words between regions which differed from each other both in the character of their inhabitants as well as the physical aspects of the country, Le Mans had for this reason alone, a particular importance .... In addition, it was one of the principal road and rail hubs of our country. Five rail lines radiated out from Le Mans in the directions of Chartres and Paris, Alençon and Cherbourg or Caen, Laval and Brest via Rennes, Nantes and Rochefort via Angers, and to Tours and Orléans or Poitiers.[14]

Le Mans is situated astride the River Sarthe, a little upriver from its junction with the Huisne. The central railway station and other major buildings were located between the two rivers. The positions which Chanzy must take up for the defence of the city were principally dictated by the course of these rivers, and by the fact that the commanding heights to the east and the west were at some distance, which meant occupying an extended line. To the north-east ran an undulating plateau, at the centre of which was the village of Sargé; at this point it is crossed by the road to Bonnétable running south-east to north-east. To the south-east the plateau slopes down to the edge of the city; to the north it falls away some six or seven kilometres from the built-up area. It is crossed by two valleys which provided good defensive positions. Along the valleys to the south-east several defensive works had previously been established in November at the time of the advance of the Grand Duke's detachment to Nogent le Rotrou.

On the left bank of the Huisne, the river is dominated by the isolated heights of Auvours. At this point the railway line to Paris runs, and the key road to Orléans via St Calais and Vendôme. To the south of the Huisne and the St Calais road the ground also rises, though not so steeply. The hamlet of La Tuilerie, above the village of Changé, which dominates the road to Chartres, and that of Le Tertre, are the two key points in this sector.

In preparing to defend Le Mans, and to establish positions along these heights, Chanzy had two principal considerations. First was the intrinsic importance of Le Mans, which he recognised that he must defend to the last. Second, there was the topographical problem caused by

13 Roger de Mauni, *The Franco-Prussian War*, pp.99–100.

14 Lehautcourt, *Campagne*, pp.123–124.

the line of the two rivers, which required him to take up a position between them. Lehautcourt challenges the belief that Le Mans should have been defended at all costs, declaring that this meant Chanzy sacrificing his freedom of movement, and that he was in this way repeating the mistakes made at Metz and Orléans. In Lehautcourt's view, only in very particular circumstances should a commander take up such a position, arguing that otherwise it is his first duty to preserve his mobility.[15]

Such an absolute precept takes no account of the nature and quality of Chanzys army or of the overall political and military situation. Still inexperienced, undertrained and only partially equipped with chassepot rifles, the freedom of movement contended for by Lehautcourt would all too probably, under the remorseless pressure of Second Army quickly become the freedom to disintegrate. Such as it was, the best chance of holding Le Mans lay in a resolute defence of the best positions that could be found. And, after all, Chanzy could have had in his mind that his army had for a long time given a good account of itself in the punishing Battle of Beaugency.

It was not, however, Chanzy's intention to sit and wait in his lines around Le Mans for Frederick Charles to arrive. His plan was to disrupt the German advance by meeting it head on along the roads which it must follow. In this way, he reckoned that he could make the best use of the advantages given to him by the nature of the country, and accordingly he pushed strong detachments forward on each of the roads which he knew the enemy must use. The consequence of this was that the heads of columns of the advancing Second Army found themselves involved in quite serious engagements almost as soon as their forward march had begun.

Frederick Charles disposed of his troops in an arc advancing towards Le Mans. His northernmost corps, XIII Corps was to advance down the Huisne, its objective being the left flank of the French army. On 5 January, Wittich's patrols had found the French in possession of La Fourche, about five miles north-west of Nogent le Rotrou, at the junction of the roads from Montlandon and La Loupe. Early on 6 January, on a bright winter's morning, the 44th Brigade advanced on La Fourche in two columns and was received with artillery fire. Supported by a horse artillery battery which ascended a steep ridge to the east, and by a heavy battery moving south from Coulonges, the 83rd and 94th Regiments deployed and advanced on La Fourche. By 2.00 p.m. they had succeeded in capturing the town, where they took three guns; subsequently the French launched a counter-attack, which was driven back before nightfall. It was however too late to resume the advance, and the 44th Brigade remained in its positions overnight.[16] The rest of the 22nd Division had reached Beaumont les Autels, and the 17th Division was at Unverre, about five miles west of Brou. The 4th Cavalry Division encountered opposition at Thiron Gardais, and bivouacked at Combres.

In the centre, III Corps was pushing forward to Vendôme, a move of which Jouffroy was soon aware. He was fearful that Alvensleben would turn south and fall on de Curten's 3rd Division of 16th Corps which was at Châteaurenault, and he accordingly launched his division in a fresh advance on Vendôme. Alvensleben's intention was to push through Vendôme and take up quarters immediately to the west of the town on either side of the road to Epuisay. Only the advance guards of his two divisions were to advance beyond the Azay; but these met with such determined opposition that the main body of the corps had to come up in support. As the leading troops of the 5th Division passed through Vendôme they found two battalions from X Corps,

15 Lehautcourt, *Campagne*, pp.125–126.
16 *Official Account*, vol. IV, p.144.

which had been left there by Voigts-Rhetz as an outpost line on the heights north of the town, engaging troops of Jouffroy's Division emerging through the woods.[17]

The engagement rapidly developed; by mid-afternoon almost the whole of Alvensleben's corps was in action. There was particularly heavy fighting around Jouffroy's position at Azay-Mazange, where General Rothmaler, commanding the advance guard of the 6th Division, launched a strong attack. In the course of this, Rothmaler himself was injured. On the left, the 35th Regiment captured the de Galette mill, and in the centre the 20th Regiment took the La Fosse farmstead, following which the two regiments then stormed the Azay position. The engagement only came to an end at about 5.00 p.m., after the French had attempted a counter-attack which was beaten off with the loss of a number of prisoners. On the extreme right of the 6th Division a detachment took Danzé without difficulty.

Stülpnagel's 5th Division had also encountered stiff resistance to the north of Villiers. Advancing in the face of heavy artillery fire from the French batteries between Clouseaux and Mazange which commanded the whole of the valley, the German infantry were for a while pinned down. At this, the French launched a series of counter-attacks from Clouseaux. Ultimately, however, after the arrival of III Corps' artillery of 36 guns which took up a position east of Le Briand, the French guns were suppressed, and Stülpnagel was able to order his infantry forward, to such effect that the village of Mazange was successfully stormed.[18]

To the left, the 20th Division of X Corps had moved out from Vendôme, advancing by way of Les Roches, while the 19th Division marched from St Amand by way of Amblay and Lavandin towards Montoire. To cover the left flank of this advance, Baumgarth's detachment, consisting of two cavalry regiments, three battalions of infantry and two batteries, was to move up the Châteaurenault – Montoire road, while the 6th Cavalry Division covered the road from Vendôme to Tours; it was then to move westward, while remaining in contact with the 1st Cavalry Brigade which had been brought up to St Amand. Frederick Charles opted to accompany the 19th Division on its advance towards Montoire, which, after the damaged bridge over the Loir at Lavandin had been repaired, it had captured without opposition.

Meanwhile, south of St Amand, de Curten's Division was demonstrating that for the moment at least it was capable of looking after itself. During the night of 5/6 January, Baumgarth's detachment had been widely scattered in a number of outposts from Ambloy to Villeporcher. The intention was that, after the head of the 19th Division had passed Ambloy, the outposts there should lead the way to Prunay. The rest of the detachment was to follow, after the 6th Cavalry Division had reached its assigned position south of St Amand. However, before it could do so, at about 9.30, a French assault was launched on Villeporcher from a position south of the village, which was successful in driving back the outpost there. The engagement rapidly developed, and the Germans were only with difficulty maintaining their position at Pias when Duke William relieved the crisis by arriving at St Gourgon with the 15th Cavalry Brigade. The French had for a while succeeded in advancing northwards to Les Haies, but were then driven back.

The French pressure continued, and the German infantry were forced to retreat behind the River Brenne, where they were supported by a horse artillery battery. Towards 3.00 p.m. the situation had stabilised; the 57th Regiment was assembling at Neuve St Amand with a battalion

17 *Official Account*, vol. IV, p.146.
18 *Official Account*, vol. IV, pp.148–149.

of the 16th Regiment; six companies from two other battalions of this regiment occupied St Amand. Duke William, as the senior officer present, assumed overall command; as the fighting died down he proposed to move the troops into quarters. However, due to a misunderstanding the garrison of St Amand evacuated it in the face of strong French columns from de Curten's Division which had worked their way round to the east. This rendered the position at Neuve St Amand untenable, and the Duke ordered a retreat to Huisseau, where the 38th Brigade had arrived. Meanwhile the 14th Cavalry Brigade had moved west to St Arnay and Prunay; the 15th Cavalry Brigade was on the right of the main road; and Lüderitz on the left side with the 1st Cavalry Brigade.[19]

News of this embarrassing setback at St Amand reached Frederick Charles during the evening of 6 January and he was, understandably, extremely displeased. When Duke William arrived later at the headquarters of Second Army, he got an extremely frosty reception. The rest of the army's advance, though hard fought, had gone well; the Duke was curtly instructed to restore the situation forthwith by retaking St Amand on the following morning, and he returned to his troops somewhat humbled. Since, however, it was realised that the French at St Amand could be reinforced by rail, Voigts-Rhetz was instructed to support Duke William if necessary.[20]

During the night news arrived at Second Army headquarters that Bourbaki, leaving 20,000 men at Vierzon, had moved with 1st Army of the Loire upon Dijon. No further threat, therefore, existed from this quarter, but the news was accompanied by a suggestion that Chanzy had received instructions to take the offensive by way of Nogent le Rotrou. If so he would meet XIII Corps in his front, while the rest of Second Army would be on his right flank. If the French had really been rash enough to launch such an offensive in this sector, they would have been destroyed in the open field.

For 7 January, therefore, the Grand Duke intended that the whole of the 22nd Division should advance on Nogent le Rotrou, supported by the 4th Cavalry Division, while the 17th Division would follow via Beaumont les Autels in support; Wittich's advance guard, consisting of two squadrons of hussars, the 93rd Regiment, 32nd Regiment and a battery of artillery, sent forward patrols at first light. These encountered outbreaks of rifle fire from isolated buildings along the road, but the enemy evacuated these as the advance progressed towards Nogent le Rotrou. On the division's northern flank, the 4th Cavalry Division encountered little opposition.[21] The French speedily evacuated Nogent le Rotrou, though the Grand Duke only learned of this at 1.00 p.m.. By nightfall, the 22nd Division had occupied the town, and pushed on along the road to La Ferté-Bernard towards which the enemy appeared to have retreated. The advance guard encountered stiff resistance at Le Gibet, about 4 miles south-west of Nogent le Rotrou. Meanwhile the 17th Division advanced unopposed to Authon, and continued its advance through St Ulphace, which its leading elements reached by nightfall.

At the headquarters of Second Army, it was concluded that there was no direct connection between Jouffroy's activity in front of Vendôme, and the advance of de Curten at St Amand. If this advance was not part of some overall scheme, then it seemed that the best way to deal with it was to press on with the general advance, so that for 7 January the task of III Corps would be to advance to the line of the River Braye, followed by IX Corps marching through Epuisay,

19 *Official Account*, vol. IV, pp.151–152.
20 *Official Account*, vol. IV, p.154.
21 Wittich, *Journal*, pp.346–347.

with orders to seize the crossing over that river. During the morning of 7 January Frederick Charles rode forward along the Epuisay road. En route he received a report from Voigts-Rhetz, perhaps sent as early as 8.00 a.m., to the effect that the enemy had withdrawn his outposts from opposite Montoire, and had evacuated St Amand, thus that problem at least was disposed of. The movements of X Corps on 7 January were seriously hampered by a thick mist. Frederick Charles, realising that it would not be until the following day that Voigts-Rhetz could move forward, ordered that if the French held the line of the Braye, III Corps was only to move up to the river, and IX Corps was to close up to Epuisay.[22]

Meanwhile Chanzy had become extremely concerned for de Curten's Division. Jouffroy's retreat had, he considered, compromised de Curten's left flank; by 10.00 a.m. on 7 January Prussian columns had appeared in front of Prunay, Villechauve and Villeporcher, as far as St Cyr du Gault. These concentrated their efforts on Villechauve, which they were not at first able to take; there, Colonel Jobey was able to repulse them in a combat which lasted four hours. The key to the French position was only taken at noon; the French launched a counter-attack to cover the retreat of de Curten's Division, which succeeded sufficiently to enable it to get away to the west. De Curten had been extremely exposed, and Chanzy was critical of Jouffroy's direction of operations in this sector. He concluded that to get the situation here under control, Admiral Jauréguiberry should go to Château du Loir, 25 miles due west of St Amand, and take charge of all the troops of Jouffroy, de Curten and Barry, which must necessarily now fall back to the positions prepared in front of Le Mans.[23] Barry's Division was already in full retreat from Les Hermites all the way back to Chahaignies and Jupille.

Alvensleben's plan for 7 January was to turn the French left flank before it could fall back behind the Braye, and to drive it back on Voigts-Rhetz and X Corps. The line of the Azay would be held by the 9th Brigade, while the rest of the corps moved on Epuisay. However, when III Corps moved out from Vendôme, it was found that the bird had flown, and the French had abandoned both Lumay and Fortan. The 9th Brigade was ordered to advance on Fortan, and the rest of the corps moved through Epuisay. For a while, it met with stiff resistance, and it was only after a sharp action that Epuisay was occupied at about 1.30 p.m. The 12th Brigade followed the retreating enemy, but before reaching Braye it encountered further resistance, the French appearing to have occupied all the houses and the heights. By 4.00 p.m., though, the village of Le Poirier and the heights to the north were taken, followed by Sargé, and the French continued their retreat to St Calais.

That night, Moltke sent further information confirming Bourbaki's march to the east:

> It was evident that General Chanzy was thrown on his own resources, but it was also seen how desirable it was to carry out the enterprise directed against him, with the least possible delay. In this sense, Prince Frederick Charles issued his instructions to all his army corps. As the left flank of the army no longer seemed to be in any danger, General von Hartmann received orders to move off the bulk of the troops at St Amand the next day to rejoin the X Corps.[24]

22 *Official Account*, vol. IV, pp.155–156.
23 Chanzy, *Deuxième Armée,* p.275.
24 *Official Account*, vol. IV, pp.158–159.

During 7 January there had been a thaw, but that night the temperature dropped again, so that the roads were once more covered with sheets of ice, seriously hampering all movement. For the following day, the orders for all units of Second Army were to continue with their westward advance. On the right XIII Corps pressed forward into La Ferté-Bernard. Marching from Nogent le Rotrou, the 22nd Division, followed by the 9th Cavalry Brigade, encountered only stragglers, but the road was so frequently broken up that it was not until 4.00 p.m. that the division entered the town. The advance guard of the 17th Division, however, had got there first, while the main body moved south by way of Courgenard and Cormes. It was soon ascertained that the French forces that had been in the front of XIII Corps had retreated south-west to Connerré. Both divisions were able, that night, to find quarters in La Ferté-Bernard; outposts were stationed on both banks of the Huisne.

Because he had expected the French to put up a stiff resistance on the line of the Braye, Frederick Charles had been concerned that XIII Corps should push its advance forward as far and as fast as possible, in order to outflank the French defensive position. The flanking detachment to the left of the 17th Division – under General von Rauch and consisting of the 17th Cavalry Brigade, two battalions of infantry, and a battery of heavy artillery – had been ordered to advance south on Vibraye by way of Montmirail. However, it found that the French had occupied the farms in front of Vibraye; it was only after launching a sudden attack that these were taken and the bridges over the Braye seized. After this the French evacuated Vibraye, falling back on Semur.

In the centre of the German advance, Manstein's IX Corps, which had been advancing on the right rear of III Corps, reached St Calais during the day. The 6th Division from III Corps had reached the place before nightfall on 7 January, and by next day had made good progress towards the west, its advance guard having marched through the Bois des Loges on the north side of the main road. South of the road, the 5th Division encountered no opposition at all during the day. To its left the 14th Cavalry Brigade was serving as the link with X Corps. It moved out of La Richardière, due north of Mont Royal, and advanced westwards through Bessé. Reaching Vancé, the brigade came under heavy fire. The leading squadrons made way for a horse artillery battery which opened fire on the line of dismounted cuirassiers that had taken up a position behind hedges, and then switched targets to a body of infantry along the River Tusson. Subsequently, the horse artillery fired with great effect on a long line of cavalry passing through Vancé, after the redoubtable Major Körber had brought two guns into position. The French, in considerable disorder, were dispersed, and fell back to Montreuil and St Georges. Schmidt led his brigade in pursuit until encountering resistance from a strong force of infantry that had taken up a position behind a series of hedges and ditches, and the brigade paused for the night, occupying quarters in Vancé.

X Corps, advancing on the right bank of the Loir, had a particularly difficult day, passing through a series of narrow defiles along a road that was frequently broken up. Emerging from the village of Poncé, the advance guard was confronted by a force of about 1,000 *gardes mobiles*, armed with mitrailleuses, and it took a long time to drive these back. The corps finally reached La Chartre at 4.00, where it went into quarters for the night. Meanwhile Woyna, with the troops that had been earmarked to reinforce the units to be employed to retake St Amand, reached Sougé and Pont de Braye.[25]

25 *Official Account*, vol. IV, p.162.

At St Amand, the situation had not changed. The French, having abandoned the place, had taken up a position in front of Vilthion on the Châteaurenault road, and remained inconsiderable strength in Villeporcher. Hartmann, reinforcing the 1st Cavalry Brigade with two battalions, launched an attack which succeeded in driving the French back to St Cyr du Gault and then to St Nicolas des Motets. Voigts-Rhetz had assumed that with the recapture of St Amand there would be no further threat to Second Army's left flank, and had sent an order to Hartmann at 10.00 a.m. to follow the rest of the corps to La Chartres. Although, when he found out that the French had not yet retreated as had been assumed, he later sent a counter order, Hartmann had already determined to begin his march westward, though he did not finally move to nightfall, going into quarters at St Arnault, Prunay and Ambloy. Theoretically, this left de Curten with the opportunity to make a further nuisance of himself with those troops of his division that had not so far marched westward, but he made no further move to threaten the Second Army's left flank.

At Château du Loir, Jauréguiberry had found General Desmaisons with 500 troops. He could see that if the Germans were allowed without resistance to advance along the Loir, de Curten's Division at St Amand would indeed be in danger, and his orders to Barry, at Chahaignies, were that he was to hold the place *coute que coute*. This was more easily said than done; Barry's troops were already exhausted and demoralised.[26]

By defending every small village and farmhouse on Second Army's road to Le Mans, Chanzy could certainly delay its westward advance, but he was under no illusion that it could be stopped. Nor did he suppose that retaining his army's mobility would avail him in the face of a determined attack by Frederick Charles. Only by a resolute defence of the positions prepared in front of Le Mans could he have any real chance of preserving his army for a subsequent bold stroke towards Paris. Remaining in the open field would, in effect, confine him to almost indefinite retreat, and the further west he went, the less chance would he have of such a stroke.

Accordingly, he ordered Jaurès to strongly occupy the defensive works at Yvré-l'Eveque, on the Auvours Plateau and in front of Sargé. De Colomb was ordered to push forward his 2nd division (Paris) along the St Calais road with a view to delaying the enemy advance for long enough to enable the rest of the army to get into the Le Mans defensive position. Paris, however, was only able to concentrate his division at St Hubert des Roches by 4.00 a.m. on 9 January, advancing to Ardenay at 11.00 a.m.

Chanzy had apparently a more ambitious task in mind for his right wing. He telegraphed Jauréguiberry during 8 January: 'It is above all necessary to recapture the crossings of the Loir. You have the command of all the troops on both banks .... Move quickly, and you will do well.' Chanzy also ordered the 75th *Gardes Mobile* to move from its position in front of La Tuilerie on 9 January and march to Château du Loir which would involve an extremely long journey. The idea of retaking the Loir crossings was, as Lehautcourt pointed out, an illusion which would soon be shattered.[27] Chanzy's task was being made more difficult by the fact that he was not being kept fully informed, getting no news from Barry, de Curten and Jouffroy; even with Jauréguiberry, at Château du Loir, his communications were irregular.[28]

26 Lehautcourt, *Campagne*, p.214.
27 Lehautcourt, *Campagne*, p.216.
28 Lehautcourt, *Campagne*, p.230.

By nightfall on 8 January the two flank corps of Second Army were at much the same distance from Le Mans, having reached the same high road which runs south from La Ferté-Bernard through St Calais and La Chartres. In the centre, III Corps had drawn out much further in advance, separated from each of the flank Corps by a long march. Frederick Charles, in issuing his orders for the following day, aimed at a further concentration of his forces by advancing along the converging high roads. He did not intend, however, to hold up Alvensleben's march to let the others catch up. He set quite demanding objectives; XIII Corps was to advance to the heights of Montfort, III Corps was to reach Ardenay and X Corps had as its target, Parigné l'Eveque. Each was to push forward advance guards beyond these points. In the centre, IX Corps would follow III Corps, and would reach Bouloire on the main road. Hartmann, with the 38th Brigade and the 1st Cavalry Division, was to be responsible for the protection of Vendôme.[29] This task was to be executed by launching a powerful attack on the French troops still in and around Châteaurenault.

As Second Army closed in on the Le Mans position, XIII Corps was to take steps to destroy the railway to Alençon, and X Corps was to destroy the line running to Tours. But as things turned out, 9 January was to prove another particularly difficult day. Snow fell heavily, limiting visibility and further hampering movement. Nevertheless, the various units of Second Army continued to make some progress. To the north, XIII Corps advanced down the high road from La Ferté-Bernard towards Le Mans; on its right the 4th Cavalry Division was ordered to advance by Bellême and if possible to reach Bonnétable, which would bring it around the French left flank. However, even with the support of its attached infantry, the division was able to make only slow progress in country unfavourable to the deployment of cavalry, and by nightfall, after an infantry battalion had been able to drive the French out of Bellême, took up its quarters there.[30]

As it advanced down the main road, the 17th Division encountered a strong enemy force beyond Sceaux. A battalion of the 75th Regiment was able to drive the French slowly back through Le Poirier and La Croix de Fer. It then had to beat off a French counter-attack, before renewing its advance. Supported by a battalion of the 76th Regiment, it pushed forward, and as night fell had taken Les Landes and Le Coudray. Progress continued to be slow, however, and the advance was held up at Duneau; numerous watch fires were visible in the valley beyond. The main body of the 17th Division was quartered for the night in and around Sceaux. On its right a strong detachment had made an important advance, occupying the villages of Tuffé and St Hilaire on the further bank of the Huisne.

Meanwhile, on the left, Rauch's detachment had assembled at Dollon, and advanced on Thorigné, which was strongly held. After a severe struggle, the village was occupied at about 3.30 p.m., but no further progress could be made. The key objective for the 17th Division had been Connerré, but it had not been possible to take the place during the day. During the night, however, the French fell back, and it was occupied by several companies of infantry. Although progress had been slower than anticipated, the various engagements had yielded around 500 prisoners; the total losses of the division amounted to some 60 men. The 22nd Division, following behind on the main road, was not significantly engaged but as it moved forward, it was hampered by the extreme weather conditions. Wittich wrote in his journal: 'It snowed so

29 Moltke, *Franco-German War*, pp.278–279.
30 *Official Account*, vol. IV, p.164.

heavily that often it was impossible to see farms and châteaux a hundred paces ahead on the road, which had become so slippery that horsemen and artillerymen preferred to go on foot and lead their horses by the bridle.'[31]

In the centre, III Corps had continued its advance from St Calais, the 6th Division along the high road through Bouloire with the corps artillery, and the 5th Division on its left, marching along the minor roads. The advance guard of the 6th Division drove the French out of the positions which had been taken up in front of Ardenay, but at about 2.00 p.m. ran into considerably stiffer resistance. This came from Paris's Division, which had occupied the château on its right, and had posted four guns with two mitrailleuses near La Butte on the north side of the road. The position was well chosen, since there was only room on the road for the Germans to bring two guns into action. After half an hour, however, they succeeded in forcing the mitrailleuses to retreat, and thereafter they continued to exchange fire with the French guns. Buddenbrock, the commander of the 6th Division, deployed the 64th Regiment in his frontline. The struggle continued throughout the afternoon, when, supported by two companies of the 24th Regiment, the 64th Regiment carried the Château of Ardenay by storm. North of the high road the advance continued through the woods leading to La Butte. After beating off a determined French attack, the German infantry succeeded in crossing the meadowland in its immediate front and establishing themselves in the copses beyond.[32]

Paris's Division had put up a brave fight, and before nightfall again attempted a general advance along and to the south of the main road. Very severe fighting ensued, which ended when the 64th and 24th Regiments charged into the villages of Ardenay and La Butte, driving the French back into the Narais Valley, taking a large number of prisoners in the process. Paris had been set an extremely difficult task by Chanzy which, all in all, he had been able to perform successfully in delaying the advance of III Corps. He only retreated at about 7.30, having resisted all day; Chanzy noted that the division was allowed to carry out its retreat without hindrance, and by 10.00 a.m. on the following morning had taken up a defensive position on the Plateau of Auvours.[33]

On Buddenbrock's left, Stülpnagel's 5th Division had encountered no opposition as it advanced along the side roads, but it had been delayed by the roads' poor condition to such an extent that it was not until the afternoon that it reached St Mars de Locquenay and Gue de l'Aube, where the Division went into quarters for the night. Its advance guard, however, had been successful in crossing the River Narais by a bridge constructed by the pioneers, pushing forward outposts through the Bois de Loudon as far as the Château of La Bazardières, and occupying the angle of the wood projecting towards Parigné l'Eveque, which had been found to be occupied.[34]

Alvensleben established his headquarters in Château Ardenay. On the whole he had had a good day; his total losses had been about 160 men, and he had taken over 1,000 prisoners. Chanzy put the losses of Paris's Division at about 250 in all. IX Corps had, as planned, reached Bouloire by nightfall. North of the road, the 2nd Cavalry Division had reached St Michel de Chavaignes.

31 Wittich, *Journal,* p.359.
32 Moltke, *Franco-German War,* pp.280–281.
33 Chanzy, *Deuxième Armée*, p 284.
34 *Official Account*, vol. IV, p.168.

The southernmost wing of Second Army's advance had experienced the most difficulty during the day. As a result of the detachment of the 39th Brigade to deal with the problem caused by de Curten's advance on St Amand, the corps was moving in three parts. Hartmann, with the 38th Brigade, advanced on Châteaurenault, where it was found that de Curten had pulled out, and was retreating westward towards St Laurent. The bulk of the corps was to advance on 9 January from La Chartres by way of Brives; its ultimate objective being Grand Lucé. Finally, Woyna, with the 39th Brigade, was to march from Pont de Braye by way of Vancy.

However, no sooner had Kraatz's 20th Division moved out from La Chartres than its leading troops ran into opposition at L'Homme, coming under fire from both artillery and mitrailleuses. Hostile infantry had taken up positions in the farmsteads and scrub to his immediate front. For once, there was ample room to deploy the German artillery, but in the heavy snow that was falling, accuracy was impossible and the three batteries ceased fire at about 9.00 a.m. Since it appeared likely that stiff resistance would be encountered, Kraatz send a message to Woyna asking him to march with the 39th Brigade to the sound of the guns, with the intention that he should come down on the enemy's left flank.[35]

In spite of the difficult weather conditions the French were gradually forced back across the River Brives. In order to follow them, it was necessary to construct a temporary bridge over the river, a task which took some time. Once across the river, though, Colonel Haberland was able to lead two battalions towards Chahaignies, from which the French retreated, with the loss of 50 prisoners. At 2.00 p.m. the main body of the 20th Division resumed its march along the left bank of the Brives. Voigts-Rhetz was, however, not having a good day, finding the going extremely difficult:

> To the inconvenience which snow and fog caused this day to all of the army, was added, in the case of X Corps, the extraordinary difficulties which were entailed at this time of year in marching through hilly country full of steep slopes, ravines, and hollow roads. Cavalry and artillery had to dismount and lead their horses; every falling horse delayed the column. The general commanding had to ride on a limber; the headquarters staff marched on foot. The corps artillery could not be employed at all, and could scarcely be brought along the frozen defiles. It was sent back at noon under escort to Lavenay, by way of Pont de Braye, with the view of advancing on the following day by the better road through Vancé.[36]

Woyna had, as requested, marched towards Brives. By the time he reached the Château of La Chênchuère, the advance guard of the 20th Division had already reached Chahaignies. Since it seemed that Kraatz would have continued his march, Woyna retired to the Tusson Brook. However, the 20th Division's advance guard under Colonel von Valentini had pushed on towards Brives, where it met with strong resistance on the heights to the north; since movement off the roads was all but impossible, there was no alternative but a frontal assault, and this was in due course successful. Kraatz now ordered Valentini to continue his advance, even though night had fallen. He succeeded in capturing the villages of St Pierre du Lorouer and St Vincent, taking over 100 prisoners and capturing a train of 100 waggons; he then went into quarters at St Vincent.

35 *Official Account*, vol. IV, p.169.
36 *Official Account*, vol. IV, p.170.

X Corps had, therefore, been unable to reach its objective of Grand Lucé. Only its advance guard had got as far as Brives, and the main body of the corps was strung out in quarters all the way back almost to the valley of the Loire. Meanwhile the 14th Cavalry Brigade, endeavouring to advance towards Montreuil, had found the enemy in such strength there and at St Georges that it could make no further progress.

It had been a tough day. Hans von Kretschmann wrote to his wife that evening from the Château of Ardenay:

> We have occupied the Château after having taken it by force; we have also taken many prisoners. The day has been hard; 12 hours in the saddle; in addition, a heavy snow storm, and the roads covered with ice. The French came out of Le Mans with one division; it appeared before us after a night march. The combat was above all a combat of infantry; that is to say, very bloody. Thank God, I am fine – actually, I am dying of hunger, I am frozen and I am exhausted.[37]

37 Kretschmann, *Lettres*, p.372.

18

Le Mans: The Battle

The day's operations had cost Second Army 276 men killed, wounded and missing; French casualties were very much higher. At the end of the day, the two wings of Frederick Charles's army were both well short of their objectives, leaving his centre a good way in advance. For 10 January, however, he was determined to press on, rather than hold back Alvensleben's corps for the rest of the army to catch up. With de Curten's retreat from St Amand Frederick Charles no longer needed to be concerned with the threat to his left flank. To delay in launching his assault on the French positions in front of Le Mans would give Chanzy the opportunity to concentrate his forces, and Frederick Charles judged that the moment had come for a decisive advance.

Accordingly, he ordered Alvensleben to push forward beyond Ardenay. The objective for the Grand Duke's XIII Corps would be St Mars la Bruyère. Manstein was ordered to send a detachment from IX Corps to support that advance, while the rest of his corps closed up behind III Corps at Bouloire. X Corps was directed to continue its advance through Grand Lucé towards Parigné l'Eveque. The orders to all of the units of Second Army stressed the need for rapid marching, which in view of the weather conditions was asking a lot. Frederick Charles saw, however, that the best way to inflict a crushing defeat on 2nd Army of the Loire was to give it as little time as possible to regroup, or to settle into its defensive positions.

In executing his orders to continue his advance, Alvensleben directed the 9th Brigade (von Conta) and the 11th Brigade (von Flatow) to unite at Changé, while the 12th Brigade (von Bismarck) continued along the high road. The 10th Brigade (Schwerin) was to move from Volnay to the left, in the direction of Parigné l'Eveque to assist the advance of X Corps. However, during the morning of 10 January it became known that the French had pulled out of Parigné l'Eveque, which made the wide sweep of the 10th Brigade unnecessary, and Alvensleben ordered it to move on Changé.[1]

Before the troops were assembled at their rendezvous for the forward march, the French moved back to reoccupy Parigné l'Eveque; a brigade of Deplanque's Division, reinforced by a regiment from Jouffroy's Division which was retiring from Grand Lucé, attacked the German pickets in the south angle of the Bois de Loudon. At first, this had appeared only to be an affair of outposts, but as the morning wore on it became necessary to strengthen the battalion

1 *Official Account*, vol. IV, p.175.

on which the French attack had fallen. The French were supported by a well sited battery of mitrailleuses at the northern entrance of Parigné l'Eveque. For Stülpnagel, anxious to push on with his advance through Changé, this was an unwelcome distraction and he ordered that the troops engaged should do no more than delay the enemy, leaving the 10th Brigade to deal with the French advance.

This brigade had already begun its march in accordance with its previous orders when it was directed to move on Challes in support of the 10th Brigade. Delayed by the condition of the roads, it was not until noon that it was able to come into action. At 12.30 four battalions of the 10th Brigade were launched in a charge on the French in Parigné l'Eveque, capturing three mitrailleuses and two guns, and then beating off a determined French counter-attack. On the right, two battalions drove the enemy out of the northern part of the village. Before the fighting died down, nearly 2,000 French troops had been taken prisoner, and the rest fell back into the woods around Ruaudin, to the west of Parigné l'Eveque.[2]

Chanzy had not given up his intention of fighting an offensive whenever he could do so; his orders for 10 January had been that Paris should again advance to the attack at Ardenay. The rest of 21st Corps was to turn north and in conjunction with Rousseau's Division of 17th Corps, to endeavour to recapture Connerré and Thorigné. Thus it was that both sides were advancing to the attack, and the consequence was a day of extremely hard fighting, particularly for III Corps.

The positions into which Chanzy's army was moving stretched for nearly 20 miles, which meant necessarily that at some points the line was extremely thin, in spite of the large number of troops at Chanzy's disposal. His plan, once these positions had been taken up, was to hold them resolutely in the hope that the Germans, exhausted by their exertions over the preceding days, would fail to break through and as they fell back, Chanzy would then launch his counter-attack. That, at any rate, was his plan; it remained to be seen whether the shaken and inexperienced troops of his army could successfully resist the assaults of Frederick Charles's battle-hardened veterans.

On the right of Second Army, the resistance which had been met by XIII Corps was principally based on the heights of Les Cohernières north of the railway station at Conneré, and a wood still further to the north. Here the 2nd Division of 21st Corps (Colin) had taken up a strong position. After Conneré itself had been abandoned by the French early on the morning of 10 January, it was occupied by several companies of Rauch's detachment. However, as the 17th Division was assembling for its further advance it was found that the railway station on the right bank of the Huisne, together with the adjoining farms, was still occupied. Rauch was ordered to cross the river, drive the enemy back, and advance on the line of the railway towards Pont des Gesnes.

Rauch's men met with a strong resistance from Colin's Division in the position which it had taken up. Although one battalion succeeded in taking the railway station, and another penetrated some way into the wood, it proved impossible to dislodge the enemy from the crest of the heights.

Meanwhile the 22nd Division had crossed the Huisne at 8.00 a.m., and then followed the main road to St Hilaire, as the railway was found to be virtually impassable due to the depth of snow. Even so, the road had to be cleared with pickaxes, and to enable horses and vehicles to use it, it was necessary to scatter sand, ashes and straw.[3]

2 Official Account, vol. IV pp.176–177
3 Wittich, *Journal*, p.363

A metalled road ran from St Hilaire, enabling the division to progress as far as Beille. The division's advance guard under Heuduck paused there, was joined by the main body, and went into quarters for the night. Wittich had sent a detachment under Beckedorff – consisting of two squadrons of hussars, three battalions of the 95th Regiment and a battery – to Bonnétable. This village had been occupied by a body of *franc-tireurs*, which Beckedorff succeeded in dislodging without undue difficulty.[4] From there he had advanced down the Le Mans road to Chanteloup, and after a brisk engagement he detachment occupied the village. Behind it followed the 4th Cavalry Division, while the 12th Cavalry Brigade moved to Bellême.

The main body of Tresckow's 17th Division struggled with great difficulty along the main road which was frozen as smooth as glass, and by nightfall it had reached La Belle Inutile. The progress of XIII Corps had been slow, and its advance lagged still further behind that of III Corps.

After the capture of Parigné l'Eveque, Stülpnagel was able to concentrate on the crucially important advance to Changé. Flatow, with the 9th Brigade, had at first made good progress on the south side of the main road, but then ran into opposition at Gue la Hart, where he was held up until the early afternoon. Alvensleben, who was riding with the brigade, ordered up fresh troops to attack the flanks of the French position. With drums beating and bugles sounding the general advance, these stormed the position taking over 1,000 prisoners, and the Germans pressed forward, reaching the line Amigné – Gue la Hart – La Girardrie:

> But still Changé, the destination of the day, was not yet gained; the foe was not yet repulsed across the Huisne. In spite of the darkness the general commanding caused the 2nd Battalion of the 20th Regiment to advance from Gue la Hart. This latter captured a barricade in front of Changé towards 7 o'clock, but then found the place itself already in the possession of our troops.[5]

What had happened was that the 10th Brigade, advancing from Parigné l'Eveque along the high road, had met with gunfire from the châteaux of Chef Raison and of La Paillerie. Stülpnagel, leaving only one battalion in front of the French position, outflanked it on its right through Boyère, and sent two battalions forward towards Changé. This detachment, under Colonel von Wulffen, advanced towards Changé Bridge and seized it, before moving into the village itself at 6.00 p.m. A fierce house-to-house struggle ensued, which ended with the French troops being driven into the market square, where they surrendered – the Prussians took 800 prisoners.

The 12th Brigade, which left Ardenay at 11.00 a.m. and advanced down the main road, met no opposition until it reached St Hubert des Rochers. Here it seized an abandoned commissariat train. The brigade paused there until about 1.00 p.m., when French infantry appeared, supported by artillery. Buddenbrock, who was accompanying the brigade, ordered an attack, and this succeeded in driving the French out of Champagné, in part across the Huisne, and in part to the heights beyond. French artillery firing from near Lune d' Auvours was met by two guns, which soon gained the upper hand, and this position was also taken.

Thus Alvensleben had been successful at all points of his advance. In the sometimes extremely fierce fighting, he had sustained a total of 450 casualties; but he had inflicted a far greater

4 Lehautcourt, *Campagne*, p.245

5 *Official Account*, vol. IV, p.178.

number of casualties on the enemy, and in addition had taken over 5,000 prisoners. His advance had taken him up to Chanzy's main position; but it had also taken him still further away from XIII Corps on his right and X Corps on his left. The latter had had an uneventful day. It had faced only some *franc-tireurs* and cavalry, who had fallen back before the German advance which, progressing slowly but still largely unopposed, had in the dreadful conditions succeeded in reaching Grand Lucé, at about 2.00 p.m., a day behind schedule. The only direct support which III Corps could expect on the following day would come from IX Corps, following along the main road from Bouloire; as darkness fell it was still some way to the east of Ardenay. Thus at nightfall on 10 January, the overall position of Frederick Charles's army was the opposite of that which he had intended. Instead of his flank corps curving around the right and left of the enemy, which would be held in the front by his centre, they were both well behind their objectives, while III Corps was well in advance.

Throughout the day both armies had suffered from extreme difficulty of movement, a problem which particularly affected the employment of artillery. On the French side, Roger de Mauni wrote of the experience of his battalion on 10 January, as it marched to take up a position on the extreme left flank of the French army:

> For some days it had been less cold, and was thawing almost everywhere. Yesterday, just as we were starting, the snow began to fall heavily, and now it lies six inches deep. From constant tramping it has become so slippery that our superior officers can scarcely continue their march on horseback. If we have far to go, as seems likely, it will be a suffering time for us.[6]

At Chanzy's headquarters, his health had been causing his staff acute anxiety. He had been unwell since 7 January, and was almost completely physically drained by his exertions. On most days he had been obliged to rest for a while in bed. Now, he was consumed by a violent fever, which was feared to be smallpox, and his doctor was gravely alarmed.[7] However, he demonstrated a remarkable recovery, overcoming his ailments to the extent that on 11 January he would spend seven and a half hours in the saddle. He was resolved at all costs to inspire his troops to make the greatest possible effort, and he was invigorated by the process of doing so: 'After several hours passing along our lines he was completely transformed.'[8]

On the evening of 10 January Chanzy had issued a general order to spell out in unmistakable terms his absolute determination to defend Le Mans to the last. He expressed his discontent that some of his generals had not executed his orders, which had meant that a vigorous offensive, the sole means of saving Le Mans, had not been possible. In some instances, units had completely collapsed and abandoned their positions. He went on to emphasise the personal responsibility of each of his generals to carry out their orders. He ended the specific instructions for the following day with a clear warning:

> The commander-in-chief will not hesitate, if the collapse is repeated, to break down the bridges behind the lines to compel a defence to the last. He demands from the War

6 de Mauni, *Franco-Prussian-War*, p.109.
7 Alfred Chuquet, *Le General de Chanzy* (Paris: E Plon, 1871), pp.123–124.
8 Lehautcourt, *Campagne*, p.230n.

> Ministry the right to dismiss all corps commanders and all officers who fail to carry out the orders given to them, who do not know how to inspire their troops. At the same time he will reward, on the battlefield, those officers and men who distinguish themselves by their devotion, their energy and their courage.[9]

To show that he meant what he said, he added that cavalry would be posted behind the lines to ensure that the position was indeed held to the last; fugitives leaving the position would be shot. He was unimpressed by the complaints from generals about the suffering of their men; Jouffroy, for instance, ended a letter to him, timed at 10.45 p.m. on 10 January: 'Tonight, after having sustained an incredible struggle since 6 January, after having gone 24 hours without food, our soldiers, in an intense snowstorm, lie in the road on the road to Tours.' Lehautcourt remarked that neither the form nor content of this letter was such that should be addressed to a commander-in-chief in the face of the enemy.[10] Nonetheless, it demonstrated just how close the French were to breaking point, and Jaurès had given a warning about his troops in similar terms.

Chanzy had now succeeded in concentrating all the troops available to him in front of Le Mans, save for de Curten's Division and part of Barry's Division which had still not arrived. Nine fresh battalions had reached Le Mans from Laval, and the units from Conlie had been formed as a division under Lalande; these were posted on Jauréguiberry's right, with only Barry's Division to the south. The admiral now had under his command five divisions (those of Barry, Lalande, Deplanque, Roquebrune and Jouffroy), together with an additional division under General Bouëdec, assembled ad hoc from the detachments of Berard and Jobey which had also just arrived. Chanzy's centre was held by de Colomb, with two and a half divisions (Paris and Gougeard) on the Auvours Heights and opposite Champagné. De Colomb, however, was given an offensive task, that of driving back Alvensleben in order to take up a position on the main road. Finally, on the left, Jaurès had three divisions (Rousseau, Colin and Villeneuve) in a position running from south of Montfort north-west to La Croix.

It was soon evident to Alvensleben, when considering the strength of the French position on the Auvours Heights, that his flank would be threatened from this direction. At the moment, only the 12th Brigade in front of St Hubert des Rochers faced any possible assault; if Alvensleben was to concentrate the whole of his corps for his own intended attack it was plainly necessary for this brigade to be relieved by IX Corps, so that his right flank would be covered. The situation had been rendered more dangerous by the evacuation of Champagné by the outposts there, in error; and the French had quickly taken advantage of this to reoccupy the village, and to post a number of guns on the heights to the west.

This was a considerable setback. Buddenbrock ordered two battalions of the 12th Brigade to recapture Champagné. Supported by four guns of a heavy battery, the infantry advanced to the assault, but it was not until after a bitterly protracted street fight, especially around the church, that the French were finally driven out of the village. This was at about 11.00 a.m., and the Germans hastened to seize a bridge over the Huisne and barricade it.[11] Colonel von Bismarck, the commander of the 12th Brigade, ordered an advance towards Lune d'Auvours, moving via Amigné because the direct road was completely dominated by the French artillery on the heights

9 Chanzy, *Deuxième Armée*, pp.307–311.
10 Lehautcourt, *Campagne*, p.248.
11 *Official Account*, vol. IV, p.186.

While the combat in and around Champagné had been taking place, the rest of III Corps had become very heavily engaged, and Frederick Charles, who had ridden forward to St Hubert, sent orders at noon to Voigts-Rhetz to bring his corps up as quickly as possible.

At the same time IX Corps had advanced through St Hubert to take up a position at Champagné. The orders given to Manstein at 1.00 p.m. were to make his immediate objective the heights on the left bank of the Huisne (which rise to about 170 feet), below Champagné village. These were known as the Plateau d'Auvours and were strongly held; the area had been arranged for defence and a battery of four mitrailleuses was posted behind Villiers, while the south slope was flanked by a battery at the south-west end of the ridge. Manstein's advance guard, commanded by Colonel Beyer von Karger, consisted of a regiment of hussars, four battalions of infantry, and two batteries. It ascended the slope along deeply sunken hollow roads, covered with snow. It was followed by the two battalions that had recaptured Champagné. The first task was to silence the mitrailleuses. A party of infantry advanced and having got within 50 yards charged forward and captured three of them. The French now abandoned Villiers; they then launched a counter-attack in an effort to retake the mitrailleuses, which failed, as did an attempt to capture the Champagné Bridge over the Huisne.

The German infantry now turned against Le Haut Tallis, which was strongly occupied. Another bitter struggle ensued, and it was not until 5.30 p.m. that the town was finally taken, together with over 200 prisoners. The French retreated, leaving the eastern part of the plateau in German hands. On the western part of the plateau the French had established strong positions in a number of farmhouses, which had to be taken one by one. This occupied the rest of the day, until the Germans had succeeded in capturing the north-western edge of the plateau. However, as dusk fell, Gougeard launched a powerful counter-attack from Yvre; after half an hour's fierce fighting, this was thrown back but then a further French attack succeeded in retaking the farmhouses along the western edge of the plateau, which Gougeard garrisoned in considerable strength. Nevertheless, Manstein's assault had succeeded in its principal object, which was to release the 12th Brigade, and to secure Alvensleben's right flank.

Opposite the front of III Corps the French had, during the night, completed the entrenchment of their position on the eastern edge of a wood in front of Pontlieue. It was supported by a considerable force of artillery on the commanding right bank of the Huisne. Alvensleben recognised that a frontal assault would be extremely difficult, while the French position stretched so far to the south that he was not strong enough to turn it on its right. Accordingly, he decided to attempt to roll up the French position from its left, a task he assigned to the 11th Brigade.

The brigade advanced along the Gue Perray brook and around the north corner of the wood. The Auvours Heights were still strongly held by the French and in the first instance it was necessary to seize the Château of Les Arches. The French launched a number of attacks to recapture it, and there was a fierce artillery exchange. On the left the 20th Regiment attempted to advance along the Chemin des Boeufs; the Château of Les Noyers was occupied, together with the nearby bridge over the Huisne. The French brought up strong columns, which were only repulsed with difficulty, and the Germans were by now taking considerable losses. They were successful however in capturing the Château of Les Granges; but, as the struggle continued, still further French troops came up and retook the château. As night fell, although the 11th Brigade had been reduced to only 2,900 men, it had been generally able to hold its position.[12]

12 *Official Account*, vol. IV, p.190.

The 10th Brigade did not begin its assault until 1.00 p.m., advancing from Changé towards Le Tertre. The farmhouse of Le Pavillon was soon taken, and the left wing of the brigade occupied Le Grand Auneau, but otherwise progress was slow and Stülpnagel was obliged to bring up two battalions from the 9th Brigade in support. With these, a concentric attack on Le Tertre finally succeeded, and a company of *Leib* Grenadiers captured two guns. A French counter-attack came close to retaking them, but was beaten off after a hand-to-hand struggle.

To the north, the 12th Brigade, only three battalions strong, advanced along the railway line towards the Huisne, recapturing the Château of Les Arches, which had been abandoned earlier; but when 10 guns drawn from three different batteries were brought up to open fire on the heights, they were, unusually, overwhelmed by a concentrated barrage from the French artillery, and the German infantry fell back upon the château. The enemy, following up its advantage, delivered a powerful attack from Yvre, which was repulsed, although the French artillery continued in action until nightfall.

As night fell, Alvensleben's men stood to their arms in positions that were close to those of the enemy. Although not a great deal of ground been gained, they had succeeded in breaking into the centre of Chanzy's position in the vital sector along the Huisne, and had reached a position only two miles from the centre of Le Mans. Their line extended from Les Arches as far as the road from Parigné l'Eveque to Pontlieue. The rest of the corps sought quarters in the rear as far as Changé. Alvensleben had lost a total of around 600 men in a very hard day's fighting, but in the course of it had captured 600 prisoners.

Frederick Charles had been watching the advance of the 18th Division from the open space in the wood near Le Bourg Neuf. From what he had seen, and the reports which he received from III Corps, it seemed to him that, although the fighting had been intense, he could reasonably feel that it had been a good day. He had, though, not heard from XIII Corps since a message sent at 10.00 a.m., according to which a stubborn defence was expected from the enemy. From X Corps he had received no news at all, notwithstanding the 'hurry up order' which he had sent Voigts-Rhetz at noon. Since the enemy clearly remained in considerable strength along the heights of the right bank of the Huisne, Frederick Charles prepared on next day to launch an attack on the left flank of the French main position. At 4.30 p.m. he sent Stiehle to Manstein to discuss with him his plan, which was to keep the passage of the river at Champagné open, while still holding that part of the Auvours Heights in German hands. Manstein sent forward the 84th Regiment of the 35th Brigade to the north bank of the Huisne, driving back the French detachments there, while the 85th Regiment remained on the left bank in front of Villiers. IX Corps had lost a total of 293 men during the course of the day's fighting. Frederick Charles remained that night at Champagné.

Meanwhile Jaurès had been putting up a stiff resistance to the advance of XIII Corps. The Grand Duke's orders had been to push on towards Le Mans through Savigné l'Eveque. Before he had received these he had already issued his own orders to his corps for the following day. His plan was, leaving an advance guard of the 17th Division on the left bank of the Huisne, for the rest of the division to cross the river at Conneré to support the advance of the 22nd Division. The enemy still held the line La Cohernières – La Capelle. South-west of Conneré, Tresckow ordered two batteries to fire on the French right wing. In the course of this bombardment, Haute Perche was set on fire and abandoned by the French, and at about noon two battalions successfully stormed Les Cohernières; three other battalions advanced through difficult country to La Chapenterie and Grands Vaux, driving the enemy before them.

On the right wing of the corps, the 22nd Division advanced on the farm of La Chêne, capturing the place and taking 350 prisoners. By now, the resistance of Jaurès's Corps was beginning to crumble. Wittich wrote: 'The feeble resistance of the enemy, after the taking by assault of the farms in the front line, was evidently due to the victorious advance of the 17th Division and the simultaneous action of Beckedorff's detachment.'[13] Early in the morning, Beckedorff was still held up by the enemy troops at Chanteloup; for the moment he was content simply to occupy these by long-range rifle fire until the 4th Cavalry Division arrived to relieve him, accompanied by a battalion of the 32nd Regiment. Beckedorff at 10.30 began an assault on St Celerin, which he duly carried, capturing many prisoners. The French fell back on La Chapelle and Lombron. That night the 22nd Division was ordered to take up its quarters on the right bank of the Huisne, and the 17th Division around Connerré. The 4th Cavalry Division had remained stationary in the position at La Croix, by Chanteloup, and it withdrew for the night to quarters as far away as Bonnétable, having failed in its attempt to cut the railway to Alençon.

During the night of 10/11 January, Voigts-Rhetz had received orders to move out from Grand Lucé towards Mulsanne, and early in the morning X Corps began its advance. The 14th Cavalry Brigade, reinforced by two infantry battalions, was to advance from Parigné l'Eveque as a connecting link to III Corps. The right wing of the advance of X Corps was covered by a battalion of the 5th Division, which had taken the châteaux of Chef Raison and of de la Paillière, and which succeeded in holding on to them in the face of French attempts to retake them. At 1.00 p.m. this battalion was reinforced by the arrival of the 14th Cavalry Brigade.

Meanwhile X Corps was making its way towards Mulsanne, an objective selected because it was believed that this was the point at which Jauréguiberry's right wing would be found. It was in fact much further north, along the Chemin des Boeufs. The leading division of the corps, Kraatz's 20th Division, was seriously delayed by the slippery state of the frozen roads, and it was almost midday before its advance guard, under Colonel Haberland, reached St Mars d'Outille. Patrols reported that there had been substantial enemy movements from Ecommoy in the direction of Le Mans, though there remained there some *gardes mobiles* and Arab cavalry.[14] A fusilier battalion which was detached to Ecommoy found its houses still densely occupied, and although it succeeded in penetrating to the main square, found the resistance so strong that it withdrew, and thereafter merely continued to observe.

The main body of the corps was by now well on its way to Mulsanne, marching through Teloche, and then Mulsanne itself, virtually unopposed. Voigts-Rhetz had decided that since Jauréguiberry's right wing was further north than had been realised, he should go into quarters for the night, but at this point, at 4.45, Frederick Charles's noon time order that he hasten his march finally reached him. For some time, the sound of heavy artillery exchanges had been heard, which indicated that III Corps was seriously engaged. Voigts-Rhetz concluded that the only way to bring to Alvensleben the assistance which was clearly necessary was to press straight on to Le Mans. Although it was already almost dark, his troops were exhausted from a difficult march and they had been unable to cook during their journey, he gave orders for the advance to be resumed.

It was a bold, dramatic and unorthodox decision. X Corps was faced by a line of earthworks and trenches which seemed all but impregnable: 'The country about to be traversed presented

13 Wittich, *Journal*, p.374.
14 *Official Account*, vol. IV, p.197.

extraordinary advantages to the enemy. Numerous ditches and banks offered cover to his skirmishers, while the separate copses and farmhouses formed points of support for the defence.'[15] In spite of this, the leading units of X Corps pressed forward and captured Le Point du Jour, before being held up at Les Mortes Aures by two batteries on the heights behind and two mitrailleuses on the main road. From the strong French positions came a continuous roll of rifle fire. In the gloom, it was difficult to distinguish friend from foe, and for some time the engagement swayed to and fro. Eventually, however, a battalion of the 17th Regiment stormed the edge of a wood into which the enemy disappeared, and Les Mortes Aures was taken. The mitrailleuses had retreated; when the drums sounded the charge the French infantry quickly fell back. Voigts-Rhetz had given orders that the struggle should be finished with the bayonet.

His leading troops now pressed forward into the wood to attack the key of the French position, at La Tuilerie. Unfortunately for the French, this was held by the hapless Breton *mobiles* from Conlie under Lalande. For a moment, the line was held; then it collapsed completely and the *mobiles* fell back in total disorder, leaving behind many prisoners. The Germans at once occupied La Tuilerie with three battalions, supported by three more:

> It was now past 8.30 p.m. Through the darkness glimmered the French watch fires north of the wood. In front and to the left were heard confused cries, the rumbling of waggons, and the rushing of departing railway trains. The patrols captured numerous prisoners, who stated that there were still large masses of men encamped in the wood.[16]

It was at once apparent to Jauréguiberry that the collapse of his position at La Tuilerie was potentially catastrophic. Before this, he had gone into Le Mans at 6.30 p.m. to report to Chanzy, and it was only when he returned at 8.00 that he discovered the scale of the disaster. He at once ordered Bouëdec to concentrate all the troops he could find to immediately retake the position; his attack was to be supported by Roquebrune. Bouëdec collected up Marty's detachment, which had only reached Pontlieue after a long march at 3.00 p.m., together with about 1,000 miscellaneous troops exhausted by the day's fighting, and his own division, and at about 10.30 p.m. advanced towards the Germans, who were ready and waiting. For more than an hour the French poured a heavy fire on the German positions with little result.[17] The columns which Bouëdec had assembled disintegrated before an effective attack could go in, as men in increasing numbers slipped away. Gradually the whole of Jauréguiberry's front collapsed, and his exhausted troops abandoned the front line, steadily making for the city in their thousands, deaf to the orders of their officers.

Earlier in the day Chanzy had been greatly encouraged, not only by de Colomb's recovery of part of the plateau of Auvours, but also by the sustained resistance offered by Jaurès to the advancing XIII Corps. Although his optimism was dampened by the pessimistic reports which later began to arrive, he believed that he would be able to hold his position in front of Le Mans on the following day. The report from Jauréguiberry which reached him at 7.25 a.m. on 12 January changed all that. Reporting bluntly on the catastrophic events at La Tuilerie, the admiral was emphatic: 'I am desolated to have to say that an immediate retreat seems to me

15 *Official Account*, vol. IV, p.198.
16 *Official Account*, vol. IV, p.199.
17 Lehautcourt, *Campagne*, p.272.

to be imperative.' It was a crushing blow. From anyone else Chanzy might have been inclined to dismiss such a report as alarmist; but from Jauréguiberry he knew at once that he must acknowledge that the hope of saving Le Mans was gone. He wrote immediately to the admiral to authorise the retreat:

> My heart bleeds; but when you, on whom I count the most, declare that the struggle is hopeless, and the retreat unavoidable, I yield. Therefore, prepare everything for the retreat, which should be as slow and as orderly as possible. Take all steps to destroy the bridge over the Huisne, once you no longer need it. But contest, I repeat, the entrance of the enemy to the city for as long as possible. It is essential that you gain the time to save the other corps of the army.[18]

That night, at Château Ardenay, Frederick Charles and Stiehle reviewed the situation. XIII Corps had been held up for a long time and was therefore well short of its objective. It had few fresh battalions available and it was clear that the level of exhaustion of the troops was high. On the other hand, IX Corps had been able to get into a strong position from which to renew its advance on the following day. III Corps was also well placed to occupy the rest of the Auvours Plateau. But it was the news from Voigts-Rhetz of the success of X Corps at La Tuilerie that told Frederick Charles and Stiehle that the Battle for Le Mans was almost as good as won, and they made their plans for the following day accordingly.

The advance in the centre would be continued next day with III Corps and IX Corps aimed at gaining complete possession of the emboli heights; a brigade would be detached across the Huisne to support the advance of XIII Corps. The Grand Duke was directed to push forward with one division through Lombron, while the other division moved further west, with Le Mans as its ultimate objective. The 4th Cavalry Division would operate still further on the right flank towards the Sarthe.

Orders had already been issued for the 17th Division to advance through Lombron to St Corneille, while the 22nd Division was to aim for Savigné l'Eveque, advancing through Sillé le Philippe without getting involved with the enemy forces known to be south of its line of march. The 4th Cavalry Division would move towards the Ballon road, on the 22nd Division's right, and make a further attempt to break up the Le Mans-Alençon railway.

The advance got under way at 9.00 a.m., still hampered by difficult roads. The 17th Division marched on both banks of the Huisne; Rauch's detachment found Lombron to have been evacuated, while another detachment under Colonel von Manteuffel advanced to the south of it. Almost at once the Germans encountered unmistakable evidence that they were facing a beaten enemy; vast numbers of abandoned arms and articles of equipment littered the roads, and many prisoners readily surrendered when found in the farmsteads. Tresckow now ordered his division to make St Corneille its objective, in order to take advantage of the better road through Montfort.[19]

During the afternoon the division closed in on the French troops in position at St Corneille. At 4.00 p.m. an attack by storm succeeded in taking the position, together with a large number

18 Chanzy, *Deuxième Armée*, p.328.
19 *Official Account*, vol. IV, p.202.

of prisoners. As darkness fell, there still appeared however to be strong French detachments in Savigné l'Eveque.

The 22nd Division had also commenced its march at 9.00 a.m. Its main body came into action in support of Beckedorff's detachment, which had been held up by Villeneuve's division at La Croix. Apart from this, and mindful of the orders which he had received, Wittich resolved not to get involved if he could avoid it, asking Tresckow whether it was necessary for his division to support the 17th Division. He halted at St Celerin while awaiting a response. Later, after the main body of the 22nd Division had occupied Sillé le Philippe, he launched an attack through Chanteloup which drove back the enemy with a loss of over 3,000 prisoners. As night fell the division's advance guard remained at Chanteloup, while the main body went into quarters echeloned back to Beaufay and Torce. Wittich was advancing cautiously due, not least, to the exhaustion and the attritional effect of the campaign on his division; he quoted as an example the second battalion of the 32nd Regiment which had been reduced to a strength of 280 men.[20]

On the right of XIII Corps, the 4th Cavalry Division had ridden towards the Upper Sarthe. As it approached Ballon it found the place occupied by infantry, and since the country was extremely unfavourable to the employment of both cavalry and artillery, no attack was attempted. By now, though, the operations on the right flank of the Second Army were no longer of crucial significance, as a result of events on the rest of its front.

As dawn broke on 12 January Manstein sent forward two battalions, supported by two batteries, along the high road towards Lune d'Auvours; two more battalions and four batteries moved up to the Auvours farm. During the morning the French began to assemble as if for an assault, but it did not materialise and the troops fell back. Advancing patrols found the country as far as the Huisne to be now unoccupied. Fog obscured visibility during the morning, but in the early afternoon this lifted, and fire was opened on the opposite bank of the river; but there was no response, the French falling back from their positions. Only at Yvre, which had been prepared for defence, did they resist.

Frederick Charles had ridden forward towards Le Bourg Neuf, and since heavy infantry fire could be heard from beyond Champagné, he ordered the 35th Brigade to advance northwards to support the advance of XIII Corps. Advancing through Fatines, the brigade took part in the attack on St Corneille before turning westward. Barricades were encountered, but they were undefended, and the brigade remained at Fatines during the night.

In the front of III Corps it soon became apparent that the enemy had, for the moment at any rate, been reinforced. Defensive works had been thrown up in the wood at Pontlieue and along the road from Yvre to Le Mans. The hedges surrounding the vineyards rising in terraces on the further bank of the river were heavily occupied by lines of skirmishers, while artillery was in place along the crest of the heights. Movement was still difficult; the deep snow was covered with a crust of ice. Considering all this, Alvensleben came to the conclusion that it would be pointless to launch an attack in this sector, and when he discussed it with Frederick Charles, the latter agreed. III Corps would, except on its extreme left, stand on the defensive. As soon as it was possible to act in concert with X Corps, the left wing, making as much use as possible of artillery, would advance towards Le Mans.

As early as 6.00 a.m. the French made an attempt to recapture and destroy the bridge over the Huisne near the Château of Les Noyers. Two companies of infantry advanced with blasting

20 Wittich, *Journal*, p.372.

materials, but were driven back, as were some later attempts. By now, the operations of the French were dedicated to ensuring as far as possible that the bulk of 2nd Army of the Loire should be able to retreat in as orderly fashion as possible.

In front of Pontlieue, the French launched an attack on the German outposts in the wood, driving them back to Le Tertre. But after an hour, the fire of the French was perceived to be slackening, and they could be seen to be retreating. Alvensleben directed the 10th Brigade to follow them up; it advanced to the Parigné l'Eveque road, and there came into contact with the right wing of X Corps.

Voigts-Rhetz had left two battalions at Mulsanne, to cover his rear against any enemy troops advancing from Ecommoy. The rest of his corps was, by 7.30 a.m., assembled for a further advance on Pontlieue. The main body of Kraatz's Division closed up on La Tuilerie, while the 19th Division concentrated at Ruaudin. The advance on Pontlieue was soon successful; the southern part of the village was taken without resistance. On the further side of the Huisne, however, the French held the line of the river bank, and at 2.00, as the Germans approached, they succeeded in blowing up the bridge. When the smoke cleared, it was seen that the demolition was incomplete, and the leading battalions of the 20th Division managed to get across the river. Two of them made their way into the high street of Pontlieue, and one turned left to the railway station. A large number of prisoners were captured, together with 150 waggons of provisions.

At Les Epinettes there had been a brisk action, where the French put up a resolute defence to the advance of two battalions in a position based on two farms. Two guns of a horse artillery battery, however, came up to support the infantry attack, and the French broke, retreating in disorder and leaving behind over 1,000 prisoners. Voigts-Rhetz ordered Woyna to advance towards Pontlieue to clear the right flank of the 20th Division.

Kraatz, now over the river, was pressing on into the city. As his leading troops advanced, their progress was delayed by bitter street fighting. The French were putting up a stiff house-to-house resistance. On the Place des Jacobins they attempted to facilitate the withdrawal of a long column of waggons. This was thwarted when the commander of the 1st Battalion of the 17th Regiment, Major von Tresckow, dashed ahead of his men, cut down the drivers of a gun that was escorting the waggons, and thereby forced the following waggons to halt. House-to-house fighting continued throughout the evening, but various battalions of both X Corps and III Corps were able to reach the northern exits of the city, taking a large number of prisoners in the process. There was a particularly bitter struggle around the Café de l'Univers in the Place des Halles, where the Germans only finally overcame the defenders by bringing up a field gun.[21]

Once resistance had finally ceased, X Corps and the 9th and 10th Brigades took up quarters in the city for the night. The outposts of the 6th Division had advanced to the northern bank of the Huisne at Les Noyers and Les Arches, while the French had finally abandoned Yvre. That night the 6th Division took up its quarters at Changé. Chanzy's retreat was being skilfully carried out. He had ordered that the retreat follow the line of the Sarthe northwards towards Pre en Pail and Alençon. This route, rather than that towards Laval, which might have been more direct, appears to have been determined by the fact that it would not take his army any further away from Paris. Chanzy, as always, had still not given up hope of relieving the capital. Meanwhile the War Ministry told him that two divisions were being sent from Carentan to Alençon.

21 *Official Account*, vol. IV, p.209.

In being able to get away in reasonably good order, the French were assisted by the late hour at which the Germans usually attacked. It was a peculiarity of the Le Mans campaign that engagements for the most part only began in the late morning, because of the time it took for combat units to move forward from their overnight quarters; and the short winter days prevented an effective pursuit of the retreating enemy. Due to the appalling weather, it was impossible for the troops to bivouac, so they were obliged to find shelter for the night, and this was frequently well to the rear of the battlefield. There, ammunition had to be issued, and such food as there was available had to be cooked, so that it was late on the following morning before the troops could be concentrated for their next advance.

During the seven days' fighting that culminated in the capture of Le Mans, Second Army had sustained total losses of around 3,400 men. During the Battle of Le Mans itself, on 10–12 January, 558 men were killed, 1,471 were wounded and 136 were missing. The French put their own losses at a total of 6,200 men; they had also lost well in excess of 25,000 men taken prisoner, while it was estimated that by the end almost twice that number had deserted. It had been a crushing victory; reporting to Moltke, Stiehle told him that Frederick Charles did not consider that it would be desirable to prolong the offensive of the Second Army towards the west, through difficult country in which it would be hard to employ artillery, while all the troops were exhausted after a brutally severe campaign. Even Moltke, usually so insistent on following up a beaten enemy, was not disposed to disagree.

In Le Mans, Kretschmann described on 13 January the situation which he found there:

> Here, the misery is immense. There are in the city about 5,000 wounded. The roads are covered with broken-down vehicles of all kinds. An army could live for weeks on the supplies that have been abandoned. Horses stand sadly in front of their vehicles; no one is giving them anything to eat .... On the roads, abandoned rifles lie among dead Frenchmen, even some civilians.[22]

Roger de Mauni, whose battalion had been operating in the region of Savigné l'Eveque but which did not get into action during the Battle of Le Mans, wrote mournfully in his diary to express his utter desolation:

> When I wrote the history of our retreat to Le Mans, I thought I should never again see a greater misfortune. I was mistaken. Our youth is destined to witness the most immense, the most overwhelming of disasters. France is sinking from one abyss into another, dragged down by the pitiless hand she has taken as her guide; half our generation is destroyed; we, unhappier than the rest, are reserved to perish the last, after having beheld everything crumbling away around us. Paris, on which the Prussian shells are now falling, is awaiting the destiny of Babylon and Jerusalem. And yet, not long ago, the papers were taking pains to inform us that active life was good for Gambetta's constitution, and that he had never been in better health![23]

22 Kretschmann, *Lettres*, p.377.
23 de Mauni, *Franco-Prussian War*, p.110.

19

Aftermath

The news of the decisive victory at Le Mans naturally came as a welcome relief in Versailles. The Crown Prince wrote in his diary: 'New important but sanguinary victories of Second Army in conjunction with XIII Corps round Le Mans and St Corneille lead us to hope that General Chanzy .... is completely defeated and rendered harmless for the time being.' He was, however, unable to avoid retailing gossip that Frederick Charles was, 'very jealous of the Grand Duke of Mecklenburg, whose successes are brilliant, but less bloody than is the case of those of Second Army; so he never mentions him in his dispatches.'[1]

Stiehle had written to Moltke on 13 January to report on the Battle of Le Mans, and to tell him that Frederick Charles did not consider it justifiable to prolong the advance of Second Army towards the west. Of this, Moltke entirely approved. He ordered that XIII Corps should move as soon as possible via Alençon to Rouen, to be ready to reinforce Goeben and First Army in the campaign in the north of France. As for the rest of Second Army, he agreed that the pursuit of Chanzy should be limited to detachments, comprising all arms. In a letter of 15 January, he wrote that, after their great exertions, the troops should remain in and around Le Mans to give them the rest which they needed. He ended his letter with an expression of his profound respect for Frederick Charles.[2]

Later in the month Stiehle wrote again to Moltke on the subject of the possible future operations of Second Army. Once the troops were sufficiently rested, they would take up a position between Chartres and Orléans, from where support could be provided for First Army if required, or if necessary to commence operations against a new Army of the Loire if it appeared likely to take the offensive. After he received this, on 21 January Moltke sent a telegram to Frederick Charles requiring that at least one corps should hold Orléans; it would be for him to decide if it was desirable to take the offensive, but if so it should be limited to an advance on Laval. On the same day he wrote to Stiehle to review the overall military situation following Goeben's victory at St Quentin, and to enlarge on his view that any offensive should not go beyond Laval.[3]

1 Crown Prince, *War Diary*, p.256.
2 Moltke, *Correspondance Militaire*, vol. II, p.671.
3 Moltke, *Correspondance Militaire*, vol. II, pp.684–686.

Chanzy, meanwhile, had still not given up the hope that an advance towards the Seine might be possible, and he telegraphed the War Ministry on 12 January to explain why, for this reason, he wished to direct his retreat towards Alençon. Gambetta replied the next day disapproving of this proposal, insisting that a retreat to Mayenne and Laval would be infinitely preferable. As for the relief of Paris, Gambetta added that Trochu had estimated that supplies would last until the end of January, and that this would give the time, with the energy that Chanzy possessed, to regain the lost ground.[4] Commenting on this, the German official history concluded that Gambetta was certainly right; the two divisions from Normandy that were to move to Alençon were not yet ready to march, while Chanzy's plan to advance to the Seine through Evreux would have meant that his army, 'would have to describe an arc, upon the chord of which the Germans could operate at pleasure. From the internal condition of the French troops, a collision in a country which allowed the employment of all arms would probably end in the complete rout of the army.'[5]

Chanzy had, with his hope of a possible advance to the relief of Paris, directed his various corps with the retreat to Alençon in mind. So that each might have a separate road, two had to move westward in the first instance, 16th Corps through Chauffour on the Laval road, and 17th Corps on the road to Mayenne. 21st Corps assembled at Ballon on the left bank of the Sarthe. Thereafter, each corps was to march northwards.

Frederick Charles wasted little time in assembling a detachment to go in pursuit. Led by Schmidt, the capable commander of the 6th Cavalry Division, it consisted of 11 squadrons, 4 battalions, and 10 guns. It set off on the Laval road towards noon on 13 January, and soon found evidence that the French had retreated in complete disorder, with abandoned waggons and firearms all along the route. The detachment reached Chauffour after some skirmishing at L'Arche.

Meanwhile XIII Corps had advanced to the Sarthe; the 17th Division sent its outposts across the river at Neuville, while the 22nd Division drove the French out of Ballon, from where 21st Corps hurriedly retreated to Beaumont. De Colomb's 17th Corps had been ordered to take up a position on the River Végre, but when it got there it continued its retreat to Laval, leaving Barry's Division as a rearguard at Chassillé.

The next day Schmidt advanced to attack the position there, sending a fusilier battalion to turn it by way of La Bretonnière and La Plante. After an artillery bombardment, Schmidt sent his infantry forward, and the French soon abandoned the position, retiring in a disorganised state to St Jean sur Erve. Meanwhile the camp at Conlie was occupied; it had been looted by the last of its French occupants, but the Germans took possession of a large quantity of war materiel, including 8,000 rifles and 5,000,000 cartridges.

When Schmidt pursued his advance towards Laval, he found the French posted in some strength at St Jean, where it was supported by artillery on the heights behind the Erve, and it took brisk fighting before the town was occupied, the French falling back to Ste Suzanne. The troops that were engaged were from the divisions of Barry and Deplanque; though reduced to a total of around 6,000 men, they still outnumbered their attackers. Meanwhile a fusilier battalion under Colonel Lehmann advancing from Conlie encountered a large part of 21st Corps which had taken up a position at Sillé le Guillaume. Although supported by four guns, the fusiliers were heavily outnumbered and sustained serious casualties; they were reinforced by

4 Chanzy, *Deuxième Armée*, pp.338–340.
5 *Official Account*, vol. III p.210.

eight companies from two other battalions, but Lehmann soon concluded that the French were too strong for him, and fell back to Conlie.[6]

XIII Corps had also met with resistance as it advanced towards Alençon on 15 January, and Wittich, with the Grand Duke's approval, deferred the attack of the 22nd Division until the following day. Next morning, however, the French positions there, and those at St Jean and Sillé were found to have been abandoned; Alençon was duly occupied, and Schmidt moved up close to Laval.

The remains of Chanzy's army, reduced to roughly half its original strength, and with a gravely shaken morale, were assembled behind the River Mayenne, and it was judged at the headquarters of Second Army that it would be some time before they could be regarded as any sort of threat. The pursuit, such as it was, was discontinued; Schmidt fell back in the first instance to Vaiges, and XIII Corps made its way towards Rouen in accordance with Moltke's orders.

There had meanwhile been a brief engagement on the Loire, when on 14 January French detachments had advanced against the German outposts at Briare, driving them back to Ouzouer. This necessitated an order to the 38th Brigade to move from Châteaurenault; this however was subsequently countermanded when the French movement was not pursued. At the same time, there came a report that the newly constituted 25th Corps at Vierzon under Pourcet was moving forward in the direction of Tours. This ultimately led to an engagement at Vienne on 28 January, when a French advance in four columns was launched forwards with the object of reaching and capturing the bridge at Blois. The German outposts at Vienne were heavily outnumbered, and retreated to the right bank of the river, blowing up the bridge as they did so. This French movement led to the concentration at Orléans of IX Corps together with the other nearby units under Manstein, while the remainder of Second Army, consisting of III Corps and X Corps and three cavalry divisions, assembled around Le Mans. This force amounted to 9,000 cavalry, 27,000 infantry and 186 guns. Since Chanzy was energetically pulling his army together between Laval and Mayenne, and had now been joined by 19th Corps, Frederick Charles assigned the task of watching the French to III Corps and the three cavalry divisions, while X Corps was withdrawn into permanent quarters at Le Mans. In the following days there were a number of skirmishes but it was found particularly difficult to assess what the strength, or the movement, of the French forces was. On the right wing of the army, the 4th Cavalry Division held Alençon, while on the left Hartmann entered Tours unopposed.[7]

On the evening of 28 January came news of the armistice that had been negotiated at Paris, to come into force at noon on 31 January. The fighting (except in South-East France) was finally over. Nonetheless, it is right to record that in the period since the ending of the Battle of Le Mans, Second Army had sustained not insignificant casualties, amounting to a total of 439: 88 killed, 214 wounded and 137 missing.[8]

The Loire campaign had ended with a victory which showed Frederick Charles at his best. For once abandoning his innate caution, he moved with impressive determination to finish off Chanzy's army, and was rewarded with a decisive success. He perhaps deserved a warmer

6 *Official Account*, vol. IV, pp.216–217.
7 *Official Account*, vol. IV, pp.227–228.
8 *Official Account*, vol. III, Appendix CXXII, pp.102–105.

appreciation than Waldersee expressed in a character study which he wrote of Frederick Charles long after the war, in which he described him as a fortunate rather than a great leader:

> Prince Frederick Charles was a man of only mediocre intellect – a man of slow understanding, as they say; he read with deliberation and did not like to have matters reported to him hurriedly, as he found it difficult to follow. By dint of iron diligence, he sought to make good this shortcoming, and he held fast by what he had once mastered; moreover, he had a good memory. His whole heart was devoted to the military calling from the close of his university career. He gave himself up to soldiering and hunting exclusively. He was one of those few princes who regarded a soldier's career as their life's vocation and had never tried to go in for anything else; and thus he developed into a real General *de métier*... As a military leader, Prince Frederick Charles was notable for his great prudence. A sort of Fabius Cunctator – if a little exaggeration be allowed – he held it as a maxim that one could not be too strong when going into battle: hence arose difficulties at times.[9]

This prudence was the source of much of Moltke's occasional disapproval of Frederick Charles's conduct of the Loire campaign, at least in its early stages.

There is really nothing new that can be said of Moltke's management of the German Armies during the war. Directing their operations from afar, while also overseeing the investment of Paris, was an enormously intricate task, not least because he was naturally dependent on the information reaching him, which was not always timely and was sometimes inaccurate. But the Loire campaign, as with those fought by Manteuffel, Goeben and Werder, demonstrated Moltke's comprehensive grasp of the strategic essentials of his situation, as well as his calm and thoughtful response to each problem as it arose. For him strategy, as he wrote after the war, was a system of expedients: 'It is the art of acting under the pressure of the most difficult conditions.'[10]

He would, however, have been the last to claim that the German success was entirely due to his leadership of the armies which he controlled; he wrote a realistic appreciation of this:

> Success principally decides the reputation of a general. How much of it is his actual due is very difficult to determine. Even the best of men fail against the irresistible force of circumstances, and the same force will carry along the mediocre man. A capable supreme commander can easily be defeated by a less capable one; but only the capable will have luck in the long run. Where armies have commanders as in 1870, and where one has to reckon only with victories, strategy has everything it needs. We have had only victories. Gneisenau, however, led a beaten army to victory. We have not yet stood this highest test.[11]

The military historian Hans Delbrück, summarising Moltke's achievements, noted that he was 'exclusively a strategist' and that 'of all great commanders Moltke is the most theoretical. The art of war that Napoleon practised with naive genius Moltke practised systematically.' He went on:

9 Waldersee, *Memoirs*, pp.83–84.
10 Daniel Hughes (ed., *Moltke on the Art of War* (Novato, CA: Presidio, 1993), p.5.
11 Hughes, *Moltke*, p.168.

> His modesty, serenity, and length in office made possible his greatness. Here we are at the point where he appears the man of pure intellect, who never falls into the temptation to operate outside the bounds of his competence …. Earnest and wise, duty true and a hard worker, these qualities are the cornerstones of Moltke's character. Heroism is hidden and wisdom and humour are united with an image of grace.[12]

Moltke had few enemies and he deserved Theodor Fontane's famous comment, who wrote that Moltke, 'embodied the Prussian ideal; he looked sound and true, with a Greek soul, the spirit of Frederick the Great and a unique character: judicious, selfless, disciplined, proficient and full of common sense.'[13]

From his quarters on the Sarthe, Kretschmann wrote on 29 January to his wife:

> I ask myself if you, or the country as a whole, can have the impressions such as those that we have here. Paris and the forts occupied today at 10.00 a.m.; from 31 January a general suspension of hostilities. For me, I have endured six months apart from my wife and child, away from my country, and have seen all the misery that war brings in its train – having endured this, even in the days of brilliant victory it is impossible not to weep for those men to whom the victory is due and now lie dead on the field of battle; and it is necessary to have endured all this to be able to appreciate in one's mind the possibilities of peace.

He noted with surprise how the French were unanimous in their opinion of their situation. All had expressed the same sentiment: 'When one has seen the Prussians close to, one is convinced that it is impossible to resist them.' This was, he thought, quite simply because the French 'do not understand our love of order and discipline; they do not understand that women and young girls can pass among victorious soldiers as safely as if they were in church.'[14]

A few days later, de Mauni was writing despairingly that the political situation was as black as night:

> Paris has surrendered, an armistice is signed, and the war apparently is at an end. Elections for a national assembly are coming on …. On the evening of 30 January, an order was received from General Jaurès for the suspension of all hostilities. But the greatest precautions are still recommended, and we continue to keep watch on the banks of the Mayenne.

He went into the town of Mayenne in the hope of finding some information in the newspapers as to what had become of the armies of Bourbaki and Faidherbe:

> If they are still in existence, no one can say what resolution the Assembly we are about to elect may not be capable of; but this silence on the part of the government and newspapers is the silence of the grave.[15]

12 Hans Delbrück (A. Bucholz, trans. and ed.), *Modern Military History* (Lincoln, Nebraska: Nebraska UP, 1997).
13 Arden Bucholz, *Moltke and the German Wars* (London: Palgrave, 2001) p.185.
14 Kretschmann, *Lettres*, pp.403–404.
15 Mauni, *The Franco-Prussian War*, pp.123–126.

Select Bibliography

Abadie, Louis, *Le Général Alfred Chanzy* (Turquant: Anovi, 2013)

Allnutt, H., *Historical Diary of the War between France and Germany 1870–71* (London: Estates Gazette, n.d.)

d'Aurelle de Paladines, Général Louis, *La Première Armée de la Loire* (Paris Henri Plon, 1872)

Barry, Quintin, *The Franco-Prussian War*, 2 volumes (Solihull: Helion & Co, 2006)

Baunard, Louis, *Le Général de Sonis* (Paris: Librairie Ch Pourrielgue, 1903)

Blumenthal, Field Marshal Leonhard von (Count A. von Blumenthal ed. Major A. D. Gillespie-Addison, trans.), *Journals for 1866 and 1870–71* (London; Edward Arnold, 1903)

Breuillac, Georges, *Campagne de la Loire et de la Sarthe pendant la Guerre Franco-Allemande 1870–1871* (Paris: E Dentu, 1871)

Bucholz, Arden, *Moltke and the German Wars* (London: Palgrave, 2001)

Bury, J. P.T., *Gambetta and the National Defence* (London: Longmans Green & Co, 1936)

Caemmerer, Lieutenant General von (K. von Donat trans.), *The Development of Strategical Science during the Nineteenth Century* (London: Hugh Rees, 1905)

Chanzy, General Alfred, *La Deuxième Armée de la Loire* (Paris: Henri Plon, 1871)

Chrastil, Rachel, *Bismarck's War* (London: Allen Lane, 2023)

Chuquet, Arthur, *Le Général Chanzy* (Paris: E Plon Nourrit & Cie, 1884)

Craig, Gordon A., *The Politics of the Prussian Army* (Oxford: OUP, 1966)

Creveld, Martin van, *Supplying War* (Cambridge: CUP 1977)

Daily News, *Correspondence of the War between Germany and France 1870–71* (London: Macmillan & Co, 1871)

Desplantes, Francois-Jemmy, *Chanzy et l'Armée de La Loire* (Rouen: Megard & Cie, 1891)

Dupuy, Colonel T. N., *A Genius for War* (London: Macdonald & Janes, 1977)

Favre, Jules, *The Government of the National Defence* (London: Henry S King & Co, 1873)

Fermer, Douglas, *France at Bay 1870–1871* (Barnsley: Pen & Sword Military, 2011)

Foerster, Wolfgang, *Prinz Friedrich Karl von Preussen* (Stuttgart: Deutsches Verlags, 1910)

Fradet, P.-A., *Campagne de 1870–71: Récit des Operations Militaires* (Rochefort: Ch Theze & Cie, 1871)

Frederick III, Emperor, *War Diary 1870–1871* (A. R. Allinson trans.), (London: Stanley Paul, 1926)

Freycinet, Charles de, *La Guerre en Province 1870–71* (Paris: Michel Levy Freres, 1872)

Furse, Colonel G. A., *The Organisation and Administration of the Lines of Communication* in *War* (London: William Clowes & Sons, 1894)

Goltz, Baron Colmar von der, *Gambetta et ses Armées* (Paris: Librairie Sandoz & Fischbacher, 1877)
Gorlitz, Walter, *The German General Staff* (London: Hollis & Carter, 1953)
Grenest, *L'Armée de la Loire* (Paris: Garnier Freres,1893)
Hale, Colonel Lonsdale, *The People's War in France* (London: Hugh Rees, 1904)
Helvig, Captain Hugo, *Operations of the I Bavarian Army Corps under General von der Tann*, 2 volumes (London: Henry S King & Co 1874)
Hittle, Colonel J. D., *The Military Staff: Its History and Development* (Harrisburg, PA: Military Service Publishing Co, 1949)
Hohenlohe-Ingelfingen, Prinz Kraft zu, *Aus Meinem Leben*, 4 volumes (Berlin: Mittler & Söhne, 1907)
Hohenlohe-Ingelfingen, Prince Kraft zu, *Letters on Infantry* (London: Edward Stanford, 1892)
Hollyday, Frederic B. M., *Bismarck's Rival* (Durham NC: Duke UP, 1960)
Howard, Michael, *The Franco-Prussian War* (London: Rupert Hart-Davis, 1961)
Kessel, Eberhard, *Moltke* (Stuttgart: KF Koehler Verlag, 1957)
Kretschmann, General Hans von, *Lettres Écrites 1870–1871* (Paris: Henri Charles-Lavauzelle, 1904)
Lehautcourt. Pierre (Général Barthélemy Palat), *Campagne de la Loire en 1870–71: Josnes, Vendôme, Le Mans* (Paris: Berger Levrault & Cie, 1895)
Mauni, Roger de (D. Clarke ed.), *The Franco-Prussian War* (London: Longman, 1970)
Maurice, Major General J. F. (ed.), *The Franco-German War* (London: Swan Sonnenschein & Co, 1900)
May, Major E. S., *Field Artillery with the other Arms* (London: Sampson Low Marston & Co, 1898)
May, Major E. S., *Guns and Cavalry* (London: Sampson Low Marston & Co, 1896)
Millotatat, Colonel Christian, *Understanding the Prussian General Staff System* (Carlisle, Pa: US Army War College, 1992)
Moltke, Field Marshal Helmuth von, *Correspondance Militaire*, 4 volumes (Paris: Henri Charles-Lavauzelle, 1899–1901)
Moltke, Field Marshal Helmuth von (C. Bell and H. Fischer trans.), *Letters to his Mother and Brothers* (New York: Harper Bros, 1892)
Moltke, Field Marshal Helmuth von (J. R. McIlwraith trans.), *Letters to his Wife and other Relatives* (London: Kegan Paul Trench & Trübner, 1896)
Moltke, Field Marshal Helmuth von, *The Franco-German War of 1870–1871* (London: Harper Bros, 1907)
Morris, William O'Connor, *Moltke* (London: Ward & Downey, 1893)
Newton, Lord, *Lord Lyons: A Record of British Diplomacy* (London: Thomas Nelson & Sons, 1913)
Ortholan, Henri, *L'Armée de la Loire* (Paris: Bernard Giovanangeli, 2005)
Renou, L'Abbe, *Histoire de la Garde Mobile d'Indre-et-Loire* (Tours: Paul Bouserez, 1876)
Ritter, Gerhard, *The Sword and the Sceptre*, 4 volumes (London: Allen Lane, 1972)
Showalter, Dennis, *Railroads and Rifles* (Hamden, Conn: Archon Books, 1975)
Stannard, H., *Gambetta* (London: Methuen & Co, 1921)
Stosch, General and Admiral Albrecht von, *Denkwürdigkeiten* (Stuttgart: Deutsche Verlags, 1904)

Topographical Branch of the Quartermaster General's Department of the German Army (The German Official Account, Captain Francis Coningsby Hannam Clarke trans.), *The Franco-German War 1870–71*, 5 volumes (London: HMSO, 1873–1884)
Verdy du Vernois, General J. von, *With the Royal Headquarters 1870–71* (London: Kegan Paul Trench & Trübner, 1897)
Waldersee, Field Marshal Alfred von (F. Whyte trans.), *A Field Marshal's Memoirs* (London: Hutchinson & Co, 1924)
Wawro, Geoffrey, *The Franco-Prussian War* (Cambridge: CUP, 2003)
Whitton, Lieutenant Colonel F. E., *Moltke* (London: Constable & Co, 1921)
Wittich, General L. von, *Journal de Guerre* (Paris: R Chapelot & Cie, 1902)

BOOKS IN THIS SERIES:

1. *The Battle of Majuba Hill The Transvaal Campaign 1880–1881* John Laband (ISBN 978-1-911512-38-7)
2. *For Queen and Company Vignettes of the Irish Soldier in the Indian Mutiny* David Truesdale (ISBN 978-1-911512-79-0)
3. *The Furthest Garrison Imperial Regiments in New Zealand 1840–1870* Adam Davis (ISBN 978-1-911628-29-3)
4. *Victory Over Disease Resolving the Medical Crisis in the Crimean War, 1854–1856* Michael Hinton (ISBN 978-1-911628-31-6)
5. *Journey Through the Wilderness Garnet Wolseley's Canadian Red River Expedition of 1870* Paul McNicholls (ISBN 978-1-911628-30-9)
6. *Kitchener The Man Not The Myth* Anne Samson (ISBN 978-1-912866-45-8)
7. *The British and the Sikhs Discovery, Warfare and Friendship c1700–1900* Gurinder Singh Mann (ISBN 978-1-911628-24-8)
8. *Bazaine 1870 Scapegoat for a Nation* Quintin Barry (ISBN 978-1-913336-08-0)
9. *Redcoats in the Classroom The British Army's Schools For Soldiers and Their Children During the 19th Century* Howard R. Clarke (ISBN 978-1-912866-47-2)
10. *The Rescue They Called a Raid The Jameson Raid 1895–96* David Snape (ISBN 978-1-913118-77-8)
11. *Hungary 1848 The Winter Campaign* Christopher Pringle (ISBN 978-1-913118-78-5)
12. *The War of the Two Brothers The Portuguese Civil War 1828-1834* Sérgio Veludo Coelho (ISBN 978-1-914059-26-1)
14. *Forgotten Victorian Generals Studies in the Exercise of Command and Control in the British Army 1837–1901* Christopher Brice (editor) (ISBN 978-1-910777-20-6)
15. *The German War of 1866 The Bohemian and Moravian Campaign* Theodore Fontane (ISBN 978-1-914059-29-2)
16. *Dust of Glory The First Anglo-Afghan War 1839–1842, its Causes and Course* Bill Whitburn (ISBN 978-1-914059-33-9)
17. *Saarbruck to Sedan The Franco-German War 1870–1871 Volume 1* Ralph Weaver (ISBN 978-1-914059-88-9)
18. *The Battle of Lissa 1866 How the Industrial Revolution Changed the Face of Naval Warfare* Quintin Barry (ISBN 978-1-914059-92-6)
19. *The Zulu Kingdom and the Boer Invasion of 1837–1840* John Laband (ISBN 978-1-914059-89-6)
20. *The Fire of Venture Was in His Veins* Major Allan Wilson and the Shangani Patrol 1893 David Snape (ISBN 978-1-914059-90-2)
21. *From the Atacama to the Andes Battles of the War of the Pacific 1879–1883* Alan Curtis (ISBN 978-1-914059-90-2)
22. *The Rise of the Sikh Soldier The Sikh Warrior Through the Ages, c1700–1900* Gurinder Singh Mann (ISBN 978-1-915070-52-4)
23. *Victorian Crusaders British and Irish Volunteers in the Papal Army 1860–70* Nicholas Schofield (ISBN 978-1-915070-53-1)
24. *The Battle for the Swiepwald Austria's Fatal Blunder at Königgrätz, the climactic battle of the Austro-Prussian War, 3 July 1866* Ernst Heidrich (ISBN 978-1-915070-49-4)
25. *British Military Panoramas Battle in The Round, 1800–1914* Ian F.W. Beckett (ISBN 978-1-915113-84-9)
26. *Onwards to Omdurman The Anglo-Egyptian Campaign to Reconquer the Sudan, 1896–1898* Keith Surridge (ISBN 978-1-915070-51-7)
27. *Hungary 1849 The Summer Campaign* Wilhelm Ramming, Christopher Pringle (editor) (ISBN 978-1-915113-80-1)
28. *Line in the Sand French Foreign Legion Forts and Fortifications in Morocco 1900–1926* Richard Jeynes (ISBN 978-1-915113-83-2)
29. *The Republic Fights Back The Franco-German War 1870-1871 Volume 2* Ralph Weaver (ISBN 978-1-915070-50-0)
30. *Controlling the Frontier Southern Africa 1806–1828, The Cape Frontier Wars and The Fetcani Alarm* Hugh Driver (ISBN 978-1-915113-78-8)
31. *The Battle of Magersfontein Victory and defeat on the South African veld, 10–12 December 1899* Garth Benneyworth (ISBN 978-1-915113-79-5)
32. *Too Little Too Late The Campaign in West and South Germany June–July 1866* Michael Embree (ISBN 978-1-804513-77-4)
33. *The Destruction of the Imperial Army* Volume 1: The Opening Engagements of the Franco-German War 1870–71 Grenville Bird (ISBN 978-1-915113-81-8)
34. *Kitchener* The Man Not the Myth Anne Samson (ISBN 978-1-804513-84-2)
35. *From Ironclads to Dreadnoughts* The Development of the German Battleship, 1864–1918 Dirk Nottelmann & David M. Sullivan (ISBN 978-1-804511-84-8)
36. *The Destruction of the Imperial Army* Volume 2: The Battles around Metz Grenville Bird (ISBN 978-1-804511-85-5)
37. *More Work Than Glory* Buffalo Soldiers in the United States Army, 1866–1916 John P Langellier (ISBN 978-1-804513-34-7)
38. *The Spioenkop Campaign* The Battles to Relieve Ladysmith 17–27 January 1900 Robert Davidson (ISBN 978-1-804513-31-6)
39. *The Destruction of the Imperial Army* Volume 3: *The Sedan Campaign 1870* Grenville Bird (ISBN 978-1-804513-32-3)
40. *The Destruction of the Imperial Army* Volume 4: *Sedan, Strasbourg and Metz* 1870 Grenville Bird (ISBN 978-1-804514-59-7)
41. *Memorandum on the Prussian Army in Relation to the Campaign of 1866* Lieutenant Colonel W.E.M Reilly (ISBN 978-1-804516-27-0)
42. *Black Week: The British Army and Defeat in Anglo-Boer War 1899-1900* Quintin Barry (ISBN 978-1-804511-86-2)
43. *War in the East. A Military History of the Russo-Turkish War 1877-78* Quintin Barry (ISBN 978-1-804517-30-7)
44. *The First Schleswig-Holstein War 1848-50* Nick Svendsen (ISBN 978-1-804517-36-9)
45. *The Hundred Thousand Sons of St Louis* Ralph Weaver (ISBN 978-1-804517-37-6)
46. *Bismarck's First War: The Campaign in Schleswig and Jutland 1864* Michael Embree (ISBN 978-1-804517-38-3)
47. *The Honvéd War. Armies of the Hungarian War of Independence 1848-49* Nigel James Smith (ISBN 978-1-804514-60-3)
48. *Radestzky's Marches. The Campaigns of 1848 and 1849 in Upper Italy* Michael Embree (ISBN 978-1-804517-42-0)
49. *The Campaign on the Loire 1870-71: Orléans and Le Mans* Quintin Barry (ISBN 978-1-804517-82-6)
50. *The British Empire's Regulars 1880-1914: Soldiers of Britain, India and Africa* Wendell Scholander (ISBN 978-1-804515-62-4)
51. *The Last Throw of the Dice: Bourbaki and Werder in Eastern France 1870-71* Quintin Barry (ISBN 978-1-804517-78-9)